A CANADIAN'S ROAD TO RUSSIA

Lieutenant Stuart Ramsay Tompkins, 89th Alberta Overseas Battalion, 1916.

A Canadian's Road to Russia

LETTERS FROM THE GREAT WAR DECADE

by

Stuart Ramsay Tompkins

Edited by Doris H. Pieroth

The University of Alberta Press

First published by
The University of Alberta Press
Athabasca Hall
Edmonton, Alberta
Canada T6G 2E8

Copyright © The University of Alberta Press 1989

ISBN 0-88864-144-3

Canadian Cataloguing in Publication Data

Tompkins, Stuart Ramsay, 1886–1977.
  A Canadian's road to Russia

Includes bibliographical references.
ISBN 0-88864-144-3

1. Tompkins, Stuart Ramsay, 1886–1977.
2. World War, 1914–1918 - Personal narratives,
Canadian. 3. Soviet Union - Description
and travel - 1917–1944. 4. Historians -
Canada - Biography. I. Pieroth, Doris H.
(Doris Hinson), 1930-   II. Title.
  D640.T64 1989   940.4′81′71   C88-091525-0

Typesetting by The Typeworks, Vancouver, British Columbia, Canada

Printed by Gagne Printing Ltd., Louiseville, Quebec, Canada

Contents

Preface

In the summer of 1955 an audience gathered in Edmonton to hear a lecture titled "The Riddle of Communism: The Quest for an Answer." The lecturer was Stuart Ramsay Tompkins, Research Professor of History at the University of Oklahoma and visiting professor at the University of Alberta for that summer term. He began by saying, "The title announced might have read, perhaps more correctly, 'The Riddle of Communism: *MY* Quest for an Answer,' for it was here in Edmonton that my quest for the answer to the riddle began some thirty-seven years ago."

Tompkins explained that it was in Edmonton in 1918 that he had been recruiting officer for the 260th Rifle Battalion, the unit in which he served in the Canadian Expeditionary Force that went to Siberia as a part of the Allied Intervention at the end of the First World War. He recalled that time as one when Canadians shared "complete *ignorance of Russia and Russians*... with almost the whole western world," and he described the near unimaginable conditions that then prevailed in Vladivostok, when Siberia "was what might be called the backwash of the revolution; [and] endless tides of refugees fleeing before the Bolsheviks swelled the city's population to three times its original number." He remembered that they "could not ignore the fact that almost to a man they resented our presence and that underneath the surface seethed unrest and intrigue," and even though he had learned more than a little of the Russian language he could not penetrate beneath the surface to reach some understanding. He ventured that they had left Vladivostok in May of 1919 "almost *as ignorant of Russia as when we landed.*" In his case the experience was a challenge "to break down that ignorance" and help to break it down in others.[1]

In accepting that challenge, he had gone on to become one of North America's pioneer specialists in Russian history. His first book, *Russia through the Ages*, was published in 1940, when the West was soon to become allied with the Soviet Union against Nazi Germany. In its preface Tompkins recalled his experience in the First World War and its contribution to the book that followed:

> *This book is a child of the Great War. In 1916, as the drumfire on the Somme was beginning to die away, a young officer, bored with the long night watches, sought to relieve the tedium of trench life by beginning the study of a language at that time strange to him. Begun thus as a means of relieving ennui . . . this study seemed at length to begin to fit into the scheme of things when the officer found himself on the fringes of the revolution that engulfed the dominions of tsarist Russia in 1917. The events in eastern Siberia. . . kindled in the mind of the soldier the passion to know more of the people that spoke this language, of their creation in art and literature, of the mighty state they forged through the ages, and of its vicissitudes. Some of the things he has learned are here at last set down.[2]*

Indeed, the scholarly career of Stuart Tompkins was itself a product of the Great War. His military record included service in France with the Second Division of the Canadian Corps, a phase that reached its climax at Vimy Ridge and was followed by volunteer duty with the C.E.F. in Siberia in 1918–19. He had received a First Class Honours degree in Classics from the University of Toronto in 1909, and following military duty he earned a teaching credential at the Calgary Normal School. He then taught in the Lethbridge High School until 1924 when he was appointed Superintendent of Schools in the Yukon Territory, a post he held for four years. In the fall of 1928 he entered graduate school at the University of Chicago and received the Ph.D. there in 1931. He went the following year as an associate professor to the University of Oklahoma, where he stayed until his retirement as Research Professor of History in 1956.

Stuart Tompkins belonged to that generation of scholars that came of age in Canada after the turn of the century and was tempered in the First World War. He studied as an undergraduate at Toronto in a classics department moulded and presided over by Maurice Hutton, a quintessential Victorian idealist.[3] Much of that Victorian idealism can be seen in Tompkins' letters. They also show an ambivalence toward

England that reflects the paradoxical attitude of early twentieth-century Canadian imperialists, a "curious mixture of affection and anxiety, resentment and solicitude," and they occasionally echo the dominant attitude toward races other than Anglo-Saxon, which was seen to be the foundation of the empire.[4]

An indefatigable letter writer, he had been in the habit of "setting down" things that he had learned long before he sent off his first manuscript. His wife, Edna, was the recipient of many of those letters. She preserved more than four hundred of them in a series of moves that took her from Edmonton, to England and back, thence to the Yukon Territory, to Chicago, to Norman, Oklahoma, and finally to Victoria, British Columbia.

His early letters, written between 15 October 1912 and 27 April 1919, provide an eloquent record of courtship and marriage; sharp observations of government and politics, both military and civil; an articulate participant's view of the war in the trenches; and discerning and sensitive reactions to the Siberia and China of 1919. In World War I, letters from the front typically did not dwell on the horror or the gloomier and darker details of life in the trenches; those of Stuart Tompkins were no exception, and while they were timely and thoughtful, they remained for the most part optimistic and good humoured. The letters recount pivotal experiences that informed the opinions and heightened the perceptions of the future historian, and they record his emergence from a comparatively sheltered social environment into the urbanity of wartime England which reinforced his conservative views on manners and morals. They show a prodigious curiosity and breadth of interest, and in their personal passages they resound with the deep love, wonder, devotion, and admiration that Stuart Tompkins held for Edna.

The preface to *Russia through the Ages* ended with acknowledgment of the help and encouragement of Samuel Harper of the University of Chicago and Sir Bernard Pares of the School of Slavonic Studies in the University of London. There can hardly have been a greater contrast in routes to Russia and Russian studies than those taken by Stuart Tompkins and his two mentors, both of whom came from families of privilege. They were advisers to ambassadors, presidents, and prime ministers, and had first traveled in Russia under comfortable if not luxurious circumstances at the turn of the century. Stuart, who was not a great deal younger than either Pares or Harper, tells a far different story in his letters that follow.

Editor's Note

The World War I Allies' intervention in Russia in 1918, in the aftermath of the Bolshevik power seizure, had always been for me little more than a footnote to world history until a Saturday afternoon in the spring of 1983, when I received a phone call from Elizabeth A.H. John, a friend who is an historian in Austin, Texas. She presented me with an opportunity to learn more about the intervention and to meet one of the most remarkable people I have ever known in the bargain. Edna Tompkins, wife of the late Stuart Ramsay Tompkins, an early specialist in Russian history, had approached her about editing a collection of letters that her husband had written to her when he was an officer in the Canadian Expeditionary Force, Siberia in 1918–1919. Dr. John, a former student of Professor Tompkins, could not then take on the project herself and suggested that perhaps I would consider doing it.

The idea intrigued me, and when I read an edited version of the letters that Tompkins himself had undertaken it intrigued even more. The editing job appeared to be no more than a six-month project at the most, and when I learned part of Edna Tompkins' own story, which piqued my recently increased interest in women's history, I agreed to at least talk with Mrs. Tompkins and give serious consideration to taking on the job.

During a three day visit with her in Edmonton, where she was then living, she convinced me to proceed not only with the letters from

Siberia, but with others in a large collection that she had saved over the years. I returned to Seattle with a suitcase crammed full with letters and audio cassettes that held more than eight hours of oral history interviews.

This book is, in a sense then, the product of Edna Tompkins' tenacious efforts. While professing to see nothing remarkable in her husband's letters, she was determined to see them published as he had once thought to do with the letters he had written from Siberia in 1919. She thought them of some historical value as, if nothing else, "a slice of life" for their time. But beyond that they mirror the course of history in Alberta, in Canada, and in the world at large. Written between 1912 and 1919, they provide a portrait of a gentleman and a scholar who was something of a Victorian idealist and a Romantic, and they record the beginning of the true and lasting partnership he built with the first and only woman he ever loved.

While the collection includes letters written as late as 1937, the letters in this selection are from those written between 1912 and 1919, during the Tompkins' courtship and during the years that he served with the Canadian armed forces. Choosing among the early letters proved to be a difficult task, and selection came down to omitting those that were clearly repetitive or less important to the story the letters tell. Deletions within the letters are indicated by ellipses, and for the most part the deleted portions were either repetitions or references to people who did not figure further in the Tompkins story. Neither the selection of the letters nor the deletions were made with an eye to censoring or to distorting the picture they form of a man who harbored his generation's prejudices as well as its strengths and attractive characteristics.

In the interest of readability, I have, without brackets, corrected the rare instances of misspelling and converted to commas or semicolons the dots that he frequently used as punctuation, and I have deleted some postscripts without the use of ellipses. In his haste of writing he occasionally omitted a word which I have added in brackets, and where a word is illegible that, too, I have indicated in brackets. Ampersands and abbreviations are spelled out, but some military abbreviations stand where they appeared more natural in the flow of a letter.

I treasure the time I spent with Edna Tompkins, an amazing woman who in her 95th year made a trip to England "for old times' sake." I am grateful to her not only for time spent in interviews, but for her gracious hospitality and for entrusting to me her collection of letters, photographs, and other documents and correspondence, which will ultimately be placed in an archive and made available to scholars. We both want to thank Elizabeth Ann Harper John for her contribution to this project; she introduced us and brought editor and letters together; without her there would have been no book.

I have had the pleasure of talking with a number of Stuart Tompkins' friends, colleagues, and former students, and I am indebted to the following people for generously giving their time in conversation and interviews: Miss Zeta Christie, Professor John Ezell, Professor Gilbert Fite, Dr. Jane C. Fredeman, Professor William E. Fredeman, Mrs. Eleanor Houston, Dr. Elizabeth A. H. John, Dean William E. Livezey, Dean Dorothy Mawdsley, and Mrs. Amy Moorhead.

Many others gave help and support along the way. I especially appreciate the time, effort, and advice of Margaret Hall, Joanne Torney Rehfeldt, and Carol Zabilski who read all or part of the manuscript. For their able assistance I thank the staff of the Western History Collection in the University of Oklahoma Library where papers of Stuart Tompkins are housed. A special note of thanks goes to Jane Fredeman, who edited the manuscript and gave valuable advice and assistance throughout the entire project. I want to thank Norma Gutteridge and Mary Mahoney-Robson of the University of Alberta Press for their considerable efforts in producing this book. The excellent maps are the work of Geoff Lester, cartographer in the Department of Geography, University of Alberta.

What had been seen as a six-month undertaking lasted far longer than that. I am grateful to my husband John, not only for support and encouragement in the face of unexpected events, but for insisting on and assisting in my conversion to the use of the word processor.

Introduction

❧ A SCHOLAR'S ODYSSEY ❧

Stuart Ramsay Tompkins was born 26 June 1886, in Lyn, Ontario, the son of Charles Abraham Tompkins and Martha Jane McNish. His grandfather Tompkins had settled early in Ontario's Hastings Township, and he recalled that his mother's forebears had left Greenwich for Canada "on the day Napoleon died in 1821." The third of five children, Stuart was younger than his sisters Louise and Alice, older than Janet and Philip. He always felt his parents' marriage had been an unfortunate one that caused suffering and emotional stress for the whole family.[1]

Charles Tompkins had an "itching foot," and the Canadian Pacific Railway's push westward across Canada attracted him to settlement possibilities on the prairies. They established a homestead in Saskatchewan, but Martha Jane did not share his enthusiasm for a place that offered little of what she deemed essential for a life of quality. She saw no schools, no churches, no future prospects, and after a short time she persuaded a family member in Toronto to offer her husband a job.

They left the homestead, returned to Brockville, Ontario, and Charles Tompkins went to work selling patent medicines. When he balked at securing personal testimonials to promote sales, he lost that job, and Stuart remembered this event as "the beginning of all our troubles." They had no money, and he later said that his father virtually did nothing for them, leaving his mother and the five children when the youngest was not yet a year old.[2]

Stuart's strong-willed mother held the family together. In a letter written to Stuart in 1934 she reminded him of those early years:

Perhaps you can have some idea how I was situated when landed on the prairie, it was not long before I found out there was nothing to look forward to there, and it seemed almost too good to be true to be settled [back] in Brockville with the advantage of church and school but this struggle was a hard one. I never talked about the effort I was making, I just made it. I had the satisfaction of knowing my children were enjoying advantages with the best. It certainly was a shock to me to find out what your father really was. . . . He did a heap of talking, spent a lot of money running around, getting ready for the west, then landed there without anything to help himself with. . . . It certainly was a shock to me, to find him out. You probably remember those two and half years he was in St. Paul, from the spring of '92 till the fall of '94. He must have had a pretty soft job, for the pay was less than nine dollars a week. He kept two thirds of it for himself and sent the rest home to the six of us. My income did not average quite three dollars a week, and he felt quite discouraged when he came home that I had gone and spent it all, that was the excuse he made for leaving us . . . [that] I never could save. . . .

What the future held for me was to do my best and make something of the children. I daresay I rather lost my head over their success at school, when I found all of them had inherited my love of books and my aptitude for absorbing learning. . . . It was a steady grind for me to try to make ends meet, you may be sure I was not having much fun and there were some humiliating experiences that were pretty hard to bear but the children were having a chance and how I did hope they would make good and I would be well paid in their loyalty for anything I had done for them.[3]

Stuart's wartime letters show some of his mother's bitterness, and it is apparent that she expected repayment from her children. While she was often severe in her assessment of Stuart, he felt keenly his obligations to his mother. He realized the extent of the sacrifice she made in keeping the family together, and he later recalled

One thing about her—she was proud and she kept a stiff upper lip, no matter how badly she was [treated]. . . . We were always down at the lowest end of the [economic] scale. We lived on [Anne Street] that took off from the main highway into Brockville and ran south and it was pretty much slum areas— but even though it was slums, my mother, who was a very, very strong minded woman, kept us in school and insisted that we learn. . . . She held her head up . . . and she kept us from being contaminated by the slum element.[4]

Life in Brockville meant attending church every Sunday, and Stuart said his mother was "very proud to march her five children down to the same seats, forward at the front. . . a pew in the front line."[5] He described the religious roots thus planted: "I was brought up a strict Presbyterian, went to Young People's Society on Sunday morning, then to the Church service at 11 o'clock then Sunday School in the afternoon and perhaps Sunday evening service, producing a peculiar brand of Presbyterian piety."[6] This piety is apparent in Stuart's courtship and wartime letters, but as the years passed his connection with the institutional church all but vanished.

Stuart's 1934 letter from his mother suggests that his father contacted the family from time to time, and she clearly regretted having once permitted Stuart to visit him: "I have always had the uneasy feeling that it was not wise to allow you to meet your father that time, for he evidently had stirred your sympathy. I never questioned you for any particulars, but I have a pretty good idea how you found him situated. . . . Your father was capable of saying things that were false. . . [and] I wish to make perfectly clear, if he said anything against me, he made it up."[7]

That trip probably came during the summer before Stuart entered university, a time when he felt a need to know more of his father, who had again taken up a homestead in Saskatchewan. He went out to see him and found him in very poor circumstances, living in a rough hut that was sparsely furnished. When his father died there a few years later, it was Stuart who went from Edmonton to settle his affairs.[8]

Stuart always thought that his mother had married his father in desperation, primarily to avoid spinsterhood. She also may well have been desperate to escape her own home where she was saddled with inordinate responsibility for a large number of younger siblings and "doing a woman's work at fourteen." The injustice of never having been allowed to attend grammar school embittered her and undoubtedly fuelled a determination to see her children educated.[9]

Stuart's sense of family responsibility extended to his sisters and brother as well as his mother, and his letters show that he loved and cared for them all in spite of the misunderstandings that came as they made their separate ways. He felt the closest relationship with his sister Janet, to whom he was nearest in age and whom, ironically, his mother had kept from school in spite of her own experience. Janet was sent to Toronto to work as a housemaid in the home of her mother's sister when Stuart entered the University; hence they were young adults together and perhaps able to lend support to one another in a

strange city. She had talent in music, and Stuart said she wrote beautifully, that "her letters were jewels—they just sparkled," and when he
wrote to his wife from France he often remarked on letters from
"Jentie," as he called her.[10]

Because of Martha Jane Tompkins' determination to provide her
children with educational advantages, Stuart began school at either
three or four years of age in a kindergarten where his mother somehow managed to pay the tuition. His early schooling in Brockville provided a sound foundation and left enough of an impression that Stuart
recalled vividly that he "just *had* to learn. The secret was constant
drilling."[11]

When he started high school at Brockville Collegiate Institute, he
found himself small for his age and among "hooligans" whose insults
he had to endure. But he "got on famously," going "through school
very fast—[as] nobody else had ever done... [taking] each grade in
five months" and finishing at the age of fifteen. He recalled that the
mathematics instruction was adequate, but said he received "poor
scientific training." Among the memorable men on the faculty were an
excellent classics teacher, a graduate of Trinity College, Dublin, and
one who, in spite of being a drunkard, was "an inspiring teacher of
English."[12]

His mother decided very early that he was bound for the university.
He said, "I didn't know how I would ever get there, but then she had
made up her mind." He chose Toronto over Queen's, which his
mother's family had always favoured and from which his sister Louise
had graduated. His mother, on the advice of her brother, decided that
he was too young to enter the university immediately, so he held back
for two years during which time he worked at various jobs, and it was
during this period that he made the trip to visit his father in Saskatchewan.[13]

His record at Brockville Collegiate had won him five scholarships to
Toronto. He could not hold them all, but he received his tuition fees
and he could start at the university. He did well the first year, but as he
later said, he took bad advice, listening to people who told him:

> you should learn more from the people you associate with and not just from
> the academic. . . . [So I listened] instead of putting myself down to work in
> the second year. . . . It was all wrong and nonsense. If you're out to attain
> anything in academic affairs, you've got to work, that's all there is to it. . . .
> In my second year I fell down for the first time in my life to third class hon-
> ours.[14]

Because of that second-year record, he was denied a Classics scholarship to Oxford even though he received his degree in 1909 with First Class Honours. The eternal optimist, he always considered that bit of misfortune to have been in reality a God-send for him. Looking back he said that he could never have taught Greek and Latin to students not interested in learning, "and that would be my fate if I were teaching classical language."[15]

Pursuing Classics at Oxford likely would also have ruled out his moving West, which he did shortly after graduation from Toronto. During his final year there he suffered a severe case of typhoid fever, but when he regained sufficient strength, he left for Edmonton and began work as a reporter for a newspaper called *The Capitol*. He recounted his short career in journalism:

> *When I was in Edmonton, I didn't have any money.... This little paper... was a purely political paper. My services were not too extensive and eventually the position in the* Bulletin *opened up. The friend of mine who held the position... wanted to go back to Ontario... and he was recommending me to take his place. So I did—I became a reporter for the* Bulletin, *which was an organ of [Frank] Oliver. I wasn't a good newspaper man because, in the first place, you have to have a thousand things under your hat that you're willing to work on. I didn't have that kind of mind, but I was reasonably successful.... I suppose I did respectable work.*[16]

He stayed at the *Bulletin* for a year and then took the job of chief clerk in the Alberta Department of Education.

The stability of this position allowed Stuart to send for the family to come from Brockville. Louise had married soon after her graduation from Queen's and she and her husband were then living as missionaries in China. Philip had joined Stuart in Edmonton earlier and had been working as an electrician, and in 1911 Stuart dispatched him east to move his mother and sisters. They gradually settled, and Stuart helped Alice to secure a teaching job in the city while Janet taught private music lessons and Philip continued in the electrical business. They all lived together with their mother during the early years in Alberta.[17]

Stuart Tompkins now bore the clear imprint of the West. He often extolled the West, its beauty and its grandeur, and he freely acknowledged its impact on him.

In the summer of 1905, fearing that he had become a regular "momma's boy," he and a cousin had boarded a "harvesters' excursion" train at Toronto, paying five dollars for the trip through Northern Ontario, Manitoba, and Saskatchewan. Farmers along the route met the train when they needed to hire additional hands, and his cousin soon stopped off to stay with a good job. The excursion trains went as far as Moose Jaw, but as Stuart recounted, "I wasn't satisfied. I wanted to go further west . . .[to] the ranching country, because I was beginning to feel that I had to assert my manhood . . . . I longed to reach the ranching country. . . in Western Alberta." He continued on to Calgary, where he was welcomed by another cousin who had a homestead and small spread northwest of town.[18]

He was hired "almost at once for haying on a remittance man's ranch and learned to gee and haw." When the haying job was finished he stayed on "for nothing but cooking and loafing," and everything went well until a former ranch hand returned and his fortunes changed. Stuart recalled that

> *[He] charged me one night with the cardinal of all sins in the west, leaving a gate open. I tried to prove I didn't; he would not hear of it. Then I picked a fight with him and hit him. Was he surprised that a mere tenderfoot would fight him? Of course he knocked me down the first punch he landed and picked up and dusted me off, not yet over his surprise. Of course technically I was the loser but no more insults. I was treated with respect.*

His next job presented him with yet another challenge. After dinner one Sunday the foreman announced that they had caught up a nice horse for him to ride and suggested that they go down to the corrals. It was all said deadpan,

> *but I knew what it meant—a challenge, would I take it up. "Fine" I said "let's go." There I found the most wicked mare they were holding blindfolded by the bridle and the neighbours gathered around to see the fun. So they helped me aboard and turned the mare loose. She tossed me around like a sack of sawdust, just playing with me, finally dumping me head over heels. Then of course with a saddle horse standing by all ready they quickly caught her and would I like to try it again. "Sure," I said, the mean mare just had fun with me bringing me down a little harder each time. At the seventh round she. . . subjected me to some harsh punishment by brushing me against the corral fence. When I came down for the seventh time, after picking me up and brushing the mud off they decided I had enough. The horse had won that one but at least I had passed the test and was accepted as equal.[19]*

He was 19 years old, and he always wondered why he, by his own admission the most timid boy in town who never fought anyone, had done that and survived. He did not tell his friends of the summer's escapades, but he remembered that when he went back to the university that fall, "although my classmates might think I was the same person who left in June for the summer holiday, I felt I was different."[20]

By 1905 Albertans had already realized to some degree the passing of the old range; some ranches had broken up range to plant feed crops, and new settlers had come both to ranch and to farm the land on a lesser scale.[21] But some of the glory still lingered, and there were still figures reminiscent of the early years who served as examples for young men in search of identity and adventure. Several years later, in an attempt to define what he found good, strong, and more fundamental than religion, what he called "the right attitude towards life," Stuart wrote of meeting the western cattleman. Nothing impressed him so much as

> the careless courage of those pioneers, the ability to take hardships with a laugh to work almost to exhaustion and then at the end of the day to kick up their heels almost in sheer defiance of the laws of nature. It is splendid and illustrates in the aptest way the essential greatness of the human soul that it can dominate its circumstances.[22]

When Stuart returned to Alberta in 1911, the old cattle range was indeed a thing of the past, but the competitiveness, the challenge and the spirit that had so attracted him during his summer of ranching still prevailed. The prairie west was a land of new beginnings, and in the new province he and his family set about to build a good life among like-minded people who shared the same values and essentially the same view of the world, a view that still mirrored to a great extent the imperialism of Victorian idealists.

Alberta's population had mushroomed since 1901, growing from 73,000 to 375,000 in just ten years. Edmonton itself had grown dramatically during this period and it had also taken on lasting social characteristics. By and large the city's leadership was Anglican or Presbyterian, reasonably well-educated, and had come from Ontario or Great Britain.[23]

Prairie cultural standards were then being set by a second generation that reaffirmed "the rule of law, the power of the church, the influence of the school lesson, and the inevitable correctness of British traditions." Western Canadians took pride in their British heritage, but they felt that frontier freedom and equality offered them opportunity to "improve upon the parent culture." At the turn of the century, the goal of prairie social leaders had been a "Protestant, law-respecting, English-speaking community in which democracy and social equality were fundamental assumptions," and in the following decade there was no reason to doubt that they would succeed in its establishment.[24]

With his strong United Empire Loyalist roots and Scottish Presbyterian grounding, Stuart Tompkins shared this western outlook, and many of his wartime letters proclaim Canada's moral and social superiority to the mother country. He had a clear sense of what it was to be a Canadian, and he held the westerner's conviction that a better world could be built in western Canada. His patriotism was unabashed, and throughout his wartime travels worldwide he did not waver from the conviction that Canada was a model of what a proper country should be.

When Stuart joined the ranks of middle class professionals in the Education Department he was at the centre of the endeavour to create a democratic and prosperous West. The schools were seen as the best instrument for the assimilation and Canadianization of vast numbers of foreign immigrants as well as a forum for imparting learning and basic skills to Canadian-born and foreign-born alike to assure their success in a world that was rapidly changing. As the population grew, the establishment of new schools became a primary task of the province's Education Department, and as the ranks of immigrants came to include large numbers from non-English speaking countries, disputes besetting the department increasingly centred on the issue of language of instruction. Stuart found himself travelling throughout the province to deal with some of these controversies.

Protestant churches occupied a central role in prairie society. Stuart had grown up in nineteenth-century Ontario, which had been "dominated by an evangelical Protestantism with a message of salvation directed to the individual,"[25] but within it new currents were beginning to run. His move to Alberta coincided with the rise of the Social Gospel which with its broader social perspective became an important influence in western Canada. Stuart's letters indicate that he retained some of what he termed his "peculiar brand of Presbyterian piety" and that he perhaps found no more compatible the progressive outlook and optimism of the Social Gospel. He became disenchanted with the institutional church, but he retained his religious beliefs until his death.

Economic struggle characterized most of Stuart Tompkins' life, from the harsh poverty of his childhood through the years of incredibly low faculty salaries while he was a professor at the University of Oklahoma. The early promise of better things in Alberta faded with the recession of 1913 when his already meagre monthly salary of $125 was reduced to an even $100.[26] The problem of money plagued him during his courtship. Since he was responsible in part for the support of his mother, he knew it would be difficult to establish a separate household on his clerk's salary. One thing that made his marriage economically possible was the fact that his bride was gainfully employed and intended to remain so.

Edna Jane Christie was an independent and determined young woman who was not easily won to the idea of marriage. She could well have pursued a career of her own, and an enticement offered by Stuart in one of the courtship letters was that she could share fully in his. That she did in fact share his scholarly career is attested to by all who knew them. As with many faculty wives, she gladly entertained in the line of duty, and she thoroughly enjoyed association with her husband's students. She participated to a far greater extent in his work than her typing and proofreading reveals, and she herself recalls the pleasure and rewards of working beside him at the Library of Congress.[27]

She, too, was an Ontario native with United Empire Loyalist roots, born in Mimico, Etobicoke County, on 5 November 1891. Her mother died when she was three, and her father, who was then a telegrapher, followed the railway west. Until she was fourteen she lived with friends in Mimico and in St. Catharines, where she attended the Collegiate Institute. Her father became a station agent in Strathcona (Edmonton) and remarried there when Edna was eleven. His new family came to include his sons, Harry and John, and another daughter, Zeta.

Edna joined them in Alberta in 1907, and she still remembers the trip through the prairies in the aftermath of the killer winter of 1906–7 when "along the railway tracks you could see the skeletons of cows." She helped care for her younger siblings and did not again attend school. She remembers those years:

> *It was quite a happy life in Edmonton. I had a group of friends and we skated and danced—and the others all went on to University, at least most of them. We went to dances and parties and the boys took us to the theatre. In those days we had a lot of artists from England and other countries who came to Edmonton in the summer... Sir John Martin Harvey—Forbes Johnson and his wife—Melba—oh I could name a dozen.*

When she was eighteen, she decided that she "didn't want to stay home and take care of children" for the rest of her life, so after finishing a three-month business course, she applied for work with the government and was accepted as a stenographer in the Department of Education.[28]

The courtship letters clearly show that Stuart was determined that she would be his wife. His suit was not made any easier by the fact that he lived north of the Saskatchewan River while the Christies lived in Strathcona on its south banks. Even the construction of a bridge and the 1912 incorporation of Strathcona into the enlarged city of Edmonton did not reduce the obstacles presented by streetcar schedules and transfers. The postal service was vital to his success, and it was his good fortune to have many of his intra-city letters delivered the day after if not later the same day he posted them.

Following their marriage in January 1915, Stuart and Edna were rarely separated until he enlisted in the Army the following August, which necessitated a resumption of his voluminous correspondence. In the summer of 1916, after he had received his commission as a lieutenant, Stuart went to England for combat preparation. It was not unusual at the time for wives to accompany the men, and Edna followed Stuart to England soon after. They were able to be together for three months before he was sent to France. Edna remained in London working at the Canadian Army Pay and Records Office. Stuart was invalided out in April of 1917, following the battle at Vimy Ridge, and they were reunited, remaining together until they returned to Canada in the spring of 1918.

In a chance shipboard meeting with a Canadian officer headed for Siberia with the British Military Mission, Stuart learned of the intended formation of a military force to be sent to Siberia as part of the Allied intervention in Russia. He had taught himself the rudiments of the Russian language while in the trenches, and the revolution in 1917 had heightened his interest in the country and its people. He saw the Expeditionary Force as perhaps his only way to travel to Russia, and not long after his discharge he volunteered again for a Siberian unit and spent much of the summer of 1918 as its recruiting officer in Edmonton. The letters reveal what he observed in Siberia with the C.E.F. It was almost a decade later before Stuart could again pay attention to Russia.

He returned from Siberia in May of 1919 and re-entered civilian life with the uncertainties common to all veterans. The Education Department had not retained his prewar job for him, and in casting about for employment he entertained a number of ideas, including farming on property they owned on the Peace River in Northern British Columbia. He chose finally to stay with education, entered a course at the Calgary Normal School, and received his teaching credential in June of 1920.

His teaching career began that summer in an ad hoc position in a rural school in the town of Alix, Alberta, where he taught a variety of subjects and even found himself responsible for military drill for the male students. That fall he and Edna moved to Lethbridge, where he had secured a teaching job in the high school. They lived there for the next four years, and the Lethbridge days proved to be happy ones in which they formed life-long friendships. A group of young teachers banded together for intellectual stimulation, all having come from different universities—Stuart from Toronto, the English teacher, Dorothy Mawdsley, from McGill, and Mr. Brodie, the science teacher, from Dalhousie. They spent many happy hours together in recreation and evenings of conversation. They felt fortunate in their common bond in a place one of them later described as "a wild west town, as Lethbridge might be said to be, [where] there wasn't a person there that you could talk about anything intellectual with."[29]

During his tenure in Lethbridge, Stuart served as vice-president of the newly chartered Alberta Teachers' Alliance, and he also managed to earn a Master of Arts degree in Education from the University of Alberta. He could do that without leaving his job, and he saw the degree as something of an insurance policy. But he had his sights set on the Ph.D., and when he was offered the job of Superintendent of Schools for Yukon Territory, he jumped at the chance to earn twice what he was paid in Lethbridge, certain that he could save half of the $4,000 annual salary and thus make it economically feasible to go to graduate school. Stuart's recommendation for the Yukon post had come from John Ross, for whom he had worked in the Alberta Education Department; Ross had himself been superintendent of the territory's schools in the gold rush days and was still consulted about candidates for the job.[30]

The Tompkins' Yukon adventure began in Dawson with the start of the 1924–25 school year. They left Alberta for a two-week vacation on Vancouver Island before sailing from Vancouver to Skagway. From there they took the railway up to Whitehorse where they boarded the river boat to Dawson. Edna later said "I was horrified when I found that we had to go two hundred miles down the river in a boat. I felt that we would never get out." Of their Yukon move, their friend

Dorothy Mawdsley said: "While it was a romantic thing to do and all that, it really was Stuart going into the wilderness to make the money to enable him to get that doctor's degree. And Edna went certainly with the greatest reluctance."[31]

They enjoyed their four years there in many ways, but it was an uncompromising and challenging environment. While they appreciated the company of good friends, the winters were harsh, and Edna complained to Stuart that she really had no desire to be a pioneer, that her UEL "ancestors made Canada, they saved it from the United States," so why should she start all over as a pioneer. They were determined that they would not spend money, but with good friends they enjoyed such things as the opportunity to "toboggan, and [go] out hiking week-ends—walk twenty miles—take our lunch with us in the middle of winter." Sixty years later Edna's memories are fonder. She remembers above all the beauty of the long days canoeing on northern rivers.[32]

Stuart's responsibilities included serving as principal of the high school in Dawson for most of the year as well as inspecting all the other schools in the Territory. In the summer he travelled by boat, and he became a skilled boatman. The Tompkins shared two memorable canoe trips down the Yukon River. They thought it marvellous to have twenty-four hours of daylight, and on the river trips they often would pull in to shore and sleep in the shade during the day and travel at night when it was pleasant.

Edna and Stuart made their first trip alone, stopping at Fort Yukon and waiting for the steamer to take them back on the return trip. The next year they took three teachers from Dawson with them, dropping them off at Circle City before going on through the Flats themselves. The Flats of the Yukon, with widths up to fifteen miles, held numerous channels and one could easily become lost. Stuart could read the currents, and he navigated the Flats with little trouble, but they had not wanted to risk taking the others through. They joined another boat at Fort Yukon and went approximately two hundred miles further down to Beaver, where they caught a steamer for the trip back up river.

During the four years they were there they did not come "outside" until they were ready to leave permanently. Edna remembers the trip out: "We came out on the longest day of the year—my it was beautiful—cascades of water everywhere as we came down the railways—the railway is spectacular... it was narrow gauge. The canyon is close to where the trail of '98 was—you see—there's a big gulch there—very spectacular."[33]

The time that Stuart and Edna spent in the Yukon provided a background interest for what may well have been his best and longest lived book, *Alaska: Promyshlennik and Sourdough,* published in 1946. As with much of his work, it was "a pioneer contribution to [a] little worked historical field." Another reviewer said, "The prose style is often equal to Francis Parkman's. The reader feels the rough waters of Alaska, the churn of a twenty-foot tide tumbling through the straits... in the distance the mighty mountains, purple, glittering, and serene." This prose style filled countless letters to Edna whenever they were apart. The Alaska book was praised for its account of the Russian occupation of Alaska and for bringing the entire Alaska story up to date, but another reviewer suggested that the account of recent years was full of shortcomings and almost echoed Stuart's evaluation of himself as a journalist: "As an historian Mr. Tompkins has performed outstandingly. As a reporter he should stick to what he does better."[34]

Because of their departure from the Yukon late in June 1928, Stuart spent the summer at Stanford, the only school that started late enough for him to enrol for the summer session. He worked in Russian history and Edna recalled that he worked hard; they both "sat up night after night 'til three or four in the morning writing term papers." They might have stayed at Stanford had it not been for his lack of a background in history. As it was, he planned to go to the University of London to work with Bernard Pares, and by the autumn had shipped his trunk and converted his money to English currency.[35]

He was ready to leave Edmonton for London when Dorothy Mawdsley suggested, "Well, on your way, why don't you stop in Chicago... just to see what they've got—you might like it." So Stuart stopped at the University of Chicago, where the only person on hand in the history department at the moment was James Westfall Thompson, the medievalist. Stuart met Thompson, who convinced him to stay at Chicago and proceeded to arrange for his admission to the doctoral program. Edna always saw the humour in this rather random turn of events and later remembered that "Stuart's trunk was down at Halifax or New York—and his money on the way to London," but everything was settled and they moved to Chicago.[36]

Stuart rented a basement apartment for them just across from the university, settled in, and sent for Edna to come from Edmonton to join him. When she arrived she found the apartment full of cockroaches; of her first encounter with those creatures she said, "Ugh. I nearly wore the skin and bone off my hands with lye and everything trying to to clean it up." This was prohibition era Chicago, and a fellow graduate student who later shared an apartment with them said of those years, "It was hell, that's what it was... there was this filthy climate and we had bedbugs and we had cockroaches and we had pickpockets and we had people—it was the time of that awful Al Capone.... What a place! What an experience!" Stuart experienced the impact of racketeering in taking his suits to a dry cleaner who charged a fluctuating fee depending on whether or not Al Capone was out of jail and demanding protection money.[37]

It was essential that Edna find a job if Stuart were to complete the degree without interruption. She said, "I used to go out... [referred] through the University... and work for two or three hours [as a stenographer], this sort of thing, you know. As a matter of fact I [even] went out charring—I helped the landlady and her sister for quite a long time—a month or two anyway." She soon went to work for the university, and in the social science secretarial pool she came to enjoy the challenging and stimulating atmosphere. She worked with brilliant scholars and felt that she truly benefited from the opportunity. She loved the work, although she worked terribly hard, and with countless wives who have supported husbands in school, she long thought, "If I hadn't had a flat [to maintain] and a husband to help I would have enjoyed my work a lot more."[38]

In a highly charged atmosphere Robert Maynard Hutchins was implementing sweeping reorganization in the university, and Edna felt something just short of conspiracy in the air at times while taking dictation. The luminaries she worked for, who either passed through Chicago briefly or were resident there, included Beardsly Ruml, John Maynard Keynes, and Dr. Franz Alexander, for whom a professorship in psychoanalysis had been created. She considered the most interesting of them all to be Mortimer Adler, of whom she said, "I did his work—I used to go to his apartment and take dictation, and in the office, too. That was when they were stirring up [things]... he and [Hutchins]. They really turned the philosophy department right on its ears.... He, I think, was the most brilliant person I've ever known. He really has a great mind—I liked him.... I really got a great lift out of being near a mind like that."[39]

Stuart Tompkins completed the graduate program at Chicago at a time when the university had the reputation of failing half of its doctoral candidates on final examinations. He and Dorothy Mawdsley, his

Lethbridge colleague, entered the program at the same time, she in English, and she recalled that "things got so grim there, because they were failing fifty percent of their candidates when we were there. It was the most awful—it was just like a pogrom really—you would see your classmates go off for the test, and then the betting would be— well they failed the best woman that we had [in English] I know .... It really was a wicked, wicked set-up." However, Stuart, then a forty-four year old scholar, always appeared extraordinarily indifferent to the pressure, and when he passed both written and oral examinations in stride, it seemed remarkable in view of the usual bias against mature students that prevailed.[40]

By virtue of having been denied a scholarship to Oxford, Stuart not only had fallen outside the early twentieth-century pattern for Canadian scholars who studied in British universities and returned to Canada for their academic careers, he had delayed his own career for more than twenty years. All historians of his generation were profoundly affected by the Great War, but for Stuart the effect was different. In a sense the war ensured growth of his field of specialization by heightening interest in the language, literature, and history of Russia, and his own participation on the fringes of the civil war that followed the 1917 revolution had made that interest more compelling for him.

James Westfall Thompson took great interest in Stuart's classical background, and tried to steer him into medieval history at Chicago, but Russia remained his priority, and while technically his work was in European history, under Bernadotte Schmitt, he did work with the university's one specialist on Russia, Samuel Harper. Stuart had continued to study Russian during the years since his return from Siberia, and he made a distinct impression on Harper in their first class meeting by reading some passages aloud with comparative ease. He wrote his dissertation, "Count Witte as Minister of Finance, 1892–1903," under Harper's direction, but the fact that Harper did not hold a doctorate prevented him from serving on the examination committee. Stuart underscored the fact that Chicago did not then emphasize Russian studies when he later recounted his experience there:

when I studied at the University of Chicago, but little was done to encourage any one [to go] into this field. . . scarcely any one did really serious work. It was impressed on graduate students that they could not make their living by working in this special field. An odd one like myself who persevered was regarded as a crank.

Stuart received the Ph.D. in December of 1931, and the following spring, thanks in large part to a strong recommendation from James Westfall Thompson, he was hired as an associate professor of history by the University of Oklahoma.[41]

It seems only fitting, after spending four years on that farthest west frontier in the Yukon earning money to study for an academic career that the next stop for a man as appreciative of the West as Stuart would be the University of Oklahoma. He was offered the appointment by E. E. Dale, one of the West's leading historians, and his professional friends and colleagues in Norman came to include some of the other outstanding historians of the West.

The years in Chicago were lean ones for Stuart and Edna Tompkins, and their lot improved only slightly with their move to Oklahoma. His appointment was for one year at a salary of $2,600, but Professor Dale made it clear that should the university receive another budget cut he would lose the same percentage as the rest of the faculty. Dale had earlier written that at the end of a first-year appointment, if everything were satisfactory the appointment became permanent and tenure was granted. The blow of salary reduction fell in 1933 when the University President informed Stuart that his salary would be $2,502, with the stipulation that all salaries would be "reduced *pro rata* in any quarter should tax collections not be sufficient." In Oklahoma, the Depression was devastating to the University, and the Tompkins lived with this reduced salary for the next ten years. Stuart remained as a tenured member of the faculty for twenty-four years, during which time the financial picture improved slightly; his salary as Research Professor of History for the year 1954–55 was $7,500.[42]

To have embarked on an academic career as late as Stuart carried something of a handicap, but on the occasion of obtaining the Oklahoma job, his age was an asset. His chief rival for the position held a Harvard Ph.D. in ancient history, but Dale felt, "On the other hand he is a little younger than you and you have distinct advantage in the breadth of your experience in foreign travel and in your very interesting work in the far North."[43]

The history department took full advantage of Stuart's unique scholarly background in assigning his first teaching load which consisted of five semester hours of Western civilization, three in the History of Greece, three in the French Revolution and the Napoleonic Era, and a two-hour seminar in European history. Dale told Stuart that the seminar would perhaps contain no more than three or four students and he could work in any field of European history he chose.[44] It would not seem amiss to assume that this first graduate seminar worked in the field of Russian history.

In correspondence with Dale, while agreeing that students should have a firm grasp of fundamentals of Western civilization, "and for that we must go to the Greeks," Stuart had clearly shown his enthusiasm for Russian history. He outlined the thrust of his work at Chicago which had a distinct tilt toward economic history, including "the economic history of Russia (my thesis was the work of Count Witte . . .). I have as a result become interested in the forms of economic and social life of western civilization and man's views on such questions. I have . . . acquainted myself with socialistic and communistic thought, especially in Russia and among the Russian historians. Of course, any live person today can hardly keep aloof from these questions."[45]

If that seminar did focus on Russia, it was the beginning of Stuart's career-long efforts to institute a program of Russian studies at Oklahoma, efforts which met with limited success. A decade later he could lament the state of the field in general and at Oklahoma in particular:

> *Meetings of the American Historical Association have not acquainted me with a body of scholars in this field. Outside of the Harvard and Yale staffs, I can recall none. That does not necessarily mean that there are not some promising younger men. . . who have just graduated and have not written anything [but they] would be known only to their instructors. . . .*
>
> *I may say that I have had a disheartening time here trying to build up Russian studies. Academic authorities have been very shortsighted about this.*[46]

During World War II, the academic world had innumerable dislocations and faculties found themselves both short handed and faced with unusual demands. The University of Oklahoma swelled with large numbers of men enrolled in the Army's V-2 program, and in the history department teaching loads increased and areas of expertise stretched to cover the assignment of classes. Stuart Tompkins, who had never taken a course in United States history, was given sections of it to teach and felt himself badly used. Never one to duck a challenge, though, he "swatted up on it" and eventually said, "You know it's fun." But the pace was gruelling for all, and because of having to meet military scheduling, there was virtually no time away for faculty.[47]

In June of 1945, the University of California at Los Angeles offered Stuart a visiting lectureship for the school year 1945–46. He was eager to accept the position, but had difficulty in negotiating a leave from Oklahoma, attributable in no small measure to wartime aberration. He explained the situation to the department at UCLA:

> *the University having consistently ignored me for over twelve years are now raising heaven and earth to keep me. The reasons are not altogether flattering to me. A patriotic but hardly prudent legislature recently chose the present critical time in academic circles to impose a new requirement of six hours in American history and government on those wishing to take a degree. . . .*
>
> *On top of everything else, I feel that I have to get away for some time. I have really had no holiday since 1942, and with extra work and writing, I must take some time off and, if nothing else, this sojourn will help. Financially it will not be too attractive since the university here made me a tempting offer to stay.*

While the dean opposed granting him leave, the chairman of the history department favoured it, and in July, President George Cross came to agree with him.[48]

Stuart accepted the UCLA offer, and he and Edna arrived in Los Angeles the day before the war ended. They drove to the coast, and Edna recalled that when they left Oklahoma they had been "given a [gasoline] allowance—and *just exactly enough to get to California*—we couldn't make any side trips." They had better luck in regard to housing, another wartime problem that had plagued California.

In the early years of their marriage, living arrangements were always unsettled and uncertain, and one theme that recurs with some frequency in the wartime letters is Stuart's promise that they would have a home of their own. Throughout his teaching career Stuart and Edna always lived in rented quarters, and the house they found in Pacific Palisades was far and away the best that Edna had known. She loved it there, and later said, "I remember we had a house at the top of an arroyo. . . a beautiful site—went right down to the sea. . . . Stuart could drive to school. . . about eight miles—a beautiful drive. Oh, [it was] a lovely house." There was a strong possibility of Stuart's receiving a permanent appointment at UCLA, but it did not materialize. Edna formed some good friendships and felt very much at home there, and she was heartbroken when they left to return to Oklahoma in the summer of 1946.[49]

Stuart devoted the ten years following his return from UCLA primarily to his three-volume study of the Russian mind. In addition to his research, he worked long and hard for the creation of a Russian studies program and especially to build a sound collection of Russian materials for the library. At the time of his retirement its then quite adequate collection was enhanced considerably by the university's acquisition of his private library. His own collection dated back to the mid-thirties when he began buying books on the international market at the time when the Soviets were selling anything they could in order to get U.S. funds. Edna recalled that "Stuart bought beautiful books—from noble libraries, you know, all embossed, bound with leather."[50]

Those books provided Stuart and Edna with a rare moment of amusement during the FBI's postwar preoccupation with past and present academicians when an agent who had been dispatched to Norman arrived at the Tompkins' house to inquire about a former Oklahoma faculty member. He was shown into the living room with its bookcase full of Russian books, and Stuart told him that while he had not known the man under investigation well, he had no cause to think him a danger. The agent then happened to turn his head and caught sight of the bookcase. He made an immediate, confused, and hasty exit, but Edna and Stuart enjoyed for years the memory of the expression that had crossed his face.[51]

It has long been necessary for faculty members to come to terms with the phenomenon of intercollegiate athletics. Stuart Tompkins' wartime letters show some passing interest in sports, including boxing, which was central among World War I sporting diversions. He shared with a friend in British Columbia his view of athletics at the University of Oklahoma in the early years of its domination of college football under coach Bud Wilkinson:

> *Your remarks about the prevailing hockey mania in Penticton sounds much like our situation here. Our football team is the pride and joy of Oklahoma. . . . Football is little more than a gladiatorial combat; the players are brought from far and near and they do everything for the stars except to pay them a salary. It is regrettable that most university presidents are taken in by this and are quite complaisant about the neglect of the real purposes of a university. Actually these games are for the students and a reasonable amount of the Rah! Rah! Rah! spirit is perfectly natural for the non-participants . . . . But people should grow out of this adolescent preoccupation with sport to the detriment of real work.[52]*

So it is doubtful that he ever joined the throngs in Memorial Stadium on a Saturday afternoon. It is more likely, as one former student recalled, that their Saturday afternoons were spent "'bird walking'. . . .

They walked many miles. Oklahoma... is a great place for birding, because it is right here on the central fly-way. So as far as I know his Saturday afternoon was birding. He couldn't have cared less about that football."[53]

In the early fifties Stuart took an active interest in the university's establishment of a program in the history of science. Predictably, he lobbied for a broad approach to the subject and was fearful of "the whole paraphernalia of industrial research with its elaborate equipment and commanding enormous sources of money, and [which] has lost sight of the slow and painful process by which the fruitful ideas that lie behind modern science were brought to life." He feared that "there is a considerable disparity between the way the historian looks at the history of science and the way in which it is regarded at least by some scientists" and that if the latter emphasis were not avoided it would kill the program "by taking from it all of its significance."[54]

One of the greatest services that Stuart Tompkins rendered the University of Oklahoma was his work on the committee that selected William E. Livezey to be dean of the College of Arts and Sciences in the spring of 1953. Livezey had joined the Oklahoma history faculty in 1937; he and Stuart respected one another, and Stuart saw in him a dean who would be unlikely to slight the humanities in coming battles over priorities in the University. He persisted in his efforts to persuade Livezey to be a candidate for the deanship and to accept it when it was offered.[55] Stuart's judgment proved more than sound a decade later when Dean Livezey's leadership helped the university through difficult days of campus protest and upheaval.

Livezey remembered Stuart as a man of great sensitivity—"an unusually gifted man" whom he rated highly in "integrity and scholarship." He knew that in the planning for the history of science program Stuart, the classical scholar, "was aware that sometimes... we historians, we social scientists, were... a little bit too restricted in our view as much as the fact that the scientists tend to ignore the humanities."[56]

Esteem for Stuart's scholarship and integrity was nearly universal in the history department and throughout the university. One colleague wrote to him while he was at UCLA in 1945, "I have often remarked to my friends that you were the most scholarly man on the faculty of Arts and Sciences" and in a later expression of appreciation said that Stuart and Edna "were among our most dependable friends... true blue."[57] A number of young men joined the department at the end of the war, among them Gilbert Fite, who later recalled, *we all had a very high regard for him. . . . He had a very broad view of history. I expect Professor Tompkins was the best educated person, you know the most knowledgeable of history in kind of the "old school" [sense], by far of anybody in the department. . . . [but] He wasn't an easy man for a young assistant professor to know. He was always friendly enough, but you know I kind of held him in awe, as I did Dr. Dale and Carl Rister. . . . There was a lot more of a class system than there is today I think in the profession. . . [and] I would never think of calling one of them by their first name.* [58]

His selection as Research Professor of History in 1950 was strong confirmation of his peers' regard for him. Such appointments were rare at that time, and the process of selection began with a department's nomination.

Among students, too, he was both held in awe and widely respected. He did not suffer fools gladly, however, and no doubt many young Oklahomans found him formidable and austere. He was, in a sense, the epitome of "old school," and while he was not a dynamic lecturer, he challenged students, especially his graduate students, to excellence. He was alert to promise in students and very quick to encourage it. He remained remarkably available to students and quick to foster special abilities. One former student later called Stuart Tompkins "a great teacher and scholar of whom it might be said, as of Goldsmith's village master: 'Yet he was kind; or if severe in ought, / The love he bore to learning was at fault.'" His appreciation of bright and able women students and encouragement of their efforts was rather unique for his time, but it echoes the regard he had for his wife's intellect and ability which is readily apparent in his letters written decades earlier. The affection and esteem which his students held for him followed well beyond their student years, and some continued to correspond with him for the rest of his life. [59]

Retirement from the University of Oklahoma was mandatory at age seventy, and although Stuart would gladly have taught another four or five years and certainly had the vigour to do so, in the spring of 1956 he obtained emeritus status and he and Edna returned to Canada. [60] They spent the next school year at the University of Toronto with Stuart as a visiting professor then turned once more to the West. They settled in the Victoria, British Columbia, suburb of Lagoon, and at last built the home that had been their promise since 1915. They selected a site overlooking the Strait of Juan de Fuca, through which Stuart had returned to Canada thirty-six years earlier from the Siberian adventure that had set him on the path to Russian studies.

When Stuart Tompkins received his doctorate and was fortunate enough to secure a job, the state of Russian studies in the United States was as uncertain as the world economy. Few people were inclined toward the field, and as he himself had experienced at Chicago, few institutions encouraged students in that direction. Without diplomatic recognition of the Soviet Union, it would be some time before American scholars would venture into the Soviet archives, but when that time arrived, Stuart Tompkins was in the vanguard of those seeking access to them.

In 1937, with the promise of a grant from the Social Science Research Council to work in the Soviet archives, he made travel plans and reservations only to be denied the grant at the last minute because he could not obtain absolute assurance of access to the archives before sailing. On the strength of Samuel Harper's having interceded for him with both Soviet Ambassador Oumansky in Washington and a Mr. Neyman of the then Commissariate of Foreign Affairs in Moscow, he felt sure enough himself to borrow the money and make the trip. Neyman secured permission for him, and, in Stuart's words,

> *I was sent to one of the Archives buildings—that on Serpukhovskaya Street, where I worked off and on for a month. . . . I was provided with a desk; was asked the subject of my study and was told a search for documents would be made. . . . These were brought to my desk. Any notes I made were picked up by the women who presided over the reading room, at the end of the day. Finally one day they informed me that they had no more documents bearing on the subject of my search.*

He then went to Leningrad and was permitted to work in the archives there. He worked in the old Senate building and found the atmosphere and conditions much freer and more relaxed. He secured more documents and no effort was made to take his notes. On his return to Moscow he applied for the notes he had surrendered there, and as he told it:

> *[I] was told they would have to be translated back into Russian and carefully scrutinized. On the advice of a Mr. Durbrow I turned over to the Commissariate also the notes I had taken in Leningrad, with a view to keeping the record straight and avoid[ing] complications. . . . [But] in retrospect I can see that it was a mistake. The Soviet government does not understand what I call*

playing the game. They expect every person to take advantage of them and failure to do so is not counted for righteousness.

He left the Soviet Union without his notes but with assurance that this was customary and that they would be sent to him. About a year later, by way of the embassy in Washington, he received a small packet with the explanation that the "handful of some half-dozen cards was all of [his] summer's work that they would allow out." The rest were denied because

> *I had . . . exceeded the limits of my project and had taken notes outside of it. The subject of research I had given was "Count Witte Minister of Finance, 1892–1903." They insisted that these latter dates set a time limit for the notes, so that nothing of a prior or a subsequent date could be allowed, no matter how much of a bearing it had on Witte's work.*

Stuart later expressed surprise that he had actually been allowed into the archives and could only ascribe it to

> *the good offices of Professor Harper and Mr. Neyman (who later that summer disappeared). But I have been even more astonished when I know what was the state of panic in Moscow in the summer of 1937 and it was probably the aftermath of that panic that led the censors to so strict an interpretation of their rules . . . or at any rate to decide to throw out my notes.*[61]

While Stuart was in the Soviet Union that summer, Edna stayed in Norman to complete the index to *Russia through the Ages,* which manuscript he had all but completed before he left. While this first book received a mixed reception, it was appreciated as an early work in English on Russian history. The reviewer for the New York *Times* noted that Stuart was then "the only native born American to attempt to present a comprehensive account of the Russian State." He applauded the declaration in the preface that the author had "not borne faith to any special theory of history and . . . endeavored to tread warily amid the still fiercely burning partisan fires," but he regretted Tompkins' "seemingly insurmountable reluctance to draw conclusions from the 'facts' he has collected."[62] This reluctance may seem incongruous in a determined, forthright, and demanding professor, but from his early letters, it should not be surprising that he did not press his own position and opinions.

Reviews in more specialized and scholarly journals ran a gamut from that in *World Affairs Quarterly,* which found it "A very good book" and concluded that it was "to be highly recommended to all who are interested in the history of Russia," through that in the *Journal of Central European Affairs,* which found that "Professor Tompkins has produced a highly commendable volume, of sound scholarship and based on extensive use of Russian sources," to a scathing assessment in the *American Historical Review,* which found the book confusing, its treatment "outmoded," and lacking in a number of details.[63]

Stuart "felt that he was a mastodon most of his life," and as a historian trained in the Classics, a firm defender of the humanist tradition, his work may well have been viewed as old-fashioned in its approach even as it broke new ground in the field of European intellectual history.[64] Among his students the view was widely held that he probably did not get nearly the recognition that he deserved. They saw this as a consequence of his geographic and intellectual isolation at Oklahoma and his being outside the Harvard-Columbia sphere in the postwar development of Russian studies. Some felt that had he stayed in California he would have loomed larger on the national scene and had his books borne a UCLA stamp they would have received more attention than they did.[65] Such speculation no doubt contains some truth.

While Stuart Tompkins was a conservative man, he was by no means a reactionary one. He had no illusions about the Soviets, and from his days in Vladivostok on he held a realistic and conservative view of their system and policies, a view not in vogue during the productive part of his career. He was fearful of a loss of balance in Soviet studies, and in 1955 wrote,

> *I have had my fingers crossed with regard to a lot of books and articles rolling off the presses which seem to be overkind to the Soviet Union. Of course, it is a sort of intangible thing and one is inclined to be ashamed to suspect respectable writers of undue tenderness. . . . But I would surely like to know whether there are other souls that have the same uncomfortable feeling that I do in the face of the evidence that seems to be accumulating of something amiss in the treatment of the Soviet Union in academic circles.[66]*

He felt that much of what was going on in the Soviet Union was rooted in historical trends that carried over from czarist objectives rather than purely derived from Communist theory. Another of his predilections was for seeing the primacy of Russian national character in historical developments, and the concept of national character, too, was not in vogue in postwar intellectual circles.

He came to think that had western statesmen and diplomats understood the Russian use of what he termed Aesopian Language they would have been less confused and more effective in their dealings with the former wartime ally. On this last point he said:

There is another factor not sufficiently understood and appreciated in the west and that is "Aesopian language." Even revolutionaries were sometimes mystified by its obscure symbolism. This practice of what Lenin refers to as "using language to hide your real thought rather than to reveal it" became second nature to the revolutionaries under Tsarist censorship and has become standard in diplomatic use in dealing with foreign powers. The best illustration is the communist policy towards national minorities proclaimed in the high-sounding "Declaration of the rights of the peoples of Russia" of Nov. 15, 1917 and embodied in the constitutions of 1923 and 1936. It is just so much humbug as one can see by the qualifications attached to it and even Lenin confessed that it was just so much window-dressing. Orwell caricatured it in his 1984 but it is far more subtle and dangerous (to us) than even he imagines.[67]

He feared the lack of appreciation in the West for conspiratorial turns, and a passage from an address given at the University of Alberta in the summer of 1953 not only stated this, but also clearly showed where he stood vis-à-vis the cold war practice of red-baiting:

at the present time, we are almost in complete ignorance of conspiratorial practice. This alone is one of our most serious blind spots. The Communist movement which thus embraces both a philosophical as well as a conspiratorial aspect quite bewilders us, with the result that we are inclined to strike out blindly. The rather indiscriminate imposition of loyalty oaths, of red scares on the campus, of reckless charges in the newspapers attests this confusion of mind. Now I am not making light of the dangers of communist conspiracy which I think is a very real one but surely some distinction should be drawn in intelligent people's minds between acts of treason and the entertainment of radical views, however wrong-headed we may regard them; and between an honest attempt to understand and explain communist ideas and practices on the one hand, and the base prostitution of intellectual powers and forswearing of all integrity of mind in the interests of the spread of communism on the other. Politicians will always make capital out of such confusion but, worse still, the intelligence agents of the armed service have been known to pillory a man because he had Russian books in his possession or because he spoke a good word for the Soviet system of education.[68]

On that same occasion he rejected the famous Churchill maxim and called for a fresh appraisal of Russian thought and life:

> *Churchill reacted to the Russian problem by saying that Russia was "a mystery wrapped in an enigma inside a riddle." Now while that is a fine piece of rhetoric expressing a natural bewilderment, it amounts to little more than a dismissal of the problem with the implied assumption that some day, the Russians will become civilized and will act in a way that civilized people will understand and that then we can get on with them. But . . . the problem has taken on an acute urgency and cannot be left to the processes of time to bring a solution in the remote future. An immediate and accurate appraisal is called for if we are to guide our actions intelligently.*[69]

Stuart had personal reason to cite loyalty oaths, having been affected by the enactment of Oklahoma's loyalty oath law in April of 1951. (The law was ultimately ruled unconstitutional by the United States Supreme Court in December of 1952.) While he personally had no strong objection to signing such an oath, there were some in the history department who did, and they received both moral and financial support from their colleagues when salaries were withheld as a consequence of their refusal to sign. The oath requirement did, however, present a problem for a Canadian citizen, and after determining from the Canadian Embassy in Washington that signing would jeopardize his status in Canada, he and Edna filed first papers for United States citizenship, which they never pursued beyond that initial application.[70]

By the summer of 1953, Stuart had completed the first of his three-volume work on the Russian mind; in it he had clarified and developed much of the thinking expressed in his August speech in Edmonton. This study had grown from seeds planted in 1946 while Stuart was at UCLA and still basking in the warm acceptance given his just completed book on Alaska, *Alaska: Promyshlennik and Sourdough*. In a letter to the director of the University of Oklahoma Press he wrote:

> *I have lately been seized with the desire to make some contribution to the distressing problems of our relations with the Soviet Union. You may or may not remember that last year I gave a talk on the Russian revolutionary tradition. That tradition (including Lenin) has fixed the Russian revolutionary mentality about which we know less than nothing and as a result we are merely sawing the air in our relations with the Russians. Of course this is not just a matter of the revolutionary tradition. It goes back to other matters. . . .*

I do not like to approach a problem with conclusions already reached. But this whole thing challenges me and I should like to at least reconnoitre it. Of course, it would require a knowledge of many other things than history and perhaps it would be just too vast for one man. At any rate I have been turning it over in my mind with a view to action.[71]

The Russian Mind: From Peter the Great through the Enlightenment appeared in 1953, greeted by the same sort of mixed reviews as *Russia through the Ages* had received. One considered it a valuable contribution to a growing body of "scholarly investigations which seek to point out the degree of continuity between the Russia of the czars and the Russia of the Soviets" and noted that Stuart had made the past a "frequent frame of reference for the present, and in this respect some startling similarities in details are brought out." The second of the three volumes, *The Russian Intelligentsia: Makers of the Revolutionary State,* was published in 1957, and while it, too, elicited varied responses, it was by and large considered a valuable "scholarly yet readable book." To judge from one reviewer's observation that it was "another valuable addition to our understanding of the Russian mind—apparently as baffling to Westerners today as it was yesterday," Stuart had accomplished at least in part his desire to aid in improving Soviet-American relations.[72]

The Russian Intelligentsia merited reissuing in 1967 (by the Greenwood Press), the same year in which the third and final volume of the trilogy came from the press. *The Triumph of Bolshevism: Revolution or Reaction?*, an intellectual history of Russian Marxism, brought the study down through the 1917 revolution. In reviews written nearly two decades since others had bruised *Russia through the Ages,* Stuart's work again met stinging criticism.[73] But there were also those who paid him tribute, as did Ralph Carter Elwood in saying, "Slavists on the North American continent owe a considerable debt to Stuart Ramsay Tompkins. Dr. Tompkins, now in his ninth decade, began his study of Russian history before the revolution and indeed participated in the ill-fated Allied intervention," and he seemed to regret that "Many readers will find Tompkins' interpretation somewhat old-fashioned." Theodore H. Von Laue said of the book, "Professor Tompkins' postscript to his earlier work on the intellectual history of modern Russia is a worthy conclusion to a fruitful scholarly career carried well beyond retirement age."[74]

Stuart Tompkins' scholarly career did extend well beyond his formal retirement. In addition to publishing *The Triumph of Bolshevism,* he researched and wrote a slender volume titled *The Secret War,* which deals with "the extra-military attempts... commencing almost at the outset of the First World War, to bring about an end to the hostilities; or, at least... to foreshorten appreciably the period of conflict."[75] He attempted to edit for publication the letters that he had written to Edna from Siberia, but rather than seeing them published he gave photocopies of them to friends.

There is an indication that in these later years Stuart regained an interest in pacifism or the means of preventing future conflicts that can be seen in some of his wartime letters. Such interest had apparently remained dormant, to resurface with the Vietnam War. In the mid-1970's, he raised the matter in what proved to be his last letter to his friend and colleague William E. Livezey, who was himself a Quaker. Livezey remembered that Stuart knew of his Quaker background and wrote expressing interest in pacifism and the story of non-violence. He speculated that having served in the army and having seen the picture pro and con Stuart had become intrigued with the possibilities of pacifism, "either as a conceivable mode of conduct . . .[or] as a counter action to his own earlier training," but he did not "think it was altogether casual with him."[76]

He had, in a sense, come full circle back to his experience in that most literary of wars that had provided the impetus for his life's work. Stuart Tompkins died in Victoria, British Columbia, on 11 October 1977, at the age of 91.

A CANADIAN'S ROAD TO RUSSIA

Edna Christie, ca. 1912.

Courtship and Marriage of a Civil Servant

❧ OCTOBER 1912 TO JUNE 1915 ❧

Edna Christie and Stuart Tompkins first met in 1912, when she joined the clerical staff of the Alberta Department of Education. She caught the eye of the twenty-five year old chief clerk almost immediately, and from that point on he was a suitor who would not be deterred. Their courtship lasted two and a half years. The letters he wrote to her during that period show the beginning of a relationship that was to become a true and lasting partnership. They reveal Stuart Tompkins as something of a Romantic in the late Victorian mode, and his letters show an inclination toward expression far more amorous and intimate than any counterpart today would permit himself. He appears as a man who placed women on a pedestal and who was to waver only slightly in his regard for women as the twentieth century progressed. The courtship letters include some written after they had just parted for the evening and some written at the end of a day in which they had worked together in the same office, but in the main they are letters written when he was away from Edmonton on Education Department business or when they were apart on separate holidays. They establish early his habit when they were not together of writing to her every day and in some instances two or three times a day, a habit that lends credence to the belief of one friend that "things just weren't quite real to Stuart until he had shared them with Edna."[1]

Two letters from 1912 survive. He wrote the first while he was away on business, and the second one found him in a reflective, prayerful holiday mood.

Christmas Eve, 1912.

My Dear Edna :—

     I suppose I need not tell you of my wishes for you on this Christmas. It has brought solemn thoughts to me and a heartfelt prayer for your future happiness There is a great deal more that might be said but I shall leave it till we are face to face. I sincerely trust that

LETHBRIDGE HOTEL
LETHBRIDGE, ALBERTA
OCTOBER 15, 1912

My Dear Edna:—

After leaving Edmonton last night, it dawned on me that I had failed to speak to you of the length of my absence and that you might reserve Saturday afternoon next, not having heard anything to the contrary. I do not know whether I should otherwise have done well in writing but I have at any rate a reasonable pretext now.

I am bound for a rather out of the way part of the province with every probability of being detained until the end of the week. Indeed it is problematical whether I can be at home for Sunday. Would it be too much to look forward to that we should go to church together Sunday evening. If I am not to be home Sunday I shall write and if I am I shall phone.

Pen and ink are a very poor medium for conveying one's thoughts. I left Edmonton last night and have made my trip so far without a hitch. One thing however I find that the further I go, the more restless I become. Believe me the one thing I look forward to at the end of my week is seeing you again. Indeed I have to admit—you have been the one object of my thoughts since leaving.

However, I suppose I should not continue in that strain. My brain is on fire and trying to express my thoughts is unsatisfactory. I do not need to tell you that I love you. I will only pray that nothing untoward may happen [to] you in the meantime.

Stuart R. Tompkins

CHRISTMAS EVE, 1912

My Dear Edna:—

I suppose I need not tell you of my wishes for you on this Christmas. It has brought solemn thoughts to me and a heartfelt prayer for your future happiness. There is a great deal more that might be said but I shall leave it till we are face to face. I sincerely trust that when you kneel tonight and on the morrow, you will include in your petition a plea for our sure guidance according to the principles of high honour and the light of love.

May Christmas dawn in gladness for you and yours. Trusting to see you tomorrow.

Yours,
Stuart

3

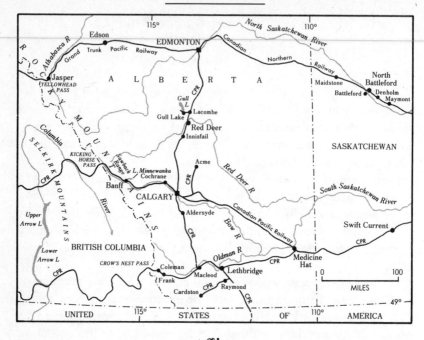

In the summer of 1913 Stuart and Edna were separated by both business and pleasure. She took her summer holiday at Gull Lake, a popular vacation spot about half way between Edmonton and Calgary, and in June, he was dispatched to southern Alberta by the Education Department on one of a number of trips that he made during his career there.

After attaining provincial status in 1905, Alberta experienced a large in-migration that required the creation of additional school districts under the supervision of the provincial Education office in Edmonton, and there were efforts at reform that would ensure a leading role for the public schools in the assimilation and "Canadianization" of the non-English-speaking. The matter of separate, tax-supported parochial schools was another element in a sensitive situation. During the 1913–1914 school year, long-simmering problems with linguistic minorities came to a head in the province. The deputy minister denied teaching permits to teachers deficient in English and took direct control of districts which refused to dismiss their then unqualified teachers. The corps of fifteen provincial school inspectors was increased to deal with these developments and at least one clerk, Stuart Tompkins, was also pressed into duty in the hinterland.[2]

LETHBRIDGE HOTEL
LETHBRIDGE, ALBERTA
JUNE 19, 1913

My Dear Edna:—

I am pulling out in a little over half an hour but thought it might be as well to drop a note before going. Nothing momentous has occurred, except that I am wretchedly tired. Our train did not get in until 12:15 last night and about one o'clock the night clerk woke me up to tell me I was in the wrong room!! He couldn't have induced me to change then at the point of a pistol. I very nearly missed the train at Edmonton, too. We met nearly every car in the city on the single track and it took me almost an hour to cross the river.

I had lots of time to think yesterday but I do not think I will put down the result just now. I guess that trip to Edson spoiled me for travelling alone. I kept turning around almost expecting to see you sitting beside me. Wouldn't I have given anything if it had been true? I guess I don't know how much you mean to me till I am away from you. Such is the irony of fate. Believe me, however, you are never out of my thoughts.

> Yours sincerely,
> *Stuart R. Tompkins*

The letter of 20 June, which follows, is an early reflection of Stuart's ambivalent feelings about Englishmen.

LETHBRIDGE
JUNE 20, 1913

Dear Edna:—

I could scarcely persuade myself it could be true when the clerk handed me a letter from you. I had just got in from the south on the train from New Dayton and believe me it was a welcome sight.

I have had a delightful stay amid the rural scenes of Southern Alberta. We had fearful rains but fortunately I was out in none of them. The country looks very beautiful and the air is delightful. I caught glimpses of the mountains as we came into Lethbridge an hour ago which is really the first time I have seen them since leaving Calgary. . . .

I don't suppose you will be interested in hearing of my trip. I learned a few things, however, particularly with reference to our department's short-comings. But I have principally had a rest. I seem to have scared up a few life sized worries lately.

Well I shall pass on your advice to me to "be good.". . . Well I'll be glad to get back to Edmonton that's a safe gamble.

Yours sincerely,

Stuart R. Tompkins

P. S. They had a bad windstorm in Raymond and the Mormon settlement. Buildings destroyed, etc.

En-route to Calgary June 21/13

P.S.   I did not post my letter in Lethbridge so you may not object to my making some additions by way of postscript: I forgot to tell you about the enjoyable time I had in New Dayton. T.M. Riches, the secretary and teacher is an Englishman but wonder of wonders is a very likeable fellow. After our meeting he took me around to the quarters of the bank clerks—also Englishmen and we had TEA. They have very delightful rooms over the bank and they gathered all the young bloods of the city in my honour. It was six o'clock before we broke up and the train left within five minutes.

Lethbridge is a very pretty city and I was almost sorry to leave. They have far better trees than we have in Edmonton although they grow under less favourable conditions. The streets and buildings also look fresh and new and after Thursday's rain things were at their best.

This would be a slow tedious journey were it not for the views one gets of the mountains. I think I have seen between 5000 and 6000 mountains since we left Lethbridge. We are now coming in sight of those you can see from Calgary which are higher than the range west of Lethbridge though not more elevated than those along the American border.

Unfortunately for me I came away without my breakfast this morning so am looking forward to reaching Calgary. G. T. promised to meet me. If I can arrange it, though I shall head for the nearest restaurant.

I have wondered several times just what you were doing but I don't suppose anything extraordinary has occurred. I expect to return Tuesday morning.

Stuart

While Edna vacationed at the lake, Stuart remained in Edmonton to help his brother Philip who was involved in the residential electrical wiring business. The following letters suggest that the courtship was of greater moment to him than to her that summer.

955 27TH STREET, EDMONTON
JULY 5, 1913

My Dear Edna:—

I have been writing a number of formal letters tonight and was tempted to start yours in the same way. I *did* receive your long delayed letter of the 3rd, with mingled feelings. Well I have not much to tell you since my last letter. I have been working hard today. My hands are getting scarred and calloused and I suppose my arms will develop a little brawn soon. I can't say I'm enjoying it and only a sense of duty keeps me at it.

Well, what about going down [to Gull Lake]. I usually know my own mind but in this case I don't or perhaps I should say I have two minds. I want to see you—never so badly, and to have the holiday... but I shall have to stick it out here at least till the end of the week.

I don't think I have anything more to say—except of course. Oh I suppose it can be left unsaid. Good bye, dear, and look after yourself.
                                                            Stuart

955 27TH STREET, EDMONTON
JULY 6 1913

My Dearest Edna:—

I am not in a very good position to write you a letter as I have no cue, not having received one from you. Nor can I write a very cheerful one. I feel kind of blue not having heard from you. I don't suppose you are to blame, only it gave me kind of an empty feeling when I came in yesterday and found nothing for me. Will tomorrow bring something? I had a little money so I went and gave it all to Alice so that I should not be tempted to board the next train for the south. I have promised myself that I will at least stick the week out.

In writing to you, I have been put in mind of something in antiquity. The letters of Cicero to his wife were couched in most affectionate terms—till the last when he grew curt and brief. No editorial explanation was needed and it was no surprise to learn that divorce followed. That sort of checks my tongue or my hand when I wish to write what my whole being longs to say. Heaven help me I have tried to be honest. I could not anyway hide hypocrisy from you. (And it is something easily nourished) but I do love you, darling, and cannot but tell you so. I have been sort of wandering around with about half my life lopped off.

Now I started off to write a nice, staid, dignified letter and feel that I have fallen away. However, I will try to resume my story where it was broken off last Tuesday. I came home and got into harness. By Friday night I was dead tired and the last straw came when Philip got up at five Saturday morning to start for Winnipeg. I stayed in bed till eight o'clock and then took a holiday the rest of the day. . . . I am going to work like a nigger the rest of the week and see if I can't forget the letter that hasn't come. I guess there is lots to do according to reports.

I was in the office yesterday and got my mail etc. I saw Miss Matilda Swenkson who is occupying your seat. I also dictated a letter to her and found her very accurate. . . .

Now I am in quandary where to address this letter. . . . Gull Lake should be a P.O. but I will trust to your first guess and if it is wrong why I am not to blame. I suppose you are having one grand time learning to swim and dive—without water-wings. What do you do with the rest of your time. Have you lots of reading matter. How is the appetite. Do you get fish. There must be some Isaak Waltons around. Well remember me to Mrs. Christie and the children.

Don't go into deep water . . . .

Yours etc.
Stuart

955 TWENTY-SEVENTH STREET,
EDMONTON
JULY 9, 1913

My Dearest Edna:—

I met someone down street this morning who said you were lonesome. It was said with a knowing nod at me which was of course quite beside the mark. It is not that I believe the remark that I am writing. I am in a mighty uncertain frame of mind and I suppose I am writing for inspiration. Yesterday the electricians struck or were locked out (no one seems to know which) but I am out of a job. I loafed around all morning but do not feel any better, in fact worse—fact is if I don't get back to work right off, I'll be pawing the air to get down to Gull Lake—a terrible state of affairs you will admit. I am just waiting till Philip comes back from Winnipeg to do something. If he needs help of course I will help him but if not I shall take things in my own hands.

It is wretchedly hot in the city today. We had quite a thunderstorm night before last and I guess it is preparing to rain again. Reminds me I have still neither umbrella nor rain coat . . . .

By the way did you know that Mr. Fife is going north to the Mission Schools. He leaves I understand today and will be gone about three months. Wouldn't I like to be going with him?

Now perhaps I am presuming too much in writing so often. If you would rather not why "verbum sapienti" a gentle hint will be enough. I don't suppose I have any right to assume that I fill so large a space in your thoughts as you in mine. However, let that be as it may, I obeyed the impulse and will leave it to you to say whether wisely or no.

You really did not tell me much about your arrangements at Gull Lake. I presume that if you do not pick strawberries you do something. Are you learning to swim or have you already learned? . . . Have you yet no pen or ink at the cottage, or do you wait till you reach the Post Office before addressing the envelope. On all of which subjects I request fuller information before I can decide whether it is a fit place for me to spend a holiday.

Now I really have nothing more to say. I wonder if I shall get a reply. Remember *I* am lonesome.

Stuart

The two letters that follow are all that survive from the fall of 1913. They were both written while he was away from Edmonton on a series of trips for the department.

ACME [ALBERTA]

AUGUST 7, 1913

My Dear Edna:—

I am very sorry that my week has been so upset that I have not been much use to myself or anyone else. I can tell you I did not leave Edmonton with any enthusiasm last night after two nights already spent on the train and for the first time in a year mother spent the night alone. However the girls will be home today. . . .

Last night I was wedged in a company of vaudeville actors travelling to Calgary. They came in about 11:30 gossiped and quarrelled till long after midnight and filled the place with confusion. (Dinner!) You can imagine with what joy I responded to the call, when you know I didn't have breakfast. I had to change at Maharg instead of going on into the city depot.

After I got on the train last night and had been asleep for some time it occurred to me that I had not taken precautions to make sure I got on the Calgary train and could not be sure but that morning would find me somewhere near Winnipeg. However it appears that Providence looks after fools.

Well I guess it is up to me to pull out as soon as possible. It is eighteen miles from here to Carbon. Don't you wish me good luck.

Yours sincerely
Stuart

THE ADELPHI HOTEL
LACOMBE, ALBERTA
SEPTEMBER 2, 1913

My Dearest Edna:—

It was my original intention to leave here this morning and to have my dinner at Gull Lake. By a combination of good and bad luck, I have to wait here till 12:30 and was mighty glad to find that I should have a chance to drop a line to you. I have really been too lazy to write since I went down to Erskine and any way there is but one mail a day and none on Sunday. My stay at Erskine was delightful. The weather has been all that could be desired. The Carruthers made such a fuss over me. I am sure I should be badly spoiled if I stayed. They have the English idea of anticipating a man's every want. I was glad I went as the son Will has been miserable with hay-fever and I guess I cheered him up some.

I hope to get through this wretched business by tomorrow night and to get off to Edmonton. I may be however one day longer and shall certainly not scruple to take all the time necessary.

I was wondering where you were and what you were doing on Sunday. I should like to have been there. I fear my heart hunger gets worse when I leave home. I felt very much down in the dumps when I left Edmonton last Saturday.

Well you will hear from me as soon as I get to Edmonton. I only wish it could be sooner.

Sincerely yours,
Stuart

If the course of true love is far from smooth, that of Stuart and Edna Tompkins was, in its early years, no exception to the rule. Toward the end of 1913, he began to press his case with greater intensity and on occasion despaired of having his offer of marriage accepted. Edna Christie was an independent woman whose plans for her own future did not necessarily include marriage. She was certainly capable and perhaps desirous of having a career and of being self-supporting; she parried his insistent pleas with interesting, evasive and, for him, frustrating suggestions and actions.

He apparently had wanted for some time to convey to her the thoughts in the following letter, and his absence from Edmonton following a recent disagreement between them provided him the opportunity. He expounds at some length on his philosophy or "right attitudes toward life," and it clearly shows the lasting influence of his first trip West.

CPR TRAIN [ON BOARD]
DECEMBER 16, 1913

My Dear Edna:—

Perhaps I am taking an unfair advantage of you in using this occasion to write to you. To tell the truth, I should like to have written before to put my thoughts on paper but probably you would not have liked it.

It is now 8:30... so I have had a wait of three quarters of an hour. I feel rewarded however. The sun is just rising and the morning is just glorious. I am sure I shall enjoy the trip if the car is not too warm. There are very few passengers travelling, not a dozen in our car.

Anent our recent argument. You are infinitely wiser than I, because you know your own mind while mine is overshadowed by one issue.

Now I don't suppose there would be any purpose in my writing, like Newman, Apologia pro Vita mea. At the same time I feel there are certain indispensable things not for success but for content and peace of mind to which I take it all men are entitled. Perhaps it borders close on religion but it is, I take it, even more fundamental. It has been the subject of discussion by philosophers for all time. I would call it the right attitude towards life. It first took hold of me when I came West in 1905 and met (to me) an entirely new creature—the Western cattleman. Nothing (aside from the bigness of the country) impressed me so much as the careless courage of those pioneers, the ability to take hardship with a laugh, to work almost to exhaustion and then at the end of the day to kick up their heels almost in sheer defiance of the laws of nature. It is splendid and illustrates in the aptest way the essential greatness of the human soul that it can dominate its circumstances. Perhaps my newspaper experience aided it but I don't know anything like my western experience that sickened me of the prospect of getting into a profession by the aid of a little extra knowledge and so dodging all the difficulties that attend making one's way in the world. I know now I was partly wrong but those, at any rate were my motives. I haven't always stuck to my own principles but it is not the fault of the principles.

Now I don't know that this has anything to do with you. Did I misunderstand you in assuming that your first essential in marriage was not the determination to make it go but the assurance that it would not interfere with your own freedom. Now my experience on that score has been that once you start bartering with circumstances you get the worst of it, that you must first accept the conditions as laid down and by the application of pluck and common sense work out your own salvation. It might be called the ability to break up your life into epochs wherein you renounce what is incompatible with conditions.

I have no written homily on marriage that I can hand you and it is a very dangerous topic for a layman to discuss. At the same time I doubt whether it is just what you think it to be. God knows it holds out the keenest allurements to me, in the way of companionship, help and the gratification of our common tastes. But common sense reminds me that that is not all and we run the risk of being fooled, if we attempt to skim off the cream and leave the milk. Mind you, I am not going to bargain. My experience the other night shows me that I cannot trifle with my peace of mind and I take it yours, by contemplating any alternative. But I think both of us have level heads and the experience of others to guide us so we would have no excuse for making a failure.

I must confess I should like nothing better than the course you hinted at—that you should for a time at any rate take up some work and that we should live together as—what shall we say—close friends with common interests. But do you honestly think it feasible. I wouldn't hint that it was a case of refusing to accept conditions. Of course I know that to you there would be no more uninteresting and blase experience than to settle down as the wife of a government employee (or professional man) with a competence to live on but the prospect of a perfect sameness till the end of your days. You would be able to look down the road and see your gravestone at the end. But I can assure you that I am ambitious that I am anxious to see the larger world and to live life to the full and you could feel that you were as much a part of my career as myself. What do you think about it?

I am going to have another talk with you. I take it you are not merely negative in the matter but that you would outline some future. I need help, you know, in this affair as well as you.

I am surprised at the dispassionate tone of my letter. It far from expressed my thoughts. Indeed the one thing that has obsessed me since Sunday night is that we do love one another and that I can bank on you. I suppose it is unreasonable for me to expect you to feel as I do. The heart seems to require no uncertain answer to its call. What does concern me is that if your life is committed to my keeping there shall be no mistake, that you will have no cause to regret but that you will find marriage the very door to heaven, the key to some of the hidden things of life, an entry by which we enter to the mysteries of God. Heaven help us dear, we may not be disobedient to the heavenly vision.

Perhaps I may seem to have said more than circumstances warrant but in view of what is at stake, not out of all proportion to its importance. And if you knew, dearest, how large a part of my life you fill, you would not wonder at it. Oh it's easy enough to put something on paper but that something comes as near it as a child does to the moon which he cries for. The sound of your voice, the glint of your hair overwhelm me with a terrible longing for you. Well, I can no more say what I want to say than I can fly to yonder sun except God bless you.

I have suddenly awoke to the fact that we are past Wetaskiwin. The sun is still hanging low over the fields but the day is getting even more beautiful. The gentleman in front in cloth cap and sheepskin coat has just borrowed my morning paper. He informs me that he has come away from home and forgot his glasses but "that feller there (the newsy) is sellin' him a pair." Imagine!! I count on getting to Castor this afternoon at 5 o'clock. If possible I shall hire a motor and go right out to Hanna. The weather is so fine and the roads so good that I should have no difficulty in reaching there at 8:30. (Our enterprising young friend has just pulled off his stunt and exchanged a bum pair of glasses for good money. Think of the torture to which those eyes will be subjected.) If I do that I will probably motor back in time to catch the morning train at Castor.

Well be sure you look after yourself. I shall probably reach home before you get this letter but never mind. My leaving home was just an excuse for writing. Goodbye for the present my dear girl.

Yours very sincerely
Stuart

The 1913 Christmas holidays, which Edna spent with her family in Calgary, marked the point at which their relationship entered a very rocky and uncertain phase that lasted well into the following spring. Edna apparently asked that they see less of each other and indicated that she was depressed by thoughts of the future. His letter of 31 December was the first of many that he would write over the next six years recounting in detail their relationship from the time of their first meeting.

1553 TWENTY-SIXTH STREET
EDMONTON, DECEMBER 25, 1913

My Dear Edna:—

For the first time today I am going to have a breathing spell, so I shall take advantage of it. We had a small crowd to dinner; indeed it is just a couple of hours since we finished and they are just breaking up for the evening, and mother and I are to be left alone—to my great content.

It seems as though it will take about twenty-four hours sleep to rest me. Last night when I bade you goodbye Jentie and I went down town, did some more shopping, loaded up with parcels and started for home. It was about ten thirty when we arrived and there were parcels to undo, incidents to tell etc. etc. with the result that I did not roll in until nearly midnight. I just soldiered around all morning and could not pluck up any courage until dinner time and now I'm going to bed just as soon as I get an opportunity.

I trust sincerely you got home all right. I thought quite a number of times of you even during the night and wondered how you fared. I suppose I should not have said so much about coming back. We will get along at the office and I suppose you will be wanted [at home]. I shall of course meet the train Saturday morning willy nilly unless I hear definitely from you to the contrary.

You were sure a brick in the thing you chose for me. I was remembered by quite a number but Santa did not duplicate. I wish to thank you, dear, for your thoughtfulness.

I really have had a very joyous time—perhaps rather in anticipation than enjoyment but it has given us all a fresh start at home and has been good for all of us.

... I shall send you news tomorrow if you are not coming Saturday.

If this letter is going tonight I shall have to close. Remember me to all the folks, and take good care of yourself and don't forget me, dearest.

Yours very sincerely,
Stuart

WEDNESDAY AFTERNOON
DECEMBER 31 [1913]

My Dear Edna:—

Your note this afternoon prompted me to do something that has been in my mind since Sunday evening—to write you a good long letter.

I do not know your reasons for the request you have made. I can only conjecture and wait for them to be revealed later. You must have some justification for it but I [am] all in a daze and cannot imagine what it can be—whether some fault of mine or some discipline you think I should undergo.

May I without undue introspection revert to our discussion of Sunday evening. I was at a loss to understand your attitude at the last but could only infer that you thought I "was not sure." Now I am going to review the whole situation and make some confidences. God help me if you misunderstand me for there is nothing I can do.

When we first met at the Department in October of last year, my impression of course was that you were a mere girl. At the same time I was afraid of you (I don't know why) and was, I am sure, ill at ease in your presence. I had other girl friends with whom I was on intimate terms and my intercourse with them continued throughout the fall, I may say that the thought had occurred to me from time to time that the intimacy *might* lead to something more definite. At the same time I never made love to them nor anything approaching it although I saw before Thanksgiving was passed that our intimacy might be construed as more than mere friendship. By Christmas, however, I found that I was in love with you. I did not know it at first, but I looked for your appearance, morning, noon and night. When you stood by me I could scarcely work so great was my agitation.

Now what was I to do? I could leave the Department but just then I could not afford to. I put off the difficulty trying to convince myself that it was a mere fleeting passion but I soon realized that I loved you and that I could not, should not, think of anyone else. Night after night I walked the street trying to come to some conclusion but could reach no other decision than to speak to you. You put me off till I should know something further of you and I waited to see if there would be some relief. Finally I made up my mind that some definite understanding should be reached. Do you remember that night when we went for a walk and I asked you. My mind had been in utter confusion and I had resolved to put the matter to you straight in some way or other. I was all on fire and I overbore your objections. You know what happened. If it was wrong for me to kiss you, I was wrong but what could I do. God knows it was the first time I ever kissed a girl.

There is no use of going over the history of the past few months. I have not departed from my idea that you are the only girl I want. Any doubt I have had was of yourself. You say yourself you were a child six months ago and I reproached myself at times that I had carried things with too high a hand and perhaps taken you at a disadvantage. I knew also that you were not *domestic* in your tastes and thought it was unfair to require you to take up with me the burden that is laid upon me. Those doubts I have expressed freely to you and we have discussed them in a dispassionate manner. There have been no other doubts. I thought there would be none in your mind.

Well I don't know why you are inflicting this anguish upon me. You told me that you loved me and how could I have any doubt after Sunday. And yet you appeared cold to me when we parted and gave me no satisfaction. I have walked around in a kind of dream since then. Tonight I don't know what to think. If you go back on me, I am undone. For Heavens sake do not take amiss what I have said. I have laid bare my whole heart. God knows there is nothing there but love for you and the pain that your note has brought. You will know now that I have no secrets from you no corners of my life into which I cannot admit you. I have never loved a girl before, never thrown myself so on one persons mercy. Why *have* you done it?

I shall not worry you beyond sending this letter. Will you let me know when this penance is to end? Since it is your wish I shall refrain from showing you attention.

I am sorry that when the old year is passing away that I should be sending such a message to you. There will be but one prayer on my lips tonight and that is that the coming year will bring you happiness, whether I am connected with it or not.

Sincerely yours,
Stuart R. Tompkins

THURSDAY EVENING
JAN 1 [1914]

My Darling Edna:—

I just got in from the south side but do not feel like rolling in. I don't know what is the matter with me—or with you. A very curse seems to hang over this New Year's day. It started out bright and cheerful but—

Well I don't suppose there is any use of putting my thoughts down on paper. As likely as not I will destroy this. If I don't you had better. I seem to have been butting my head against a stone wall. I wish to heaven I knew what it was. Something seems amiss with all my plans. I contemplate the future with such joy until I find there is some nameless pall hanging over you. It fairly crushes me and takes all the kick out of me. You have assured me that I have nothing to do with your pessimism but if a nameless and purely mental foe can so chill the blood what of the future when I lean on you more and more for encouragement. I am not playing for sympathy. I can take my medicine if I have to but I wish I understood. The experience today was like tearing one's vitals. I know I should not get worked up, but I cannot help it under such circumstances.

I must confess the idea has sometimes suggested itself to me that you are quite pessimistic about your married life. If that is the case I am asking a terrible self sacrifice on your part and would feel guilty. If that is the case let's get together and talk the thing out and put this distress of mind at an end. I scarcely know what to do. I am torn with my love for you and the feeling that I may possibly have got you in wrong. Believe me, dearest, I want nothing but your own happiness and that we both should be without spot or blemish when we present ourselves before the throne of God.

Look here, Edna, I hate preaching but surely you know that the battle is fierce, that to keep our faith we must enshrine it in the inner sanctum whence we can draw inspiration in our hour of need. I suppose the root of my trouble is that I have hopes to enshrine you in that inner temple—and you would not, you prefer to be human. Perhaps it is all right but it distresses me to see you so apathetic and cheerless. The light of my life goes out in such an atmosphere. Well goodnight and God bless you, and lead you out of tribulation into a quiet land. You may answer or not. I shall see you soon. Be sure however that I love you and that you are with me day and night.

Yours in love and sincerity,
Stuart

SUNDAY EVENING [JANUARY 1914]

My Darling Edna:—

I have brought up the coal and done my chores and sat down to think. Alas though I left you only an hour ago I am possessed by a longing to see you again and to hear your voice once more. That is the thing I was trying to talk of tonight. I cannot love you without feeling the awful responsibility that is laid upon [me], not perhaps to live up to your ideals but to build our love and life on a solid foundation. You said once that husband and wife should have separate lives. I do not see how it is possible. I do not seem able to bear separation from you; and yet I should do so if I thought it were for our good. God knows I cannot see ahead and the lives and characters of people sometimes take queer turns. If I thought however that I should attempt to develop other interests I would do so if it costs me my heart's blood. But honestly dear, I don't see the purpose. Our lives will be spent together we will develop side by side, and I have felt lately that I should like to surrender to the tremendous desire I have to be with you. Granted that there are times when people should be apart and I know that sometimes it has done me good to be away from you for a few days. (never of course away from your memory) Still I am obsessed with the idea that our destinies are one and that we should be together as much as possible. It is not now a matter of impulse. It is something vastly deeper.

I don't know whether you can help me, whether the currents of duty have ever run counter to your likes. I wish you could help me. It is your problem as well as mine and I am groping in the dark for a helping hand.

Well God bless you dear. I look forward to seeing you at least Tuesday evening. If anything should intervene I will let you know.

Stuart

[JANUARY 1914]

My Dearest Edna:—

I started in tonight to read but your face has kept coming up before me till I had to take my pen in sheer desperation. I don't know whether you care for me to do so. If it in anyway embarrasses you, you have but to speak the word for I will not in any way take advantage of you. But my heart keeps crying out that I love you and I cannot deny it expression. Dearest do not blame me.

You were in a very abstracted mood last night. It was a time when it seemed as if our hearts and lives touched at very vital spots, moments that I treasure up for days. Do you know one thing of which I have been convinced that you have been for months back in an abnormal physical condition that has preyed on your mind. I can't think you are harsh or ill-tempered by nature and yet it worries me to think how you assume the role at times. I know because I have suffered. I wish I could take you away for a year or so from these so ever-present scenes and let you get a view of life in perspective. It is not such an ignoble thing as we sometimes think, and honour and heroism are more common than we think. One needs to constantly renew his life at the fountain of youth in order to avoid pessimism and I think both of us must learn it.

Now I must not weary you with a lecture for you don't want it. . . . Life has abundant things in store for us all if we would but reach out and take them and I am going to do so and when I have something to say about your mode of life. I hope you will get a chance to reach out towards the sunlight.

I fear that I do not always commit you to the care of the Eternal Father but I shall tonight. But I can assure you that in my dreams it is your face I see and that when I awake thoughts of you are the first that enter. I love you, I love you darling and I cannot keep my heart from singing a paean of praise whenever I think of you. May God grant that I be worthy of your love and have enough decency and manhood to command some affection from you.

Pardon these broken lines. They ill express my thoughts but they come from the heart.

Yours very sincerely
(and may I add constantly)
Stuart

From that time in early 1914 when he was so uncertain of their future together, Stuart's letters were full of expressions of the hope that he would prove worthy of her and genuine admissions that he needed the strength of her love and support in whatever he undertook. The months of January and February continued full of uncertainty and frustration for him, but toward the end of February his letters indicate that the ice had begun to thaw a bit. By March they show that Edna had finally accepted his marriage proposals.

[JANUARY 1914]

Dear Edna:—

I am awfully tired but inasmuch as I have undertaken it, I will write a short note. I was a long time getting a car on Fifth St, had to wait ten minutes at Ninth St and to crown all was dumped off unceremoniously at Short Ave leaving me to walk home from there.

No I was not helped by the sermon this evening. I guess I am falling from any interest I had in church work but it all seems so childish in face of the real things in life. No rule of thumb goodness will do. I want a living vital touch with the power which one touches only in the great moments of life.

I suppose I have a grouch on tonight. With mediocre ability, I have had to stack up against the impossible to attempt things beyond my powers. Do you wonder I want strength in the hour of need. And a helping hand. I must confess I have never had a real help yet. So few understand your problem or give you any vital assistance. And just now when things are at their blackest, I don't want to be soothed with teething syrup. I want something to help me understand the facts, to face them and play the man. There is no use blinking at it. Life is a hideous cruel thing at least on the surface and tonight it has me buffaloed.

Well, good-night. Health and strength for the morrow.

Stuart

MONDAY EVENING

[FEBRUARY 1914]

My Dearest Edna:—

I do not know what hand guides my thoughts tonight but it is you on whom they are centred. A solemnity has possessed me when looking back—and forward—and wondering what the future has in store. In a way I am frightened. I suppose in detached moments, the momentousness of one's decision are more or less overwhelming. Why should we two [have] been chosen as mates out of all this great world? And those bonds of love stronger than steel been forged that even death cannot break and which will last through the dawn of the life that is to be.

I must confess that I am haunted by one fear—or anxiety lest we allow our line of communication to be broken. Perhaps I am too much inclined to look for hidden dangers. It is not altogether the desire for mastery or possession. I have at times seen your face light up with joy and of course I dread that anything might occur to mar it. My own character is that for which I fear most of all. I shall certainly be glad when my present shackles are broken and we are in a position to discover one another as we cannot hope to do now.

I fear I have been prodigal of rest tonight. I sat and read the Boer War for nearly four hours and have just laid it down. The rain is falling and will I hope lull me to my rest. Has it already wooed you to sleep?

Well I shall probably go over for a short time this evening (already it is a.m.) if I may, to return the book.

May God bless and guard you this night.

Stuart

MONDAY EVENING [MARCH 1914]

My Dear Dear Girl:—

My brain is playing tag with my ideas tonight but I must sit down to write a few words to you before I go to rest. I must confess my heart expands with solemn thanksgiving for the treasure I have been given. I know you are a doubting Thomas and your hard head like mine must needs critically examine anything that promises well. As I said last night my heart sometimes has chilled at the thought that you were afraid that I did "protest too much." But even my good sense cannot persuade me that the gold is dross. Perhaps after all we men are the creatures of circumstances and that whether we love or hate we are good or bad, happy or unhappy as fate determines; but my heart refuses to believe that. There may be no such thing as the soul finding its mate, but I realize that I am about to step out into manhood, by my side a comrade to share my ill fortune as well as my good fortune.

Now we can bring our good sense into play. We have *both* to learn domestic efficiency in every sense of the word and there will be many failures before our efforts are crowned with success. Now please please don't be a pessimist. I am one myself but by your good help my dear we can transmute our lives into pure gold. Am I overpainting the picture. Are you so impressed with the failures that you cannot believe in ultimate triumph. It is a severe process but such as refines the gold. Don't be too hard on me, but you mean so much to me that perhaps my wordiness is to be condoned. Goodbye until Wednesday.

Stuart

MARCH 11, 1914

My Darling Edna:—

At the risk of incurring your grave displeasure, I am going to write a few lines tonight. . . . I must confess I felt like a boy who has been caught stealing apples after revealing to you my financial condition and my perseverance in my determination. But I have something within me that says I am right, that financial conditions have little do with happiness. At least they have very little bearing on the sum-total. Now I suppose that the confidence one feels may have little to do with the success one attains; at least everything must be qualified with a Deo Volente, but dearest I feel at last that what small powers I have latent are now ready to be drawn forth for the struggle before me for there will be a struggle. But it means life to me and love and work—a fine combination and I am going to dare it all for your sake.

Another thing. Naturally your attitude toward things and my own critical nature has led me to scrutinize myself very closely. I don't know of course whether I am better or worse than my fellows. Who among you will cast the first stone, but I feel a growing conviction that God does not abandon those who try. I will admit the awful abysses I have contemplated make me shudder but I have a small but glowing spark of faith and a trust that there is such a thing as a pure and divine love of which we are a part. God knows our own love only catches the divine fire when we do our best to purge it of its dross.

I have not much to say except that I love you. Your face is with me by day and night. When will this yearning be satisfied and our hearts be at rest?

Yours very sincerely,
Stuart

THURSDAY EVENING
[MARCH 1914]

My Dear Edna:—

... I am tired tonight and yet it is sort of a peaceful tiredness. My heart naturally turns to you and to our future. Really I can not be pessimistic. I think I can see all the rocks. I know my own weaknesses (and probably yours, too) and yet something tells me that I have at last got a grip on life and realities. I don't believe much in panaceas, but when your heart sings a paean of gladness at the future, you cannot help but think that you have turned a corner.

I often wonder whether you don't know a vast more about life than I do. You are very noncommittal on most subjects but when you have an opinion it is very decided. . . . [W]hen I begin to discuss things with you, I sort of lose faith in myself. Of course on the surface I agree with a vast number of the things you think and have a cynical distrust of human nature but down underneath I am an optimist and believe that life should be a great and good experience with victory at the end. I dare not give way to discouragement for to do so would mean defeat and defeat might mean loss of you. After all that is where I come back to. Right or wrong, my life has come to revolve around you. . . . I have been let into a new world through you; now I have weighed the thing pretty carefully pro and con and believe that it has been a good thing for me. I suppose that is why I am sometimes chafed at your distrust.

Well I am very glad like you that I have to work hard. If hard work serves no other purpose, it keeps your mind from undesirable thoughts into which one naturally drifts. I hope that I am not boring you in my efforts to release some of the thoughts that crowd my mind. It just seems as if I must find expression for my yearning and love. It keeps me from worrying about the delay.

23

I hope you do not forget to offer a prayer on our behalf. I am something of a heathen but I do it myself. Well good-night my dear dear girl.

Yours sincerely,
Stuart

COCHRANE [ALBERTA]
MARCH 21, 1914

My Dear Dear Edna:—

My heart smites me with reproach for not having written you enroute but to be candid, I could not. My brain was numb and my will fagged out so that all I could do was to try to forget the incidents and scenes of the past few weeks. . . .

I reached Calgary at 10:10 (after having spent the trip reading Anna Karenina) got my room at the Alberta and went out for supper. I rolled in about eleven but could hardly sleep for the heat, called up the bell-hop and together we fixed things; then followed a brief respite till five thirty when I was called. I got out and took the train. Cochrane was reached at seven thirty. Oh how the mountains stood out with a glistening whiteness. I don't know when a place aroused such thoughts within me. This is the first place I spent any time in the West some nine years ago. I climbed the Big Hill back of the town although it nearly played me out. Arrived there; what a panorama—one vast skyline of snow peaks towering over the gloomy foothills and endless miles of plain and valley with the river wriggling at the bottom. I was at least five hundred feet above the valley. My eyes ached with the length of vision so I lay on my back and watched the light clouds that flitted across the zenith. For some few moments I was happy except that you were not there to share it. I should have given anything if you had. . . . After the meeting I think I shall try to get out to the Beaver Dam where my cousins live. I am going to spend Monday looking into trouble in the Westminster District so shall not be back till Tuesday. I shall look forward to a letter on Monday.

Good by dear
Yours very sincerely
Stuart

My Darling Edna:—

I am miserably wretchedly tired but before rolling in I am prompted
to write you a few lines. May I be pardoned therefor? I suppose yesterday will live in my memory as a red-letter day. You don't know of
course what an inspiration a day like that can be. . . . One needs so
much help to do the right thing and our temperaments are so much
alike that we go down at the same time. But this is neither here nor
there. We are both suffering from work—and ennui. I am reconciled I
can tell you to a good prolonged holiday with you and a chance to
make the acquaintance of my own soul (If I have one). And after we
are married (I hardly dare say it) we are going to live in the real sense
of the word if I have anything to say about it.

You must get tired reading my literary lapses. I suppose you gather
them up once a month and set fire to them. Well I don't bear you any
grudge.

I am sorry I forgot to ask how your mother was today. I should be
glad to know. Meantime good night dearest. When may I see you
next?

Stuart

May I see you Wednesday night—I leave for Battleford probably
Thursday or early Friday morning.

Stuart

Dear Edna:—

Where are you going Dominion Day? Coming right after pay day
you should not complain of lack of the wherewithal. Can we arrange
for a short jaunt. I am sick of work. Personally I should like to go as
far afield. Surely you don't contemplate working. How is your
mother?

Stuart

Stuart and Edna were together during most of the summer of 1914,
that last summer of peace which is recalled by many of their generation as being almost idyllic.[3] There are no letters until August, when

Edna and her younger sister Zeta left on a fairly extended trip to Ontario to visit family members in St. Catharines. He once again became the faithful correspondent, writing almost daily. During the time she was away, Stuart combined business and pleasure while on a trip to southwest Alberta for the Education Department. He scheduled a short side trip to Banff, where he and T. W. Henderson, a colleague in the department, spent a few days in needed rest and relaxation. The war became an increasingly frequent element in the letters, but daily routine, accounts of his activities, and soaring protestations of love remained their primary content.

EDMONTON, AUGUST 25, 1914

My Dear Edna:—

I was heartily ashamed of myself when I got up this morning (at 11) to have a letter confront me when I was about to leave my room. I knew I should have written yesterday but physical weakness seemed to overcome my good intentions. However I slipped up to the [government] buildings and pinched some paper tonight to write a few lines before turning in.

I slept in this morning till eleven and have scarcely spent three hours at the office. Henderson and I are arranging a trip to Banff. I know it can't come any too soon for me.

I am afraid I have not been very heroic lately but I have been dogged with a weariness that is oppressive. For your sake more than my own I am going to try to climb out of the slough. Indeed you are the only star on my horizon. . . .

Aren't we getting terrible war news. The war machine is working well in spite of what people said. What about the English? They don't seem to be doing anything remarkable. Everyone is depressed.

Your mother misses you more than perhaps you are aware. She seemed glad that I called.

Well goodnight. I shall try to write more tomorrow.

Remember that I love you.

Stuart

The Province of Alberta, as did all the prairie provinces, contributed manpower for World War I far in excess of its ratio to Canada's total population. The early, somewhat piecemeal efforts to form an army rested entirely on volunteers. The new 10th Battalion, authorized on 7 August, attracted most of Edmonton's 101st Reserve Battalion, and by the end of the month they were in training at Valcartier Camp in Quebec.[4] Stuart's brother Philip was among the first of those who left from Edmonton.

EDMONTON, AUGUST 26, 1914

My Dearest Edna:—

Positively I am ashamed that I am a man. A woman when she gets sick braces up and is a brick while a man is a curse to himself and the world. Today I have loafed. . . . I feel lazier than ever; in fact I am doubting whether I shall go out for supper, but of course I shall go out to get the news even if it is raining.

What are my thoughts; very very unhappy, if you must know the truth; for I am in the depths mentally more than physically, despising myself for being a cumberer of the earth and a very useless appendage. Man cannot live by bread alone and you know as well as I that only the ideals we cherish and cling to keep us close to Heaven. I am walking in a kind of trance wherein real and unreal are blended together. My life for years back seems a useless feeble struggle against the current. I long for the peaceful reaches where I shall be alone with you. . . .

Well, I have been filled with a fierce longing today for you. You are the harbour where all my thoughts find anchor and I know that I cannot do without you. Our farewell was very brief and undramatic which is I suppose better. . . .

I ran over to see your mother last night. The girls and I go over tomorrow afternoon. Your mother generously agreed to give us storage room for our garden truck but I am going to try to persuade her to use it. . . .

The 101st sent off another contingent of 250 today. Edmonton certainly has done her duty. The turn of events of late leads me to believe more will be wanted. [Field-Marshal Lord] Kitchener is calling for recruits. Even the London Times is urging men to enlist. Things do indeed look black but thank Heavens there are men at the head of the government that we can trust. . . .

I hear the continued cheers of the baseball fans. Neither war nor rain serves to dampen their ardour.

I will enclose a note to Zeta. Need I say I close with much love.

Stuart

EDMONTON, AUGUST 28, 1914

Dearest Edna:—

Your second letter reached me last night or rather I found it when I came back from the office. I was sorry to hear you were tired after your first night on the train but you will have lots of time to recuperate.

The girls and I were over at your place last night for tea, discussed the war pro and con pretty thoroughly and had a very pleasant time. They still miss you but seem to be somewhat more reconciled. . . .

It is now nine thirty a.m. I have just arisen after lying in thought for an hour and a half. I get little comfort out of thinking, though. Things seem in such an inextricable turmoil. I am oppressed with a terrible sense of failure. Not that alone but the feeling that our happy days are as far off as ever. I seem unable to see any silver lining.

We have had a few spatters of rain lately but today is warm and bright. I think Henderson and I will leave tonight for Banff (if I can get my money); and I will be glad to get away to find rest unto my soul. I regret I did not send this letter yesterday but I think I have been pretty faithful. . . .

With best wishes and all love,

Stuart

The letter below suggests that Edna had been among the hundreds who invested in oil shares when the first Dingman well came in near Calgary in May 1914. The reference to "pure gasoline" hints that Stuart either was gently chiding her or was not yet fully attuned to the petroleum industry.

C.P.R. TRAIN
SATURDAY, AUGUST 29, 1914

Darling Edna:—

I am running away as fast as the train can carry me. I lit out this morning at 7:30 as per schedule and will be in the mountains tonight.

My only regret is that I shall not be able to get your letters. I was indeed glad to get the one from Winnipeg; I think you have done very well—better indeed than I deserve. I had a busy day, yestreen. I dug up our garden stuff and inflicted it on your mother, cleaned up things at the office and other business. I called on your mother in the evening.... I did not sleep very well and felt very very tired this morning but had to get up at 6. The girls saw me off.... I blew myself to breakfast on the train and a good one I had, too.

Was that not great news we had this morning of the night attack on the Germans off Heligoland. That certainly is the best news we have had to date. It is certainly a relief after the discouragements of the past two weeks.

My plans were to go up to Coleman tonight and do some work for the Department, to return to Calgary Monday, and get up to Banff Tuesday. As Mr. Henderson is probably going up tonight I think I shall change my plans and go on up to Banff. I am anxious to have a rest. Then I will enjoy my Coleman trip better. I think I will not stay very long probably a week. The weather is delightful—I should like to take advantage of it....

Did you know that Dingman No. 2 had struck pure gasoline at 1600 ft? You may get something out of your shares yet.

I shall write again from Banff. Be a good girl.

Goodbye for the present

Stuart

Later:—

Say—look here. I am a smug hypocrite I must admit without qualification. I thought I should enjoy this run to Calgary but, I am beastly lonely.... I feel a great gap and you are two thousand miles away. How am I going to fill up the emptiness until you get back. I am glad you won't be getting this letter for another week. Really I have been very philosophic up to now but I begin to see things differently; God grant this waiting period will be soon brought to a close. Really I think we should both be better off living our whole lives together instead of a small fraction.

Well be sure to tell me of all your experiences. Not only your goings and comings but of other things. I take it life lends us all new side lights on things from time to time and we are led on, we know not how, to a higher plane....

As you will see, it is in the nature of trains to rock and to ruin naturally good handwriting. But I get a sort of a mournful solace out of such in which imagination and memory play a part.... I trust I shall

find a whole sheaf of letters waiting for me when I get back.
Good bye dear and don't forget to write.

Stuart

While at Banff, Stuart and Henderson enjoyed the grandeur of the resort's magnificent setting and such recreational opportunities as hiking, climbing, fishing, and swimming.

BANFF, AUGUST 31, 1914

Dear Edna:—

I suppose I have neglected you, not having written since Saturday, but so much has happened in the meantime. I arrove Saturday 8 pm. located my boarding house and went to bed. Bright and early I was up and climbed Tunnel mountain before breakfast. Afterwards up the Cave and Basin road and off along all kinds of bypaths into the thick bush where I lay and ruminated. I can hardly put my thoughts on paper. It was a regular soulwashing process. How I wished you were here. It seemed to lack just one element to make perfection. Darling you have become so near [sic] to me that there is not one plan or calculation into which you do not enter. Don't think this imaginary. It is the straight truth.

Well it does not make things any better when you are 3000 miles away. After supper, I went down to the station. Two trains leave and one arrives between 7–7:30. The 7:30 brought Henderson (and incidentally ran off the track almost in front of our eyes) also a War Extra from Calgary announcing that the allies were crushed and that the Germans were within 75 miles of Paris. I hardly slept last night at all.

We have not done much today. T. W. H. went into the Basin for a swim. I was too tired. I am going to have a snooze now, so goodbye.

I will look forward to a whole stack of letters when I get back to Edmonton.

Stuart

BANFF, SEPTEMBER 2, 1914

My darling Edna:—

To think that I skipped you yesterday. We did all sorts of things, played like kids in the Basin and fished all afternoon in the Bow [River]. So I could not work in a letter and I have felt guilty. Perhaps that was why I did not sleep well last night.

To make a long story short, Henderson and I got rods and lines and spent yesterday afternoon trying to lure the trout from his native haunts. I got the first blood in five minutes but we caught nothing more. It was very beautiful though; I am sure I enjoyed the dancing of the river and the colour of the mountains more even than the sport. Once I caught my line and had to wade in after it. Imagine my feelings in the ice cold water. We came in at 7:30 and weren't we hungry and tired. Today has been pretty much a repetition of it, but tomorrow I think we shall climb Sulphur or else go out to [Lake] Minnewanka.

I don't need to tell you I have wished you were here. It is more than that. I don't think I can put in much longer here. It is only now I am feeling it. It seems as though it were months since I saw you.

But I keep all this to myself pretty well and I suppose the time cannot be long. Things are very quiet at Banff since the war broke out as you may imagine.

I have under my writing material an extra of the News Telegram issued on Sunday with 3-inch block type "Foe nearing Paris; Canada asked for half a million men." It spoiled every body's Sunday in Southern Alberta and gave me a bad night.

Well, I must go for the rest of those fish.

Stuart

C.P.R. TRAIN
EN ROUTE TO MACLEOD
SEPTEMBER 4, 1914

Dearest Edna:—

And now for home. I bad goodbye to T. W. H. and Banff this morning with the mountains all shrouded in smoke. I decided it was time for me to be turning homeward—

And now I have leisure to tell you of things. Yes I enjoyed my stay there but it was quite long enough and I am glad it is over. . . .

I suppose you have been enjoying yourself immensely, bushels of apples and grapes etc and your cheeks are filling out. . . . I put on several pounds at Banff and three or four shades of colour. But my hair is awful—refuses to obey orders any more . . . . Possibly it was the sulphur in the water.

We lived a pretty strenuous life the first few days, so we were glad enough to rest yesterday by driving out to Lake Minnewanka. . . . We came back about three and instead of driving into Banff turned west and drove up the river to Sawback where we had a splendid view of Wellington's peak and the Sawback range. Henderson was anxious for me to stay but I could not and decided to pull out this morning.

What do you think of the war. Banff is fairly paralyzed by it. All the hotels are empty. We were up to the C.P.R. [Banff Springs Hotel] the other day. It was untenanted except by the help. Indeed they fired all of Austrian or German lineage (giving them I presume the alternative of naturalization) to prevent a riot. How soon we get used to this sort of thing. . . .

They are just harvesting around here. I have been surprised in most places to see things so late but of course there has been no frost (on the prairie). Strange to say though around Calgary the country looks green, probably owing to the late rains.

Now, what more can I tell you. My wanderings are nearly over, though I anticipate more holidays. Naturally everyone thinks of the war. I fear we are in for a long gruelling contest. I trust every Canadian will do his part. Do you know they sent about 2000 from Edmonton, the largest contribution in the West, the largest without doubt in proportion to the population and the largest unit from Canada—the 101st. Be sure you tell everybody!!

We have just passed Aldersyde—on the gallop. Do you know that one cannot see the slightest trace of the mountains which are usually so distinct. Heavy brush fires have blotted them out. I am going to make my first trip into the Crows Nest tonight and am wondering what it will be like.

I am counting the days as you perhaps know. . . . I wonder if there will be a pile of letters waiting for me when I get back.

Well I am going to close now. Please do not disappoint me in the writing. Trusting to see you soon, safe and sound.

Stuart

The Crowsnest Pass area was one of Alberta's leading coal mining districts early in this century, and one of the most productive mines was at the town of Frank. The Frank Slide, which is described in a following letter, occurred on the morning of 29 April 1903 and is considered one of Canada's worst natural disasters. Stuart made his trip through the Crowsnest just two and a half months after an explosion in the Hillcrest mine, located a mile down the valley from the Frank Slide, had killed at least 189 miners.[5]

COLEMAN HOTEL
COLEMAN, ALBERTA
SEPTEMBER 5, 1914

My Dear Edna:—

I have just finished a much more arduous day than I had planned. I pictured myself finishing by noon and spending the afternoon fishing and tramping over the hills. Instead I was going until eight o'clock interviewing people and digging up information of all kinds. I have just now been off for a tramp with the chairman of the school board, a dour auld Scot but a very good fellow. It is a beautiful moonlight night and we tramped down the valley for a mile or more while the distant hills are shrouded in smoke. We could see Turtle Mountain, the top of which fell on Frank some eleven years ago. We are all now waiting for the train due at 9:53 for the war news. What will it be? It was reported here today that the Russians had captured 150,000 German troops but the report was unconfirmed, in fact later denied. So everyone is on the *qui vive.* I have had a pleasant time. This is a mining camp of about 2800 population and as a rule quite prosperous. It is violently socialistic but I have found some fine fellows here. It seems as though this Pass has been a regular trail of disaster—the Frank slide, the Bellevue explosion, the Hillcrest disaster. Today I saw a miner carried home on a stretcher—fortunately not seriously injured but the experience is common enough.

Well I am glad this is over. I am anxious to be home and to make some plans. Don't forget to write. . . . I shall write on the train tomorrow.

Goodbye for tonight
Stuart

INNISFAIL [ALBERTA]
SEPTEMBER 6, 1914

Dear Edna:—

Enroute again for home! I have been travelling since 8 o'clock this morning. I was rather late getting up and had a fine scramble getting around. The morning was very bright the smoke had somewhat lifted and the mountains stood out clearer than they have done for days. I had my breakfast on the train and so had a good view of the awful Frank slide. Turtle mountain is on the south side of the pass—a long ridge . . . . Through some freak of nature a mass of rock detached itself from the northern or rather northeastern face, rushed to the valley below and spread out in a huge fan shape, ploughed its way across the valley for two and a half miles burying half the town to a depth of fifty to a hundred and fifty feet. I could not from the train discern how the strata lay. They must have formed an anticline to have acted as they did, a portion of the crest of the mountain came down this apparently; the strata dipped toward the valley. The remarkable thing is that although the mountain is not very high, the slide almost crossed the valley and created far greater devastation two miles away from its base than in the valley immediately at its foot. The school board chairman was there at the time and describes vividly the horror of the whole thing which happened at dead of night. Of the 96 who perished only six bodies were recovered.

The train I was on made good time to Calgary but allowed us only 15 minutes so I had no time to go around and only got a bite. . . .

Well I think I shall get ready for supper. I can assure you I need cleaning up and I am hungry. Excuse the writing.

Stuart

Letters from Edna did await him when he returned to Edmonton, but their perfunctory style did not satisfy him. A note of uncertainty on her part plunged him into a negative, introspective mood, and the next few letters show how much he had come to rely on her.

EDMONTON SEPTEMBER 8, 1914

My Dear Edna:—

What are my thoughts this wretched night as I sit down to my desk. Not despondent but somewhat sad, as I look back over the past year and all its follies. I believe I at last have a grip on myself and that I now can contemplate things with more equanimity. I confess to a feeling of shame for some things I have done or left undone. Death bed confessions are not pleasant but it relieves and I suppose strengthens me to admit my weakness. It is largely due to sourness of soul which has taken possession of me, and I blush to admit it, I have sometimes thought that the selfish self indulgent person really carries off the palm of life. . . .

Well, dearest, in addition to the letters awaiting me I have received two since I came home. Do you know, to be frank your letters sometimes are a bit unsatisfactory. (I believe I have been told that mine are). Perhaps I want too much but I know you have some gift along such lines. I think people are inclined often to take letter writing as a bothersome duty, to be got rid of as soon as possible. "I now take my pen in hand.". . .

I wonder how you would take it if I told you again how I missed you—or is that subject tabooed. Does it ever do any good? I suppose it is one of the drawbacks to forming such a relation and I must take it as such without appealing for sympathy. Heavens! I have felt like jumping on the first train.

Did you hear about all the Hindu troops that were taken through Calgary and Edmonton without one soul being the wiser. I heard of it at Banff and it has lately become common property. The troops went through towns with blinds drawn; the newspapers had the story and were not allowed to use it. What terrible progress this war is making and the fearful carnage; someone will surely pay for it! Do you know, I purchased a scrapbook and am going to make clippings from the Globe. I am quite proud of my experiment and shall show it you when you return. It is quite a unique idea and I have the wall plastered with maps, also. . . .

Now, without saying anything to hurt your feelings, I wonder sometimes if it wouldn't be all right to break through reserve in your letters to use the three simple words "I love you." Do they look too bold on paper or is it condemned as unmaidenly. For heaven's sake do not think I am trying to be sentimental but I have a great loneliness and surely two tried and trusted comrades may express the confidence they have in one another and speak magic words of cheer and comforts. The heart cries out at the presence that is gone and bespeaks some things in its place. I can assure you, darling, there has not been an hour when you have been absent from my thoughts or when I have not wished myself better for your sake. If you condemn such I am afraid you condemn the mainspring of a man's life.

. . . Let me know your plans.

With kindest regards and (may I say?) love
Stuart R. Tompkins

The war became a greater reality to the men of the Department of Education as autumn brought with it plans for their possible mobilization but no guarantee of partial salary while on duty. Stuart mentioned "hopeful news" from the Western Front in the letter below, a reference to the Battle of the Marne, which began on 5 September and ended on the ninth with a German retreat. A few weeks later, however, there would be less optimism as both Saint-Miheil and Antwerp fell to the Germans, and as the Allies held in the First Battle of Ypres (12 October to 11 November), the front became stabilized, developing into the trench warfare that became the hallmark of the Great War.[6]

EDMONTON, SEPTEMBER 10, 1914

Dearest Edna:—

Alas for me, I am no writer. I put off writing you until last evening and as I spent the evening out, it was neglected. However, I have nothing much to do this afternoon so will write a short note. The weather has cleared and it is now delightful. I think I shall go for a long walk this afternoon—go over to see your mother perhaps. . . . I worked a scheme to get transportation down to Calgary for my trip. The Department had a case at Coleman (the establishment) of a separate school so I took that on. I went down Friday and came away Sunday. I did not think much of the case; it was awfully delicate and you could feel the Catholic strings pulling behind. . . .

Henderson has not returned yet, I left him in Banff on Friday. It turned cold later and snowed, perhaps he is immured in the mountains. He still has a couple of weeks holidays to run.

The whole city is now astir with a mild form of mobilization. Last night coming down town we passed a squad of citizens marching to the tune of "A Hundred Pipers . . . ". A whole regiment is being formed to train bellicose citizens. The civil service are forming a squad but in view of the announcement in this mornings Bulletin, a copy of which I enclose, there is much less enthusiasm being displayed. Strong exception is being taken to the stand of the government in refusing to allow men any part of their salary while on active service. A regular indignation meeting (on a small scale) occurred in the corridor this morning. I suppose you are following the war with keen interest. Everyone is keyed up in view of the more hopeful news this last few days. The British have certainly covered themselves with glory. Did you see Tranch's report of the retreat and the courage shown by the troops.

We have heard from Philip. He is now a sergeant in B Company.... I am not going to ask you when you are coming home for you are to stay and have a good rest. What about Zeta? I have not heard anything of her movements at all....

I suppose I shall have to close without saying anything. You surely will get one right royal welcome when you come back. Your mother is very lonely.

Goodbye dear
Stuart

EDMONTON, SEPTEMBER 12, 1914
[NO. 1]

My dear Edna:—

You were shamefully neglected yesterday with only one short note. Today, however, it will be my first task to write down my thoughts before the day obliterates them. I was out last evening to a "New Thought" meeting. The subject was not, however, very high brow. "Resolved that by reason of territorial restriction Germany is justified in seeking more land" and WE WON. Write that in large letters so that he may read that runs. Mrs. O. M. Wallace, whom you possibly know (She is working at the office) was the hostess and champ*ee*on speaker for the affirmative. We had a pleasant time. It was nearly twelve when I got in. Thank heavens I live close.

The weather has turned a trifle colder of late but is quite fine. I begin to think of zero weather. Do you know I have not had a letter for two days? You went at it too hard and ran out of wind, I guess.

Everything jogs along at the office just the same. Mr. Alger is doing his own typing and making out his own debentures lately.

Don't hurry back of course. Remember me to Zeta.

Stuart

EDMONTON, SEPTEMBER 12, 1914
[NO. 2]

Darling Edna:—

There is a sabbatical hush over things tonight although it is only Saturday night, and I feel constrained to write you a letter in a burst of confidence. . . . I have perhaps no startling disclosures to make so calm yourself, but as you will scarcely get this letter before you leave it is not amiss for you to know how much I missed you. . . . I think I may say that I did not pine for I tried not to trouble you or worry myself but there has not been one moment in your absence when I have not longed for you and almost trembled at the thought of your continued absence. These sort[s] of statements are perhaps wild in your ears but they are cold facts, and show me most conclusively that you are the heart and centre of my life. Now I have done; I think sometimes you discourage and dislike such protestations. They are however not used even to impress you, but I love you and long for your return.

Today, the civil service held a meeting to discuss military training. As a result, I think we shall try to form a troop to have attached to the 19th. Several in the Education Department are quite enthusiastic. There will also be a civil service company attached to the 101st. . . .

Tomorrow I am going to spend in the country. Should I not be happy. Alas, there is no gilt on the gingerbread. All such pleasures are very stale indeed under the circumstances, but I go under compulsion.

Yours truly,
Stuart

EDMONTON, SEPTEMBER 13, 1914

My dearest Edna:—

I have a guilty twinge of conscience at not having sent off your letter yesterday and today I have spent having a good time, but as your parting instructions were to get some more flesh on my bones, I am not so far amiss. The weather has been very cold and raw today. In fact, this afternoon it rained in town as we discovered when we reached here this evening and it has been blowing ad infinitum. . . .

I am going to debate again. . . so you see I must have made something of a success at it but I expect we will go down to defeat next time. I am really glad to exercise my slight mental powers in such a way. It is quite refreshing and brings one into keen conflict with people which is very stimulating.

Now there is not much to tell. I have resolved not to confide in you any more as to my personal feelings. I shall spare you. In fact the best way to do is not to have any; or to persuade yourself that you have not. When you write please tell me all about your plans; and don't forget to come back.

With best wishes and —

Stuart

Stuart and Edna Tompkins were married on 27 January 1915, in the Christie home. The wedding was attended by members of the family and one or two close friends. One family member conspicuous by her absence was the mother of the groom, of whom Edna later recalled, "His mother wouldn't come—she was disgusted at his getting married."[7]

They made their first home in Edmonton, within walking distance of the government office building. While they knew a hard time economically, they pursued their favourite activities which required little or no expenditure. They were both accomplished skaters, and that winter they also made skiing a daily event on the hill that lay between their apartment building and the river. They were avid readers and shared both the classics and current literature. Stuart decided to teach her to read Greek, and she remembered, "we would have a light supper and then go out and ski and then he'd come back and expect me to learn Greek when I was just tired and so sleepy I could hardly hold my eyes open." It was then that they established their life-long habit of walking several miles every day, a habit remarked on by friends in Oklahoma, some of whom felt that clocks could be set each evening in time with their outings.[8]

The first six months of married life were obviously a very happy time for Stuart, even though the war in Europe caused increasing concern. Few families in Canada, even at that early stage, had not felt directly the effects of the war, and perhaps he could see that he would himself soon be in uniform.

The Education Department experienced some dislocation because of mobilization, and Stuart was again sent out into the province and beyond on official business. Three letters written in June of that year were from a trip to North Battleford, Saskatchewan, and the nearby towns of Maidstone and Denholm. This may well have been their first separation since their marriage, and his letters bespeak an assurance about their relationship that the courtship letters never did.

SOMEWHERE IN SASKATCHEWAN
TUESDAY MORNING, JUNE 22, 1915

Dearest Honey:—

Now how am I to write a letter on the rocky road to Dublin. We are careening along like a drunken man at a speed of say twenty miles an hour. We have just come in sight of the Saskatchewan river which we left at Fort Saskatchewan and which we will cross at Battleford Junction. It is somewhat wider and has smoother more gently sloping banks. What a night I put in and what an ass I was. When I left you, I retired to the lounging compartment and smoked a long black see-gar, result[ing] in my present state: sick. I was alright after I turned in but I did not get a wink of real sleep, till after we passed Lloydminster. Only once I suspected I had been asleep. I rolled out about half an hour ago and dressed because I must get my breakfast on the train. I am really feeling very well considering and it promises to be a beautiful day. . . .

Well, Hon, I have had occasion to size up things and to appreciate the intense happiness that has been my lot for the past few months. Of course, I was lonely for you and yet the realization that I took with me your love and the memory of the things that have been spoken and the lives we have led together were sufficient comfort. Indeed they seem to have in them something of immortality and divinity. Indeed I sometimes think were it not for you, I should gladly die. There can be no higher happiness in store for me.

I hope you were not alone last night. Still no doubt you would not worry. We are now in Battleford (North) and the diner has just been switched on. I think probably it would be a good thing for me to drop this letter in here. I can or could see Old Battleford just a minute ago on a beautiful plateau at the junction of the two rivers away to the south and off beyond the Battle [River], the Eagle Hills. . . .

Well I shall close this unpretentious epistle. Don't forget to look after yourself and be a very good girl.

As ever
Your lover
Stuart

Prohibition was one of the social reforms that accompanied the war into the prairie provinces. Stuart arrived on a raucous scene on the eve of its implementation in Maymont, Saskatchewan.

DENHOLM, SASKATCHEWAN
JUNE 22, 1915

Dear Honey:—

After a showery afternoon, the sun has come out and flooded the prairie in green and gold. . . . When I reached Maymont this morning I found it to be the day set aside for their annual sports and all the farmers from the whole country side were scheduled to arrive in town. Alas they were also scheduled to get intoxicated and other foolishness and I spent the greater part of the day in vain attempts to get some business done. . . . It was nearly train time when I finally got my business done and indeed I was overjoyed to be able to go on. The whole day has been most unpleasant. So obedient to instructions, I had a supper, a light one, and am feeling fit once more though tired. . . . I shall probably get through at Lloydminster tomorrow and reach home Thursday morning but don't expect me till you see me.

Now you have heard enough of my griefs. The prairie really is beautiful dear. I wish you were here. There has been little rain but lots of frost. Many of the crops are ruined in places, though not right around here.

Do you know I cannot regard drink other than an unmitigated curse. To realize that it is the sole recreation and source of enjoyment to some millions of the earths inhabitants is a sorry revelation and the scenes today were certainly revolting to me. The one bright spot was the good natured mountie who smiled through it all but was firm and soldierly. We had several pleasant chats. He used to work in Edmonton and is certainly a fine fellow. To me it was a great comfort that such scenes are not likely to be repeated. The sale of liquor ceases in Saskatchewan a week from Thursday. I expect this was a ruse of mine host to dispose of his stock. His churlishness to me is ample evidence as to whence his revenue is derived.

Would I like to be going home tonight? Would I? Just ask me. But just one night more. You won't of course be lonesome will you. Will you speak a little prayer for me tonight. I think it would help me for I need it. I am mentally and physically tired.

We are rolling into Battleford and I think I will get some fruit etc and perhaps post this letter. Look after yourself.

Your ownest own
Stuart

Dearest Hon—

The sun went down in a blaze of glory at 8:55 standard time—and you are going to get another letter thereby exhausting my note paper. By the way, it is interesting to watch the avidity with which the natives devour the daily newspapers carried by this train. That serves instead of a "bulletin" I suppose. I have just been trying to argue with a down east Yankee who wanted to know why "if England knew Germany was getting ready, she didn't get ready too" but really I have not thought about the war today except when discussing it with Constable Balmer in Maymont, he says they may send a squadron or two of mounties over.

Well, I wonder what you are doing now perhaps "sie kamt ihr goldenes Haar" and will you miss me—or is Jentie there. . . . As tomorrow night's train does not reach Lloydminster till 11:35 I should be able to drive till ten or ten thirty and then for home—sweet home. The country here is thinly wooded & there has been nothing to see since we left the Saskatchewan [River] at sundown. The scene was truly magnificent.

Goodnight dear. . . . For fear you forget, I will remind you that I love you always

Stuart

2

One Man's Mobilization

✦ AUTUMN 1915 ✦

When war was declared in August of 1914, Canada's position within the British Empire determined that she was at war even though she had had no part in the diplomatic manoeuvring that led to the final outbreak of hostilities. There was never much doubt that her support for the war effort would be firm and that her contributions in men, materiel, and food stuffs would be large, but in the beginning her military resources were confused and limited.

In 1910 the Militia Council had undertaken a reorganization and by 1914 had drawn plans for mobilizing six Canadian divisions and a separate plan for the mobilization of an overseas expeditionary force. When the Conservatives came to power in 1911, Prime Minister Sir Robert Borden appointed Colonel Sam Hughes as minister of militia. At the end of July 1914, Hughes inexplicably ordered the plan for the overseas force to be dropped and proceeded instead to improvise an inefficient and uneconomical mobilization of volunteers who assembled for training at a hastily built camp at Valcartier near Quebec. This First Contingent sailed in convoy for England on 3 October 1914.[1]

Early in the raising of the First Contingent, a private battalion of former British regulars and Canadian veterans of the South African War was raised and equipped by Hamilton Gault, a Montreal millionaire, at a cost of $100,000. The battalion, Princess Patricia's Canadian Light Infantry, was named for the daughter of the governor general; the "Princess Pats" embarked at Montreal on 28 August and landed in France on 21 December, eight weeks in advance of the first Canadian Division. No other private battalions were allowed, but the ranks of wealthy militia officers, businessmen, and politicians provided "newly minted CEF colonels" for Hughes' volunteer force.[2]

Although the concept of "When Britain is at war, Canada is at war" prevailed, Canada was able to control the form of her forces' participation. There were ultimately four Canadian divisions committed to action, and they were maintained as a separate Canadian Corps rather than being absorbed into the British Army.

Response to the first call for volunteers was immediate, and it is remembered that men literally camped in the streets to be first in line at the recruiting office. Battalions were raised locally and for the most part they trained together and went overseas together as locally identifiable units. As the war dragged on, enthusiasm for enlistment diminished. By the spring of 1917 flagging recruitment neared crisis proportions, and the consideration of conscription became an overriding political and military issue.

On 1 July 1915, Stuart Tompkins enlisted in Edmonton's 66th Battalion, an infantry unit in which there was at least one other recruit from the Education Department, a former school inspector named MacGregor. The 66th trained at Sarcee Camp, a site near Calgary that, incidentally, medical officers had protested as being unhealthy. The seeming disarray that the following letters reflect is but a microcosm of that at upper echelons as Canada confronted the problems inherent in mobilizing and equipping a volunteer army. There was no precedent for the training and dispatch of troops. Rumours about the 66th ranged all the way from possible reassignment back to Edmonton to immediate transport to England in one of the frequent drafts of men sent to join Canadian troops already stationed at such posts as that at Shorncliffe where they trained in anticipation of being sent to the Western Front.

Converting to the military and relinquishing civilian status was slow and fraught with political overtones. Stuart went to Sarcee as a sergeant, and Edna later said that from the beginning he was really not happy, that "he had been at the mercy of the non-coms."[3] In November he entered the ranks of officers in training. Many of the following letters from this period show that Edna offered strong support, if not pressure, for his own half-hearted, half-formulated plans for seeking a commission.

The first of the wartime letters extant was written on Sunday, 22 August. The 66th had left its Edmonton barracks the previous Wednesday, and this was the first opportunity that Stuart had to write.

SARCEE CAMP,
66 BATT. I COMPANY
CALGARY, AUGUST 22, 1915

My dear little girl:—

I know what sorts of things you are saying up in Edmonton but I don't know what I shall say in my own defence. I had faint hopes of getting away almost immediately on our arrival but it has taken so long to organize things that my leave has kept receding from me. I expect, however, to get away this week... and should be able to spend next week end with you, if all goes well.

There is so much to tell that I don't know where to start. Wednesday was a day of continual hurry. The grounds were fairly saturated and I was soon puddling around in mud and water. I had not a moment to myself, barracks to inspect, meals to arrange for. Finally at 4:30 we were out of the barracks, everything packed, and we had supper, dry bread and ham and tea (an earnest of things to come). At 5:45 we fell in and at 6:00 marched off through Edmonton to the C.P.R. depot. We halted in front of the cars, doubled into them and in two minutes were off. . . . We were quite comfortable and had a good night's sleep. Dry supper, dry breakfast was not very reassuring, however. Hot coffee was waiting for us at Calgary and after imbibing we were off for our tramp. The morning was cool and the walking good; we reached camp about noon and found dinner ready. After dinner, tents were fixed up, baggage claimed etc; it was quite dark, however, and rainy so we did not have drill, but we were on the go all the time. Next day, Friday, was largely spent in "redding up" the camp, building gravel walks etc. Saturday the weather cleared and the camp began to dry out. We had drill and I guess everyone felt better for it. Today has been very lovely. We had divine service this morning attended by the whole brigade. The colonel complimented us on our appearance. It was a mad rush though to shave, clean buttons and boots, etc. I have been very lucky, however, in every way. I had no time to pack up my stuff but detailed a couple of men to look after it. I got everything in good order on Thursday night. My sleeping bag is a daisy and I have been fine and warm at night. Under the circumstances, my summer underwear has been all I needed, but I shall draw my winter stuff soon. I ruined my boots of course and shall need to paint them I guess to restore them. Four of us sergeants have a tent between us—Graham, myself, Jones and Taylor. The latter has been very miserable and off duty since we left Edmonton. Graham has taken a fancy to travel with us rather than the staff sergeants and as a result we see a good deal of one another. There is a good deal of camp gossip around here that might interest you. The camp lies in the valley of the Elbow and is sited in a very low, damp location. It is said that the doctors have held a meeting to protest to the government. It is interesting to conjecture what results it will have on our going back to Edmonton. I have felt well but they say there is a good deal of rheumatism going the rounds among the regiments that have been here. You know, we have five battalions here, the 50th, 51st, 56th, 63rd and 66th besides two mounted regiments. The majority are now away on harvest leave or are about to go, but I think the inaction has had a bad effect on the men. They were certainly very sloppy on parade this morning. Things are bound to be very quiet for the next few weeks which leads me to believe I shall get my leave all the more readily. I will certainly be glad to get back, as we are so far from town, one cannot think of leaving the lines to go into town.

Now, dear little honey, I have gabbed away to you for quite a bit, without saying very much. We have had what might be considered a hard time but except for Thursday evening when I was all in, I have been quite well. The camp life will be more enjoyable than lying around a dirty barracks. We have our own sergeants mess started and are getting good meals again. The first few days we ate with the men. I was pretty sick of it Friday night when I went without my supper from rustling for the men. Saturday we ate with the 51st but this morning everything is lovely.

. . . [H]ow unconsciously my thoughts turn to you as the pole star of my being. As soon as we get a table in our tent, I shall use my odd moments to jot down my thoughts from time to time so as to keep in closer touch with you. Please let me have a line from you soon. I think I will get anything addressed to No 1 Co. 66th Batt. without any difficulty. The postman knows me quite well.

Well I shall let this do for the present. If you want to send me a little piece of cake once in a while it would be all right. . . .

Dearest little girl:—

I write this letter with sort of a heavy heart. I have been working hard expecting [the captain] to get me my leave and up to date it has not come. . . . If I do not get fixed up, I shall go before the adjutant or the colonel. We have had nothing to do all afternoon and everyone is off to town and I am still sticking around here. Of course I am broke. What money I had is lent or spent and I am absolutely strapped. They are not allowing us a cent till the end of the month. How I am to get home, I do not know but if I get stuck I shall have to phone you I suppose.

Well never mind all this. We have had delightful weather lately and I am feeling fine. The work has been only reasonably hard. We have lots of time for sleep and lots to eat. I don't know that I am gaining any flesh.

By the way, I had a card from Philip dated August 5th stating that he was in France on his way up country. . . .

I hope you have not been lonely in Edmonton. I am all right as long as I am working but at night and when I am not occupied I get to thinking of things, not regretfully, yet longing to be with you. There have been all sorts of rumours afloat as to our movements. Some say huts are to be built for us in Calgary or here. Some say we go back to Edmonton. Others that we leave for England. It seems to be generally understood that one or two more battalions are to be recruited in Edmonton (one to be commanded by Major Hopkins). I wish you would keep your ear to the ground. If he gets command I should get something. MacGregor was at the orderly room puffing me up to the skies. I don't know what his purpose was; and I sometimes doubt whether I live up to my reputation. It is stated here that MacGregor could have got command of a battalion but that he does not want it, his intentions being to go back to the department after the camp is closed.

As to what our move is to be I am much in doubt. During the fall and winter Calgary has no advantages to offer, except in the matter of [firing] ranges and those advantages are rather offset by the extra barrack accommodation in Edmonton. You see the armouries are to be finished this fall or winter. But political pull may decide the matter. . . .

I do wish you would write something to cheer me up. Once in a while, when things go wrong I need it. Graham gets at least *one* letter a day and poor *me* I get nothing. Never mind I will be home soon for a few days, but I would like to know how you are getting on. . . .

Your own
Stuart

SARCEE CAMP, AUGUST 30, 1915

Dearest Honey:—

I know the things you are thinking of me but really I have had so much to do that it has been impossible. Friday night and Saturday, I was on guard and Sunday my duties as orderly sergeant began. It was pretty busy at first but things are running very smoothly. I am not on parade this morning under instructions from the captain so have a little leisure for writing. . . .

The weather has been very nice lately; in fact, it has been almost too warm. I guess I must be getting hardened. I get up at 5 o'clock without a whimper. The mornings are glorious here; the last day or two we have seen the mountains quite distinctly. Then I am inclined to be satisfied with the place. At other times, I am disgusted; it is certainly not healthy and some of the men have had bad colds. Our grub is very good and the boys are happy. I wrote home last week but have had only one letter. I suppose things are running quite smoothly at home.

It is settled of course that we are going north in three weeks. The relations between the O.C. [Officer Commanding] and the D.O.C. [District Officer Commanding] are quite strained and it may affect us. By the way I saw MacGregor on Saturday and had quite a long talk with him. I'll tell you about it when I get home. He was very nice. By the way, can my little girl keep a secret, MacGregor is to be second in command of an Alberta regiment to be authorized shortly. It was quite a shock to me, in view of what I have heard lately. Now don't mention what I said.

Now, I haven't more to tell you just now, except that I love you dear and think of you all the time. Of course I may not be home tomorrow night but should not be later than Wednesday.

Good bye dearest
Yours
Stuart

Stuart spent the anticipated leave in Edmonton, and on Monday, 6 September, he was on board a train back to Sarcee Camp, resolved to pursue a commission. The following letter is one of many in which he expresses his desire to do the "noble thing" for her sake.

ENROUTE TO CALGARY
SEPTEMBER 6, 1915

Dearest Honey:—

We are rolling along at a good clip and now that I have settled down for the trip I can talk to you. There is a sort of quiet exaltation in my mind in going back. I don't know what to ascribe it to save a sort of "hunch" that everything is coming out OK. Really dear the longer our married life lasts, the more it seems to me to be the opening up of vast vistas of growth in character. Perhaps introspection is not good for one and yet I am possessed with a quiet confidence and joy in the future both in this life and beyond. I was rather interested in knowing how I would measure up when thrown out among men after living for some months continually (almost) in your company. The results were somewhat surprising. I found that something had entered my life that rendered me almost impervious to temptation; not only that but I have been seized with determination to try to do the noble thing at all times to do the thing that you would have me do. Truly honey, I am confessing not boasting. Is it any wonder I look for letters from you. It is not news alone but the strength I draw from knowing that you think of me and the need for strength which makes me rely on you. For that reason I beg of you dear to write even if you are sick and disgusted of things. Write as often as you can and I shall do the same.

When I got on the train I met that 66th lad we saw talking to two girls. He is from No. 1 Company and goes [to England] with the draft. He was refused a pass to come home... and as a result ran away. Penalty—oh about a week's pay, extra fatigues, and 3 weeks confined to barracks. Of course he won't work out his sentence. I gave the boy a good fatherly talking to but I don't blame him.

We have just passed Ponoka and are coming into Morningside. On all hands signs of a most bountiful harvest. The country indeed looks lovely. I just wish you were here.

By the way I am travelling in a first class coach so you see I have apparently impressed the conductor. There are a few fellows on board from other regiments. I imagine however the great majority will come back tonight.... There are not more than 25 or 30 passengers on the train. *Sic transit gloria mundi.* Even the C.P.R. will have to unbend and entice people into travelling.

Well now little honey, I am going to keep my ear to the ground good and plenty for a few weeks re that new battalion and am going to raise heaven and earth for that commission. I may not get it but I am going to know the reason why....

By the way, in case the folks should forget, I wish you would keep me informed of Philip's movements. I shall be anxious for some time at any rate and they are so uncertain at home. By the way I noticed something that would explain the movement of troops to France. The British line has been lengthened from 40 to 100 miles necessitating a total army of 800,000 men. What this presages of course no one knows. We seemingly cannot look into the seeds of time as we should like. No doubt the British line will be made as impregnable as human ingenuity can make it. I do not think a forward movement is likely on the British line.

Well I don't worry much about the war when I am working. I expect we will have about as much as we care to do during the next two weeks without carrying the burdens of generalissimo. If each of us does his bit that is enough. . . .

Now I want you to be a good girl and look after yourself. I don't think you eat enough when I am away. Never mind, when I get home I shall show you how to handle a steak. Write long and often.

Your own
Stuart

SARCEE CAMP, SEPTEMBER 7, 1915

Dearest Honey:—

As you see by the address I am here o.k., though after what experiences. The trip got pretty monotonous after leaving Red Deer but I discovered Miss Fisher and Miss McCarg of the Calgary Normal and whiled away some two hours with them. Although there were very few when we left Edmonton a large number of duck hunters got on and I was crowded out into the smoker. It was raining when we reached Calgary, oh blessed raincoat. So I took the car with some trepidation. At the end of steel—no jitneys. Fortunately there is another route so we went out 14th Street. There were jitneys apparently but after a long wait we started to walk. Some of the boys from the 17th helped me carry my suit case. About a mile out a dozen of us held up a jitney and turned it back to camp. We were dumped out in the dark and left to find our way through the lines. I was not challenged but the mud and the water—I was wet to the knees when I got in. The camp was in confusion; the draft went in the morning. The battalion was in town during the day and as a result drunk and disorderly. It rained all night and we rolled out at 5:45 with teeth chattering. But for the first time the mountains stood out with snow white outlines extremely beautiful.

There was a fine fat orderly room this morning—sore heads [and] fat heads. Alas for those who fared not wisely but too well.

We are getting back to work. I tell you I am glad that I was not here. The whole battalion was confined to barracks all day Sunday while the draft was being selected.

Well honey, I must close. Please send me some envelopes.

Stuart

Throughout his stay at Sarcee, the hope of the battalion's being sent back to Edmonton remained high and rumours to that effect were constant. He knew of recruiting problems in his own unit, but his references to the war itself still showed optimism for its early end, and he adopted the soldier's less than reverent attitude toward the governor general and the minister of defence. The Russian victory mentioned below may be a case of the press putting the best light possible on the end of a German offensive that had cost the Russians dearly in both men and territory.[4]

SARCEE CAMP, SEPTEMBER 9, 1915

Honey Dear:—

... A good deal has happened since I came back. The draft went on Monday and there have been a lot of changes. I now have charge of No. 1 Platoon or rather I should say I am platoon sergeant.... The regimental sergeant major has received a commission and has left us. He was very decent to me after coming back and I guess a lot are sorry he is going. But I tell you they had to overlook a lot on Tuesday morning. The whole battalion was in town Monday. A big rain came on and those who were sober found difficulty in getting out.

We are going to have great doings here next week. His R. H. etc etc is to be here and possibly Sham Shughes. We have practiced a review twice and I think have done very well, I guess.

But best of all, honey, we are informed that we leave for Edmonton Monday week, that is I suppose the 20th. Do you know in spite of the wet cold weather, the time is passing rapidly; it is now three days since

I left home. Unfortunately I go on guard tonight for 24 hours. The weather has cleared somewhat however and it promises to be a fine night. We had a terrific hailstorm here on Tuesday night and the camp was flooded. It was some storm all right. I hope you will keep me posted on news. We get so little here, we are so far out of the world. There was great news in the paper today of the Russian victory. Do you suppose the tide has turned. I believe it has you know. All that is needed is patience and determination.

I hear they are having trouble getting recruits in Edmonton. I suppose the harvest will attract a lot of men but 750 men is a big bunch to take out of a city so soon after being depleted. Well honey I'll be glad to get back and sleep in a bed once more. It has been beastly down here I can tell you. And a lot of the men are suffering from rheumatism. But I am feeling really better than when I was here before. . . .

Well dear I will close for the present. Think of me tonight, will you, and write lots. . . .

Good bye dear and don't forget that I love you.

Stuart

SARCEE CAMP, ALBERTA,
SEPTEMBER 10, 1915

Dearest:—

I have a dandy chance to write a few lines. I am on guard and things are pretty slow and will be so for the afternoon. I have had a lovely time for the last 18 hours. It wasn't so bad last night so we rolled in and slept but today it has been pretty chilly sticking around. We have one comfort that we did not have to go on brigade review today as the others, so to that extent we have fared well. Also we have had good meals etc, etc, and now we are looking forward to being relieved. . . .

Rumour has it that the 66th has had trouble raising men. The adjutant and the colonel are both going north to recruit, the latter as far north as Spirit River, where there are said to be 200 men waiting. Do you know, I don't believe they have 2000 men in training here. Of the battalions left about ⅔ are away on harvest leave. It is scandalous; that is why we have so many guards to do; and on top of everything else, the others are given 24 hours leave after guard; we get two.

Well goodbye dearest and let me hear soon. I hope there is a letter for me tonight.

Yours
Stuart

SARCEE CAMP,
SEPTEMBER 13, 1915

My Dear Little Girl:—

I know what sort of things you are saying of me but . . . I have had no leisure and really no opportunity of writing you. Saturday it came on cold and wet and Sunday was a corker. We messed around all day trying to keep warm and busy; but really it was no use. I had a lot of writing to do. I simply sat in the orderly tent with sweater, great coat, etc on and plugged ahead. It certainly was not enjoyable. I expect everyone might have said it was the most miserable day he ever put in. . . . This morning it was about 10 above zero—eighteen degrees of frost or more. It was hard turning out but I had a lot to look after and was not long in getting warmed up.

As you know the Duke [Duke of Connaught, governor general of Canada] reviewed the troops this morning. We have been practicing "fix-bayonets" for several days and everyone had his buttons shined and boots cleaned; but luck had that I was to be battalion orderly sergeant. That kept me in the camp all day and all I saw was seen through a glass. The 66th did exceptionally well I understand but then we always hear that. I took advantage of the occasion to shave and wash in warm water. They did not get back until 12:30 and everyone was famished.

But listen, honey dear, that box you sent me was the best ever. Saturday afternoon I saw the postman hiking towards me with a big parcel. I thought he wanted to borrow some money but he handed it to me. We opened it and say you don't know how good the contents looked to me. I never appreciated candy before and I know the fellows have enjoyed it. We still have some left.

Well we heard today that the 63rd are going north tomorrow. It came out in orders today so we may go north Friday. We will be tickled to death to get away from here, somewhere.

Well dear, ring [my] mother up and tell her I can't write for cold hands. You can see the scrawl.

Goodbye and take care of yourself.

Stuart

Stuart Tompkins had been thrust into the role of head-of-the-family, and he continued to take a keen interest in his siblings. His concern for his brother Philip is evident throughout the wartime letters. Having left Canada with the first contingent, by September 1915, Philip had seen active duty in France and had acquired an English wife.

SARCEE CAMP,
SEPTEMBER 14, 1915

Dear Little Girl:—

I have now a quiet hour before rolling in... I have not much to tell you dear but it really is a great satisfaction to sit down and write you. One gets so immersed in the routine of army life.

I have been thinking a good deal today of the past and of the future and of ourselves. I take it a man may think of himself at times even in the army. Do you remember asking in your last letter, what strength I could draw from you and really it is in my heart to tell you. I have always been afraid of your judgments. Of course you have been charitable and you love me, but I have been so afraid that you might some day discover that I was not all you thought, that I was a little less than high-minded.... [Y]our love has been my guiding star and I have sought to follow it.

Do you know I heard indirectly from Philip today. Kit, who was in the 9th, apparently keeps up a correspondence with Philip's wife's family. He tells me Philip was in the trenches for ten days then went back to England and had again returned to the front.

And now about going north. I know just as much as I did, wars and rumours of war. I am now from Missouri. We are going north but don't know when and won't know until we get orders.... The weather is clear today and we got warmed up, though I didn't get a bath. Pay day tomorrow. Hurrah.

Goodbye dear. Say we have enjoyed the candy. Send all you like.
Stuart

SARCEE CAMP,
SEPTEMBER 19, 1915

Dearest Girl:—

Sunday morning again and still in camp. It came on cold and rainy last night so we closed our tents lit our candles and made ourselves comfortable. The sergeant major was away so we occupied his tent for the night. We lit his oil stove, read, talked, and smoked while the wind howled and the rain beat outside. The morning has been wet and blustery; still we had church parade out on the open prairie. Somehow for the first time it seemed a fitting thing that two thousand men should lift their voices in worship of the Creator of the universe. The very bigness of the great out doors and the feeling of Divine immanence made it all seem so natural and my heart rose for the first time spontaneously as though impelled by an instinct I could not deny. All little things seemed to fall away and one stood alone before the great things of life. . . . Above, beyond and through all runs our love which has become the one great fact and the inspiring motive of my life. And really my dear, it makes things easier and duty more readily born than before. For I cannot do other. I cannot tell you dear what an infinite joy your love has been and is to me nor the rare good fortune that has been mine. As I talk and meet other men and learn their sorrows and mishaps and think that nothing has ever sullied the deep joy that has been our lot, there wells up in me a . . . determination that with your love as my support, I shall do what I can to relieve the anguish and suffering of other men and women.

The weather is now clearing and I shall probably spend the afternoon outside. I might go to town. . . . By the way, that reminds me, I somewhat depleted my pocket book and may need money before the end of the month. . . . I was disappointed not to receive a letter this morning. Mother wrote last week and I shall write this afternoon in reply. I was very glad to get Philip's letter. Do you know, I don't wonder he complains of lack of news from home. Their letters contain all sorts of items but not the ones you want to hear always.

. . . I shall let you know definitely when we hear about going north. Don't forget to write dear.

Yours
Stuart

SARCEE CAMP,
SEPTEMBER 21, 1915

Honey Dear:—

I have just obtained my leave and am writing to advise you of the fact.... I hate to ask a favour dear but I am almost broke and must come to you for financial assistance. Can you lend me the price to come home.... You will I hope let me know at your earliest convenience.

By the way I understand the 105th regiment is authorized to be commanded by Major Naismith. It appeared in the *Albertan* this morning so I am going... to follow it up to see what I can get....

Today at noon I was warned out for a 24 hour guard. I spoke to [the captain] and he at once took the thing up, with the result that Graham went on [guard duty instead]. Graham has been attached to our company for two months with no duties although he is not attached to regimental staff. Consequently he has escaped all duties. With the change in sergeant majors he... is now out for his first day at squad drill.... It strikes me he has been carefree long enough and it is about time he assumed some responsibility....

Well work is going very well but it is time I was cleaned up so good bye dear.

Stuart

Stuart spent his eagerly awaited week-end leave in Edmonton and was back in camp on Monday morning. The Allies mounted a series of offensives in the fall of 1915; the first reports from this Second Battle of Champagne (25 September to 5 November) hailed initial successes, but the fierce fighting yielded limited final gains. British troops fought the section of the battle that took place at Loos, and Philip Tompkins could well have seen action there. Philip was not noted for writing with any frequency, and in the following letters Stuart expressed some worry about his brother.[5]

SARCEE, SEPTEMBER 27, 1915

Dearest:—

Just a few minutes before first post sounds to write a few lines. Do you know I have just a touch of rheumatism, the first I have felt in years—nothing serious, of course. I reached here uneventfully at 8:30 just as fall-in sounded. The camp was dry and the day fairly pleasant, but it was a long time till dinner. Company parade this morning, battalion parade this afternoon. The colonel is back, came down on the same train as I did. Wasn't that glorious [war] news this morning—and the end is not yet. Really, it has cheered us all up, but I am afraid of the price to be paid. I have been wondering all day whether Philip was in it. I trust you will let me know at once if he was, the papers give no news of the Canadians. . . .

Camp gossip—yes all kinds of it but nothing conclusive. We know no more than a week ago.

Well honey dear, my trip home was a great blessing to me. I realize more and more what you mean and such experiences are a tremendous inspiration to me. Our love and companionship seem to compass all there is in life worthwhile and I pray all the time I may be worthy of it. . . .

Well goodnight honey and look after yourself.

Stuart

SARCEE CAMP,
SEPTEMBER 29, 1915
[NO. I]

Dearest Honey:—

I got your little letter just now. . . . I am writing this now as I hear we are to bivouac tonight. . . . When you are reposing in your nice downy cot tonight just think of me out under the vault of heaven in the moonlight. Last night it froze very hard and as it is not warm yet you can imagine what tonight will be. . . .

Don't believe any rumours you hear until you see them. I hear something new every hour; one of the most original that we are to march to Edmonton. I could write a whole volume of stories. I shall tell some of them when I get back.

The British rush in France seems to have petered out. I wonder if it is lack of munitions this time. Such negligence (if there was any) would be nothing short of criminal. The English-speaking world will be anxious until they are taken into the confidence of the war office. I hope there will be good news from Philip. Be sure to let me hear as soon as you hear anything.

Well honey dear, I wonder if you know how often I think of you. I feel sometimes as if your presence were with me all the time. The parting was quite a wrench lightened only by a feeling that I was doing my duty. . . .

Well good bye dear
Your own
Stuart

Stuart Tompkins grew to manhood in his mother's strict, Presbyterian home, and earlier letters have revealed his inexperience with women and his awe at the "love of a good woman." In the army he encountered men from a wide variety of backgrounds, not all of whom shared his moral values, and while he does not appear to have been unduly self-righteous, he did maintain his own high standards and on occasion noted the erosion of the standards of others and of society in general.

SARCEE CAMP, OCTOBER 1, 1915
[WRITTEN ON A CAMP MEMO
FORM]

My dear:—

I sit in the guard tent, not confined, but in the capacity of jailor to write you a few brief words before I roll in. The camp is quieting down after a very strenuous day and my mind or what is left of it is becoming clearer. I got your letter today dearest and though I got only a scant moment to glance over it, it did not mar the great joy with which I read it. You nearly always have something worth while. But after all, it is not so much what you say as what is implied—I am so ashamed sometimes at the love you have shown me and tremble almost to ask myself whether I am worth it all. For a man has to be mighty good to be worth a good woman's love and devotion. I never cease to wonder at the fact that you love me. Indeed it seems a miracle both in its causes and its results—how indeed the very world in which I live and move is transformed and takes on an other worldliness.

Well honey, I often wonder over the question we were discussing. Of course it cannot be approached without a sense of awe and mystery and there attaches to it no less sacredness that it is too often the subject of vulgar jocularity. And thereby hangs a good deal of the trouble people have; indeed they must comport themselves in such manner that there attaches to their conscience no blame if they are to be able to regard such things as sacred. Of course we must all crave forbearance. There are so many forces at work in human life and in the human soul that it is very hard to be dogmatic. Heaven knows I am not perfect. But you know all my faults and they cause myself I think more pain than they do others. We have had some arguments between ourselves (Jones and I) on the matter of purity and I believe that one should absolutely discountenance questionable remarks. I have started to do so and already notice some change in the attitude of the tent. . . .

Well the weary hours of night draw on and I become more wide awake all the time. On returning from the route march this afternoon I was nearly exhausted and very sore but it has gradually worn off and except for the cold I shall not mind it. It is a great relief to think of other than military matters for a while each day. . . .

. . . I really enjoy writing you these letters my dear, if they mean anything to you. I put more into them I may confess than any writing I have ever done for the simple reason that new well springs in my life have been tapped. I have so many things to say it scarcely seems possible to find words fast enough to frame my thoughts.

Well honey, the latest is we go to Edmonton on October 15th. That is a fairly safe bet, though we may clear out of here before that. I have enjoyed the life here. The surroundings are very beautiful and the air almost sparkles like wine. I am feeling very fit, the touch of rheumatism I had is gone. . . .

Let us look forward to the future dear with confidence. Ring up mother and ask about her for me. Tell her I received her long letter and shall write at once.

With all the love possible,
Stuart

The constant rumours of his unit's return to Edmonton began to take their toll on Edna, and Stuart wrote reassurance for both the short and the long term. His vision of a better postwar world put great faith in another of the social reforms that came to wartime Alberta: woman's suffrage.

SARCEE CAMP, OCTOBER 2, 1915
[SATURDAY]

Dear Honey:—

I have at last got down to a letter after making innumerable unsuccessful attempts during the afternoon. But the day has been about as bad as could be imagined and one's work degenerates into puttering. I got your two letters today, both due yesterday, that gave me severe heart tugs. . . . I was minded to sit right down and write a comforting letter. . . . [Y]ou may rest assured we are going back to Edmonton. There is not any doubt in my mind as to that. When is only a question of the D.O.C. and the weather.

And now my dear little wife may I tender a little bit of philosophy and that is not to anticipate things. I think you are very brave and I want you to rest in the assurance that all things work together for good and I want you to look always on the bright side of things and cheer. I believe dear you will reap a thousand fold for any sacrifice. I am becoming more convinced of that every day.

No, you need not worry about our returning to Edmonton. That is certainly assured. Will you give us a welcome.

Well, it is time for first post to sound so I must leave you for tonight. Offer up a little prayer for me will you. I need that more than pity even though I am wet. Goodnight.

Your own,
Stuart

Sunday p.m.: When I wrote the other side, I sat in the orderly room shivering and trying to keep cheerful. I really did lose myself in what I was writing but woke up to the horrible reality at 9:30 when first post blew and I had to get out in the mud and rain for roll-call. I don't think things were ever more cheerless than when I rolled in. The rain was falling, our lines were soft and "squishy" and one row of tents were almost like a quagmire. When we got up this morning the sky was clear and light frost had stiffened the mud. The day broke clear and each hour has seen the temperature moderate and the air become more delightful. Tents are all rolled up and blankets piled. I spent some two or three hours cleaning up (I haven't however had a bath) and now after a good dinner I am going to sit down to enjoy life. The only fly in the ointment is that we have not yet got yesterday's mail. The postal wagon was mired outward bound from Calgary and we are still without. (I rather suspect the postie was sampling good whiskey last night). . . . I intended to go out to town today but I really must write to

Philip and to mother and Sunday seems the only time for writing such extra letters. I can work in yours it seems. . . .

Well things run on about the same here. I have been chosen for the school of signalling which starts tomorrow. I do not know how long it lasts but I shall probably start it. If it continues after we leave here I shall certainly drop out. By the way, Major Hopkins has resigned his commission. What that means I do not know. There have been all sorts of rumours for some time. . . .

Well the news from the front is much better these days. At the same time I suppose there is no occasion for excessive optimism. I do not anticipate the war to last much longer however. The moral element in the world will not stand for it. Do you know I am so glad the women of Alberta are to get the vote. I want to see a tremendous effort made after this war to adjust the political organization of the world so that there will be no more war. No one is more entitled to inaugurate such a movement than the women who have suffered and sacrificed. We need a tremendous moral upheaval and it is the women, who will really have won the war, who are the ones to lead the way. It will be indeed the creation of a new world and the ushering in of an era such as we have never anticipated.

Now honey dear, I don't want you to give way to any nervous fears. We can surely contemplate the future with calmness and leave the ultimate results to another power. Now that is what I feel and I am sure it will be all right. I think this will be a great experience for both of us.

Well, I must get this letter off right away. Let me hear as often and as soon as possible. I must write to mother if possible.

As ever,
Stuart

Albertans had volunteered for the Canadian forces almost immediately upon the declaration of war, and one of the first units to reach the camp at Valcartier was the 19th Alberta Dragoons, made up primarily of veterans of the South African War. They went into action in France in February of 1915, and the bitter reality of the war came home to the prairies, but heavy casualty reports were yet to dampen the spirit with which succeeding troops departed for Europe. Units recruited from every city and town and ranch and trained in camps such as Sarcee continually replaced the killed and wounded. One such battalion was the 12th Mounted Rifles, whose send-off is described in the following letter.[6]

SARCEE CAMP, OCTOBER 5, 1915

Dearest:—

I have already written you a note today which you perhaps will not appreciate but I could not help inscribing another today. I was touched by a statement of yours that life was taking on more meaning. I am very very glad of it dear; I know I have done right and I believe out of it much good will come to both of us. Moreover to be able to sit down and write in the quiet of evening or in the lulls of work brings me great joy. . . .

I am in somewhat of a quandary at present. I was put on to attend the signalling school at Headquarters here and have already attended for one day. I find it is to last until the end of the month and I simply am not going to stay here after the troops leave. Signalling is not so very important but it adds one more qualification which is handy. So in the meantime I am taking it and waiting to see. . . .

We have had a beast of a day here. Rain and squalls all morning and this afternoon a gale. The Y.M.C.A. tent was blown down and a man seriously hurt. There was no parade but the Signalling School had a lecture (no field work). I am sitting in the orderly room shivering with my great coat on (waiting for supper). The marquee is tugging at its ropes threatening to go any time. I expect snow before night fall—then good night. We may be moved at once if something desperate happens. . . .

A young fellow, Christie, has just transferred to the 66th from the 12th Overseas Mounted Rifles. He was in my firing squad yesterday and I was quite taken with him. He used to work in the Dominion Bank, Edmonton. Would he be a relative. . . .

The 12th O.M.R. went off last night with great eclat. They worked all day breaking up camp and packing their impedimenta. Towards evening they fired all their tables and boxes and had a huge bonfire. All the regiments around camp gathered around to help celebrate. At 9:30 they marched out with five bands. The streets of Calgary were packed. One could not move around the station for the crowds. Some said 40,000 people were congregated. It was a great occasion. There was however nothing published in the papers; at least not the morning papers.

Well, dear, the supper call has gone so I must beat it. Will there be a letter tonight.

Stuart

(I was going to say the 12th were as fine a set of boys as I ever saw. They were very popular around camp.)

SARCEE CAMP, OCTOBER 6, 1915

Dearest:—

It is hard to realize that I have already had two letters today both just brimming over with cheeriness. And indeed I need a little encouraging all the time. Things get a trifle monotonous at times in between letters. Still I find life really is interesting on the whole. I can't really tell you what it is but our relation seems in a quiet mysterious [way] to be changing. I think our separation with the consciousness that we have done our duty has seemingly consecrated our union and we have made amazing strides in spiritual growth. Do you know our love has meant more to me almost since we have been away. It gives me a sense of great joy to carry with me the feeling that in our life and thoughts we are one. Do you know I have seen a great many married people and I don't think very many gave me the impressions that they really were very soul mates. It is a great pity people do not more often find an affinity in married life. Honey dear it gives me a great comfort to know that your thoughts are with me and that in all my actions I have consulted you and that our motives have been in accord. . . .

Dare I confide in you the latest rumour. It is that we leave for Edmonton the first of the week. It seems to come from "Good Authority" (reputed the worst liar in camp). There seems to be something in it and in the meantime I am trying to run it to earth to test it. If it is true I shall not go north on leave. In fact I have not much hope of getting away otherwise.

Of course I shall not let the signalling interfere with my going home for it simply is not worth while to me.

How I wish there would be a letter for me tonight. But no chance. I have been too well served today already. I have so much to talk to you about, that I can hardly wait. . . . Be sure and write me tonight.

Your own
Stuart

While Stuart found some challenge in his work and great satisfaction in the knowledge that he was doing his duty, life in the military left much to be desired. The letters that he wrote to Edna each day provided him with his major intellectual stimulation and substituted for meaningful conversation.

SARCEE CAMP, OCTOBER 7, 1915

My Dear:—

I feel a trifle blue this afternoon or rather as if the taste had gone out of life. Your letter which I got at noon contained I imagine just a wee bit of reproach for not having been more active. I know it is well merited and I am trying to live down my indifference but I fear it will take some months to eradicate it.

It has been a beastly raw cold and windy day. Our signalling was not a success, as it was difficult to make the flags go. Still one becomes accustomed to almost anything and our day did count for something. I almost wish I were going to continue the school but you bet I am not going to sacrifice other things for that and certainly I am not going to stay here after the battalion goes. . . .

. . . We have had some very beautiful nights here and some very fine northern lights but it is too cold as a rule at night to stay out. Indeed I usually roll into bed and spend some hours there before first post. I find I can drop into the necessary mood [for writing] easier then than when there are a good many around. . . . I find my own thoughts better companions than a good many others. . . .

I do wish I had more time for reading. Do you know I do crave mental pabulum. One grinds away for days at the same old routine without realizing there is anything better in life than three square meals a day and a bed at night. Still it is one comfort that from time to time one does meet a comrade to cheer one up and inspire one to do one's duty enthusiastically. It is no time to shilly shally. Even if I did not have a good little comrade to bring the very best out of me. For you are doing that dear and thereby lighting up a common place existence with the colour and warmth of idealism. For that surely is the end of life and the one thing worth living for. . . . Did you ever stop to think what would have happened had I not left newspaper work and sought a fat government job. The other alternative appalls me and yet I accept the saw:

> There is a divinity that shapes our ends
> Rough hew them how we will.

I must confess, I have been drawn somewhat reluctantly to believe in such. In these scientific ages one tends to analyze, criticize, etc etc. Years before I ever loved, I dissected love or rather shall I say resolved it into its component parts. (You see I studied psychology and had a thoroughly critical instructor) I had them all labelled and as soon as I saw the right kind of girl I would put them all together and manufacture my love. How I pity now such inane stupidity now that forgets the soul God puts into a man (genus homo) and how there be innate in his bosom the forces that can set the universe on fire, that can exalt him to the heavens if he so will. And side by side with the spiritual forces that be dormant is the passionate longing for a helpmeet and the pure and passionate devotion that every man carries in his heart for the perfect woman. Do not think I have made my pedestal and put you on it. I love you indeed for what you are and I don't want to make you different. . . . I love you dear, I love you and am trying to be worthy of you for I know I am not yet. Goodnight dearest.

Your own
Stuart

Military inconsistencies and politics compounded Stuart's problems in securing a commission, but by 15 October he had begun to explore the avenues that eventually led to officers' training.

SARCEE CAMP, OCTOBER 15, 1915

Dearest Honey:—

Imagine my writing down and attempting to dash off a few lines before I have to report to my evening class. It has been a horribly busy day. I tried to get time to write at noon but it was impossible; and really you deserve a letter even though there has been none for me today.

I made my bow before Colonel Naismith, Officer Commanding, 105th, today. This begins the first act—impression very favourable. . . . I introduced myself you see and talked. Colonel N. is a toughened veteran now though not very old. I like him very much—nothing of the bully about him like our O.C. I have not yet come under McKinery's ban, but he does cut loose once in awhile; he is no gentleman. Now I cannot tell you more at present. I have nothing.

I have to meet Captain Sievwright so will have to close.

Your own,
Stuart

[later]

Dearest:—

I have been out for a long evening and am just back. I *am* tired but do not like to roll in without telling you that I love you. I wish you were here; it is a lovely night; the moon is shining and some one is playing when "The sands of the desert grow cold" and I am reminded that not till then will I cease to love you, dearest. It is one of those rare nights in camp that are almost idyllic when one is freed from the heat and the burden of the day and one is withdrawn into one's self and away back in the inner chamber you trim once more the lamps of the soul that have been lighted from the divine altar. Back there I find the spring of all my joy—the love of a pure woman—worth more than all the riches of the east. Well honey say a little prayer for me. I need it often.

I could tell you more fables re our return to Edmonton, but won't.

What have I done that there was no letter for me today. Must I merely live in hopes.

Stuart

SARCEE CAMP, OCTOBER 16, 1915
[NO. 1]

Dearest:—

What have I done that I have been without a letter for two days. I have been very busy but have managed to get a letter written every day.... I just had a letter of recrimination from mother... Am I, honey, as selfish as others see me? Mother has been blaming my lack of success as due to my failing to think of other people, which is of course ridiculous. The man who attains to the world's standard of success is a frankly and brutally selfish individual. I confess I am indifferent and procrastinating which is perhaps a negative form of selfishness. There's one thing "chez nous", no one would get an exalted idea of himself. . . .

It is a very very beautiful day and looks as if we might stay here for months. The D.O.C. will be back next week and the camp will probably be broken up then. The signalling is progressing fine but I don't think I shall continue after the regiment leaves. Probably arrangements could be made for my finishing it in Edmonton. We had a delightful day. The mountains presenting a glorious panorama, peak and cliff and rugged foothill. . . .

How I wish you were with me tomorrow but cheer up. We will be together soon. I must confess I have a sneaking fear I have offended you. I hope you will tell me if such is the case.

Meanwhile goodbye dearest.

Stuart

Fear of having offended her, and perhaps fear also that Edna shared his mother's recent harsh assessment of his character mentioned in the letter above, set him to soul-searching and self-recrimination.

SARCEE CAMP, OCTOBER 16, 1915
[NO. 2]

Dearest:—

I am going to write very confidentially tonight. I am I admit very tired but there are some things I should like to talk about. You remember that letter you wrote me was it only last week. . . . I plead guilty to indifference and procrastination. I suppose as mother says I [have] inherent physical weakness which weakens my spine but it certainly hurts right to the bone to be called selfish. When mother says it, I think nothing of it, as I lay part of it down to exaggeration but if it comes from another source it does stick. Now this new experience has brought me face to face with realities as I perhaps never saw them before and I feel as though I had got down pretty near to rock bottom. Perhaps religion itself does not appeal to me, but when one's whole being, life and ambition and love—in short all that life means—come up before you as clearly as I have seen them you do some thinking. And in times like these I turn to you for it seems as though you and you only had my soul in your keeping. Now honey I am talking up in the air and yet my reasoning is correct. You know that in ordinary everyday life one talks and acts somewhat cynical but deep down in my heart as you do in yours I don't believe in cynicism. I honestly do believe in the life lived by Jesus Christ and the ideals for which he sacrificed himself; of course I don't go around telling people about it. I follow very falteringly, inclined to adopt rough and ready methods to get through life without weighing the moral principles. But honestly honey our love has brought me back to these basic things; I simply could not love you and not want to be better and nobler and I feel it horribly when I fall back. With anybody else I perhaps should not care but before you my soul stands naked and I simply must make good or feel humiliated before you. I suppose my love is almost my religion. . . . I cannot make you responsible for me but for heavens sake if I am astray I want to be put right. I suppose one can't expect a process of correction without some pain. But I have gripped myself and life and faith with a new inspiration and I want to keep the vision before me.

This is a wild rambling talk but it is very earnest and tonight I shall pray a little, I think, over it. I find a great solace in the natural objects around. One never feels so near to the Almighty as when within sight of the everlasting hills and all man's troubles and petty mundane affairs are dwarfed into insignificance. How slight and feeble are our efforts compared with the vast creation in process around us and how eternal and unchangeable the cosmic forces that are going on in and around us.

"In Thee we move and live and have our being."

He is indeed not far from any one of us. And when one takes up his duties in the light of such knowledge. . . how easy things are, how easy it is to sacrifice to exert ones self to help the other to align oneself with the divine power. My own dearest, when one grips such things he feels life is worth living i.e. the kind of life that counts. . . .

Well the bugles are sounding with a cheerful air; outside the moon is shining with a romantic glow down on a camp that is almost at rest. A calm fills the air as it were with a sense of other worldly things and the soul can withdraw into itself for peace—the joy in memories of the past and the no less glorious vision of the future. I have come through the gloom and the way shines clear before me.

Do you know what I saw in the paper last night. Rev. Robert Pearson is to take a commission in a new regiment and will go to the front as [an] officer. He [said] some time ago he would not go as a chaplain if he went and I admire his spirit. I feel more at peace with myself now, for if Bob chose it he was right. Now I have a lot of work to do and must stop. I do hope Monday brings a letter.

Your own
Stuart

SARCEE CAMP, OCTOBER 17, 1915
[SUNDAY]

My own Darling:—

I don't know whether you like to get such a scrawly letter as I write with a pencil but it is to be your fate tonight as I am in bed very, very tired and there is no pen nearer than the orderly room. . . . I feel the need of talking to you. . . . So here I am honey snugly wrapped up in blankets and coat, leaning on my elbow my suitcase alongside the bed serving as writing table. I must confess I am at peace, though so many miles separate us for have I not a vision of your sweet face as I go to sleep, and shall we not shortly be reunited again. I confess the memories of your being with me have braced me up through many a stiff and unpleasant task.

My utter weariness today is due to a night escapade in which I figured. We signalled yesterday afternoon—at least I did and the use of muscles not ordinarily employed tired me. I was just preparing to turn in when [the captain] came along and asked me to stand by till 10 o'clock. I was spending the intervening time lounging around the tent. . . when my attention was attracted to a commotion at the end of the No 1 Company lines. Apparently some one had called for the men to fall in; when I investigated I found Lieutenant Dodsworth drunk as a lord with his men lined up for squad drill; he was reeling and his voice gurgled drunkenly in his throat. I was sick I can tell you but could not interfere. From indications, however, it was apparent something was doing so I was not surprised when at 10 o'clock the whole company was roused and the tents searched for liquor. Of course the search was a farce as the searchers were not expected to find liquor; but although I searched only one tent I found it and turned it in. It is disgraceful how smuggling it in is connived at; and it is going to ruin the battalion if not cut out. Things are much worse particularly among n.c.o.'s than when we were in Edmonton. . . . It was 11 o'clock before I turned in and nearly midnight when I finally got to sleep so I am not much good today and have done very little.

Well dearest. . . goodnight and sweet dreams

Stuart

He did not write again for several days, during which time he suffered a severe respiratory ailment. The letters he had pleaded for caught up with him in the hospital and apparently contained pressure from her regarding the commission, so he was grateful for his father-in-law's support in having enlisted as he did. Letters that follow contain several critical appraisals of the Army's medical services and of ineptitude and perceived fraud at command levels.

SARCEE CAMP, OCTOBER 21, 1915

Dearest Honey:—

Now where do you suppose I am this fine autumn morning. Nowhere else than in the hospital. You won't be alarmed of course for it is nothing more or less than a bad cold but it quite laid me out and this is the first day I have felt like myself. . . . The night work last week and Saturday night's vigil, on top of which came an early church parade, and to crown all we were kept standing in front of our tents nearly two hours waiting for a distribution of Testaments by the Bible Society. The latter was really an imposition. I did nothing but loaf the rest of the day and went to bed early. I fully intended to get up Monday morning but it was beyond me. Graham brought the doctor around at 10 o'clock to see me, all he did was to grouch that I didn't line up for sick parade at six o'clock and give me some cough medicine. That's characteristic. But the corporal came up to see me, took my temperature, and insisted on my going to the hospital. I could hardly get down here. I was not sick but just very, very weak, wanted to sleep all the time. I guess I just naturally wanted a good rest and indeed I got it.

I have had four letters from you since I came. They certainly looked good to me. The first I could hardly read for the mist in my eyes. There were so many things raised in your letters I scarcely know where to start.

I certainly am glad I had the approval of your father in what I did. Your father is a man's man and his opinion means something, besides I know how much he means to you. Regarding the points you wrote of in your long letter which reached me yesterday, I can't talk now. My plans are all knocked sky high, I am afraid, by this outbreak. . . .

The 55th Battalion left last night for the old country. We are bound to leave within the next ten days, maybe sooner. I shall be good and glad to get out of here.

Well I had a nice luxurious shave this morning which made me feel 50% better. I wish I could have a bath as well. . . .

Well honey I have made quite an effort. I hope you did not worry at not hearing from me. I took the very first opportunity.

Don't forget dear that I love you.

Your own
Stuart

SARCEE CAMP, OCTOBER 22, 1915

Dear Honey:—

Twenty four hours have gone round since I wrote you and a good deal has happened since then. First of all I received a letter from you (also one from mother). Yours was indeed very satisfying and in mother's case some of the sting seemed to have gone out of her pen and I felt better. Secondly I took a real turn last night and have felt quite normal today; chances are I shall get out of here tomorrow at least. I am getting a little to eat now so should begin to pad out. Really I am lucky compared with some of the fellows here. One poor chap from Grande Prairie is doubled up with rheumatism—a fit specimen he is, too, and just my age. He stands his pain well. One fellow sufferer who sleeps next me is just the opposite, lays it on thick when describing his physical troubles and is very qualified in his remarks re his improvement. To disgust me more he is a Canadian from near North Bay or somewhere. Just now he asked me who General Joffre (imagine such ignorance) was!. . .

There has been all kinds of trouble in the 66th. You knew Major Hopkins had resigned. Well the adjutant resigned early in the week. . . . Of course, there must have been trouble with the Colonel [McKinery] but what it was I have not heard. There are all kinds of nasty rumours which have been afloat for some time. You see, every activity of the regiment centres in the Colonel (and to a less extent in the Adjutant). I have been surprised to know to how great an extent he can dictate in little matters. Some of these activities involve considerable money—the sergeants mess, officers mess—regimental institute and canteen. The latter it appears has caused considerable suspicion. To begin with we were all taxed $1 a total of nearly $1700—then the canteen by stiff prices has been making enormous profits—for which we have nothing to show but that Thanksgiving turkey feed when the men were given a mere pittance of fowl. Very little money has been spent on sports or recreation for the men. In fact they have no means at all. McKinery has rather an unsavoury reputation in money matters and so the talk grows. There seems to be lots of room at the top.

Apropos turkeys. The sergeants were served but just 30 pounds as their portion for 78 men. So the sergeant chef hied himself down town in the morning, by gentle guile and a judicious use of the glass succeeded in buying 40 pounds more together with sundry delicacies. The account for which was duly presented to His Imperial Majesty to o.k. Would he. See him snort. Were not 30 lbs of good fat turkey from out his larder, I mean the regimental institute's, sufficient for near a hundred sergeants. In wrath he smote the table. "Sergeant Major. I recommend this man's dismissal. He is too extravagant." I expect he was peeved at the exposure of his own niggardliness. The last news was however, [the chef] was still on deck.

Were it not for the weakness, confinement to a hospital would be intolerable—the long night watches—the fever, the smoking lanterns. . . . You get a little satisfaction when you hear reveille sound and just turn over on your side. I did very little reading before today, it wearied me so and I was too tired to talk. . . .

I fear the signalling will have to go by the board. If the battalion stays all week I shall perhaps go to the classes but don't suppose I shall be able to qualify. I don't care much as there is to be a school in Edmonton this winter.

Nothing from Colonel Naismith. . . .

Today has brought no mail.

> Goodbye dearest
> *Stuart*

SARCEE CAMP, OCTOBER 23, 1915

My Dearest:—

. . . Here I am back in bed at 4 o'clock in the afternoon on a beautiful fall day. But I found the atmosphere outside too intoxicating, my head would float away and leave my feet behind. The Grande Prairie man across the room was joshing me telling some friends that I had to cling to the tent rope and wait for the door to come around before I could dodge in. Whatever the reason I don't feel as well as I did yesterday but I am doomed to be turned out into the cold world tomorrow after one square meal. . . .

Did I tell you my doctor here was Ferris' partner Dr. Gunn. He seems much improved and they all like him. But Ferris that beast. This Grande Prairie man has been suffering the torments of the damned, he went to Ferris Wednesday morning about nine and because he had not been out to sick parade at 6:00 a.m. [Ferris] sent him back to his tent with the excuse that the hospital could not admit him during the day. Such rot. He goes out of his way to show his authority and to dodge work, is never to be seen during the day and cares less for the health of the soldiers than of his horse. He is simply battening off the government and having a holiday, while good men like Mersereau who gave up a farm can be around in their cold tents because he won't take the trouble to see they have better. Our militia system is driving me mad. When King George is calling on the empire to steel themselves for all kinds of sacrifices, fat blood suckers like this Ferris—yes and McKinery—are having a good time drawing fat pay and doing nothing. It's criminal for that is what may lose us the war. I hope they get *their* reward. The country should hang them. Such consummate stupidity and cold blooded sacrificing of the country's interests to that of a few heelers is disgusting. . . .

There has been a fresh crop of rumours grown. . . . One was that [the adjutant] was appointed Brigadier General and was going to the front. I was hoping it was true in the hope something would happen to him when he promptly denied any knowledge of the matter. Another that the 60th was going north a week from today; a third that we are going Wednesday so there you are; one thing only we know—there is sure to be a church parade tomorrow. That is like death and taxes.

Do you know I don't like to let men like Ferris and McKinery poison my mind against patriotism but it seems that the weakness of the present government is allowing patriotic self sacrifice of the many to be exploited for the few. What do some of those men give up— Ferris will not even go to the front while hundreds of fellows who left stakes are treated just like food for a machine or really worse than that. The present surely calls for extreme measures and the government should recognize merit alone.

The weather has turned a bit colder today and it is not comfortable outside except for a couple of hours. There must be brush fires for the mountains are fast receding in smoke. Indeed, we had a young prairie fire right close here the other day, up on the hills just where the South Calgary cars come in. Everything of course is as dry and inflammable as paper. . . .

Well I must close as it is nearly supper time—not much like the suppers we have at home—when will we have another eh. I just . . . dream of the time, honey.

Well look out for your self dear.

Your own,
Stuart

While at home in Edmonton on medical leave following his release from the hospital, Stuart received a transfer to the 89th Battalion, which placed him in the officers' training program. He returned to Calgary and to greatly improved circumstances.

SOMEWHERE IN ALBERTA
NOVEMBER 2, 1915

Dearest Honey:—

We have just crossed the Blindman River and will be rolling into Red Deer shortly so I will indite a song to my well beloved—with apologies to the author of the Song of Solomon. . . .

I have felt very, very sleepy since getting on the train; in fact I fell asleep at Leduc. I have been reading constantly for the last hour or more and the time has gone very rapidly. (We have just passed the Edmonton train so there is no use mailing this till I get to Calgary).

I was just thinking about Mrs. Emslie's case. Of course one cannot be around a military camp without knowing that such situations do arise. One cannot be dogmatic of course. I think the woman is much to be pitied, married to such a thing. On the other hand surely it is not possible to cheat life. Why are people tempted to think that by admitting another to the chambers of the soul life can be made to yield lasting fruits. Naturally though, nature abhors a vacuum, the call to love and self sacrifice is persistent in the human heart and if things are such that they cannot be bestowed on one person I suppose the other is inevitable.

You know it would be awful if a woman were untrue to you. I couldn't forget her you know. I believe I should love her all the same and keep on till my dying day. Because you know it is not a thing you can take on or off at pleasure—it is without doubt the most primal instinct in the human heart.

Well, little girl, I didn't intend to preach a sermon when I sat down. I am sometimes awed at life, its perplexities and complexities—how easily we could have trouble and friction all along the line and how smooth things run. You are serenity personified (I shall say in all kindliness, despite a peppery nature). I have not a little marvelled at what I might call a transformation in you, at any rate you are away beyond what I expected of you. . . .

I am awfully hungry. I did not feel hungry when supper was called so passed up my chance. . . . However I shall get a good meal when I get to Calgary.

Well honey good night and write soon.

Your own,
Stuart

THE GRUNWALD HOTEL
CALGARY, CANADA,
NOVEMBER 3, 1915

Dearest one:—

Behold me just making ready to settle down for the night—yet not able to till I narrate the day's incidents to one I love better than the whole round world. The day has been rich in experiences. . . .

First of all imagine me ensconced in commodious quarters finished in mahogany, substantial walnut furniture including a double bed, hot and cold water and—a sumptuous bath room tiled and nickelled to your taste. Therein shall I disport myself this evening and many others (bear in mind evenings) as well. Last night I stopped at the King George [Hotel], alas now the abode merely of departed grandeur. It has indeed fallen from high estate and is sadly down at the heel; also the service is very poor and I was very uncomfortable so after 24 hours I checked out and beat it for this fair abode inhabited by numerous specimens of the 89th and other southern Alberta species.

But I must hasten on. My train got in at 9:35 and after sending my luggage over to the King George I went to the Club and had a bang up supper—then home and to bed. (Of course your letter was first posted). This morning up bright and early and to breakfast. . . . I reported to the Officer Commanding, was instructed to register and furnished information pertinent to myself. He asked me of my knowledge re drill and I confessed to possessing some information re the rudiments. About 9:15 we prepared to fall in—on the the horizon looms up the herculean figure of Bob Pearson—joyful greetings etc, then the fall in, and out. I was trotted along with Goddard and others—as instructor!! That was bad enough, but listen. In the ranks in my squad were first and foremost George Alexander McGill quondam sergeant major, No 1 Company, 60th Battalion, now Lieutenant—Lieutenant McGuire veteran of how many wars, formerly instructor in the 63rd, and shades of departed Banquo, Lieutenant Emery of the 58th Battalion formerly camp sergeant major with a string of ribbons nearly a foot wide across his chest. Where was my kind mistress Fortune. My knees wobbled at first. I knew McGill was looking for a chance but I plunged blindly forward—right turn, left turn, stand at ease etc, making a few slips but getting through some way. This afternoon ditto—with a different squad and a little more confidence but a little less voice. I had several non coms from the 66th—some of them sergeants senior to me but I did fairly well. I must have a terrible reputation but I am going to live up to it or bust—even if the O.C. decides to come into my class. But I am more than delighted with the men I am to be one of for the next year—clean, well set up fellows—a trifle citified but keen and full of good humour—even the veterans are anxious to help you.

I may say that under the able chairmanship of Rev. Bob a committee sat or rather stood today and made final arrangements with regard to uniforms. They are to be uniform so I am conforming to the rest though in some particulars our outfit is hardly regulation. But we are getting good prices, a good discount, and a genuine guarantee. I left my measurements tonight. We are to wear brown leggings, bedford cords, tunic of dice cloth, service caps much like my old one [and British warm coat]. The only question still is, should I get slacks. They are $11.00 and I think would be very nice to wear around when the others would be most uncomfortable. As far as I can figure out, the cost will be $93.00, less of course a discount. We will of course have shirts and gloves to purchase and boots if we have not got them, but the whole should be well within $100.00 and be it understood, the merchant is to wait for his pay till the Government grant comes through, so I shall not need more than $15.00 or $20.00 at present for my outfit. I am at present in a room at the Grunwald at $20.00 per month. I do not think I shall stay; it seems almost too much although I shall be very comfortable. I think I can save a little on meals by getting meal tickets. I did some running around today for rooms but was not very successful, saw a number of suites $15.00–$20.00 unfurnished, but no rooms in houses. McGill is renting a $40.00 suite and bringing down his wife. I may say I get an allowance of $1.50 per day till we go into barracks which will be at least a month. I should think we could save money by setting up housekeeping.

I was very, very tired tonight despite the fact that we quit at 3 o'clock but the strain and the unaccustomed exercise was too much for my throat and I am quite hoarse tonight, but after a bath I shall feel better. I shall not tell you more of the regiment; instead I shall send clippings from the local papers. Quite a number of well known people are joining, not all as officers. So honey you will have to be satisfied with this effort. How I wish you were here. Things would be brighter. . . . I have something more to tell you but will reserve it for my next letter.

Your lover,
Stuart

His transfer into the officer program made it possible for Stuart to consider seriously Edna's joining him in Calgary, yet he showed some reluctance for her to jeopardize her future by leaving the position in the Education Department. The wishing, hoping, and planning expressed in the following letters reflected life lived in constricted economic circumstances. The reality of the war, too, weighed heavily in November when the fighting at Loos wound down, leaving the British with little to show for the heavy toll taken.

GRUNWALD HOTEL
CALGARY, NOVEMBER 5, 1915
[NO. 2]

My Dear:—

I have a very big bone to pick with you. Do you realize this is Friday evening and that I have not heard from you by mail, wire or wireless since I bade farewell to you on Tuesday afternoon. . . .

Dearest, I should like to spend an hour or so telling you all that is in my heart tonight. I get so lonely for you down here all by myself and I vow that when we are together again I shall be so good to you. My waking thoughts are always filled with you dear, particularly when I come home to a cheerless hotel room. Now I must be exceedingly practical for there are some tough problems to meet. I have thought long and seriously over your coming down to Calgary. Financially there is no reason why you should not. There is just the problem of your future. I feel horribly selfish in asking you to give that up for me. My heart and soul cries out that I want you; yet conscience tells me I must not consult my own wishes. Honey, I haven't very much, but all I have is yours. It will not assure you very much, but will be something and I am going to work hard and try to rise. I do not like to put it up to you and yet feel it a great responsibility for me to assume. I really do need you dear, and if you just speak the word I shall get quarters right away. . . . Now as to finances; all the expenses I shall have re my uniform will be covered by government grant—everything for some months to come. You now have nearly $200 in the bank, I have $25 coming to me from the 66th. . . . Now it seems to me $40 will cover all expenses re moving to Calgary. Ticket $5.75, cartage two way not more than $10.00, leaving almost $25.00 for freight and packing which is a substantial amount. Even if I am painting things in roseate colours I am earning money all the time and we will have over $100 coming in by the end of the month. As to expenses in Calgary, an unfurnished apartment will cost us $20.00, light 75 cents, gas $1.50 per month. Surely we will have ample to live on with a margin over. There should be very little carfare as Calgary is not nearly so scattered as Edmonton. Then for six weeks I shall have lots of time to myself and perhaps more, but above all I want you. Be sure you let me know what you think of it. I shall go out tomorrow to look for houses and things. . . .

I shall be on pins and needles till I hear from you. In fact I am on them already not having heard from you. I don't suppose you will get this tomorrow but I shall post this tonight without fail. I wish you would write . . . so I can prepare to make some move.

. . . I am going to get in a great lick tonight studying. I am really getting down to business. It is really funny to see the changed attitude of the 66th men who are here. It's queer how long merit goes unrecognized. . . .

The news from the front is indeed very black but there was a flash tonight that the Allies had achieved a great success in the Balkans. Pray God it is true.

Well good night dearest.

Your own
Stuart

Stuart thrived in the officer training program, and the following letter shows a rarely expressed self-confidence and satisfaction with his accomplishments. It also finds him confronting the alien and uncomfortable matter of marital infidelity to which he had alluded in an earlier letter.

GRUNWALD HOTEL
CALGARY, NOVEMBER 7, 1915

Beloved:—

Your two letters were waiting for me when I came in for lunch yesterday. . . .

I slept in till nearly eleven o'clock this morning so breakfast and dinner coincided. . . . I spent over an hour last night looking at and for suites. There seems to be a big demand for them now and janitors and others feel very independent. I located one fairly good one the other day in the Underwood Block, but had no luck last night. I shall probably just stumble on what we want one of these days. Of course I am assuming you are coming down. Dearest I did try to look at the matter unselfishly. I don't think I allowed myself to be swept away by the terrible longing. Still it looks to me now as if it would be a want of trust to the all-guiding Hand if we remained parted now. What do you think? Well my mind is made up, in fact the whole question is as clear as the noon day sun. You have not led me to believe you thought otherwise so I shall go ahead. . . .

The classes are going along very pleasantly. It seems to be taken for granted that I am one of the most proficient. I am called out every morning to take a squad. Mr. Goddard who is one of the instructors assures me that I know as much about it as he and is very deferential. I have found out that some of the new men know more than I do about squad drill but I expect with my practical experience, I can show them aces in spades in battalion drill and interior economy. However I am not going to trust to my knowledge, but intend to work. Lectures start tomorrow but as they are from 4:30 to 5:30 we will have our evenings free—don't I wish you were here dearest. By the way, how long notice will they want at the department do you suppose. . . .

My relations here with everybody are certainly the happiest. Colonel Naismith is very thoughtful. He could not get that 66th pay fixed up, so he promised me an advance on my November pay. He was also very very kind when I was not well. He is a vastly different type from McKinery. Thank heavens this is a Canadian outfit.

I fear you will be disappointed about my uniform, we will not get them until *next* week. Some things I shall want your advice on e.g. slacks for walking out. They will cost $11.00 or $12.00 but of course are not absolutely necessary. We will have to pay $20.00 or so for swords. Still everything we get we will get at rock bottom prices so should be well within our allowance. Everything is being bought through the purchasing committee.

I am very anxious to hear from you tomorrow to know what you think re plans. I have really missed you more since I came down this time than ever before. Of course, I am alone more. . . .

I fear I have some reputation as I was saying. It's Mr. Tompkins this and Mr. Tompkins that; and not just sergeant. I fear though sometimes that these fellows do not realize that in camp life the platoon commander is scarcely as important as the platoon sergeant however little honour the latter may reap in several matters. But it is strange how the attitude of the 66th men has changed, even Emslie. I feel sorry for the poor fellow. . . . I scarcely understood what you said re Mrs. Emslie—whether to put a sinister interpretation on it. I certainly hope not. It certainly is rough treatment for a fellow who has heard the call—no matter what he may be like. Heaven grant I might die before anything came between us. No, with me it would not be a matter of respect. I can scarcely explain what. The way it has acted on me would prevent me. I have sat for some minutes trying to frame words to express it. Deep calleth unto deep, the very foundations of my life would have to be swept away. No I could not, I could not.

Well I have rambled away at great length, dearest, though the time has gone pleasantly enough. I do hope I shall not have another Sunday to pass alone. . . .

Do you know I have a sort of religious streak on today. I am a heathen as far as observing the average rules of the church-goer but there seems to be a growing element in my nature that cries out to the Divine Power. I am as sure that the Father is leading us all and that as we call on Him serve Him and strive to know His will, will the Kingdom of Heaven be established among men. Be sure that the Kingdom of Heaven is not here nor there but is within you of course. I am ashamed at how little I live up to my ideals. I believe a new life is opening up for both of us and vast and unexplored vistas of thought and character stretch away into the distance. In moments of peace I have that feeling. God help me that I am so little able to translate it into the language of action.

Well honey good bye and write soon.

Your lover
Stuart

GRUNWALD HOTEL
CALGARY, NOVEMBER 8, 1915

Dearest:—

Apartments and apartments and apartments; I think I have seen every block in the city where you can even hang up your hat and the end is not yet. I have seen cheap ones and dear ones, high ones and low ones, nice ones and the other kind, and the one that appealed to me was a very plain ordinary suite (unfurnished) on 16th Ave. W. There is no fireplace and the floors are not hard wood but it is bright and clean and there is a homelike atmosphere around the place. I like the people or what I saw of them. The apartment is a small one and the rooms are on the first floor.... The price is $24.00 but I believe I could get it cheaper, possibly $22.50. It is about 12–15 minutes walk from Victoria Park....

I fear I have almost overdone it today, it is snowing and blowing but in spite of that I undertook a trip out. However I am just a bit tired that's all and will not be able to study. You need not worry about me. I am feeling fine now I can assure you....

A troop train from the coast has just gone through. I could hear the cheering.

... I would like to write reams tonight but I know I should not; I shall try to write more tomorrow. Remember dear some one who loves you.

Stuart

P.S. I got a check today from the regiment so am all right.

Stuart

GRUNWALD HOTEL
CALGARY, NOVEMBER 9, 1915
[TUESDAY]

Dearest:—

I just want to sit down and dash off a letter to my own darling. The day is stormy and disagreeable but I feel quite cheerful within (having partaken of breakfast). I wrote my letter in such a hurry last night without reference to the ones I had received from you. What was it made you feel blue on Saturday, you did not say and I can hardly imagine. . . . Now I shall not get back to the apartment question. I suppose I bored you to death over it. I feared I should be tired this morning after my efforts but I feel quite fit. Be sure you write at once and let me know what you think. . . .

Do you know this promotion has done a wonderful amount to hearten me. I was growing discouraged and indifferent. Of course I can't tell you how blue I felt all summer but I feel now as if I were among friends and comrades and should get a fair show and am going to do my little best. Life is rapidly changing for me; a new note is creeping in that I can't tell you about. Dear I am so glad I have you, we can work together and cheer one another up when the way is dark. Well I must not write more this morning but get to work.

Stuart

Tuesday evening
Carissima:—

I have only ten minutes as I promised myself I should get down to work at 9. . . .

I can't tell you, dear, how much I think of you and how I miss you. What a blessed experience to be together again and all the things we will have to talk over. I am just bursting now.

I should like to ramble on but I have long exceeded my time and must get to work. I shall post this tonight. Please let me hear from you as soon as you can. I may say I have not drawn my 66th pay but have an advance on the other. I hope to have it straightened up tomorrow.

Your own
Stuart

Stuart selected an apartment that obviously proved acceptable to Edna, and she joined him in Calgary after a few more days of his anxious waiting.

GRUNWALD HOTEL
CALGARY, NOVEMBER 12, 1915
[FRIDAY, NO. 1]

Dearest:—

I don't know when I felt so disappointed as when you told me you were not coming till Tuesday. I suppose I have been getting worked up over rooms. Of course I swallowed it and shall have to forget all about it till you get here. I have no plans for the next few days. I was thinking of moving into the suite tomorrow but I get really so very little time that it would be hard to do the unpacking. Still if I feel like it that is what I shall do. We'll just have to forget we haven't the nicest suite in Calgary and be cumfy where we are. . . .

There is little to tell outside of the grind of the classes. I was thinking last night of our life together, its ups and downs, and wondering how you regarded it. You know two people can go through the same experience and it means something totally different to each. But no matter what love may bring I suppose there is a certain amount of pain in contemplating that even people who love one another are not necessarily happy and that so many wrecks strew the tides. Then I have been wondering about ourselves and what the ultimate result will be. Do you know love is the perfection of friendship. The Greeks had one word for both [phylia] and we should constantly walk in the light of the fact that we are bound with these ties for all time and that one must show one's self all the Christ's teaching demands before one is really entitled to the self sacrificing love of a friend.

Post-prandium—all of which goes to show, honey dear, that love is the most abiding thing in one's life or in one's self—a golden strand running through the cord of life that cannot cease even with death. . . . But perhaps in that far off life when all secrets are revealed I will be permitted by the Good Father to walk with you and tell you how hard I tried in my poor way to be worthy of that which you have bestowed on me.

Well I must away as it is late. I regret I did not post this for the morning train but then my poor head is gone.

Your lover,
Stuart

Stuart's next letter was not written until May 1916. The period that he and Edna spent together in Calgary was one of the happiest of the early years of their marriage, even though they both knew that when he received his commission he would leave for England and ultimately duty at the front. They formed some lasting friendships among his fellow officer candidates and their wives, several of whom went on to spend the war years in England, as did Edna.

3

Troop Train and Steamship

❧ EARLY SUMMER, 1916 ❧

The 89th Alberta Overseas Battalion left Calgary on 25 May 1916. Stuart and Edna Tompkins chose to keep their parting private, and they said goodbye at home rather than at the Calgary railway station. The 89th and most other Alberta infantry battalions were destined to be dispersed and absorbed into other units on their way to the trenches in France, but the province sent off its own with great pride and enthusiasm, as the following letter attests. The troops received a welcome befitting heroes at almost every stop along the route to Halifax, their port of embarkation.

ENROUTE, MAY 25, 1916

My Dearest Honey:—

At last the peace that passeth understanding. You can have no idea of the relief of all—particularly those of us who can subside into upholstered seats.

This afternoon has been quite an experience. I really calmed down a little after I got back to barracks, as there were things to do not a few. I did get my shoes shined but that was all I had time for. When I got back I found all my men there drunks and all. At 5 o'clock we fell in with full marching kit; when we moved on to the battalion parade ground we found a troop of mounted police and a platoon or so of the 137th forming an escort. It was very prettily arranged. We moved off

This photograph of newly commissioned Lieutenant Stuart Tompkins was taken just before the 89th Alberta Overseas departed Calgary, May 1916.

with our own band; the HQ staff went off with the right half Company 4 about half an hour before us; the escort going with us, i.e. the battalion. We found the streets thick with people. . . . Such a jam, the streets choked with people so we could hardly get through—sweethearts etc etc etc. Even the [station] platform was thronged. We were soon in the train and a further spasm of farewells. It was real touching how sentimental some of these callow youths became. Perhaps it was safe now and it made the girls feel nice. I had to shoo the boys back on the train time after time and I know I became in a short time most unpopular. However, "kind but firm" is my motto.

The Red Deer train was there. They went just a short time ahead of us. Well we did get off and oh the luxury of sitting down. Dinner was very late as we had to see the men fed first. But it was worth it, soup, turkey, cranberries, chocolate pudding, coffee, and now to bed.

I caught a fleeting glimpse and a sweet smile from Mrs. Pavey. Mrs. Gilmour was also at the depot. . . . She wished to be remembered to you. There is heaps more I could write of, so much that is interesting and amusing but I am running out of paper! (I have lots of stamps). Captain Whittaker admired the portfolio, thought it a beauty which it is. I will write tomorrow and tell you how I love you.

Stuart

EN ROUTE, MAY 26, 1916
[NO. 1]

My Dearest:—

Lunch is over and we are still rolling merrily on through the scrub country of Eastern Saskatchewan. I am just keeping awake till after roll call at 3 o'clock and then I am going to make up. I wonder what you are doing today, whether you stopped off at Wetaskiwin. . . .

We have been getting along fine as far as comfort etc is concerned. For all the colonel is very easy going, he insists on things being right. I have had a glimpse of a harsher side to his character. One of my men applied for his discharge at the last moment; I was inclined to yield to the tears of a woman but not so the colonel; he is a stern disciplinarian when it comes down to brass tacks and I guess he is right. Of course he is sacrificing as much as any of us, when it comes to that.

Well, honey, I know that I am doing my best and I am going to make it my business to spare no pains to make good. Every bit of approbation I get I shall pass on to you and every bit of encouragement. I am satisfied that things are going all right and I shall try to keep them.

Life is full of such possibilities just now; I know I shall not ever have occasion to regret it.

That reminds me, there were so many amusing things happened yesterday. The catch word seemed to be the old garbage collectors "Shawnt be round tomorrow." It really was very pat. Really Calgary did herself proud for us and I must confess my heart swelled. The music though was unnerving as it nearly always is and I was glad we could not hear it. I am sure we must have been quite a sight.

I know everyone is envying me my travelling arrangements. Not only my toilet articles but writing material ink etc. I feel most luxurious, I can tell you, and I know everyone thinks what a thoughtful wife I have. Domnie says the portfolio is a quiet hint about writing.

Well I am going to get some telegrams off and settle down to snooze. . . . we are sailing from Halifax and not from Quebec. . . . We have seen troops all along the route. Did you remember reading of the sudden death of Colonel Bruce of the 181st. CPR officials say he jumped off the train and was killed.

This is a very scrappy letter but you may look for better later. I will write home tonight. Goodbye for the present.

Your own
Stuart

Stuart had convinced Edna to make the trip to England while they were still in Calgary, and from the very first he looked forward to having her join him. The fact that a fairly large number of wives did go to England indicates a seeming casualness in regulations that still prevailed at that stage of the war. Edna recalled that "A number of us did go. There were a number that I knew who went over. They hadn't any restrictions—you know, they were so accustomed—nobody had had a war since the Boer. And we went."[1]

ENROUTE, MAY 26, 1916
[NO. 2]

Dearest:—
Swift Current, Moose Jaw, Regina, Indian Head [Saskatchewan]—all have passed like a flash without my sending a letter. However I have had some difficulty getting writing material and of course I have

been orderly officer. I did not sleep well last night until well on toward morning so today I feel kind of light as though I might blow away. I was up at 7:00 just as we rolled into Moose Jaw. Of course everyone wanted to get off and I had to shoo them back in the train. The discipline is none too good. Still we manage. Their breakfast—baked apple, corn flakes, bacon and toast, marmalade. Not bad is it. What surprises me is the remarkable time we are making. We are to be in Winnipeg this evening at 7 pm, just a trifle over 24 hours. We are to have a march out. Everyone will be glad I guess to stretch his legs. We had train inspection this morning and things are in very good shape. Really the CPR has things wonderfully organized. The men have tourist cars and we have a standard sleeper and a tourist car turned into a diner. Then there is a cooking car which they use on these troop trains. Everything is complete and everyone is happy.

We have just passed Sentaluta where mother and father used to live. Of course it is just a name to me as I was never there. I have bunked in, did I tell you, with the chaplain, he below and I above. Really we are a congenial crowd and I am very contented. Everyone has been asking about you honey and I am sure you will be glad to see the fellows in England when you arrive.

I sometimes catch myself wishing you were in the seat opposite me and that your dear eyes were looking across. Of course, that will come in time. Meanwhile I am very contented just to have your love and to feel across the vast distances that separate us, the love that binds us together. God bless you, dear, for what you have been to me. . . .

Well now good bye dearest. I must away to my duties. Best wishes. Once again I want to tell you how I appreciate the portfolio. It is a jewel. With all imaginable love.

Stuart

EN ROUTE, SATURDAY MORNING
[MAY 27, 1916]
[NO. 1]

Dearest Honey:—

Nine o'clock and all is well. Now I have so many things to tell, I do not know where to stop or start. My last note which I intended to post at Brandon [Manitoba], I neglected till I got to Winnipeg. At Brandon it was pouring rain, but a lot of people turned out to see us—and such good looking girls. Believe me, they weren't a bit bashful. One came up and introduced herself and Mr. Dunn somehow picked out the prettiest one and brought her around to meet us. I am sure a number of hearts were lost. The YWCA and others went around with literature for the men. We had a very cheering reception. We reached Winnipeg about ten o'clock p.m. It was intended to march out but orders have been issued forbidding it. As I stepped off I heard a cheery Hello Tommy, turned and saw Bob Pearson. "Meet Mr. Tompkins," he said. I looked up at a tall military gentleman with red band on his hat and crossed batons. I had the presence of mind to salute before I shook hands and only then did I realize I was speaking to Gen. John Hughes. There were quite a lot of people in the station. We were there for half an hour. More YWCA people, more books etc but no pretty girls. Then to bed. This morning is really beautiful. We are now in Ontario well east of Ignace which we passed at breakfast time. Fort William will be reached at noon. Again I am metaphorically hugging myself (or you) for the conveniences I have on the train. I never had the like—toilet articles and writing material. It is fine and is adding to the pleasure of travelling.

Well honey I thought of you a long time last night. Not that I was lonely, only I love you. I wonder what you are doing today and how you are. I hope you are getting better than we have been. It was rotten crossing the prairie and the whole country was just flooded. We are now back in the land of trees and lakes and it is lovely.

Now I hope you will have a good time and a little rest before moving again.

Don't worry about me. I am just fine and eating well. I will write again today when I will tell you perhaps something more interesting.

Meantime goodbye dearest
Your own
Stuart

EN ROUTE,
SATURDAY MORNING, MAY 27TH
[NO. 2]

Dearest Honey:—

I probably have not much to tell except that I am back in Old Ontario once more. We stopped off at Ft. William for a walk. How dull and sleepy everyone seemed after the west. The natives did not seem to care anything about us except the youngsters, who tagged us about.... I have been thinking about you this afternoon wondering at life and the changes since I came west six years ago before I knew you.

Once again a profound change is coming in things. I some times wish by some miracle I could leave myself behind and take on a new man. Yet I suppose the Almighty has not willed it thus; so we must struggle on and do the best with our poor personalities.

Still, when I look back and think of the happiness we have had in the last year I am content; and I trust the next year will make me more a man. I am so far from what I would be. Still I am confident that with your love and with what efforts I can put forth I shall become some what more like my ideal. Meantime; good bye and good luck. We get to Ottawa Monday morning.

Goodbye

Stuart

SUNDAY MORNING [MAY 28, 1916]

[NO. 1]

Dearest:—

An exquisite day. . . . It was almost seven when I awoke, the sun shining in the windows. Really it is good to be alive these days, and rolling merrily eastwards even though our surroundings are the rock bound desert of New Ontario. We had a slight accident this morning. The train parted in two but nothing serious occurred and we were soon patched up.

Last night we ran into Schreiber about five o'clock when the whole native population turned out to see us. . . . Dear how frowsy Ontario looks after the West. You cannot get away from it. The scenery coming into and going out of Schreiber was extremely beautiful—around the headlands of the north shore.

Today things have not been going so well. We had OC's inspection and Whittaker of course got excited. Things were not just right but instead of calling me down he just insinuated. I was so mad I could not speak but I am going to forget it. It is childish to keep anything like that, particularly when we are bound on the mission we are. And above all I must make good for my honey's sake, so I shall forget it all.

Well we will soon be in the [Toronto] "Globe" belt. We have had almost no news since leaving home and don't know whether the empire is still standing. Au revoir dearest

Stuart

❦

One break in the tedium of the troop train came when the regiment acquired a mascot along the way—which Stuart describes in the following letter. In 1986, on the occasion of the sixtieth anniversary of the publication of *Winnie the Pooh*, a spate of articles identified the model for that famous bear as a cub named Winnipeg that had arrived in England with Canadian troops during the Great War and had been donated to the London Zoo. It is quite likely that Stuart's regimental mascot went on to become Winnie the Pooh.

STURGEON FALLS, ONTARIO
MAY 28, 1916
[NO. 2]

Dearest:—

What a hot almost oppressive day it has been. We have been seeing sights since morning. At 12 o'clock we stopped at Cartier and had a walk down the track and back. It was not enjoyable in the dust and heat. We were at Sudbury an hour and half ago. It has become a real smart progressive looking place and even the ladies were out to see us. It was quite interesting. One demure maiden went the length of the train and shook hands with the 484 odd on board. She didn't seem enthusiastic, doing it apparently as a matter of duty. How like Old Ontario. She came up to a group of us officers and for the life of me I could not think of anything to say to cover our embarrassment. But she didn't worry. She hoped us shyly a safe return and left it at that. By the way I must tell you of our b'ar—which was taken on the strength of the regiment at Jackfish. I don't know its length over all or its weight but it is about the size of a pup. He has been appointed provisional regimental mascot and will still have to qualify before the imperial authorities. His appearance is always hailed with shrieks of delight but everyone clears passage when he lunges with his tiny paws.

The conductor on the train came along an hour or so ago and catching a profile view of him I was much struck by a familiar look which took me back 20 years. He is a boy with whom I attended school for a short time. I suppose I had forgotten his existence. Curiosity prompted me to question him and sure enough it was Walter Peverly. So he came back when disengaged and we had a bit crack together over old times. He was asking about the girls i.e. Louise and Alice.

Well honey we are back to the land of the elm and maple. As I look out I can count an odd dozen, and the whole country side is the most luscious green and cows and chickens and barns everywhere.

I bought an extra supply of stamps at the last station so look out for letters. . . . I know they are illegible and not worth while but maybe you will find a few grains of wheat in the chaff. Captain Muncaster and I have been discussing *wives* this afternoon.

Stuart

When the train reached Ottawa, the troops turned out for a parade and inspection by the governor general, the Duke of Connaught, and by the dominion defence minister, Sir Sam Hughes. Stuart withstood the ordeal, which he described in some detail in the following letter.

TURCOT, QUEBEC, MAY 29, 1916

Dearest Honey:

I have just saved a life, meaning instead of waiting for dinner I just bought a banana. I did not eat much lunch and as a result am suffering from after effects. However with the prospect of a speedy departure, my stomach is beginning to take hope that dinner also will materialize.

Well what a red letter day this has been for all of us. First we awoke in the C.P.R. yards at Ottawa. Reveille went at five. I was up at 5:45 shaving and dressing. After breakfasting I saw the men and warned them all to be ready. At eight o'clock we tumbled out of the cars and lined up, with perhaps just a little too much confusion but at 8:30 all was ready and off we went. How strange to be in an eastern city once more. Smoke and grime and neglect apparent at every turn—toil worn men and women without the joy of hope or the bloom that comes of contact with God's fresh air—and just a little dirt and squalor. Up the winding streets and finally onto Parliament Hill, the little quadrangle of green backed by the Parliament buildings and fronting on a street (I forget the name) where are a number of administration buildings. How our hearts beat and our breasts swelled with conscious pride as we marched through the crowds on to that historic ground. We formed mass, fronting on a small square two sides of which were formed by the 88th (Victoria) and the 90th (Winnipeg). The crowd formed the 4th. About 9 o'clock Gen. Sir Sam appeared with his staff, gold braid etc. He came over and spoke to the officers of each regiment in turn, handing out the usual line of dope—fine bunch of officers, need for further training with a few little variations. Then the Duke appeared, battalions in turn come to attention, Duke inspects. Our men lay as long as possible owing to great heat and the heavy packs. Finally they came to No. 10 who stood stolidly at attention while I saluted grandly as we (i.e. the Duke and I) came around the first end of the platoon, Sir Sam apparently thinking I needed jollying said, "I suppose you think you're the best looking officer here; and by George you are next to the adjutant." My knees trembled almost but I smiled and apparently it was meant for a joke the same as if a bear hugged you or an elephant stepped on you—for everyone laughed. However I was proud of the boys and treated them to oranges afterwards. We were introduced to the Duke in turn after forming up and listening to a little speech of his. We received a great ovation when we marched off, particularly "C" Company and I just knew my boys were doing their prettiest; hand clapping and cheers followed us right down to the station. Here the Volunteer Society of St. John's Ambulance had a treat for the boys, cigarets and oranges for 3000 men. The fellows were tickled. I met some of the young ladies and fine girls they were, too. . . .

We got off at 12 o'clock, the 88th clearing in two sections ahead of us and the 90th behind. Our trip down the Ottawa was beautiful, the countryside a vivid green and the river a dream. Nothing momentous occurred except that everyone was sort of overwhelmed at things. We passed Dowal where we switched to the G.T.P. [Grand Trunk Pacific] and Turcot where our old crew left us. We are now in the hands of the I.C.R. [Intercolonial Railway] and in a few short minutes will be going across the Victoria Bridge. . . .

Well so much for today.

Later.

I rather dashed this letter off with the idea of getting it off at Turcot but there was no post office so this will have to be posted in the morning. We have still a run of over 800 miles so we expect to be nearly 40 hours on the way. I am going to tell you a secret. The three battalions inspected today together with two others are to sail on the Olympic White Star Liner on Wednesday. As she is a fairly speedy craft we should make the trip in good time.

. . . I hope and trust the war will have a steadying effect on me and will make me the real man I want to be. You know I feel in the bottom of my soul that a man is not good enough for a girl even if he were perfect; and how far we fall below perfection. God only knows. Well dearest that is the way I feel. Ah how I love you and how I try every hour to be worthy of you. Every day I shall try to make a step upward. Every day a real spiritual experience. I think we shall have revealed to us in a new and startling way the true meaning of human life, the relation of man to woman and both to the state. We shall the better understand one another and that life of which we form a part. Let us both try to play our part in the great drama now being enacted.

I am just dying to hear from you. You must write long and interesting letters re yourself, dearest.

Your own—*Stuart*

SATHER POINT, QUEBEC,
MAY 30, 1916
[NO. 1]

Dearest:—

During the past 24 hours we have been ushered out the new into the old world—the land of fishing villages, the habitant and of the church. This morning we turned into a grey land, farms and hills, houses clinging to hillsides but covered with a thick blanket of rain and fog and the smell of salt water in the nostrils. I wonder what you are doing back in that sun blest land where it "never rains."

There is little to tell about. I discovered this a. m. that there are 9 troop trains ahead of us, from which we can infer there will be 5 regiments on board our transport—some body of troops.

You know, at every point the train stops troop trains are welcomed with open arms particularly where there are petticoats around. Every man in the train then claims to be single by some strange chance and indeed you would think so. I was just wondering whether these men really forget those they have left behind. Light hearted and all as they are, I do not think so, for to be with a woman for months and years together has [had] a most profound influence on me. . . . If there is one thing that our love has done it is that it has lit up all the dark corners of my soul and made me ashamed to harbour a wrong thought and so I live in daily exaltation at the greatness of the destiny before us and confident that the love we have for one another will go down throughout all the life to come. . . . [A]s time and eternity go on, the ties will grow stronger and the life will grow deeper; we will be led out of our

grey and colourless past into a new world where love and peace and
mutual service shall reign, supreme. Funny, I can't measure things by
conventional standards. Technically, it would be prudent for you to
stay at home and get a job, but if it meant that the mighty epoch in
which you were living would go by without the adding of one inch to
your mental and spiritual stature, to stay home would be most lamentable. Prudent indeed but not wise. Oh my darling, how much more
will we mean to one another, when we have lived through the stress
and strain of the present, when our souls shall have been lifted out of
the common world on to the heights whence we will have caught the
vision splendid of that new world which is to be.

Everyone is happy this morning at the thought of embarking tomorrow. We will be the last troops on so will hardly get choice of
quarters. . . .

Well honey we catch glimpses from time to time of the great Gulf of
St. Lawrence—everywhere there is a great stretch of foreshore (the
tide is out) like at Vancouver. . . .

Goodbye and good luck
Stuart

CAMPBELLTOWN,
NEW BRUNSWICK
MAY 30, 1916 [NO. 2]

Dearest:—

It has been a rotten miserable day and just now one cannot see more
than a hundred yards away. We have just had a stop at Campbelltown
where a large part of the native population turned out to meet us in
spite of the pouring rain. Campbelltown lies at the foot of the
Matapedia Valley where the river which runs through that valley empties into the Bay of Chaleur. The ride down the valley was very disappointing. Doubtless it was very beautiful but one could see nothing;
now and again the dim shapes of mountains loomed up through the
fog on either hand. Campbelltown is a town of 4,500. Four years ago it
was burned to the ground. Today it has a fairly prosperous look. . . .
We are now skirting the Bay which is very close but can see nothing of
the country to our right. It is not yet a week since I left home but it
seems ages. Will there be a letter awaiting me when I reach England.
Still I am not lonely.

I think Captain Martin has developed into the champion lady
hunter. His motives are not hard to discern. The last time he came in

he shouted in triumph, "Ah, a box of cigarettes every week." The shameless fellow is making a business of it.

I am sending a couple of cards showing scenes near here. It is not hard to see we are in a seafaring community, all kinds of sailing ships in sight.

We have made all arrangements for embarking tomorrow. We expect to be a bit crowded to be sure but then it should not last more than a week.

The time has again changed so we get supper shortly but I am not hungry. Wouldn't a bit of toast and coffee tempt a little.

I wonder how you are getting on, what your plans are. I will be impatient to hear. Do you think of me just a little.

Really I have never travelled in such comfort. Even slippers to put on when my feet get wet. I can never be grateful enough for the portfolio. . . . I had a couple of accidents—left my tooth powder can open and sprinkled its contents in the bed, lost the contents of the camphorated oil bottle, but nothing serious. I am learning to look after myself.

Well good bye darling.
Your own
Stuart

As the troop train neared Halifax, security restrictions tightened. Censorship became a burden that would last throughout the war, and Stuart himself served as censor for the men in his battery.

TRURO, NOVA SCOTIA
MAY 31, 1916
[NO. 1]

Dearest:—

Here we are at the farthest east almost and the weather still muggy. Nova Scotia is something like Ontario and yet it is not; it is far more old fashioned and staid. We passed one beautiful place this morning, Wentworth Valley; skirting the mountain that formed its southern boundary, we could look down 300 feet on the farms and houses below.

In case I did not get time to get a letter off I dropped you a card. I now find that from now on all correspondence is to be censored, so I suppose I cannot tell you that I love you eh!. . .

We will be glad to get on board ship today and get away. While our trip has not been monotonous, it is beginning to tire us physically owing to lack of exercise and probably overeating.

I am so sorry I shall not hear from you till I reach England, though I will be busy I expect. I resumed this letter in the hope that I could post it at Truro and get it away uncensored, but we are now off.

To our other restrictions were added a kit inspection on the train to discover possible spies etc. I hope that this terminates our pleasurable activities till we get to Halifax. . . .

Now little honey, I want you to have a good rest and a good time before starting on any peregrinations. Don't forget that I am always thinking of you and trying in my own small way to do the things you would like me to. I am hoping that I shall in some way prove worthy of the one who has cast in her lot with me.

Sweetheart I love you day and night. Do not forget.

Goodbye,
Stuart

To be booked on the sister ship of the *Titanic* for one's first trans-Atlantic crossing might not seem the best of omens to some, but Stuart Tompkins did not let that stand in the way of enjoying this adventure, and he shared as much of it as possible with his wife.

ON BOARD S.S. OLYMPIC
[WEDNESDAY] MAY 31, 1916
[NO. 2]

Dearest Honey:—

I am next thing to all in but I cannot refrain from writing you a note before turning in. I have an upper berth in a stateroom for three with the comfiest little reading lamp at my head. There are so many things to tell that I shall not attempt. We hardly know where we are at and I am just all in expecting to be more so tomorrow.

Well, dearie, I trust everything is ok, and that I will hear in time. Do not forget how much I love you ever.

Thursday:—

The long neglected epistle—But we were so busy this morning with rearranging the men. . . .

And now I have to tell you a whole new reef of experience. It all seems so unreal that I almost have to pinch myself to believe it is me. We reached Halifax about 2 p.m. yesterday—cold mist and drizzling rain. Glimpses were caught of the harbour as we drew in with the shipping and we pulled up within sight of the docks. After an unconscionably long delay we were trundled off, formed up and marched in file by twists and turns through the muddy slimy freight yards to the wharves. Here lying along side her pier was the vessel we were to board. I was disappointed in her. She was behind a large shed but it did not seem that she came up to advance notices. It was not until we had traversed the length and breadth of this shed several times that the immensity of the boat dawned on me. At every door and window down the full length of the building showed through the steel grey side of the vessel, and I afterwards discovered she extended 200 feet beyond. The boarding was tedious. Filing slowly in fours or file down the building to a stairway, up a flight of stairs, around and around the next floor, a vast living snake. It all seemed unreal, in the gloom of the murky afternoon, the men all excited and singing deliriously. At last we looked [up] our stateroom and were aboard. Then baggage to bring up, batmen to find etc. All exciting and leaving us no time for worrying, but alas we wasted hours finding our way around. Great corridors leading back and forth, elevators, stairs that dipped down into the cavernous maw of the vessel. One could lean over the balustrade and imagine he was looking down an elevator shaft in a huge building. Hundreds of men lost their way for hours; the common cause was travelling in a circle. The difficulty is the vessel is apparently divided laterally into compartments between which there is no connection, so to get between compartments on the same deck you have to go up above and the stairs and corridors and landings are legion. I attempted to bring order out of chaos down among the men but with little good result though most of them did get to sleep. I retired at 10:00 o'clock and I tell you I was dog tired and had a real luxurious sleep.

This morning again the confusion. Some of the men got no breakfast. There seemed to be no one to direct the men what to do and indeed we knew no better. I suppose lack of experience explained the lack of cooperation. Eventually though Major McRae took hold and we finally succeeded in making the necessary dispositions and now comes leisure. I am going out on deck later on. The wet weather is breaking and the clouds look discouraged enough to take to flight. The harbour reminds me of Vancouver, in fact others say the same thing, a long rather narrow inlet flanked by wooded hills. Dartmouth to the north corresponds with North Vancouver, the entrance to the inlet is of course just opposite. At anchor less than half a mile away lies a cruiser, the "Corona." There is no sign of life on her and her dull grey colour, with absolutely no stir or colour is something of a disappointment. But she has steam up and I know everyone is alive on her. This morning I saw her signalling with the flashy naval flags. Another liner is anchored just abreast of us (probably an Allan liner) also painted a conventional grey and no name visible. A patrol boat with the neatest little 3 inch gun mounted on her stern, patrols her beat in a most workman-like manner. There is a second cruiser in the harbour somewhere, also a destroyer, whether to escort us or not I do not know. This harbour is, you are aware, a fortress with the 2nd or 3rd finest harbour defences in the world. In addition to the harbour defences I am informed they have now a net across its mouth. We cannot of course see the forts as they are not visible.

We hear all kinds of rumours about sailing. There are now 5 regiments aboard. . . . The latest rumour I have heard is that we sail at 5 o'clock. I hope it is true. As you know every merchant man has a gun mounted on its stern. We have a 4.7 on our stern, looks quite business-like.

This is a delightful experience for a landlubber. I should have been perfectly happy this morning if my honey had been here. Just to see things together would be such a treat. Still we will see a lot of things yet.

Ah honey dear I did not know I loved you half so much. What would I not give for the sight of your face and the sound of your voice. Do you know, it seems as though a woman becomes more and more sanctified as time goes on. To live with a man is to discover all his weaknesses, his foibles, his eccentricities and selfishness but to walk with a woman is to discover her strength, her courage, her love and fidelity. . . . Oh you are laughing I suppose at my discovery. (I suppose you may) but alas I am discovering now that I have entertained angels unawares. Ah dearest, I love and adore you more every day, the more so that I realize the courage and love that is enclosed in that plucky little body. God bless you dearest.

Stuart

R.M.S. OLYMPIC, JUNE 2, 1916

Dearest:—

At last we are at sea. We pulled out at 8 o'clock and now at 11:30 are pounding off our 2 knots per. Things are humming merrily along and we have great hopes of something to eat soon. It was a great sight to see the boat leave the harbour. It seemed surprisingly easy to swing out and get under way but two tugs lent their humble aid till we got our general direction. Then we moved slowly down the harbour past the boom that blocks its mouth and out into the roadstead. When out about two miles we slowed down and dropped our pilot; a ticklish job, too, necessitating a slow down ten or fifteen minutes before the small boat was reached and even then the liner had considerable way on. Since then we have been standing out a general easterly direction, probably south of east. The morning is lovely—quite bright and clear with a long swell that makes the boat rise just perceptibly. It certainly is glorious on deck. I have been out up till now, almost 12 o'clock. I am now in the luxurious smoking room, the most magnificent I guess I ever saw.

I shall tell you a secret. We put on our life belts this morning and are to keep them on from now on; a very wise precaution. You won't always need to be after the men. I am feeling quite fit and hope now to get down to the serious business of eating.

You may be interested in knowing some of the dimensions of this ship, sister of the ill-fated Titanic. Length over all 882.9 feet. Extreme breadth 92.6 ft. Depth from keel to A deck—the highest inhabited deck—104 ft. It would be impossible for me to describe her as I don't half know it, and I am running onto something new all the time. Upstairs they have a gymnasium (so called) containing all sorts of fancy contrivances most of them run by electricity, three horses, one of them a bucking horse, a jiggler, a roller, exercisers, etc etc. I hope to have some biceps when I get to the Old Country.

I wrote you a long letter yesterday and mailed it so it could go ashore. Whether you will get it or when I do not know. It is possible you will get it before you leave. I thought often yesterday how much you would have enjoyed it being here. When the clouds lifted there was so much to see—the harbour, shipping etc. In the evening I was out on deck most of the time up till eleven. When I got back I found the officers all away up town. At the last minute leave came to go ashore but I did not go then. It was getting late and I wanted a sleep. I got up once in the night for fear the vessel would go off without my seeing it.

From now on we will take every precaution, sentries everywhere and the most elaborate arrangements in case of an emergency. If the Germans do get us they won't catch us napping.

There is one thing I forgot when leaving i.e. to get a picture from you. I wish I had one. Better get one taken right away if possible, if you can get a good one. I am awfully sorry about forgetting that.

I wish now I had asked you to write me at Halifax. We were there 36 hours and I would certainly have got a letter if it had been thought of.

Well I suppose you are hustling around making your plans complete. I do hope you get things fixed up all right without trouble. I shall be anxious to hear from you. I hope we will see one another in England at no very distant time. It seems hard to realize we are separated after less than a year of real married life. . . . [The] memory of that blessed time should keep us buoyed up in doubt and darkness. I know it a source of ineffable joy to me. . . . I do not exactly hope that your experience has been the same for I fear that would be a measure of self conceit.

Well honey dear I shall say goodbye as there is no further news at present. Keep a brave heart and come soon.

Yours as ever
Stuart

The Battle of Jutland (31 May to 3 June 1916) paralleled in the North Sea the stalemated land war in the trenches. It ended more or less a drawn battle, the German fleet escaping with a moral victory by avoiding the destruction that vaunted British sea power should have wreaked on it, and the British taking comfort in having forced the High Seas Fleet back into port. But "the spell of Trafalgar had been broken," and the battle "was in fact a defeat for British technology." The indecision of the battle produced strategic results that included the eventual resort to all-out submarine warfare by the Germans. "Jutland had closed the one open flank; at sea as well as in the trenches strategy withered into attrition; and the last military chance of avoiding a long war and utter mutual exhaustion had gone."[2]

First news of the Battle of Jutland reached RMS *Olympic* the second day out, disturbing the faith of Stuart Tompkins a bit, but at this early stage he was coolly objective and analytical in regard to the relative merits of the British and German navies. The following letter is the first to reflect something akin to antipathy to England that Stuart and other Canadians frequently expressed during the war.

R.M.S. OLYMPIC, JUNE 3, 1916

Dearest:—

This has been a dull dreary day; in the early morning we ran into a fog bank and since then we have been running slower and slower until now we are almost at a stand still; there is one consolation, however, the sea is quite calm and there is practically no roll or pitch to the ship.

We got our first news of the North Sea affair, over the wireless during the night. After finally straightening it all out, my confidence in the British Admiralty has gone down a few points. Perhaps it is unreasonable to expect sensational coups to be pulled off by our fleets once in a while. At the same time, the average Briton is pretty sensitive on the navy question and he won't listen to excuses where there has been so much publicity re our boasted superiority. However, possibly it is just another knock that we are to recover from as we did from the surrender at Kut-Al-Mara.

I must confess my enthusiasm does not rise as we approach the shores of the Home Country. As Canada receded from our view, it seemed that it would be a long time before we saw a better country. Everything is English on board and English money is used as well as Canadian money. . . .

You know the Germans, it must be acknowledged, have done admirably with their navy. It is not yet 20 years old and yet they have brought it up to the 2nd position; and the way in which the attack was conceived and carried out calls for the highest praise. To produce such an instrument in one generation is a great achievement and I hope it will make England rub her eyes. I think we all need to wake up.

I am wondering how many of my letters you will get. I probably am not yet wise to the things the censor loves to pounce on, so you must not be surprised if there is a gap in my correspondence. I shall probably learn someday. . . .

I am going to have a nice warm bath tonight before going to bed so should be comfy. I hope to get a good night's sleep and clear out my head.

I trust you won't worry any over the affair in the North Sea as far as we are concerned. The Germans did not by any means get out and England is still sitting tight. I only wish they had drawn more blood.

I think I will draw my little epistle to a close for today. I feel lazy and not a bit like writing. Everything is so dull and close I hope there will be a letter for me in England when I get there.

Yours,
Stuart

R.M.S. OLYMPIC,

SUNDAY JUNE 4, 1916

Dearest:—

I fear I made a very poor attempt at a letter yesterday. I felt so wretched my heart was not in it. However after my sleep I perked up and at dinner time managed to partake somewhat abundantly. I did enjoy my dinner. It was something of an event with the 90th band in attendance. Some one sang "Darling I am growing old," with an accompaniment by the band which was very effective. The king's health was drunk (in wine for the first time) then more music. Something seemed to stir up the college students for first thing I knew over in the corner, out broke the Toronto yell, followed a minute later by the Queens. A very pleasant half hour was spent and it is one of the pleasant recollections of the trip. . . .

This morning we woke to find the ship going at full speed, the weather needless to say being somewhat clearer. I did not have time to go to communion at 7:00, but we had church parade at 10:30. I felt much better today and being about on deck felt in better spirits. The weather is quite calm and clear. We got further particulars this morning by wireless of the naval battle. Hard to explain isn't it; but after all is said and done, we accomplished our purpose and the Germans failed of theirs. Nobody on ship is worrying.

We had for the second time an alarm drill today. This time it came unannounced just as I was dropping off to sleep. I had my belt on. I dashed out and headed for the general direction in which our men are and the well by which they would reach the deck. The siren was blowing, bugles and whistles as well. The sentries were all at their posts and were closing the water tight doors over which they mount guard. They close doors on the floor beneath. Any persons caught in compartments by this closing escape by emergency exits which are I understand worked from the bridge. In addition to being divided longitudinally and laterally the ship has a second hull inside her. She was on the high seas at the time of the Titanic disaster; in fact was one of the boats rushing to the rescue when informed by the Carpathian that all was over. She was at once put into dry dock and fitted with an inner hull to prevent such disasters as overwhelmed the Titanic. The skipper is a very cautious man; during the fog no chances were taken.

After the dismiss I turned in and finished my nap. I was on deck a while after lunch. For the first time since leaving Halifax, we sighted a vessel, a sailing vessel some miles to our south.

It was curious to observe how her sails only were visible, the hull being entirely below the skyline. Several whales have been sighted but I did not see them. They may have been dolphins or porpoises such as we saw off Vancouver Island.

I wonder if you know what a boon the little things you made for me are. I never felt so completely outfitted in my life. I expect I will need some few things when I reach the other side.

What are you doing today. I suppose you are now going to bed in little old Edmonton. I do hope you have laid your plans so that you can come over soon. . . .

Really, there are so many things to see, I am sure it will be a tremendous education. Already everything is so English and one must perforce talk in English money. I got most of mine changed at Halifax into gold so should be all right.

Well, beloved, I find these letters a great source of satisfaction to myself. They enable me to find my true centre and bring me to realize the meaning and purpose of this separation. The process of hardening and purging through which we are passing should make us more worthy of life and love and of the sacrifices and devotion of those that love us. Only in such times as these can a man really prove he is worthy of the country which brought him forth and of those women who reared him and who have entrusted their lives into his keeping.

Keep a brave heart.

Stuart

Stuart worried about censorship from time to time, as in the letter below, but the only evidence of censoring in the entire collection of letters occurs in a few instances in which a word was deleted by his own pen. The reference to Major MacGregor in the following letter suggests that after almost two years of mobilization informality of commitment and ease of resignation or transfer still prevailed for some in the officer corps.

EN ROUTE [TUESDAY] JUNE 6, 1916

Dearest:—

... Orders have just come out re censorship of letters. I am between the devil and the deep blue sea in the matter. I suppose I have been sort of promiscuous in my mention of places and incidents and they may hold my letters over. I have not posted any however, except one. I am not anxious to tell details of military interest and will do my part to prevent such becoming known. Still one hardly appreciates having one's personal letter perused by the jealous censor.

I was somewhat taken aback to hear that reports were current in Canada that we were sunk. We of course are somewhat in the dark as to whether this is true. I sincerely hope you had no such occasion to worry. We hear a fresh rumour every hour. Some of them come in over wireless, some are manufactured out of the whole cloth. We heard this morning that in the big sea fight, the odds favoured the British.

I wonder when there will be a letter for me or will you arrive in person soon. I am beginning to feel the frigid English atmosphere descend on me already and know I shall need someone to cheer me up. This boat is quite English and you feel what is coming.

Everything is running smoothly on board but we do not know what is before us. We are in the dark absolutely as to where and when we are to land. The voyage has been great and I don't think anyone has been sick. . . .

I am picking up new ideas about the war all the time. Most of the ship's people have been more or less closely connected with it since the start. Some of them speak as though it would last for years—when one feels quite discouraged. There is no doubt it comes closer home to the average Britisher than to us. This troop ship made several trips to the Mediterranean and one can see the names of famous British regiments scrawled on the woodwork. The magnitude of the efforts made to meet the Germans shows that they are not to be despised; still I think this naval battle is an indication of the extremes to which they are being driven.

I am discouraged and exalted by turns; sometimes I am inclined to feel this is not our fight and we will get nothing out of it. If I thought the insular British spirit would prevent us from reaping the full fruits of the war I should quit right now. But when I think of the other things we are called on to uphold for the sake of civilization and the human beings that make it up, I feel different. You know the world pretty much progresses or retrogresses in accordance with the honour or dishonour accorded women. If there is one thing to be impressed on us, and this I shall strive to adhere to, is that we must guard as our lives our own ideals with regard to womanhood. For therein is more involved than might appear. We can learn more of selflessness and of purity of character by being brought under such an influence. I think with awe and wonder of the power of love in the heart and life and of how it can transform the most commonplace life and cause it to be exalted. . . .

This morning the gun crew gave a little demonstration of target practice. At a given signal the ship swerved in her course and doubled back in her track performing a long S-like turn, at a certain point barrels were thrown out and when the ship in her swerve came abreast of them, the two guns were let fly. It was a fine exhibition. . . .

I trust you will have no trouble . . . getting away. Don't forget to get a good photo if you have the chance. If you don't get a chance to travel with Mrs. Cameron [wife of a fellow officer], I should go by an American boat if possible. Still I don't suppose you will get this advice in any time to be of use.

As soon as we disembark I am going to try to get an opportunity to cable. Some say they do not allow it, but I will make a stab at it. By the way do not forget to have sent to me an Edmonton paper. Otherwise we will almost lose touch.

We had a mess meeting yesterday at which I had the misfortune to be elected a member. That reminds me. Major MacGregor refused to pay for his one meal per day last winter . . . and appealed. . . . This after drawing subsistence and separation allowance all winter. Everyone was mad and it was decided (on the suggestion of the Colonel) to strike him from our mess from January 1st and inform him of it. Whether this will affect his separation allowance or not I do not know but it surely will sting. Major MacGregor is discredited as far as the 89th are concerned. He got out when he could get nothing more out of it.

Well this is a long letter and you will be tired by the time you read it. . . .

Goodbye dearest
Stuart

EN ROUTE, JUNE 7, 1916

Dearest:—

As we are drawing near land, I have decided to write a short letter synopsizing our voyage. The letters I wrote on board I fear would have to be heavily censored and I do not wish my communication to be delayed. I may say by way of introduction that I am cabling you tomorrow re our arrival which I trust will set your mind at rest.

We left our port of embarkation last Friday after one day's delay in the harbour. The weather out has been fine with the exception of a day and a half of fog off the Newfoundland banks. When that cleared we speeded up and have been making good progress. We were somewhat excited re the reports received by wireless over the North Sea Fight. Apparently the British came off all right and later reports have been more reassuring. This morning we were shocked to hear of Lord Kitchener's death. Really one wonders what next will happen. It certainly is the most astounding event that has happened to date.

Today for the first time the ship is rolling and pitching. It is amusing to see people trying to keep their equilibrium, and sick—dear—there are literally thousands sprawled over the deck and down stairs. . . .

Luncheon was not nearly so popular a meal as it has been. In fact there were a great number of vacant chairs. Still I have managed to keep going and nothing dire has happened. . . . One of my men, Ingham, has been making frantic efforts to get discharged. His wife is an invalid and is wild because he has gone. But the colonel will not hear of it.

It has been a wonderful trip all around. H[is] M[ajesty's] Transports are all armed with naval guns and yesterday we had a trial of them. We are now travelling with an escort so feel pretty safe. The boat herself, so the crew assures us, could look after herself.

I hope there will be a letter for me in England. However don't forget to come yourself. Meanwhile keep up a brave heart.

Yours
Stuart

The death of Field-Marshal Lord Kitchener, noted in the letter above, and the loss of his leadership shocked the British Empire; as secretary of state for war he had rallied the Empire to mobilize. When Kitchener issued a call on 7 August 1914 for 100,000 recruits to form a new army of six divisions, the contingent was raised in a few days.[3] On 5 June 1916, while on a mission to Russia, he went down with HMS *Hampshire* when it was torpedoed off the Orkney Islands.

4

Shorncliffe

By the time the 89th Alberta Overseas Battalion arrived in England, order had been brought out of the chaos besetting other units earlier when they had endured deplorable conditions in dreadful weather at the first Canadian tent encampment on Salisbury Plain. Canadian forces bound for France were now concentrated around Shorncliffe Camp, near Folkestone in Kent, in such places as St. Martin's Plain, East and West Sandling, and Westenhanger. In the following letter Stuart describes his last day at sea and tells of the trip to Westenhanger, his surprising greeting there by his cousin Harris McNish, and of plans to meet his brother Philip who was stationed at Shorncliffe.

WESTENHANGER, KENT, ENGLAND
JUNE 10, 1916

Dearest Honey:—

In England at last. You have no idea how funny it seems. Wouldn't you enjoy it to the full and wouldn't your eyes have stuck out. Indeed I can't keep my own from doing it.

Where shall I start. About 3:30 Wednesday afternoon ... somebody announced that you could see the coast of Ireland. There was an immediate rush to the side and there off the starboard bow a line of cliffs loomed up through the mist at a distance of ten miles or so. It gradually drew near and we were soon running along a rather beauti-

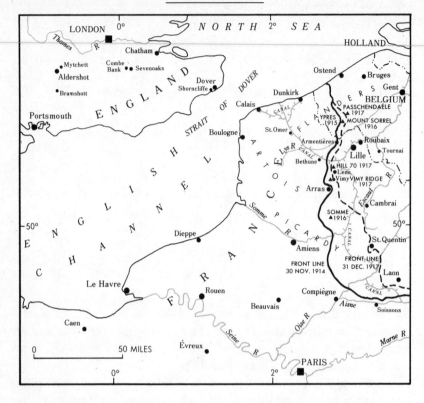

ful and typically Irish coast, a succession of cliffs and hills clad in a pale green with clusters of white buildings here and there. The scenery became more striking as we went along, numbers of high rocky islands appearing on our left with sheep and goats grazing over them. At places, buildings of some age could be seen. I am sure I saw one old castle perched up on the brow of one of these island crags. The waterway became narrower like some of the places off the western coast and finally we saw off our port bow the Mull of Kintyre a long narrow peninsula stretching southwestward from Argyle County to within 12 or 14 miles of Ireland (it really looked much closer) right near the narrowest point is the Giant's Causeway.... One by one we passed the promontories turning south and running past Belfast into the channel and Irish Sea. No one slept much; we were up at 3:30 and there ensued all the routine of disembarking. About 6 o'clock we stopped outside the bar of the Mersey and took on our pilot. Our destroyer dropped to the rear and disappeared. We then moved into the mouth of the Mersey and up to Liverpool.

You can imagine my feelings as we drew up towards the landing place and could see the buildings of a great city also the homes and gardens. Of course there was no one to welcome us except a few officials. We were the first troops to disembark; we formed up at the wharf and filed through the buildings to the train platform. Oh, the train. You would think it had been built for children to play with. About the size of piano boxes the cars were. The Royal Transport Officer saw the men split up into the groups of sufficient size to fill the compartments. Entraining was a short job and we were off through the city. Nothing much to see but it was interesting to me none the less, miles of warehouses, sidings, shipyards all jumbled up together—then finally out into the open country—if open country you can call it. Groups of houses everywhere—homes rather—every one representing the thoughts and plans and efforts of bygone generations. Of course it is all superlatively beautiful. . . . This through the whole delightful morning till we got to Rugby where the men had lunch. Everything well planned you see. Baskets were provided for all officers at 3 shillings per. Of course it was good but a pretty stiff price for a cold snack even with chicken in. Typically English with mustard and watercress. As the afternoon drew on we approached London and for some fifteen or twenty miles were running through the outskirts, Crystal Palace, Shepherds Bush etc etc. We cross the Thames on the [deleted] bridge, and at some junction . . . changed to the South Eastern Railway. Then on into Kent. Kent is a more rolling country than the Midlands but is just as beautiful. All the towns are emptied of male population, no indication of soldiers save at the bridge culverts (very numerous). The railway line unfortunately runs for a great part of its length under ground or beneath ground level so your view is restricted. At 5 p.m. we reached our destination, Westenhanger. I got out [and] got my platoon out. First thing I hear some one say "Hello Stuart." I turned around and there was Harris large as life with a grin on his face. I was dumbfounded. It seems he had been sent up with his truck and men to move the 88th and happened to get there in time to meet me. Wasn't it fine. Well we detrained and got into our quarters, very comfy ones, too—huts but very commodious and dry. Harris came back that night to meet the second 88th train and we had an hour together. I had arranged to go down to Shornecliffe in the evening the next day to see Philip.

In the morning we had a massed parade and while the Major was addressing them they were allowed to sit down. I lifted my eyes, saw somebody approach towards me, salute then turn to the Major and salute. It was Philip just as dirty as he used to get in Edmonton. I was excused, but more later for I must get this off.

Goodbye for today

Stuart

Stuart's discussion of Philip's economic and physical health in the letter below is but one example of concern for his family that is apparent throughout his letters. (While on leave from the trenches, Philip had returned home with a souvenir shell; it exploded leaving one eye and a hand with impairment that ultimately led to his discharge from the Army.) The following letter also shows Stuart's pique with English disdain for Canadians and is the first of several that indicate his concern about the direction in which he perceived the war's impact to be taking English women. The concentration of Canadian troops near Shorncliffe afforded opportunities for reunions among comrades who had gone separate ways, as in the case of Stuart's meeting up with the 66th Battalion which he had left in Calgary the preceding November. His comment below that news was better from the Eastern Front was in reference to a Russian offensive, launched on 4 June, which had yielded a penetration of the Austrian lines to a depth of fifty miles by 10 June.[1]

WESTENHANGER, KENT ENGLAND

JUNE 11, 1916

Dearest:—

I expect this will not be [a] cheery letter for I don't feel that way I can tell you just now. . . . [W]e are liable to be moving pretty often so in addressing my letters I think I should address mail care of Army P.O., London, as per instructions until I get stationed permanently.

Now as to things in general, nearly everyone is blue today and there is a pretty sad funk all around. As for myself, I am resigned, prepared for all eventualities. But I cannot help feeling depressed a little or is it disappointed, but I shall discuss that later.

Well as to events from where I left off. I saw Philip for the first time on Friday and spent the afternoon and evening with him, also yesterday afternoon and evening and of course have met the wife. . . . Philip looks surprisingly well but quite thin. I was surprised to see his hand so well; in fact it hardly bothers him at all and does not impress one as a disfigurement. . . . His wife is a really fine girl I think; she seemed so taken aback when I kissed her and I felt very awkward. Of course she is reserved and I have found it very hard to get acquainted. That characteristic British reserve makes one feel so awkward oneself. . . .

Philip is pretty near down to bed rock as far as money goes so that I feel guilty at eating there as I have done. Of course, Emily may not be used to anything special and she may be reconciled to straitened domestic arrangements but I do not think it right that she should have nothing at all. She idolizes Philip of course but that is not enough. But English people are all pinched these days and there are mighty few pleasures going. Still I am going to insist on a difference. It makes me rather peeved at the way mother and the girls talk. If they knew what it were like here they might feel different.

As to the English, they may be a great people but they certainly are far from cordial. I should like to be fair to them for they are engaged in a serious business but it makes me sick the way they fuss over Gen. Joffre and then cold shoulder the "comedians" as they call us. They are not a bit glad to see us and the only welcome we have had has been from our brother Canadians. Even the Englishmen among us feel the atmosphere and feel more Canadian than ever in their isolation. There is one thing here which has saddened and disgusted me, and that is the attitude towards women. Of course, I have yet to see the better class women but the women of the poorer classes hold themselves cheap. Why in Canada even the poorest little steno holds her head high and has her distinctive womanliness, but here they regard themselves as common and their womanly charms as something to get men—and they are not particular how they get them or what kind they get. This attitude has shocked me. I could not explain my first impressions of English girls but I have found them borne out by what I am learning from day to day. I also understand more about English men.

As to our future, we are prepared for anything so are not worrying. I was warned for a 3 month course at the Canadian Military School, Shornecliffe, which is supposed to be the immediate successor to active service but that has been cancelled and I am to stay with the battalion. It is quite evident we are going to be broken up as we have been warned to get ready a draft.

I saw the 66th this morning, the [Signal Corps] were moving them from Lydd to St. Martin's plain and I went out with Philip; got there at 2 a.m. and left at 5:30. I saw everybody. . . . I came back with the convoy along the coast to where the London road leaves the coast and turns inland. Here I walked, reaching camp at 7:30. . . . As it was I was up before the others, had my breakfast earlier and was first ready for church parade (the captain was late so I took charge). There was a heart to heart talk to the officers after parade. Major McRae is going to make good and discipline is being made stricter all through, which will be good. This afternoon I spent sleeping. Tonight I have a bath.

Now don't think I am downhearted. I am prepared to play the game but I am writing down first impressions which are not of the best. After I have seen the Englishman in action I may change my mind.

Well dearest I think of you night and day and wonder when we will again be united. There is better news from the front lately particularly from the East. Of course people have ceased to prophesy. The British Government is calling up the 24th class, who report on Tuesday for training but I must not tell you any war news or the censor will think I am babbling. We are being afflicted with inspections just now which may be good for the soul.

. . . I wish I could hear from you soon. I must confess to a tiny bit of disappointment at not getting [a letter]. However Philip got one last night dated I think May 17th, so I do not feel badly. Take care of yourself.

Stuart

WESTENHANGER CAMP, KENT
ENGLAND, JUNE 13, 1916

Dearest:—

I think I am nearly heartbroken or homesick or something at not hearing from you. . . . [W]e have been here nearly a week and still no letter. Have you forgotten all about me.

. . . [We] have learned our fate—89th Reserve Battalion. What mine is to be, the Lord only knows. At present, I am taking orderly officer every other day with the only other sub left in camp—a pleasant prospect eh?

Today has been a long hard day. We were at it hard from 8 a.m. to 4 p.m. When coming in at 4, we were turned back and sent out for an hour's ceremonial. I was quite disappointed as Philip was here and I could have gone on into Shornecliffe with him. As it was we did not get in till 5:00, wet and cold and hungry. I may add it has been raining steadily almost since we came.

I tell you a lot of the officers would like to be back in Canada. Personally, I don't mind it. We are lucky when I think of Sarcee, fine warm quarters and good paths or roads wherever we go. Just now I am basking in the heat of a coal stove in my own room with my portfolio on my knee. The men though are getting the worst of it. The fare is not what it was in Canada; it isn't the quality so much as the quantity. One good thing, they can keep warm and dry in their huts.

I had rather an uncanny experience today. We adjoin a race course and spent the morning drilling around the stables where there is a good deal of concrete laid. This afternoon we went beyond, passed through an arched gateway into a farm yard and past what looked to be an old stone barn. A wing jutting out from the north side of that barn had two entrances partly glassed and looked a little like a chapel. I sort of rubbed my eyes to take it in and mentioned it to the captain, wondering what strange kind of a a structure it was—and how dilapidated. "Why don't you know," he said, "that is a castle"—and all the time I had been gazing straight at the habitation of some medieval baron. Back among the oaks was the vine covered tower; scattered at various points around me were ruins of the wall crumbling away and right in front was this old outhouse, barn, dwelling, or whatever it was, still almost intact with the summer ivy growing out of the very rock and clasping the old building in its cruel embrace. There was the old moat spanned at one point by the building itself supported by an arch. . . . [O]ne could trace the ruins of the wall along the moat which no longer encircled the structure but babbled off like a rustic stream. . . . What a queer feeling came over me to see this bit of hoary antiquity set down in the midst of modernity and to think of the faces that had looked out of those old windows and the hearts that beat behind those stone walls. How the old owners of this must have plundered and oppressed the neighborhood.

Well, honey, I can see now, if you come over you are not going to see very much of me. . . . At present there is no leave at all. What will be forth coming in a few weeks time I do not know. I hope however that my knowledge of England and English people is not going to be gathered solely from my casual observations of country folk. I should be moreover perfectly satisfied if you got some place in England where you could be satisfied and content—no matter what it was or where—even if I could not see you. It fills me with a feeling of dismay to think of you being 6000 miles away.

I think it will be a great experience for all of us. As I told you we have selected a draft for the front, and it is grand the way the men are anxious to go. At a time like this when you might think they would hesitate every man is keen and anxious to do his part. The officers can do no less and I really feel that I can draw inspiration from such men who have nothing to gain and everything to lose.

I have been struck lately at what a hallowed memory you have been to me. . . . Listen did you ever sit back with a sigh of content that what you had wished for and imagined all your life was visualized before you and that you had at last cast anchor in the harbour of your dreams. Dearest that and more than that was my lot. . .

Well these are momentous times and call for what is best in a man. And while I may not go to the front with my men I can at least profit by my contact with them and resolve that I too will be prepared to sacrifice no less than they.

I just heard today of Colonel Griesbach's death also of Stanley Fofe. The grim reaper is taking a great toll. God grant, it may not be much longer.

Be sure to write soon.
Stuart

Although the role of the 89th was not yet fully determined, it had already been selected to provide draft reinforcements for the front, and the early letters from England reflect the uncertainty that was their lot. They also show a man unhappy with no letters from home, and it appears at one point that Stuart even had second thoughts about the wisdom of her coming to join him.

WESTENHANGER CAMP, KENT
JUNE 14, 1916

Dearest:—

Another day and no letter. . . . It is now three weeks tomorrow since we left Calgary and it seems as though that part of the world had dropped out of sight as far as news is concerned. We get practically no Canadian news here at all.

There has been very little happening of late. . . . The men's rations are a big problem; they are not what they were used to in Canada and I really feel sorry for them and do all I can for them which is needless to say very little.

I have been wondering whether you have made as yet any arrangements re sailing. It is unsatisfactory of course not to have heard from you; but the others are almost in the same boat. Captain Whittaker though has heard from his wife.... I suppose England will be my home for some time to come and I feel if only you were within reach I could go down for a week end probably and I should have my regular leave after going to the front. I must admit I had cold feet about the idea, when I first came, but I still think if you got something to do to take up your time we could both be fairly contented and I should probably be a better soldier for it. I must admit to getting a bit lonely. It is quite a hard tug for a person who has adopted fairly regular habits of life to adjust himself to the soldier's life.... Just now of course we are feeling a sort of reaction from the events of interest on our trip and we have not yet been caught in the swirl of great things going on around us. We feel isolated here and almost ostracized so one is thrown back on one's self and sometimes the heart fails just a little and one is inclined to remember what one has left behind. When I think of the others and of the sacrifices being made all around us, I am content and satisfied with the future, glad that I could do my part and realizing that the things the Great God has in store for us are greater than what we are leaving behind. Still in moments of weariness of the flesh one is apt to think of nothing but fatigue and cold and hunger; only at times does one catch the vision.

Then, too, I have nothing to regret with regard to our married life. If I lived twice three score and ten I could not have greater happiness than has been mine. It has but inspired me the more to do my duty and try to be worthy of it. You know men seldom prove such worthiness of the love of a true woman; indeed it seems as if it were only in times like this that they can measure up to their responsibility. Do not blame me if I am a bit sentimental and if I rejoice in the fact that I am given an opportunity to prove the power of a woman's love in a man's life.

Goodbye dearest
Stuart

WESTENHANGER CAMP, KENT
JUNE 16, 1916
[NO. 1]

Dearest:—

Would you believe it, I actually got a letter yesterday from your own self. I must have had a kindly hunch about it for when I got back from Seabrook at 10 o'clock last night I went into the anteroom and by the fading light discovered the epistle. I went to my room covered the windows and read it. . . . Still it was something of a comfort at least to know you were o.k. but of course it told me nothing of your plans etc. Since last writing we were inspected (yesterday) by General Alderson, Commander in Chief of the Canadian Forces in the field. He was kind enough to be very complimentary to us and to hold out hopes that we might get to the front as a battalion in the Fourth Division which is now being organized. It is hard to realize isn't it that all the Canadian Forces at the front are not more than ⅓ of the Austrian forces taken prisoners by the Russians since launching their great offensive. To return, we were up at 5:00 o'clock—breakfast at six and were off shortly before seven. At the Royal Oaks Inn about ¼ mile south we met the 88th and together took the London road through Hythe and Seabrook to . . . Shorncliffe. It was about 6½ miles but the morning was cool and I know everyone enjoyed it. . . . As soon as the inspection was over, we marched back, halting about two miles out from camp for the men to lunch. We had nothing till we returned; was I hungry? The Colonel is a good soul and let the men go for the day. After finishing my duties . . . I met Philip so I went down to Shorncliffe with him and home to Seabrook to supper. It is truly a lovely walk. The view from the hills above Seabrook gives over a wide expanse of sea and coast. Dover cannot be seen as it is around a bend in the coast, but the shores of France can usually be seen, away to the west is Dungeness Point sweeping away to the southwest, nearer [are] Seabrook, Hythe, Lydd. The whole country is full of interest—the old Martello towers, built in Napoleonic times and the canals dug just behind the beach to prevent a landing. For miles and miles along the coast there is an esplanade with parks and drives at intervals. Off Folkestone there are usually dozens of ships lying at anchor. Yesterday we saw a submarine. (Of course airships are very common) Now and again we could hear the Dover forts at practice, the heavy boom of the guns.

I stayed till 9:15, caught the train back to Sandling from where I walked across the fields.

Well, honey, this must do for the present as I have duties to perform. I am sorry you had only got one letter. I certainly wrote my share on the train.

I am feeling much better than I was. The climate oppressed me at first. . . .

Your own
Stuart

In the course of putting things in order so that she could leave for England, Edna went in person to file on a homestead located "five or six miles out of Peace River ... [where] Stuart always had a yen to have a farm." As he realized, this trip north meant even fewer letters for him.[2]

WESTENHANGER CAMP, KENT
JUNE 16, 1916
[NO. 2]

Dearest:—

You no doubt are not expecting two letters in one day but you must not be surprised that I am writing my second one. This has been the first bright clear day since we landed. Were we in Alberta, I should say there would be frost tonight, so cold is the wind. However we are enjoying what we have and piling up the fire with good coals....

I was of course disappointed that there will be no letters for me soon. The mail service is quite irregular anyway and your trip to the Peace River will further postpone writing so I can hardly expect to hear for ten days yet.

When I came home from Seabrook last night I had to walk the last mile and a half. I was minded to walk up the track but on due consideration decided to cut across country. Do you know there are established foot paths all over with gates or stiles through the hedges and fences, so I had no difficulty whatever in finding the way. It was really a delightful walk. The walks here are always a treat, a great many of the country roads are paved so one never gets one's feet wet.

We hear more talk about draft so everyone is upset. It will be hard to be taken away from one's men....

... A small detachment of the 63rd is here waiting orders for moving. Both the 63rd and 66th are shot to pieces...

By the way did I tell you we are all ordered to refrain from shaving the upper lip....

I wish I could drop in on you for a few minutes to find out your plans. It is a wee bit lonesome here at times. Bob Pearson is feeling blue about having to leave his little girl and wife. We were just condoling with one another. Oh I don't mind it very much but 6000 miles does seem a long way off and letters will come so seldom.

Well this must do for tonight. I must get some reading done if possible. You must write to let me know your plans. . . . Philip wants to rent a house in Seabrook. I am not sure how you would like it. It would be a good thing for Emily. She is inexperienced and needs to be taught something re housekeeping.

Don't forget

Your own

Stuart

The letters from Westenhanger contained accounts of long expeditions on foot and by train through the Kent countryside. With informal and close connections among men and units, news of friends was often easily available as troops shuttled back and forth between camps in England and trenches in France. Rumours abounded, and together with press accounts of Russian victories on the Eastern Front, they no doubt contributed to expressions of premature optimism.

WESTENHANGER CAMP, KENT

JUNE 19, 1916

Dearest:—

I am compelled to admit that today things are pretty quiet so that I shall have time for a short note. Since I wrote I have had a weekend at Hythe for which I feel very much better. I made the necessary arrangements and got away at 1:30 with Bob Pearson. We walked down to the Royal Oak Inn where the London road is reached. From here we walked for a few minutes till we caught a truck going into Folkestone. Philip was not in when I got there but arrived later. We had supper and went into Folkestone. Say it was an experience. I think all the Canadian soldiers in England were there. I saw nearly everyone I knew. There were few imperial troops but some French and Belgian soldiers could be seen, the latter in khaki with a sort of Glengarry on—the French in blue and grey. There was quite a contrast between the two—the Belgians appeared light hearted, the French very sombre. The streets of Folkestone are the worst I have seen—narrow and steep—sprawling up the face of the hill. One of the streets was so narrow I am sure an auto could not have got up or down. There were of course no lights. A walk on the Leas is very pleasant, a long spacious esplanade along the cliffs overlooking the channel. The residential parts are quite fine and reminded me of Montreal—the dull grey stone and the abundant foliage. We took in a movie before coming back. There were just the two, Philip and myself, so we walked back. I got a room next door and slept till 9 o'clock—a dandy rest. Philip brought over word at ten for breakfast—which I hastened to second. We had a meal of fresh mackerel—the most delicate morsel I have ever eaten I should say. We had a walk on the sea drive and saw the fishermen hauling in their nets. Hythe is quite a watering place although there are few there this year—the men mostly in khaki—in fact they are nearly all Canadian soldiers. In the afternoon we got a boat and rowed on the Hythe canal which empties into the sea close to where Philip lives. After passing through Hythe you get into a beautiful piece of rural England with cows and sheep grazing along its banks. Most exquisite scenes. Although my leave was good until reveille I came back last night—by train as far as Sandling from which I walked. . . .

I suppose I must needs be reconciled to not hearing from you soon. The irregularity of the mails and your long trip. It is no doubt over now. I was wondering when I should see you in England. . . . What I am afraid of is that you will get cold feet at the last minute.

I wonder sometimes whether this Russian offensive can really be the beginning of the end, and that we are past the crisis of the war. It is too good to be true. We are always expecting the Russians to be doing so much. There is no doubt that the Germans are pretty close to the end of their rope in men at any rate. Wouldn't it be great if the war were to finish soon and wouldn't there be unbounded rejoicing. Germany should begin to realize that whatever else she might hope for from a prolongation of the war, she can never beat England. She is as supreme as she was two years ago and her aid to the allies in money and munitions is sooner or later going to deal Germany a crushing blow. I think the Allied Powers almost have success within their reach. Well, dear, it would be great to be together again. Believe me though we are going to see London first and . . . also knock around rural England a little and see some of the castles etc. There is one between here and Hythe. I think it is called Salton. It was there that the three knights slept—the night before they killed Thomas a Becket in Canterbury Cathedral. This is probably one of the oldest and prettiest parts of rural England—though I don't like the people, at least the women. . . .

I think this is enough for this morning. Particularly as you have only written once since I left. Remember me to your mother and the children. Kindest regards to your father.

As ever your own

Stuart

The wives of Stuart's friends Norman Weir and Fred Shouldice had already arrived from Canada and were living nearby, causing him to feel Edna's absence more acutely. But for the delay and inconsistency of mail service he would have known that she had in fact already left Edmonton and would reach Westenhanger on 4 July.

WESTENHANGER, JUNE 21, 1916

Dearest:—

Do you know I have neglected [you] for two whole days. Still that is nothing when you consider how I have been neglected for a whole week. I just have to gulp hard when I come in at night and find no letter awaiting me. . . .

This has been a very tiresome week. With most of the battalion away on duties and most of the rest quarantined, there are hardly enough to form fours. Yesterday, we were up at brigade headquarters for an afternoon lecture after which I went down to Hythe. I was late for the train so I walked; from Hythe, I went on to Seabrook. Just as I got off the bus, I saw Mrs. Shouldice and her husband so I overtook them and shook hands with her. Both she and Mrs. Weir arrived in Folkestone Sunday. Mrs. S wanted to know when you were coming over. I saw Philip for just half an hour or so as I had to catch the 9:20 train. At that time of night I cannot make connections for Westenhanger so I have to walk from Sandling Junction through the bush and fields. It is very beautiful and I enjoy it. . . .

I think I got just a little lonesome when I saw Mrs. Shouldice. Still I can find some solace in the memories which are after all a sure comfort. . . . I cannot tell you of the peace and joy that come to me when I think of doing my duty and when I realize that to you it is of more importance that my life should be an expression of and a sacrifice to what is noble and to the great purpose in view; I am buoyed up with confidence and hope. May God grant that I be not deterred from my purpose. All these things will bear fruit an hundred fold in years to come.

If you were here you would be running to the window every few minutes to see the aeroplanes which are becoming common. I cannot get over the wonder of them though.

Well I must get to bed as I did not sleep well last night. Let us hope tomorrow will bring a letter.

Your own
Stuart

WESTENHANGER CAMP, KENT
JUNE 23, 1916

Dearest:—

Alas another day and still no Canadian mail. There are anxious hungry hearts around here, I can tell you though the face would fain hide what the heart speaketh. . . . [V]ery important news!! I am to go to the Canadian Military School at Shornecliffe next week. This is I know but preliminary to going to the front which will likely be without delay. Whether I shall see you at all before going depends on your plans. I rather imagine I shall be at the front by July 15th at the latest. I am sorry now you did not come when Mrs. Weir did. It would I guess have been better. As it is now things are very indefinite and uncertain but I am learning to live from day to day and allow things to work out by themselves.

Every time I use this portfolio or my travelling case or some of the things you got me, I am almost overcome by the tenderness that seems wrapped in every object. I never had anybody to do me things of that kind before and it seems too good almost to be true. How good I shall have to be to you to make up for it. Really though I am trying to live in the spirit of our common ideals and to have your "well done" which is more to me than the benediction of angels. . . .

Last night on an impulse I jumped on the train and went down to Fokestone with Andrew; we had supper together and went for a walk on the Leas. . . .

Well honey I had the comforting assurance that Canadian mail is often held up for six weeks here when troops are moving. Something will have to be done or Canada and England will drift apart.

I have been making some small purchases, only minor ones. Still I am surprised at the way they stick you for everything. There is absolutely nothing cheaper than can be got in Canada and even clothes are dearer. I am going to begin to make up my list of things for the front right away so that I will not be caught short.

Well I must to sleep—Pleasant dreams, dear.

Stuart

Sunday evening [June 25]:—What do you suppose happened today. I had three letters from my honey each one of which was devoured greedily. . . . It was just like a glimpse of heaven from this old earth to see my dear honey's handwriting.

Confusion and uncertainty continued for Stuart and the 89th. The cancellation of his assignment to the Canadian Military School at Shorncliffe added to his anxiety about Edna's future plans, but it ultimately proved advantageous in that it delayed his departure for the trenches until October.

WESTENHANGER CAMP, KENT
JUNE 26, 1916

Dearest:—

. . . Yesterday for the first time we worked on Sunday. Apparently the situation has become very acute and reenforcements are badly needed at the front; hence a rush order for our first draft to be trained in musketry, result haste and confusion. I was withdrawn from the C.M.S. to instruct. In fact we were in the midst of it when chancing to go into the mess I found a neat little pile of letters awaiting me. . . . It all seemed unreal. After almost months of waiting to get a line from you. I was disappointed that your latest letter was dated only June 4th. However I was revived and felt really interested in life once more. So Pat Andrew and I beat it down after supper to St. Martin's Plain. Here I met all the old worthies of the 66th and 63rd etc. . . . The 66th is sending the last draft this week. But we nearly missed the train. The last train before midnight leaves Shornecliffe at 10:10. We left it so late that we had to run the last half mile. Maybe it wasn't a funny sight. . . .

So here I am still instead of at the C.M.S. and may be lodged here for some weeks to come. . . .

There has been trouble about leave for both officers and men. I do hope that it will not be denied us altogether. Some of them will be sore.

I really can hardly push my pen. I am so tired after my days work I think I shall get off my clothes and get into bed.

Goodnight

Let me hear soon

Stuart

WESTENHANGER CAMP, KENT

JUNE 28, 1916

Dearest:—

We have been in for about an hour but I must confess that I am not enthusiastic about writing. We have had a hard day and I have not been up to snuff so it's bed for me shortly. We have been rushing our draft in musketry and today we took them down for their first shooting. It was a walk of about 5 miles through Hythe and west along the sea shore which is lined with rifle ranges clear out to Lydd. . . . Lunch was curtailed on account of time. We left the ranges at 5:30 came straight across country which involved a climb of about 500 feet. Do you know the men dropped out in scores. I was tired enough goodness only knows and I did not have a pack. I was carrying a rain coat and the sweat was just running off me. Though I was hungry I made up my mind to have a wash. I did but nearly [missed] my supper. I raised a strong protest however and managed to get boiled eggs and tea. . . .

I have been looking for a letter from you since Sunday but I suppose I have no right to expect one. I should however, like to know your plans. What mine are goodness only knows. I suppose I shall be here for ten days more till the rest are through with their shooting. . . .

We saw the most extraordinary evolutions carried out today by some airships, just over our heads down at the ranges. One of the machines had a gun mounted and the pilot had some target practice at balloons loosed for the purpose. The machine travelled at full speed all the while and circled and plunged into the bargain. It was one of the finest sights I ever saw. I wish you had seen it. Once the pilot turned clean over. Well I feel I must get to bed. Don't forget me in your prayers dearest and remember to write.

Your own

Stuart

WESTENHANGER CAMP, KENT
JUNE 29, 1916

Dearest:—

... It is a beautiful morning clear and cool and we are looking forward to a nice day at the ranges. I had a great sleep and am feeling fine this morning, got up at six o'clock, had breakfast and am ready for anything. The papers this morning say that the British guns were busy yesterday and last night. Several of the officers claimed they heard dull reverberations from them. Whether so I am sure I could not say.

I am wondering (later) and wondering what your plans are. Since beginning this sentence I got your two letters dated respectively the 8th and the 10th. I was between laughter and tears on reading them. . . . In fact although it is raining my spirits refuse to be damped today.

I am of course disappointed at your not having made plans to come sooner. Still I am not in a position to tell you what to expect. . . . Whatever else may happen our men are doubtless going to the front in the course of a month. Whether that means we go with them or not lies still in the lap of time. I do not see how they can hold us back much longer unless some untoward incident occurs. Philip of course has been urging me to hunt up some staff job but I will wait and see what turns up.

As to Lord Kitchener, you can imagine how that depressed us on board the steamer. Now however I see things differently. His work is done and he has gone to his rest. There are others now who can take up the burden and see his task finished. Over here you look at things differently. From here we can hear the roar of the British guns and realize that behind them is not only one nation in arms but several and behind these in turn a dozen nations manufacturing supplies for the Allies. The might of England (and she is mighty) is being gathered and thrown into the scale and Germany's doom is sealed. It is now only a matter of time. Germany's lavish expenditures of men and munitions has wrested some hard won victories but when the time comes (in fact it draws on apace) that her reserves are all in front line and she has lost her liberty to manoeuvre, things will take on a different aspect. In fact that is just what I see now in passing events. There are to be I believe no more sensational triumphs for Germany. Meanwhile at home, according to latest information here, her people are entirely deceived as to the true state of affairs and it will need more than one crushing victory to bring it home to them. Germany is still united and confident but such refusal to see the truth cannot last forever.

Meanwhile the Russians hammer away and if I am not deceived they are going to get away with still more swag. Austria it seems to me is doomed.

Do you feel sorry for me going out in the rain, dear. I don't.

Goodbye

Your own

Stuart

Stuart came to take the loss of Kitchener philosophically and expressed optimism and confidence in an early end to the war, not knowing that some of the costliest battles were yet to come. A combined French and British offensive launched the Battle of the Somme on 1 July 1916; it was to last into mid-November. There was some Allied success, but the Somme's toll in casualties was high: 420,000 British, 195,000 French, and 650,000 German.[3]

WESTENHANGER CAMP, KENT

JULY 2, 1916

Dearest:—

Another Sunday and I am glad to say a day of rest and peace. I really was very tired last night but today or rather this afternoon I have been sleeping and reading in the quiet of a beautiful English summer afternoon; for we are seeing England at her best, all green and luxuriant with a fresh moist breeze always blowing and endless vistas of country road embowered with trees and green shrubbery.

Has the great drive started? For days we have been hearing the distant rumble of the artillery and last night it was announced, well you already know. Of course we must possess our soul in patience and not expect too much. Such are the fortunes of war. Of course, I do not know much of the English mind; still I know how a Canadian feels about the matter.

I have been very blessed within the last week, three letters from you. I was disappointed that you had no more definite plans for the future; things are so uncertain. One never knows what the next few days will bring forth and it would have been a great comfort to know that you were comfortably settled until after the war at something. I scarcely know what advice to offer you. I did expect to be away shortly, then things altered but with the recent changes there is a probability that we will soon go to the front. Of course I think you could get things here to do; there are so many channels opening up to women but I leave it to your own judgment. I do not see how we can go to the front until our men have shot on the ranges and it will take at least two or three weeks for that. However I have no doubt that in a month we shall all be at the front.

I have been thinking of you lately, especially your letters. I do not think your letters are censored. As to mine I am not so sure and I don't think any reasonable censor would want to read too closely an impassioned paragraph. By the way that reminds me of Ingham the fellow whose wife is a cripple and who wanted his discharge. He showed me a letter (which he insisted on my reading) from his wife. It actually pained me. You know one looks at what is apparently a commonplace life and fancies it drab and conventional and if you look below the surface you see the divine fire glowing. This poor woman whose days are bounded by the four walls of her room actually worships this very ordinary man while he on his part for fourteen years has lavished on her a wealth of tenderness that one would not expect from a man "whose calling" it is recorded is that of "labourer." Such is human life. I must go over to see him this afternoon; he has worried himself into the hospital and goodness only knows what will happen to him.

Well honey dear. . . your letter was certainly most enjoyable. You certainly ran the gamut of nearly all the emotions. As to my cable, it looks commonplace and yet we went though a rather nervous week on the transport, the North Sea Battle and the death of Kitchener—we also heard it had been reported throughout Canada that the transport was sunk. So I thought it a couple of dollars well invested.

Well goodby till tomorrow.
Your own
Stuart

WESTENHANGER CAMP, KENT
JULY 3, 1916

Dearest:—

I found your letter of the 13th awaiting me on our return from the ranges this afternoon. . . .

I was heartened at first and then depressed by your letter. What I feared has happened, you have had to postpone your departure because of monetary consideration and as a result it is extremely unlikely that I shall be here when you arrive in England. We were examined medically for overseas service and I understand that all the officers they can lay their hands on are being sent overseas during these momentous times. I do not grudge going but it will be a terrible disappointment not to see you. Even if I am spared it will be three months before I can see you again. . . . Well I will get this off my chest and not worry any more about it. If I have to go I shall leave some instructions with Philip for your plans temporarily. Beyond that you will probably have to arrange yourself.

There are a number of possibilities open. You can practically always get Voluntary Aid work in connection with the care of convalescent wounded. You might get into some of the new openings for wounded and lastly you could probably find employment with the Government. If you are furnished with a recommendation by Hon. A. L. [Alberta Premier A. L. Sifton] that should go quite a way in a country like this. Once you have settled it in your mind to come don't be downhearted. I will try to do anything I can and you will of course accommodate yourself to circumstances until after the war.

The old days in Strathcona are certainly pleasant memories and thank God their promise has not been belied. I do not need to repeat how radiantly happy I have been. . . . Some day we will be rewarded for the pain of separation.

As to the casualty lists—they surprise you more than us. We probably heard the truth sooner than you. The lists you are getting are I know weeks old. But when you hear the thunder of the British guns and know that victory is within our grasp, you understand that there can be no sorrow for the dead, only regret that they did not live for the triumph but that their life and death has indeed become sanctified by their self-sacrifice. . . . It will come as a shock to the home people that war is so real; but no less real is our determination to see the end.

Well honey you have got more of my letters now—probably those written from England and know of my first impressions. I expect they will improve. I find England very lovely when the weather is fine.

Goodbye and God bless you

Your own

Stuart

Although Edna had left Edmonton by the 20th of June, Stuart had continued to write almost daily. The journey to England remained strong in Edna's memory, and sixty-seven years later she recalled: "I sailed on the *Andania*—we were eleven days—the most beautiful sail— the ocean was like glass. I got to England—we were supposed to land at Plymouth, but owing to submarines we went to Falmouth and we got on the train there and I got into London about three or four in the morning—pitch black, and of course the lights were out.... I got to Westenhanger—it was a milk train—and Stuart was away on a route march. But I went to the camp and the colonel took me in."[4]

Stuart arranged for lodgings at nearby Stanford House where they lived for a few weeks that summer; by late September Edna had moved to London to share a flat with Mary Williams, the wife of a sergeant in Stuart's battalion. They now spent weekends together, either in London or in a town near the Westenhanger camp. Edna had secured a job in the Canadian Army Pay Office in London, and a reference in the following letter implies that it was not customary for an officer's wife to be employed.

WESTENHANGER, OCTOBER 1, 1916

My ownest sweetheart:

And now my first Sunday without you is drawing to a close. It has indeed been quiet though pleasant in a way. I went up to Ashford on the chance of seeing Philip but they had gone on leave to Bristol. Fortunately I caught the same bus back and was here in time for dinner. It has been very dull since dinner, I can assure you. I slept, bathed and talked, that is the extent of my industry. And now I am going to another school, this time the bombing school. I shall write you from Shorncliffe so you will have my address. I shall go in the morning. The course will last three weeks so before it is over the camp will probably have been moved.

You have said very little in your letters of your work.... By the way, you probably have already seen Sgt. Williams. Like a fool I posted all those letters instead of sending them by him. You might remind him that he did not come over to say goodbye. I am wondering how his arrival will affect your [living] arrangements....

I may say I have told everyone quite frankly you have gone to work. No comment was made one way or the other. Strange to say, others' minds seemed to run in a like channel. Fred Shouldice went to the same place to try to get "Jessie" a job but I gather he was not successful. She is going to stay here for a while and is then going visiting. I told her to let you know if she goes to London. . . . It seems to have been getting colder today. I put on my heavy underwear so have been feeling much more comfortable.

It seems a long time since I saw you. It is hard to be parted but I certainly am proud to feel that we are doing our part and not shirking. Indeed I am very proud of my honey for the grit she has shown. At times I realize I do not appreciate you. You have been everything to me a wife could be and your goodness makes me feel small. . . . God bless you darling for all you have been to me. . . .

Now be sure to write often.

Your own
Stuart

The next letters were written at a time when rumours ran rampant as to the future of the Battalion, much as they had in Stuart's early days at Sarcee. For a few days he found himself billeted in Hythe, near the lodgings of his cousin Harris McNish and his wife.

101 SEABROOK ROAD, HYTHE
OCTOBER 2, 1916

Dearest:—

. . . This has been a long hard day—up at 5:45 a.m. breakfast at 7, up at headquarters at 8, Sandgate at 9. As I told you I was instructed to attend the grenade course at Shorncliffe. I got down in good time to find there was no accommodation and I was reduced to coming here where Harris is. It's horribly mixed up. There are so many officers up there they don't know what to do with them and a new mob coming tomorrow. . . . The weather is raining and generally wretched.

No mail today. What is wrong? Have I offended. Surely I deserve a letter every other day. I know I should have sent a message by Sgt. Williams but I did not see him.

I certainly wish we hadn't been in such haste to break up housekeeping in Hythe. It would be just heaven if you were here now but of course—. . . . What of your first Sunday in London. Did you see the Zeppelin. I heard bombs and turned out once but was so wretched shivering that I got back to bed and stayed there. . . . I wonder how often I have cursed the whole tribe of Zeppelins.

I really am neglected—no word from home of any kind. By the way the regiment is moving up this week to Shoreham. What they will do with me I don't know. I suppose I shall follow later.

By the way do you want me [to come up] this week end and can arrangements be made. Be sure to write and let me know tout de suite. This letter is not satisfactory I know. I am cold and it is cheerless. But I know you will forgive it.

Don't forget to write lots. I really need some consolation.

Goodnight dearest. . . .

Your own
Stuart

101 SEABROOK ROAD, HYTHE
OCTOBER 4, 1916

Dearest:—

Now who do you suppose I am sitting down to write to tonight— who indeed but my own sweetheart. Indeed I am heaping coals of fire on her head as she has not written to me since Saturday. What a week this has been. I never thought I should miss you so much but every time I thought of you I had a terrible heartache. It just seemed unbearable today. . . . There is no definite news about moving yet, only rumours. I suppose though I will be in this billet for a couple of weeks anyway, so I can settle down to it. It is not bad in the evening. Harris' wife makes tea and invites me in (nuff said). . . .

One learns day by day. I suppose one never rates at the full value companionship with sensible people till deprived of it. I have been trying to understand and appreciate my new cousin but it is impossible. She talks enough but says nothing. It is as hard to carry on a conversation as to keep step with a puppy dog and then I thought of sitting down to talk with you. I do like, when I start to talk about a thing, to keep on talking, but her idea of conversation is to shoot as many squibs into the fire as possible—most exhausting to her hearers. Oh honey you will have to rescue me from boredom. If we ever get back home again I am going to pay perpetual court to you. I do so love to see you really roused in conversation to see your eyes work and the most intense look come over your face as you lay the law down to the multitude. I am really not kidding you. Those are some of the most exhilarating moments. . . .

I suppose I should not go on like this but be sensible and write about my work. As a matter of fact I am getting down to business, but it has been raining and is horribly depressing wading around in mud—and I am dirty all the time.

Well I shall have to close. Be sure and let me know about week end plans, where to go etc etc. If you would rather come down here I can arrange it. . . . Have you heard from Philip yet. He will probably hunt you up. Wasn't that too bad about Bert Scott.

Your own.
Stuart

IOI SEABROOK ROAD
OCTOBER 6, 1916

Dearest:—

. . . Now am I going to London. I confess for the moment I thought there wasn't much encouragement but I have since plucked up courage and applied for leave truth to tell. It would be a very little short of terrible to spend my week end here, though conceivably there might be compensations, but alas as to getting boots etc. I shall not arrive in London till p.m. Saturday. I think the train leaves at 1:40. . . .

. . . [E]xpect to be in Charring Cross about 3:30.

Stuart

Friday evening:—

I really have been put to it to find writing material but when I went in a store and told the girl I was a poor Canadian soldier without money or paper to write my wife she said she would give me an envelope. She knew a Canadian fellow onst [sic] who was poor but honest. If all is well I shall arrive Charring X 3:20 tomorrow. I shant have much money. Till then goodnight.

Stuart

Every weekend in London could well have been Stuart's last. Given the uncertainty of plans for the 89th's departure for France, there was no way of knowing when they would see one another again. Edna earned the admiration of his comrades for the way in which she coped with the situation.

Dearest, Dearest Honey:—

Your letter written on Sunday evening was handed me this morning; how could I fail to be moved by it? So I have remembered my promise to you last night to let you hear from me; so here are Norman Weir and myself comfortably ensconced in a room (rather smoky at that) in one of the huts, my batman frantically striving to make the fire go. We had a comfortable trip down last night, Bob and I; we both managed to sleep most of the way. At Ashford somebody shook me. I looked up and it was Philip. He had Emily with him. . . . [H]e apparently took a chance on catching me at the train. Do you know he was pinched by the M.P. that Sunday he came down without a tunic and was doing 7 days C.B. [confined to barracks] but managed to get a pass. I am going to wire him today and will probably be able to see him again. . . . When we got to Shornecliffe there were five officers going out. (Norman Weir joined us at Westenhanger) so we came out in a taxi. I got a bed o.k. and had a fair nights sleep, what there was of it. It is very quiet around here today so I should get some work done.

I certainly felt very proud, honey, of you yesterday and of your courage. I should like to have said more but I could not trust myself. I do not know yet what comfort to hold out. In fact you seem to have risen to the occasion a great deal better than I. After all I feel that doing my best is simply being worthy of you and your trust. I think someday your courage will be justified. I shall take good care of myself honey. There will be lots to write about and we will both keep busy and our minds occupied. We will steady down. I know I feel at peace. . . .

We really had a most delightful day. There was not a cloud to mar it. Always by my side there was my honey, game as could be and I knew I could rely on her. My heart just swelled with pride. Bob thought you were a good sport. "She doesn't look it you know. She seems so frail." Well dearest we will smile on and trust that things will come out all right. In many ways they are right now of course. We have found ourselves in the greatest crisis of life and know that we can count on one another. God bless you, dear, and take care of you. I shall pray for you.

Your own
Stuart

Two Alberta battalions, Edmonton's 49th and Calgary's 31st, suffered heavy losses in the Battle of Flers-Courcelette in mid-September 1916. This battle was distinguished somewhat from all the other painfully costly "over the top" trench assaults by two innovations that were expected to provide the infantry with unprecedented support. The creeping artillery barrage, designed to precede an infantry charge across no-man's land, had recently been adopted when sufficient ammunition made it a plausible tactic, and the tank, developed to combat the deadly machine gun and enemy barbed wire, made its debut at Flers-Courcelette.[5]

News from the front continued to circulate among the reserve troops in England who were ready to take the place of casualties, many of whom were friends from home. Disappointment with the Russians, noted in the letter below, stemmed from heavy losses in late September that blunted their offensive. Stuart's comment about the Italians apparently referred to the 8th Battle of Isonzo that began on 10 October and ended the day he wrote the letter; it was the eighth of eleven such encounters fought on the Italian Front between 23 June 1915 and 19 August 1917.[6]

Stuart knew that time often hung on one's hands in the Army, and he made plans before sailing to invest such time in studying the Russian language.

9TH RES. BATT. ST. MARTIN'S PLAIN
SHORNECLIFFE, OCTOBER 12, 1916
[NO.1]

Dearest:

Apparently I gave you an unfortunate impression when I left you night before last as I have received no letters. While there would be no use of sending me any letters en route, we may be here indefinitely and I certainly should like to get word from you. . . .

Now I have some news for you. Major Flint had a letter from Yuell (or is it Yule). He was one of the officers who went out with Bert Scott, I think it was at Courcelette, apparently to take or hold an advanced position. I am not sure whether McKnight was with him or not. At any rate you know the result. Yuell and Scott got back and the former is to get the Military Cross. I knew you would be glad to hear it.

They get lots of news here as there are very few of the Alberta officers who have not passed through here. . . . There are quite a bunch of 66th officers around here. They are certainly a motley crew. All ranks, sizes and ages. A bunch of them put up a sing song last night. One fellow gave the greatest imitation of Harry Lauder you could ever imagine. It did not tempt me though. I was glad to get to bed.

Well there is better news from the theatre of war today. The Italians seem to be still on the job. Everyone I think is silently disappointed in the Russians. They did so well for a while; we think they should go on. I suppose it will work out all right. There is not much more time left for fighting this year.

And now honey, take good care of yourself. I hope you manage to get moved all right and that you like the place. Write and tell me all about [it]. Don't forget to get me that Russian grammar will you and if you can, pick up a good first aid book. I want to know something about it.

Well dear, if I think of any more news I shall dash off another letter today. If we are here till Sunday would you like to come down Saturday afternoon. Be sure to write and let me know. I know I could arrange for you to be accommodated in Hythe. Let me hear from you.

Your own
Stuart

As the time to depart for France neared, Stuart began to arrange his affairs and told Edna of his decisions in the following letter. They indicate his feeling of responsibility for his mother, and it can only be imagined how those decisions were perceived by his wife.

OCTOBER 12TH, SHORNECLIFFE
[NO.2]

Dearest:—

No doubt you were surprised to get my extraordinary telegram yesterday. I decided however to risk the smiles of telegraphers and send it as I need the articles mentioned. I trust also that my telegram gave you the needed clue that I will be here for a day or two and that you will write so that I can get a letter before I go.

There are one or two things to which I wish to refer. First I am going to ask you to pay mother that $750 life insurance in case I do not come back. Also I have arranged with Philip that I will contribute towards a monthly payment to mother, i.e. the present arrangement is terminated and only an allowance of a personal nature will be made. I suggested $15 per month of which I should pay $10. Philip will let you know the amount and I think I had better pay ⅔. This arrangement is to last only during my lifetime. . . . I may say I am going to make a will to straighten out affairs with regard to the lots I have in Edmonton. The title to the one in Hayman and the equity in the other will go to mother. Also my interest in the farm. That will have to be adjusted, anyway you will know from this that it is my wish that any interest I have in the above property should be assigned to mother. Have I made myself clear?

Another matter, I have turned in my revolver and binoculars, for which I am to receive credit in my account. The total will be approximately $72.50. . . . There will probably also be a credit of $15.00 for billeting allowance. . . . So you see our shattered fortunes will probably be restored. I may have to draw on my account for a revolver and ammunition but nothing else. That should give us at least £30 clear. Be sure to let me know how things stand. . . .

I am all packed up ready to go. My kit is quite a comfortable size. The big double blanket I am sending up to Philip. That has considerably lightened my outfit. My toilet bag I shall carry in my haversack. I had qualms about taking it but thought
[This letter remained unfinished.]

9TH RES. BATT.
ST. MARTIN'S PLAIN
SHORNECLIFFE, OCTOBER 13, 1916
[NO. 1]

Dearest:—
Still we are here! Isn't it depressing that I had so short a stay in London and I might just as well have had longer. I have absolutely nothing to do beyond writing. . . . I did not contemplate so long a delay of course.

After writing to you, I went up to see Philip. I only had a little while there so it was hardly worth the effort. I came back on the bus. . . . I got back about 8:30.

I told you, did I, that Norman Weir and I are together. More good luck than good management. . . .

It is raining lamentably here this morning—started in about day break and has been keeping it up ever since. The camp is fairly dry though, like Westenhanger, so no one suffers. They are expecting all the officers to go this month. Whittaker is away on leave with his wife. Domnie and MacRae are at the school, Dunn is up at Westenhanger having a great time looking after the camp. Martin is away. Mooney is going overseas. Thus endeth the 89th. The band are anxious to go overseas and join the 31st band. I am going to try and work it if I can. Now little girl look after yourself and don't forget to write. Let me know all about the new dress and is it going to be a new hat? Give my regards to Mrs. W. Tell her I have enjoyed the cigarettes very much.

Meanwhile good bye

Yours,

Stuart

What do you think of the idea of coming down Saturday. Be sure to let me know. I would wire in case we went before you got here.

ST. MARTIN'S PLAIN

SHORNECLIFFE, OCTOBER 13, 1916

[NO. 3]

Dearest dearest Honey:—

I have already written twice to you today but cannot refrain from doing so once more. I had a nice comfortable supper of tea and toast and here I am in my room making myself comfortable as best I can after a wearisome day. . . .

I ran across a most interesting article in tonight's evening news re German use of the Press. It struck me as a most illuminating description of what is most obvious and yet what has distorted the minds of not only most of the neutrals but even belligerents. We say we see through their press agents and yet I find myself at times unconsciously half won to their point of view. It [is] the most deliberate, audacious perversion of the truth and its effect is a million fold more far reaching than we realize. If you use enough skill and enterprize apparently you can colour the thinking of most of the civilized world. Really, Germany's proselytism is just begun and we are going to see German press agents set about redeeming a military and economic defeat. Astounding isn't it? I consider this article very able and am clipping it for you.

My stuff is all packed and is going in quite a small compass. You would be surprised. . . . I certainly hope there will be a letter for me in the morning. We may not get away till Monday.

We fellows are very happy anticipating the change and I am sure we will be fine. The 2nd Division is said to be at Armentieres for the winter. That means no more Somme. Be sure to let me know if you are coming.

Stuart

The stay at Shorncliffe did not end until 16 October. The final days saw the 89th Alberta Overseas broken up, its men and officers distributed among units destined for France, and Stuart was assigned to the badly decimated 31st Battalion in the Canadian Second Division. Edna heeded Stuart's pleas to join him in Kent, and they spent the weekend of the 14th together. Her journal entry on 18 October 1916, said: "Well, it came at last. Stuart went to France on Monday last. We had a lovely day on Sunday at Seabrook, the day was grand and there seemed to be sort of a serene calm over everything in spite of the calamities around us. . . . I hope and pray the Good Lord to spare me the trial that Mrs. Scott has to bear."[7]

SHORNECLIFFE, OCTOBER 16, 1916

Dearest:—

We are about to be off and in anticipation of that much hoped for event I am setting myself down to write. First did you get home all right? I shall be anxious until I hear from you as it was a somewhat risky thing. Next *do not get book Eclipse or Empire I bought one* [sic] here at the station.

We are a happy bunch going this morning 100 or so of us. We have been delayed and did not get off till 10:15. . . . Our luggage went about six. I have come off very well financially. My mess bill was smaller than I anticipated and it cost me less than I expected for the batman so I expect to make the grade. We are going by Guildford and not London. . . . We will embark some time this evening and get to Havre tonight. From there I shall write. Now, if you don't like your work, get into something congenial. . . . It would dearly please me to see you get into something you would like.

We are just going through Sandling. . . . Mrs. Weir left for London at 9:40 this morning so you should see her. Now I can see Stanford. It certainly looks fine this morning.

Well dear look after yourself and write lots.
Goodbye
Stuart

5

Impressions of France
At the Front with Alberta's 31st

Stuart's unit disembarked at Le Havre where they spent one day before moving for a short stay at a nearby Canadian Base Camp and then by train to the front. He continued to share his widening world with Edna, sending her his general impressions of France as well as the day-to-day details of life at the front. On occasion he used words that now are racist, words that were commonplace in a world of colonial troops and defence of Empire.

On his last leave in London Stuart had ordered a pair of boots from Randall's and expected to receive them soon on his arrival on the Continent. The following letter is the first of several in which he castigated the store as he came to need the boots in the trenches.

SOMEWHERE IN FRANCE,
OCTOBER 17, 1916

Dearest:—

Here we are at last, not right up to the front line, but on the way. We had a good passage across and are now at the base having got here this morning. The principal thing to be noticed is the high cost of living. "Dix francs monsieur" for everything. If I lived for long on the scale of the last twenty four hours I should not last long. It has been raining here for a couple of days very muddy. The camp is very cramped in a poor location. Of course it is only a clearing house so any kind of a billet will do. I have not met anyone outside of our own little party of five or seven including those going to the 49th, but we are a happy party and very agreeable. We leave tomorrow for the base. I am going into town this afternoon to look around, see and be seen. I should certainly like to walk around the French stores and talk French with the ladies. As a town this place is not a shining example of French civilization, in fact quite disappointing at the start. I shall be able however to tell you more later. . . .

I had a good sleep last night and am feeling fine this morning. . . . By the way it looks to me as if English papers were pretty scarce here. I could not get any this morning and there are none kicking around the mess here, so I shall certainly be glad of some. That is a dandy book I am reading—a terrible indictment of England. . . .

When I see the mud here I am glad I got my boots though I should like to have them soon. I am also glad I turned in the binoculars and revolver. I will need money at the rate it is going now. My only hope is we will get away from here before it grows worse. As for news of the front, we know absolutely nothing and probably less the further up we get. Now remember I shall look forward to a letter when I get up to the battalion. Don't forget to write and to think of me.

Your own
Stuart

FRANCE, OCTOBER 18, 1916

Dearest:—

A wet muddy morning with a tramp over the hills and far away does not put me in a very good mood for writing. One has moreover a curious detached feeling as though one had stepped out of the world and as though there were nothing to write of. There probably is lots to see around a base camp if one cared to go below the surface. But your feelings are sure to be that you are "fed up." You've seen it all in the first two hours and you are seized with a violent desire to get away. I thought it was to be my good fortune to get away today but nothing doing. At least another day of enforced waiting. Yesterday we went to town in the afternoon, a curious little French train which we caught down the road—crowded into 3rd class cars, with seats running like in English cars but no partitions between departments. Englishmen, Canadians, French Canadians, Frenchmen, two French women going shopping. The conductor locked us in, blew on a little horn such as the kids get at Christmas and we were off rolling and pitching, through back yards, gardens, country lanes, off the seven or eight miles to town. Arrived there we found we had to pay four sous each or twopence. Then for the town. We took this in in a very mild way, walked nearly all over it and saw the inevitable cinema. The cinema I suppose is essentially American even here, but there was one French plot, very poor but of course very dramatic, the inevitable young girl led astray in her dramatic career and ending up with a suicide. Poor Charlie C[haplin] was quite a relief after that. We walked after that [and] found a little restaurant, not bad. I had a little vin blanc. The fellows insisted on coming back in a taxi. . . . We got home in good time for dinner, which is at seven p.m.

Our quarters here are just fair. I don't know whether you have any idea what a base camp is. It sprawls all over the country with depots of every imaginable kind. Just here it is not a favourable spot as it is up and down hill, mud and bad roads everywhere. There seems to be no cohesion. One very comforting thing in the camp is the mess here which is really good. Since we reported yesterday morning, we have had little to do. This morning we went up to what they call the training camp, about two miles away, where we were introduced to the mysteries of gas, helmets, the lethal chamber etc. The first experience was putting on the helmet and going through a long low dugout filled with chlorine—the deadly gas first used at Ypres. I did not enjoy it at all, for the gas and chemicals together went for my throat. I was glad to get out, felt as though I were being gassed all the time. We went from there to the lachrimatory gasses. This time we went down one runway below ground and up. The gasses were lying at the bottom of the dip. I went in without my goggles as the gas is harmless. It has a peculiar fruity smell and just as I started to come up I got a whiff that wrung the tears out like water out of a sponge. Gee I blinked, but a breath of wind blew it out of my eyes. Then we saw the phosphorus bombs used for deep dugouts. . . . It was quite an interesting morning and I was hungry when I got back. Lunch is quite a ceremony here. It is served cafeteria style but during the present congestion is worse than lumberjacks style. At noon today, there was a crush. I managed to rustle some food and get a seat also—trust me eh. There certainly is no kick coming on the grub.

We are not going up to the front today for some reason or other.

Apparently we are not wanted. I am very hard up for my field boots and may decide to get a pair here. The ones I have are almost useless against this French mud.

Do you know I have probably got the cart before the horse in my narrative, telling you all about the camp and nothing of our trip which began on Monday morning. . . . Our run down to the port of embarkation was very enjoyable, broken by a very enjoyable lunch and a very gay supper. That was my first experience of high life. We did not leave till 7 p.m. and were out long enough to go to bed. I unrolled my bed and had a good sleep. Our debarkation was a little delayed but by 8:30 we were off up town for some breakfast. We passed gangs of German prisoners on the way, also Turcos, Sengalese etc. We even saw what looked to be Chinks in French uniform. They were probably soldiers from the Straits settlements. They certainly looked odd. The town for all it is bigger looked for all the world like a reproduction of some place in Quebec, shoddy and down at [the] heels. There are really very few fine buildings. We sauntered up town till we discovered a restaurant where we were invited to enter. I had rolls and coffee, Norman a little more but we paid 4 francs. A good cigar for 2 francs. Think of it! That shot the first hole in my pocket book. Not knowing the way we decided on a taxi and at 10 o'clock we reported at British H.Q. from where we left for the Canadian H.Q. Here we were assigned tents and batmen. That constitutes an outline of our itinerary. I could tell you more if I might of various things in the way of warlike preparations. One thing here they do not seem to be bothered with Zeppelins as lighting restrictions seem to be absent. Still everything seems to be abnormal, as English goods are shown everywhere and there are English faces in all public places. In fact the English have taken possession. What struck me is what a good time the French Canadians have. There are quite a lot of them in our crowd and they seem to get around. I gather that this is the part of France from which they originally come and it is a reproduction almost of their native province. . . .

I shall certainly look forward to getting up to the front as there will probably be letters waiting for me there. Meanwhile I shall have to content myself with writing. Don't forget dear that I love you and will be wanting to hear from you often. Let me know of any news you get from home. Good bye dearest.

Your own
Stuart

While Stuart's letters often reflected pride in the British Empire, he frequently expressed disgust with the English, and his assessment of the French was often harsh. He thought constantly of his wife, and his letters from the front continued to hold the same expressions of love and discourses on the nature of love and the nobility of womanhood that had characterized his courtship letters. He relied on Edna to send both necessities and luxuries across the Channel, and very early in the game he included reading matter as a necessity for keeping his mind constructively engaged.

CANADIAN BASE DEPOT, B.E.F.
FRANCE, OCTOBER 20, 1916

Dearest:—

It is hard to realize that I have not written you for two days but I can assure you the circumstances justify such an omission. We were up at 6 a.m. yesterday and moved off at 7:30 to the training camp several miles away. Although it did not rain, it was wet and cold, still we managed to put in a very busy and very interesting day, musketry, skirmishing and looking at the artillery. I have not been so hungry in a long time, ate every opportunity that afforded itself. We were back about 4:30 and went in to tea. Who was there but Pat Allen—somewhat subdued. He has been in hospital at the base. His heart gave out a couple of weeks ago and he had to be carried out of the front line. I heard from one of his brother officers. Pat has certainly seen some scrapping, I can tell you. We had dinner fairly early and I rolled in soon afterward. A "topping" (as they say) night's sleep has put me in fine shape. . . . Today we are in camp and this afternoon I shall go to town with Norman. We have to censor the mail in the morning. During the afternoon we are allowed away. I suppose I read about 50 letters this morning. One fellow was writing to his wife who was expecting a a child. I don't think I ever read a letter that touched me so much, breathing the utmost tenderness and affection. There are apparently lots of fine fellows in the army. It set me to thinking of you, dear. I suppose men do not know what their blessings are until they are torn from their grasp. Still I feel that our love is not lost but that every day and all day it bears me up in the midst of discouragement and dejection and inspires my every action and thought. I am so glad we had the courage to marry without worrying over the future. As you can surmise, I have no word yet of going up the line. I am hoping though that we will be away by the end of the week at least. It is not very enjoyable here. The worst is that I get no mail. I suppose mine has all gone up country to the battalion.

I was just thinking this morning that I had not yet heard whether you got home on Sunday night. I regretted afterwards that you had waited for the late train. It really was a late hour for you to be poking around the streets of London alone. Under ordinary circumstances, it would have been wrong. . . .

It is strange what an education it is to knock around the world and see people. This war is really an eye-opener to every Canadian soldier. I am not sure it opens their eyes to the right things always. You can see it in their letters. One thing recurs everywhere: that everyone will be glad to get back to Canada. France is not I think so attractive as England. The lower classes are not only untidy but dirty—their houses close and shabby—no neatly trimmed hedges and lawns. Of course the poor people are too busy tilling the soil. The children though very courteous are not naturally so attractive as the English children. In fact there is an air of poverty and squalor everywhere. The country is very pretty though the roads are not to be compared with those of England, but every foot is tilled. Even the hillsides are planted with trees. It was such a surprise to me to see their groves planted just like corn, straight rows both ways. Of course the country is at a great disadvantage, all the men are away at the war, only the children and old men and women working. You see the direct results of war here far more than in England. Today the sun is out and we are drying out. I have been very comfortable, though one cannot keep one's feet dry. But all your troubles are forgotten when you roll yourself up in your blankets at night and dream of home.

I certainly wish I had more reading matter here. We get the Times and the Chronicle here but that does not seem to satisfy. I don't want to hear anything of the war. I think I should like to have a serious book or two. If you could get them in a cheap binding—the Golden Treasury or some of the really good novels. It would keep my mind functioning properly and healthy. Because here, you just grub along, play cards, go to town for amusement. There is companionship of course but one's mind never soars to great heights—meals, bed etc. You should have a great opportunity in London to see things and to keep your mind active.

Give my regards to Mrs. Williams and Sgt. Williams when you see them. Don't forget to write. You might drop a line to the above address.

Don't forget, dearest

Your own
Stuart

At Thiepval Ridge, one of the Battles of the Somme, 26–28 September, the First and Second Canadian Divisions, including Calgary's 31st Battalion, had advanced against heavy German machine gun and rifle fire, to achieve only limited success.[1] Casualties returning to the rear met fresh reserve troops advancing to the front, and the limited geographical area in which the Canadians fought insured that former comrades would have chance meetings from time to time. Stuart found himself in the 31st, which was then with the main body of the Canadian Corps in the general vicinity of Bethune, near the Lens-Arras sector and north of the area where the Somme Battles continued on into November.

The following letter records his introduction to the trenches and is the first of many in which he mentions men whom he had known previously and with whom he was now serving. The trip he describes remained clear in his memory; sixty years later he said, "I well remember when we went up to the front. We had these ordinary freight cars, you see, and I had trouble keeping warm in them."[2]

FRANCE, OCTOBER 22, 1916

Dearest:—

We are now nearing our destination so I shall drop a little note to you when we get off. We left the base depot yesterday. Such a mix up I never saw in my life. We were away up at the training camp three miles away at 10:30 a.m. when we were warned to be on the parade ground ready to move off at 11:30 a.m. I got off in a terrible rush, forgetting to pay my mess bill. I was sure I had forgotten a dozen other things. However my batman did manage to get them all together. We entrained at 1 o'clock and left about 4 p.m. It was fierce trying to get something to eat. There was a canteen fortunately and I rustled some biscuits, beef and jam so we have survived. But it was very cold last night. I rolled in at 9:50 on the floor with my coat over me. By midnight I was frozen stiff. Later on the train stopped and I went out to the baggage car and got my kit to roll my bed on the floor. From that time on I began to warm up and had really a fine sleep. At our first stop this morning we had a cup of coffee which made us take interest in life once more. It really has been colder than it would be in Alberta at this time of year. I do not yet know what my movements will be for the next day or so. I have a party of reenforcements to look after before joining the 31st, but that should not take long. By the way, I met several of our fellows going up country. They were in the big scrap on the 26th, were hit and were going back. . . .

I shall be glad to have some mail again. It seems nearly a month since I left home though it is only a week as a matter of fact.

Well we are coming to a town so I must get out and look after the boys.

[much later]

Alas that this letter should have been postponed. It is nearly 36 hours since I wrote the first part and I am now in the trenches—not the front line but the supports. I am comfortable seated in a dug out with a grate fire burning and a table on which to write and am going to have a very comfortable evening though alone. We reached rail head yesterday about 1 p.m. Just after we embarked two German machines flew over and the archibalds [anti-aircraft guns] turned on them. They were a way up but the sky was punctured all over with little puffs from the shells bursting. The planes went right overhead and I thought of bombs dropping but as Bob Pearson says I had to look brave and pretend they weren't there. At any rate Fritz was not daunted and they flew whithersoever they listed. I turned over my drafts to the Royal Transport Officer, met the transport officer of the 31st, went and had a shave and some lunch and at 4:30 started for the battalion lines. It was a good way. We soon cleared the village and came out into the open fields going south. We climbed a high ridge from which we made a continuous descent through a couple of villages finally turning due east towards the German lines. As darkness fell the East was illuminated with the star shells going up all along the lines. We gradually descended a long low valley till at a point where it widened out we reached a large village—in ruins. The village was the scene of a big scrap and it surely showed traces of it—not a house intact. Battalion headquarters was in an old inn where we were welcomed to the mess and made comfortable. The battalion were coming out of the front line so we waited until the 2nd in command arrived. Hewgill is his name (from Edmonton). Then supper, a good one too, and we spread our bed on the floor. Some guns around us started action and kept me awake for a time then the firing died away. But the rats—running around me and over the bed all night. I scared them away with my flash [light] at first. But do you know what they did—ate a dozen holes through my British warm for some biscuits inside—absolutely ruining it of course though it will do for trench work. Say I was mad. I am gaining some experience; still several of the officers said they had never known it to happen before. This morning after breakfast some scouts came around to conduct us to our quarters and I started up here. On the way up I asked about Bennet [a friend of his sisters], found out he was still here and went to see him, large as life I found him without a scratch. He promised to come up tonight though I have not seen him yet or had a talk with him. I have seen a goodly number of the 89th boys. Many of them alas I will never see again. . . . I found my quarters and have spent the day getting acquainted and fixing up a dug out. Tomorrow I work.

I spent part of the afternoon nosing around the neighbourhood and seeing the sights. There must have been a fierce fight here. All kinds of paraphernalia—several unexploded shells, aerial torpedoes, bombs, rifles, equipment, the earth torn and pitted with shell holes. Towards evening, our guns opened fire. Lord knows where from as you never see our batteries but it was quite close and you could hear the huge shells tearing Hunward on their task of death. They burst along the skyline with great black puffs. You could not tell their effect as the day has been very misty. As evening came down, the usual activity opened on the front line, increased machine gun fire—our guns speaking away up and down. Far off one dull continuous boom from the Somme battle, I even heard a spent bullet go overhead.

The battalion are now in a quiet part of the line and are to be here for some time. I find I made a mistake not bringing more stuff—particularly an automatic. I do not like to ask you to get things but I should certainly like to get an automatic .45 or .38 calibre preferably. I have indented but will probably not get one. I also want writing material, cigarettes, heavy gloves. Such as I can I shall indent for but we are a long way from Battalion HQ and still farther from stores. Also any dainties in the eats are mighty good—candy, jam etc etc. The rations are light.

Well honey this is quite a letter so I shall close. Remember to write often. I have not had a letter from you yet.

As ever your own
Stuart

When the war began in the summer of 1914, few predicted a long and protracted conflict, and none could anticipate that it would take the form of trench combat and stalemate. Nothing in their military past had prepared any of the participants for trench war,[3] but by October 1916, when Stuart Tompkins joined the 31st Battalion on the Western Front, an elaborate and relatively uniform trench system had evolved and adapting to life in that system had become a science for all ranks, if not an art form.

Trenches on both sides were usually built in triple lines, although in some instances the Germans might have as many as ten lines of trenches. Typically there were the forward or fire trench, the support trench, and the reserve trench; they were designed in zig-zag or traverse formation to break line-of-sight access and prevent direct line of fire the length of a trench. A trench was usually dug deep enough for most men to stand upright; it was lined with sandbags, and shored up with timber reinforcing. The three lines were connected by zig-zag communication trenches that enabled troops to move forward or to the rear with some safety.[4]

The dugout, described as an "indispensable feature of any piece of trench," provided bunk space or a mess area and offered protection from the weather and artillery fire. Dugouts varied in size and comfort even in the front lines; they might range from a ten-foot-deep hole with a layer of logs for a roof to a 4′ × 7′ "room" containing a bed and a table with its walls and corrugated iron roof lined with sand bags. Dugouts further to the rear were deeper and more elaborate. A reserve trench in the Arras sector in early 1916 is reported to have offered at a depth of thirty feet two small rooms that were wallpapered and furnished with bed, easy chairs, stove, and mirror.[5]

Troops served rotations in the three lines at the front and were occasionally removed to reserve billets in French villages. Stuart's letters reported his various assignments in and out of forward positions, and he turned to describing the effects of combat and the circumstances of trench life.

FRANCE, OCTOBER 25, 1916

Dearest:—

I received this morning two letters from you dated 20th and 22nd. Your first letter dated 19th I got day before yesterday.

Oh dear! Honey I have been censoring letters. Mind you with a company strength of about 80 it takes 3 officers all their time to censor the letters when the company is in reserve. I never saw the like of it. However I am done for tonight.

I am sure you want me to tell all about my experiences. Of these none yet. But every few minutes a shell whistles over my head followed by a loud report. There are several [artillery] batteries in our rear and at times, convenient for them but not for us, they open up. Between 12 and 1 and at dark are favorite times.

Well what is it like here? I can hear you asking. To tell the truth. The line we are holding runs across a battle field made famous earlier in the war and the ground around us is replete with relics from that conflict. I wish I could go more into particulars. The position which was taken by the French is now two miles or more behind the front line. The ridge behind which we feel so safe commands a wide valley to the east and looks over on the German lines. Just where we are the ridge ends abruptly and the valley which cuts the ridge and up which the main road lies is exposed to view from the east. Naturally the village in the valley is in ruins and no transport can come down the valley road except at night. To our rear are scattered batteries of artillery. It is amusing what an impression they make on you when you first hear them. I was dozing at headquarters the first night when I heard them speak. Just one hoarse bark followed by four or five others; then silence then another salvo and you hear the shells sing over your head and if you listen well you hear them burst way off. Then we have some "heavies." One gun in particular. You hear a loud boom and s-s-s-s-right over your head skips a huge shell rushing like an express train off into space. . . . It is interesting to try to spot where the guns are. On all sides you hear their fierce bark. At times the heavies shake the ground. Things seem to be fairly quiet in the front line. Things liven up a bit at night. Machine gun fire can be heard on every side and always the flares. But beyond that you see and hear nothing. You might just as well be in sunny Alberta.

Bennett and I went for a walk this afternoon out the road we came in on. It was quite beautiful, particularly when we got on that part of the road which is out of range of Fritz. But the country is almost deserted and desolate. He told me all about himself and his experience both here and in England where his father refused to own him. . . . He wears the ribbon for his Military Medal. We got back about six in time for dinner, steak, potatoes, peas, bread, butter jam, figs and tea. Then I fell to censoring letters.

Our mess room is just a dug out built into the rear of the trench and faced with sand bags. We have a grate, a smoky one, benches and table. My own diggings is quite a similar one. I have rigged up a fair bed on engineering wire—have a brazier [and] a block at the head of my bed for a candle. So I get into pyjamas, crawl into bed, don my sweater, put on my glasses, prop my back against the wall and am ready for any contingency. We have little to do now as we are in the reserve trenches. Saturday though, we go into the [forward] trenches. I do not see anything of Norman Weir. . . .

The weather till today has been wretched now it is clearing but getting cold. We fortunately can make the raise of coal near at hand and our chaps are great rustlers. . . . I wish I could write and tell you all the things I think of—all I am learning about life and about you. Every day your dear face becomes dearer. I shall write again before we go in.

Your own
Stuart

As he made ready to move into the front line trenches, Stuart's need for the boots he had ordered from Randall's grew more critical. The excitement and anticipation of seeing first action may have mitigated the bad news mentioned below; the German offensive in the Balkans had seen Constantza fall on 23 October, and by mid-December would see a near rout of the Russian and Romanian armies.[6]

FRANCE, OCTOBER 27, 1916

My own Dearest:—

Another day this time rainy and disagreeable with one bright spot—a real "Oliver" bath. This afternoon I went down to battalion HQ where (so it had been announced) we would be able to go through our ablutions. We had only a tub but unlimited quantities of H2O and soap. So I washed from head to foot. . . . So I feel like a new born creature. This morning we further reconnoitred the battle ground around here. It was all seamed with trenches and plentifully scarred with shell holes. About lay all the debris of the battle field—equipment, rifles, bayonets, barbed wire. We found a huge trench mortar literally buried by the explosion of a shell—not far away an unexploded shell about 7 or 8 inches in diameter, also a small trench catapult. The numerous graves around bespeak the desperate struggle. We were all very tired when we came in climbing up and down the shell holes. Really I have been very comfortable here. The meals have really been good. We have been able to rustle fresh eggs and cabbage—also to buy Quaker oats, tinned fruit, milk and numerous other delicacies. I fancy we will fare not too badly in the front line. We go in tomorrow. I am much disappointed at not getting my boots. It is nearly 3 weeks now. I shall clean and oil the ones I have and shall get along not too badly I hope. I find my bed a godsend. My clothes are fine particularly that sweater and my underwear. I have not suffered the least bit from cold. I am taking in my British Warm, slicker, two extra pairs socks, shaving material, towel, [and] my old uniform so I do not dread it at all. The only drawback is that it has been raining this afternoon so it will probably be wet. Bill Emery got a box from Canada today and has been sharing his cigars. Emery is from the 56th one of those old soldiers I had in my squad when I went to the 89th school first day—remember? . . . I am getting on fine but Norman [Weir] and Bob [Pearson] are both in other companies so I have not seen either of them. I may see them tomorrow.

We get practically no news—except bad news. We heard of the capture of Constantza by the Germans. It is real disheartening. Still nobody worries here. We peg along. I have been instructing in the Lewis Gun will probably do musketry later so do not feel that my training is altogether wasted. Everything has been fine so far.

. . . Do you ever hear from home or from the girls? I must arrange to write to the girls and to Philip tonight. I shall have leisure unless there are a lot more letters to censor.

There is really no news of any kind except small talk. Things are very quiet around here and away from the British lines there is nothing doing as the country is almost desolate. I look forward to getting the books as I wish to keep my mind healthily occupied. I shall try to write from the front line when not otherwise engaged. . . .

Will I get a letter tonight. Nobody knows I guess but I shall look forward to something. Goodbye dear and God bless you.

Your own
Stuart

FRANCE, OCTOBER 30, 1916

Dearest:—

Now you are not going to get much of a letter tonight but I felt I cannot turn in without saying something. I was rather sick when I came in [to the trenches] Saturday night when I tore my boots all to pieces coming in. I said some things about those Randall people for the way they have fallen down. It means I shall have to purchase a pair from the Quarter Master. If you want to do some good work for me, you might give them a bit of my mind. I received the parcels you sent. It makes me think I do nothing but ask you for things. You have been awfully good. The reading matter I am enjoying immensely and have already learned the Russian script. . . . We have had quiet time as you may see in the papers. The Minnenwerfers [German mortars] are the only things that have bothered. Most of the battalions get out without any casualties. . . .

I have asked you for so many things that I hate to ask for more. But I should like the Times if you could arrange for it. We suffer from a dearth of news.

. . . I have really been very comfortable since coming in. You might send socks any time. I suffer from lack of footwear—also more writing material.

I have found a lot of our [89th] fellows in this battalion. They had a very severe time and seem glad to see a familiar face. The relations between men and officers out here is very fine and the fellows are all fine.

I am glad to hear that you will like it at Mrs. Williams. I think you should enjoy yourself. Norman Weir was here this morning for a few minutes. I am very tired tonight as one of our officers was not well last night and I had to take his place. So I shall close.

You might send a pair of heavy gloves (and some candy?) We are revelling in mud these days but I have rubber waders and keep fairly clean. Let me hear from you soon. No mail tonight.

Your own
Stuart

It took only one tour in the trenches to convince him that he needed the revolver that he had relinquished at Shorncliffe, and he added a Colt .45 to his list of requests. Sending packages across the channel was an easy matter, but a revolver posed some problems. Edna's hours at the Pay Office precluded her shopping, so Sgt. Williams's wife Mary tried to buy the .45 for Stuart at Gamages; they refused to sell it to her, but agreed to ship it to him in France.[7]

FRANCE, NOVEMBER 1, 1916

Dearest:—

Never mind the paper as I can write just as well on signallers paper as on Vellum. Still it will intimate to you that I am out of writing material.

I was out of the trenches yesterday, i.e. behind the lines attending a gas school. We left about 12 reached there at 2 p.m. and reached home by 6. It was a long walk but very interesting. I met Mr. Yule and had a long talk with him about his experiences on the Somme. He was with Bert Scott on the 15th September but very luckily was taken off and sent to a grenade school. . . . I came back with Major Piper, Co F Commander and the M.O. [Medical Officer], a very fine fellow. When I was at the M.O.'s Norman Weir came in to see him, had a bit of a cold. He was sent out to the hospital. It is nothing serious probably something like I had at Sarcee. . . .

As I had had a good deal of walking yesterday I took my tour of duty last. I was just coming back when Fritz started up a fine row with rifle grenades, a terrific noise. It really was a joke for nothing happened and nobody paid any attention to it.

I wish you would raise cain with H.E. Randall. I was pretty mad yesterday when I had to walk 8 or 10 miles with rubber boots on. As it was I was dirty as a pig as I did not get warned in time to clean up. However you get used to dirt. If you can wash and have a shave once every other day, you are lucky. But those Randall people have let me down and its rotten. My feet were in good condition and I do not like to have them become otherwise.

I am sorry you suffer from the cold and have a cold. Surely you can heat your room up in some way and don't forget that warm clothes help to keep you warm. There is really very little to tell this morning. I am very tired anyway and you won't get a satisfactory letter till we get out which will be Friday night. By the way I don't believe I am going to get a revolver here. Do you think you could get me one in London. Try to anyway. A Colt preferably. Of course I shall have to have ammunition. I was delighted needless to say to get your letters of the 26th and 27th.

I almost forgot the purpose of this letter, which was to wish you many happy returns of the day. Too bad honey I can't send you anything. I am thinking of you though dear. . . .

Now to bed after reading my Bible. I carry it in my inside pocket, honey. God bless and keep you.

Your own

Stuart

Stuart received some news from a colleague in Edmonton which he shared in the following letter. His R.B.B. reference to is to R. B. Bennett, the future prime minister, who was then a powerful Conservative representing Calgary in the Alberta provincial parliament.

FRANCE, NOVEMBER 5, 1916

My Dearest own:—

I had two letters last night, the second one being handed to me at supper.... [I]magine my pleasure in... knowing that my revolver was on the way. I don't mind telling you now that I felt nervous last week when in [the trenches]. We had a fairly long line and it was lonely patrolling. I tried carrying a rifle but it was too cumbersome particularly when floundering in the mud. Please thank Mrs. Williams most cordially for her trouble.

Well I guess I have quite a bit of news now that I have the opportunity to tell it. We were relieved night before last but say it was 9:30 before the relieving Company F marched in. I got my pack on at once and beat it off with my platoon. Although the moon was bright I decided to go overland rather than through the communication trenches and although we took a chance it was the only thing to do.... It was a hike of over two miles through the bush but we made it all right. But say I wanted to be down. I had the waders on my feet, my slicker on, a pack with my British warm, books, etc, two smoke helmets, haversack, water bottle, rifle, and walking stick; still it had to be done and I felt happy when we got to our billets and found supper waiting and my bed made up. We are quartered in huts, men in one part, officers in another. Aren't we comfortable. I rolled in without asking any questions either.

The day we came out there was a bit of a show on; it cleared off in the afternoon and a bunch of aeroplanes went up. I don't know what happened but the artillery opened up—not rapid fire, but say it was enough for a new comer. It seemed to be all concentrated on one spot and soon a fire broke out in houses behind the Hun lines. It blazed up furiously as though fed by oil and at times figures could be seen between us and the light. Fortunately it distracted Fritz sufficiently to prevent his evening hymn of minnenwerfers. I think he got an awful drubbing that day with huge H.E. shells. We were not molested in any way during the relief. The fire burned fiercely all night.

Yesterday I was orderly dog. The most onerous duty was the round of the guards which took five hours. It was very interesting as I saw a good deal of the country around here. There are no fences, the country being quite open. The roads are very poor particularly when they are cut up with transport and artillery. It was very interesting to stand on a hill and follow the German lines marked by their flares, the guns roaring at all points from our sides, the explosions of the shells reverberating through the night air. Just where we are the country begins to be cultivated but between us and the Hun it is a waste—ruined villages, shell holes, barbed wire and weeds weeds every where. The evening when I finished was very clear and warm; the whole war seemed more or less summed up in the sights and sounds around.

I don't know that there is very much I can tell you of our tour in the trenches. It was not very hard but the mud is *fierce* underlined sixteen times. We are fairly busy at night and sleep by day. I think I made a fairly favourable impression on our Company Commander, perhaps just by comparison with . . . the other platoon commanders. . . . Both of them are liable to be shunted. I am not a real soldier perhaps, but I try to do the right thing. It really is funny how a man shows up in the trenches. I must admit yet that I duck but you can hardly help it. I really don't mind the life. We feed pretty well and sleep well and you always look forward to coming out. I cannot tell you how your letters comfort me in the trenches. We get mail every evening about 7 o'clock. I look forward to a letter I can tell you, though I only had one every other night. The people at home have absolutely forgotten me. I have not heard for weeks. The same with Philip. . . .

Really honey I am pleased over that revolver, though it has not yet reached me. Several of us in the company are without and really we were given to understand that we could not get them. I am really delighted that you arranged to get it. I am getting an extra pair of boots. My feet were wet all the time I was in the trenches so I am going to try to obviate it by having a change. I shall not wear waders except at night and shall have a change in boots. Socks are simply indispensable. I can usually draw dry socks from the Company Quarter Master but one's feet get wet so often that you need a change sometimes twice a day. The trenches are different from what I expected but not so bad as painted (yet). The M.O. says there is very little sickness among the men and they are all so cheerful. I have seen quite a number of friends from the 89th. Even one man from my old platoon in the 66th. By the way, I am afraid poor Sharon is gone. The boys all say he was missing and nothing has been heard of him. I wish you would write to his wife, dear. I had quite a letter from Barron tonight. He was telling me... that elections were on and that R.B.B. was leading the faithful against the hosts of the Amelekites. You don't hear much of that little corner of the world over here, do you.

Dearest honey, I go to sleep every night thinking of you and of our consecrated love. It bears me up in discouragement and temptation and is my only source of comfort. You have been a darling wife and I am prouder of you than I can ever tell. May you have your reward in time.

I did a very foolish thing today. The paymaster was here and I had him cash a cheque for f128.... I know I am extravagant but I will try to do better. I told you of indenting for some things from the Q.M. but really they are dirt cheap. I have no word yet of boots from Randall. They have surely used me rotten. My feet were badly chafed when I got out of the trenches, but they are better now.

I could write whole chapters to you on the war but will refrain. I trust it will be a good lesson to Britishers the world over. We have been tempting Germany for years to do this sort of thing. Heaven grant that greater ills do not follow.

And now of the future. No one knows, and yet I believe peace is nearer than we realize. If Germany is beaten in Romania I think she will talk of peace before spring. She is being bled white and cannot stand it. I know whereof I speak. There will be a crash next year despite all her bravado.

Well honey dearest, I shall write every day while in billets. Do the same if you can. I need your help.

Good night darling, Your own
Stuart

FRANCE, NOVEMBER 6, 1916

Dearest, dearest Honey:—

Afternoon has come and the leisure to write again and say things that need saying pretty often, that I love you more than ever. My heart goes out to you dearest at all times and I long for your words of encouragement and cheer. Believe me mail is mighty welcome in the trenches, particularly when it comes from one who means so much to you.

I have been speculating of late on the causes of the war and what is likely to be the cause of peace. There is no doubt but the Germans have had enough, but they are owned body and soul by their Kaiser and his clique, [and] that it will be almost impossible to set in motion the forces that will bring an end to it. Germany is beaten, is bled white and yet is forced to go on fighting. They are something like the English, it is deuced hard to persuade them they are beaten. However, I suppose the revelation will come in time. . . .

I am very glad of this time out and to get an opportunity to get my stuff fixed up so I should go into the trenches fixed up. I must though ask you to get a few things yet, notably a battery for my lamp or rather two. It comes in mighty handy I can tell you. Oh I am learning what I need but to tell the truth I came over from England insufficiently equipped. It would have been all right but I was unable to get to the ordnance at Havre. . . . However now that you have got my revolver I feel quite set out. I don't know about ammunition. You did not tell me the calibre, so I shall have to wait till I see it.

I am still getting driblets of letters from Havre. I think I have received three up to date. They come drifting along weeks after, but of course they are none the less welcome. . . . I receive everything within three days as a rule from you. Parcels have to be allowed a bit longer. . . .

Will you feel very hurt when I tell I have determined to burn all your letters. . . . So you need not fear, they will scarcely fall into other hands. As for my letters I censor them myself or get an officer to censor them which means that I assume responsibility that there is nothing military in them. Of course I must be careful just the same; indeed you yourself will admit that I am pretty guarded. . . .

This has been a most unsatisfactory letter as I have been interrupted so often. However I shall try to drop a line tonight or tomorrow. Will there be a letter tonight?

What word have you had from home? Nothing for me. Good night dearest.

Stuart

Later.

I feel as though I must write more. Really if one's mind is open, there is so much to be learned in experiences like this. You find that life takes on nobler colours here where all the false ones drop off like a garment. It would surprise you how many men you find to be right good fellows and how dearly they love their wives. It would do you good to read their letters and see how much they think of the folks at home. Of course there are the other kind. But a man cannot live here without being affected for the better.

... Glad am I that we had these almost two years together, of the many blessed memories and the part you have played in my life. You will probably never know how much I must admit. I had always an ambition to measure up in part to your ideal of me. ...

I was indeed glad to receive the writing paper; though my batman had already swiped some at the Y. I shall be well fixed for most supplies if my boots come. We shall be back in division reserve the end of next week so I expect to enjoy some of the comforts of life. I shall really be glad of the papers and any reading matter though we keep our minds fairly well occupied.

We are fearfully overrun with rats here. They are already prowling around. I only hope I don't get lice. If you can get a preventative I would be grateful. Most of the men are scratching all the time. ...

I have been making inquiries re Sharon but cannot get anything definite. I have heard him variously reported as wounded and killed. ...

... By the way I forgot to bring a diary with me—a hint eh! I have not lost anything yet but am going to look after things well.

Now be good to yourself. ...

Stuart

FRANCE, NOVEMBER 7, 1916

Dearest:—

I don't know when I have felt so disgusted with things (which I suppose are all my own fault) as tonight. My boots have not come from Randalls, there was no mail, I got my revolver but no ammunition and find I can't get it. I am going into the trenches as badly off as I came out. I don't know what to do about boots unless I can get away [to Bethune—crossed out] but as I have already indented for a pair from ordnance I don't like to load up. I am not blaming you for any of these things but I do feel that everything has gone wrong. I was particularly disappointed that there was no letter either tonight or last night. I was tickled to get the chocolate which really is good. ...

I had a letter from Philip last night also one from Jentie. Jentie's was full of all the casualties and was not very cheering. Philip said he had not received mine though it is over ten days since I wrote him. Your letters seem very short dear. I don't know whether you are vexed with me or not. I suppose I have asked a good deal of you, but do you know you are absolutely cut off from the world here. Today I have not been outside the hut hardly—rain and wind and cold—no papers, no magazines, no letters. . . .

I really have absolutely nothing to tell. We are so shut in here, nothing to see or hear but the guns, and how they do roar, particularly at night. Fritz must be having a terrible time these days. But the rain and the mud. Our meals are our only variation. I am going to try and vary them, get as good meals as we can to keep up our courage.

Now you must not mind my peevishness tonight because it is not personal. . . . This life gets on your nerves in a lot of ways. I really get more fed up on the coarseness than on the hardships. I don't like to talk of these things but believe me contact with European ways is going to do our boys a lot of harm. It will be many a year before we recover from it. I think they might very well keep back part of the officers' pay. It would be a mighty good thing I believe. Oh honey I need you to talk these things over with. I don't meet many congenial spirits here I can tell you, but of course we are soldiering.

Now I haven't asked about your little self and about Mrs. Williams. You seem not to be very well satisfied, overworked in fact. Don't take it too seriously and for heaven's sake don't work too hard. It simply will not pay.

Janet had a lot of apologies to make for mother which of course did no good. It made me feel inexpressibly sad and disheartened with life as I have not felt in a long time.

Well, honey, write soon and don't forget to think of me a little.

> Your own,
> Stuart

An afternoon's leave and a trip into Bethune did much to improve Stuart's depressed state of 7 November, and not even difficulty in securing ammunition could dent his good humour. The following letter contains one of many indications that the army experience assailed his Canadian innocence and propriety.

Dearest:—

You will observe the new paper. From that if you are a Sherlock Holmes you will infer that I have been to town and blown a bunch of money. . . . Seeing that my London shoemaker has let me down, it behooved me to bestir myself for a pair of shoes so I got leave and went to town. The name of the place for obvious reasons must remain unspoken. Suffice it to say that permission having been applied for and given, I borrowed a wheel from the signallers at Brigade Headquarters and set off in the rain. The latter cleared off and I had a nice run in over the cobblestone roads, through several towns and villages. I arrived about 11:30 and decided to make my purchases before lunch as I was not hungry. The first place I attempted was a shoe store. A nice little French lassie waited on me and insisted on my essaying the bouties [sic] and lacing them herself. She also took it on herself to point out the hole in the sock, no not in the toe my dear. I pointed out that I had no wife now to darn them. She then remarked on the curiosity of the children looking in at her at her unwonted task. When I cut the string on a box of boots for her, she remarked, "Tous les canadiens sont tres aimable" sic. This very effective flattery induced me to buy a pair of bouties at quarant franc—eight dollars—nothing cheap. I tried to get some ammunition for my revolver, a clothes brush, soap etc etc. I was absolutely unable to buy any ammunition for my revolver so my dear I shall have to ask you to send it along with an extra clip. I am very sorry. I thought I mentioned it. If the revolver had been a .45 I could have drawn ammunition from the stores but with the .38 I shall have to buy it.

. . . After making the rounds of the town. . . I landed up at the [censored] Club for lunch. It is a real club but a non member can get lunch, so I was informed by an "out since Mons" Seaforth Highland Sergeant with a burr that would stick in your throat. I had lunch in French style—hors d'oeuvres of four kinds, fish, veal, bread, butter and coffee. Each course I thought was the end of the meal but I kept on, bravely. It certainly was a fine place and I did my part. I had a bit more shopping to do so did not get away till three. (I spent over an hour at lunch). Just as I started it began to rain. I got on the wrong road and had to cut across to the right road and then it came on worse. Then in spite of the wet I developed a fearful thirst and had to stop to get a drink at a town half way. A very nice French girl waited on me but I had to go on. The rain let up just as I got into Bde. H.Q. and I was glad to get off the wheel and walk home. . . . The trip gave me a nice break and was a good test to my French. It would certainly improve if I had more of an opportunity to use it.

Well, we go into the trenches tomorrow but we will be in support so I guess we will be not badly off. So you needn't worry, if only I get the ammunition before we go up in the front line.

. . . I tried frantically to get papers today but they were not to be had—also no mail. I should have died if I had stayed here. I certainly hope it is not raining when we come here next. Quite a number of our lads arrived yesterday. . . . There was a little family reunion out here tonight. My old sergeant Gilbert and the band. They seemed to [be] glad to be here.

I think I shall have to send my watch back to get repaired. It has fallen down on me. If it is going to cost a lot to fix it I wouldn't pay it. I can get along with an Ingersoll. I tried to buy one today but—nothing doing.

We have had a new arrival in the company—a Captain Blair who has been at Corps HQ. He spent some time in Germany and in addition to being a soldier is something of a man of the world. His opinion of German[s] will hardly bear publication. Really, honey, it has just come to this that we are at the parting of the ways; and if Germany wins, we go her way to moral dissolution. On the new order of things which would be set up there would be no such thing as tender sentiments, purity or uprightness. Everything would be valued according to what it would do for the state or the physical pleasure it would give. To think that we would throw aside all restraint imposed by finer sentiments and our higher nature and simply follow our natural instincts; wouldn't it be horrible, or is it that we have been brought up wrong and all our training is in the reverse direction.

He cited instances of German women, shocking even Englishmen with their amazing animalism. I think I am made of clay similar to other men but there is something in that that horrifies anyone no matter how coarse. Won't I be glad to get back to Canada where our women are pure and straightforward and honest and where men know they have got to play square with the other sex.

Well I cannot write more tonight as I am tired and there will be a lot to do tomorrow. Goodnight dearest. God bless you.

Ever your own,
Stuart

In the following letter Stuart mentioned Maconochie, a canned concoction that usually consisted of sliced carrots and turnips in a thin gravy; its great virtue was that it provided respite from canned corned beef or bully-beef as it was known among British troops.[8] When the premature report of the victory of Charles Evans Hughes in the 1916 United States presidential election reached the trenches, it produced little reaction from an obvious Roosevelt admirer; later letters show that it might have been otherwise had the actual victor been known, because Stuart grew increasingly impatient and disgusted with the policies of Woodrow Wilson.

FRANCE, NOVEMBER 9, 1916

Darling:—

Once more in the line. We were up bright and early this morning with the sun shining as he has not done for weeks, and making a desperate attempt to undo the work of the recent rains. A battalion can move very easily out here as one finds. Our Lares and Penates disappeared by magic; packs were made ready, lunch was served and we were off. The weather was perfect but warm and before long I was dripping with perspiration. But one just goes on and pretends he enjoys it. We had not many hitches despite mud and water and now we are installed in the support trenches. Didn't supper taste good—we had a "Mulligan" made from what they call Maconochie's—[and] a dried preparation, compote of fruit that tasted for all the world like tear gas. Later in the evening we had coffee made over the kerosene stove so really we are not so much to be pitied. Our duties are not so strenuous as before and I shall have lots of leisure—at least a moderate amount of leisure. Our quarters are comfortable although the water does manage to trickle through a little. Still we have no reason to complain. . . . If only one has lots of fuel inside and outside the rest is tolerable at least. By the way that chocolate came in fine tonight. When we came in hungry waiting for supper a few discs did wonders to brighten things up. Our culinary arrangements are not perfect but are improving.

I was so disappointed tonight to receive no mail. I think it is the fourth night, not even a scratch. . . . We have not seen a newspaper for nearly a week. I heard them being cried about breakfast time so chased one of the batmen out. The result was we had a regular carnival of reading for a while. Still there was nothing important in it. We did learn later from the Paris papers of the election of Hughes. There has been quite a stir about it but it can make no difference in this war. If only it were T. R. eh? Did you hear anything of the elections in Alberta. I wonder if my job will be waiting for me. What think you?

I have been thinking of you today, constantly and of our life together. It hardly seems possible that it is almost two years since we were married. I often wonder why the experiences of courtship and marriage stand out so in one's life. I suppose it is not because they are so intense but rather because they mark a crisis, the end of one epoch and the beginning of another. How clearly I remember everything— .... You have taught me the deep and abiding power of affection and loyalty.... [O]ut of the age long yearnings and strivings of humanity two souls cleave together each finding in the other... a trusted fellow voyager and companion for all his thoughts with whom his richest experiences can be shared, to whom his closest confidence can be given, the perfect love that casteth out fear, that mocks at death, that challenges destiny. Oh, my love, how much do I owe you!...

Could you guess that it is almost 1 a.m. and that I am on duty till 3. It is getting beastly cold owing to some confusion about bringing up the coke. I hope it will be remedied tomorrow, for we can at least be warm. The army you see furnish coke which is burned in braziers in the trenches, the idea being of course to prevent smoke. As I sit here, the rats are having a midnight carousal. They start without waiting for the human occupants to retire. We have a little dog around but he is busier sleeping just now than chasing rats. I do hope they don't prowl around my face. It will drive me mad if they do.

I am really ashamed of the number of things I have asked of you. I am an extravagant and selfish individual I know. I am going to get along without things for a while. Our mess fees I may say are quite light. While in the trenches, they are next to nothing. When we are out they amount to about two francs a day. Of course if we were close to town they would be more for one can buy very few things around here. The Y.M.C.A. have numerous canteens also there are a number of B.E.F. canteens everywhere. As far as articles for wear go, the French stock a great many English articles; you see the country is dominated by British troops.

I have been wondering about Christmas. I looked in the shops yesterday but I fear you will have to go presentless. I'll have to write you a particularly long letter. I hope though you have not forgotten my request for a photo—one of those you know in a case for carrying in your pocket. Nothing could give me greater pleasure.

You will be interested in knowing that our bandsmen are on sentry tonight and not a bit pleased either. They will be in the front line, I suppose, till their instruments come. . . .

Well goodbye sweetheart. Don't forget to write.

Your own
Stuart

FRANCE, NOVEMBER 11, 1916

Dearest:—

I have been used most shamefully or else there is something radically wrong. Again the mail came in last night and nothing for me. . . . I can't understand it.

Yesterday was a lovely day; one of the rare days of real weather such as we have in Alberta and it had a wonderful effect on the spirit of the men. They worked with a will and the trenches underwent a transformation. You can now get about almost every where. I was out quite a bit and was pretty tired when supper came so after our steak etc. I climbed to my upper Pullman, lay and read for a while and then went to sleep, since when I have passed seven hours of slumbering repose. I think the soundness of my sleep was due to the fact that in our portion of the dugout the air lies stagnant and this combines with the effect of smoke and gas from the brazier at the entrance to our room to more or less intoxicate me. However I shall soon go up above and take the air when I shall fill my lungs good and full of the morning breeze. I rather look forward to a turn in the open as the weather is so fine and the moon shining bright. . . . [O]ur dugouts in this part of the line . . . may have been built by the French though of course I don't know. They really are commodious and quite dry but they get musty if you stay in them too much.

Our artillery was a bit lively yesterday and for 15 minutes there was quite a racket. It is quite funny. You really cannot help ducking though you know you are safe.

We saw a paper for the first time in a week on Thursday and managed to get another yesterday. The news continues good or rather is good. I don't suppose there is anything a soldier gets so hungry for as news and of this he gets mighty little. And letters. I don't know how many they get but the number written is legion. I know from having to censor them. Parcels are pretty common, too. They certainly need them to eke out their living. Sox are supplied when in the trenches dry. . . . If only I had those boots; that's what galls me. I think I shall write and cancel the order.

If you want to send anything chocolate is always acceptable. . . . One seems to have a craving for sweets. Then I have lost my little knife and if you see a pen knife cheap, you might send it. I remember using it in town the other day to cut the string on a parcel but it seems to have gone. My watch I shall not send till we get out into reserve again. I tried to buy an Ingersoll to take its place but they don't seem to sell them in France.

Do you know I am getting on fine with the Russian. After while I am going to get a story of some kind and a dictionary and read it. I shall probably learn more that way. I am glad I brought it because otherwise so much time would be merely dawdled away.

Well I am going to read a bit and then turn out so I shall wish you good morning, sweetheart.

As ever yours
Stuart

FRANCE, NOVEMBER 13, 1916

Dear one:—

Still another day without mail. If you knew the state of mind of the occupants of this trench, you would at once take steps to remedy it. The major is grouchy, Captain Blair has had letters so has nothing to say, but Emery and I are both threatening to get divorces. The night after the mail comes in, drags on to day, the day drags on from breakfast to lunch, lunch to dinner and all we live for is the mail we expect (but which does not come; and then we are disappointed.) I pity poor Norman Weir. . . he is worse off than I.

Another day in the trenches. This time the gods have favoured us and the weather is topping. This morning (3 a.m.) I was out for a walk. It can only be described as glorious—a moonlit night with soft sounds and breezes. Even the Boche must have felt its influence as he has been very quiet tonight. . . .

Seriously, dear, I shall become alarmed if I do not hear from you today. It is certainly exceptional whatever the causes. Don't forget to write.

Stuart

Later:

I have been discovering that I have been spending too much money.

There is no use in blinking at facts. To begin with, I travelled in too good company coming over and there were lunches and taxi cabs to pay for. In addition of course there is the revolver, my boots purchased in England, in addition to the pair I purchased in town and a third pair ordered from the ordnance. Also of course I imagine that Philip drew on you, though to what extent I do not know. My expenses in the last month have been

	Pounds	shillings
boots	6	6
expenses, trip	2	
boots	1	6
mess fees	1	6
Revolver	5	
Batman		9
expenses		18
incidentals		15
[total]	18	0

In addition of course are a number of things you bought for me. . . . You have never told me whether you have got a raise or what your expenses are. You know dearest I wouldn't for the world do anything unfair to you and if I have spent lavishly perhaps, I shall not continue it.

I can't tell you how anxiously I am awaiting a letter from you.

Stuart

Stuart's anxiety mounted as days passed with no word from Edna in London, but the news from the Somme afforded him some optimism. The final action there, the Battle of the Ancre, began on 13 November, and it was fought in snow, sleet, rain, and unspeakable mud. While the British had some success, not the least of which was destroying the illusion of German invincibility on the Western Front, one historian has concluded that "At best the five-month campaign that had opened on 1 July with such high expectations had resulted in a costly stalemate."[9] The Canadians who fought at the Ancre rejoined the Canadian Corps on the Lens-Arras front at the end of November.

My own beloved:—

I cannot tell you how anxious I am, another day having passed without word from you. I cannot think it is due to carelessness. All sorts of possibilities have passed before my eyes; yet my mind is in a chaos. . . . Do you know a whole carload of mail came in last night—letters and parcels galore and never a one for me. . . . I cannot think the mail service is disturbed for there was so much mail in. Surely you will let me know what is amiss.

The weather has been ideal in the trenches. Two whole days were bright and sunny. The wild geese have been flying over. Yesterday was one of those golden autumn days with that mellow peaceful light over all the world. It was hard to believe we were at war. Today one of the men brought down a goose with a rifle, quite a shot eh.

It is quite strange in here at times. When you get up in the morning everything peaceful and quiet, sometimes the stars shining with their heavenly light, all the mystic influences of nature throw their subtle spell over you, and all the trammels of civilization are thrown off. I have never been very religious. Still one cannot help thinking hard as never before and coming to a clear realization of things vague and indistinct before. But you don't want to hear all this. One needs to be here to appreciate it.

Will there be mail tonight. . . . I feel very lazy today and beyond my usual attention to Russian, not very much doing. . . .

We heard last night of the further good news from the Somme. I tell you, it bucked us all up and made us throw out our chests. We don't discuss the war here very much of course. You feel too amateurish. Well, good bye, honey, look after yourself and let me hear from you.

Your own as ever,

Stuart

My Dear:—

. . . Honey, dearest, I can't tell how delighted I was with the parcel I got last night. We got here about 5:30 footsore and weary and hungry. . . . But when two parcels came, it sort of made things seem different. The gloves are simply great. I wasn't quite sure whether I could credit you with knitting them or not but they are certainly the finest thing I have seen. The glove problem is one of the most difficult ones there is. Then the socks. I must admit I like fine socks and I have enjoyed having them on. Are they your work? You see I got my new boots last night and with the new socks they go swell. The boots are certainly everything I expected. They are absolutely a perfect fit. The leather appears to be the very best and they sure look swell—almost too swell for the trenches but I shant wear them in deep mud. One has to use waders then. I have been wondering whether they are worth the price but when I think of the comfort I have had all day I believe I was right. Really they are fine.

Emery got a box of knick knacks—cakes and things so we had a feast of reason and flow of soul, and on top of them the cigarettes. I am getting to be a creature of carnal desires but dearest, it is all we have to think of so don't blame us. Captain Blair who recently joined us as 2nd in command of Co. F is away today buying up eatables. He is going to lay in a supply for two weeks. We expect to live well anyway.

Blair is a very fine fellow—an Englishman, too. He received part of his education in Germany, finished in England, joined the Guards and later went to Canada to follow his profession (mining engineer). He is very sensible and curses the Englishmen for their prejudices and stupidity. He thinks a great deal of his wife.

Goodbye,

Your own, *Stuart*

The satisfaction of having finally received letters and the long awaited boots warmed him even though the weather had turned very cold. The prospect of Edna's joining him on leave in Paris, although remote, helped Stuart's morale, and he felt optimistic enough to suggest that she quit her job in the Army Pay Office where she now worked an additional hour a day at no extra pay.

Politics, military decisions, his lack of administrative ability, and his own style finally caught up with Sir Sam Hughes. The headstrong minister of militia triggered his dismissal with a letter to the prime minister that bordered on insubordination in which he protested the appointment of Sir George Perley as minister of overseas military forces from Canada in the United Kingdom. Borden requested Hughes's resignation and received it on 11 November 1916.[10]

Dearest:—

You will wonder at the abrupt termination of my last letter written just before the mail went out. . . . I chopped it off in order to get it off.

I cannot say that our stay in reserve is an unalloyed pleasure. The weather turned very cold the night we came out. I have not slept any too warm at night but thanks to a generous supply of fuel and a brazier I expect to do better tonight. There was almost half an inch of ice on the water in the shell holes.

Funny that this weather does not seem to hurt your health. . . . I have been out for a bit of exercise today and am feeling fine. Yesterday Captain Blair went off to a neighbouring village to buy grub. It is a stiff 3 hours walk and although he got several lifts, it was 9 o'clock when he got back. He carried two packs full of provisions, so we expect to live high for a while. I should have gone but they do not allow many away at once.

I was very pleased to get your letter of Sunday. Do you know there have been rumours of a great air raid on London. I do not believe it but it can't help but make me anxious. I shall look for letters to reassure me.

I cannot tell you how pleased I am with the gloves. I wore them all day and they certainly are warm, the warmest yet. The socks too were fine and I am sure you would be delighted to see my new boots. I am certainly a swell in them. . . .

I went down to see Norman Weir this morning but he was not in. There is always quite a bit of fussing to do when we get out so I suppose he was away on duty. I wonder if he has yet heard from Mrs. Weir.

I don't know how I manage to spin out my letters, but there seems a good deal to tell somehow. It would be very interesting to take you around the ruined villages and defences—miles and miles and miles of them. Captain Blair says he is going to take his wife around through the ruined districts after the war, provided he has the money. Wasn't that splendid news from the Somme front. We can hear the guns warring continuously for days at a time, though we never know when an attack is on. Does it presage something big. Who knows? We hope and pray it does. Do you know I have been tempted to ask you whether you would like to spend a leave with me in Paris. It can be arranged, i.e. from my point of view. Let me know what you think of it. . . . Of course I know I have laid out a lot of money lately re boots, revolver etc etc. Why not arrange to drop what you are at if we can afford it. You are not getting any further ahead where you are and apparently you are going to have to work harder for what you get. Did you get that promised raise on November 1st. You never told me. What do you think of Sam Hughes' resignation. I guess there is a lot leading up to it. Sir George Perley is possibly responsible for the extra hour. . . .

I must try to get this letter off tonight. Be sure to write a long letter and let me know how you are. I am sorry the folks at home have neglected you. Look after yourself.

As ever your own
Stuart

FRANCE, NOVEMBER 18, 1916

Dearest:—

Another letter last night. One written on the 14th so I really have been in luck. I feel life is worth living once more. . . . I also got a parcel from the ordnance containing one or two articles I had requisitioned— another shirt, a scarf and a pair of gloves—. . . all for 4 shillings. The scarf is good for tying around my head at night. I have been mighty lucky all the way round seeing that the weather has turned cold once more. . . . The weather reminds me of Alberta, the ground covered with snow, the water all frozen, the ground hard. I was really cold at night and am already thinking of having that quilted blanket sent out. . . .

It is strange how ones point of view alters with regard to the relative importance of things here. Nothing bulks so large to the mind of the soldier as the mail. True he is not allowed to tell of anything more important but his letters are full of questions of home, of the letters he received, how he is, but nothing of military matters. In fact after a time he ceases discussing them except very occasionally.

I do hope you can do something about getting me ammunition. I don't like to send the pistol back to try to exchange it for I might not be able to get a .45—but of course it is useless till I get ammunition. At present I have a borrowed one, so you need not worry. . . .

I keep thinking of you constantly these days and wondering how you are. I do hope you will not have occasion to regret having come

over. You must not overwork because it is of no use; you have better
things to do with your energies.

It is amusing work to censor the letters out here. I am afraid our
good Canadian soldiers have the art of getting around girls. Some are
making love to half a dozen and I am sure they have no other purpose
than securing parcels. Bill Emery is absolutely shameless, receives letters from at least a dozen (most of them women) and parcels; he has
had three since we came out and two more coming. . . .

I cannot tell you how I appreciate the things you have sent me. You
can ship along as many pairs of sox like the last as you want. The
boots are fine and I am the envy of the regiment. I want to thank you
especially for that Bible. It is a great source of comfort to me being as
it is a book for great crises. You realize as you read it how great the
struggles through which the human heart has passed on the upward
path and how it has by some strange Providence won through in spite
of man and devil. This world is a queer mixture. The mystery deepens,
the longer one lives and yet one is, at least I am, forced back on the belief in a loving Father. Am I right?

Well I must not write more just now as I have things to do—a bed to
rig up etc etc. I hope to be comfy tonight. Will there be a letter
tonight? Remember me to Mrs. Williams. God bless you dearest.

Your own
Stuart

FRANCE, NOVEMBER 19, 1916

Dearest:—

I received two delightful letters written on the 13th and 15th respectively. Needless to say I read the last one first, according to scrip-
ture; your remarks re myself and my needs duly noted; that I should
command such loyalty and service from you is indeed a matter of pride
and also humility. . . . I know I have asked a lot from you in the last
month. I can tell you one thing that you need have no doubt as to
whether I appreciate what has been done. Everything done has been a
matter of exquisite joy to me.

You I am sure are aware that I never neglect you. Ah dear one, you
know that I am the lover first and cannot but be filled with thoughts of
you. Never do I drop off to sleep in my dugout without thinking first
of you and what you are doing. Never do I wake without your face going before me. . . .

So you think you know where we are do you? Well I shall not sat-isfy your curiosity by telling you whether you are right or wrong. I must not dally with the censor. Your failure to get ammunition fills me with peculiar rage at English methods. Why should Gamages sell a re-volver and then refuse to sell ammunition for it. I am therefore going to suggest this. I shall enclose a letter to Gamages telling them the sit-uation and asking them either to sell me the ammunition or let me have a .45 in place of it. Meanwhile I will retain the .38 till I find out what you can do. If necessary pay or give a deposit for the .45 pending the return of the .38. I can send the latter home by some one. But I must do something right away. I have a weapon but it is borrowed and as you can imagine, one should not be in the front line without one. Do you understand. Present that alternative in most pungent terms. Point out that a revolver is of no use without ammunition and as I can-not get .38 am. around here the alternative is to let me have the other for which I can obtain ammunition. *Also* in any case get at least *one* ex-tra clip and if possible a lanyard. I can use my present holster till I get a chance to get a better. . . .

You needn't worry about me. I take no chance with things. . . .

I know I have asked a lot of you. Like Bassanio I know from the past I can count on you. . . . Good bye dearest.

As ever yours
Stuart

FRANCE NOVEMBER 20, 1916
[NO. 1]

Dearest:—

Just a line tonight to reassure you. I have a great pile of letters to censor, consequently I have an evening's work for me. There was no mail last night at all. Connections missed somewhere so I am busy wondering whether I shall have one tonight. It is beastly depressing when nothing comes. By the way re ammunition. In case it cannot be got at Gamages, I understand that it can be bought at The London Armoury . . . the agents of the Colt people in London. I will enclose a letter which you can mail if you prefer; they can send it to me and send the bill to you. How will that be?

Today has been lovely. I was out a good deal of the time and among other things had a bath. I certainly enjoyed it immensely. It is wonder-ful how well one keeps at this work. By the way I went over to see

Norman Weir yesterday. He was out, however, and I learned today he went to see his brother. . . . We have no news to speak of although we get papers as late as yesterdays.

Well dearest I must close for tonight to get this off with the mail. Good luck and God bless you.

Your own
Stuart

FRANCE, NOVEMBER 20, 1916
[NO. 2]

Dearest:—

How can I resist writing to you before I roll in tonight. I am in bed with a candle perched on a beer keg at my elbow, the Spectator lying read beside my bed, and a dandy comfy fire burning in the fire place just three feet away in the corner. Without can be heard the rumble of transport along the road; the sound of voices has just died away and my ears are still ringing with the thunder of the guns (ours) firing into the German lines—first the deep reverberating note from their throats, the rush of the shell like a train through space and then far off the explosion. But it does not affect me. I sit here in comfort. The only disturbance has been a big rat who without waiting till I blew out my light and went to sleep slipped through the partition and was just starting across my bed when I caught him with my eagle eye. I grabbed my stick but he had already gone. Do you know a few minutes ago I heard a bugle sounding "Last Post," the only bugle call I have heard near the front line. . . .

Do you know I am getting on very well with Russian. Someday I am going to ask you to get me a Russian dictionary a small one and a Russian novel paper. Size is an important consideration. I am making an effort to get the fundamentals of the language down and will learn the rest later by reading. . . .

Well honey I shall not write more tonight but will close. I try to write at least once a day but you will probably not hear every day. I shall be reduced to field post cards at times. Be good to yourself and let me hear about all you are doing.

Your lover and husband
Stuart

Tuesday November 21st—a bright and beautiful morning. I got up without waiting for my batman and started my own fire. . . . By the way I am out of shaving soap. If you are sending a parcel some time you might send something in that line. A small tube of shaving cream would be the very thing. . . . I fear I cannot write more. I have a lot of letters I ought to write. I have been writing to Rev. Mittamillon [in Edmonton]. His son was killed in France.

Wednesday November 22nd.

Everything fine, am feeling a little tough as sleep was curtailed. Had a letter last night from you dated November 17th also one from Jentie. I believe I forgot to thank you for the Times you sent. No word of parcels yet. By the way I meant to ask you if you knew of some simple prescription for taking out iron stains. These corrugated iron roofs sweat and leak and my tunics are stained with the drip. This is merely a request for suggestions.

Well I shall close to get this off. Good luck. May there be a letter tonight.

Stuart

FRANCE, NOVEMBER 24, 1916

Dearest:—

Just a few lines before going to press so to speak it. I am in charge this p.m. and more or less by myself. The weather has been quite fine in fact superfine and I have been feeling very well. I received last night your letter of the 20th inst. also the package of Times which were gratefully received. We had a paper today announcing the sinking of the Britannie. I saw her on the way over do you know—a fine beautiful ship. The loss of life does not seem to have been great. . . .

I am going to return your mother's letter. . . .

Your mother seems quite cheerful. They worry more about the war though at home than we do here. Do you know the men go about with the shells flying over quite unconcernedly. It is quite funny. I don't think I should be giving anything away in saying that the most of the shells we receive here are trench mortar shells if that conveys anything to you. Minnenwerfers as Fritz calls them. We have seen several small bombardments (of our own). At close range, they are something to see.

You must not wonder, dear, if my inspiration runs out at times. I do not work in my sleep very well and I feel pretty tired during the day. You can't very well sleep when there is a show on. I wish I had more news but you know it is from you the news must come as I have not. I am mighty glad of those Times for they give you an idea what is doing. Am I to expect another parcel. I am not sure yet. My boots are fine. I am well satisfied. They are warm, comfortable and look well. The only fly in the ointment is that one gets so muddy—even my hair. We were short of water for a day or two but now I wash and shave once a day whether I need it or not.

Goodbye dearest

Yours ever

Stuart

6

Further Impressions
Transfer to the Trench Mortars

In November Stuart transferred into the Trench Mortar battery that would be his assignment for the rest of his time in France, and the move improved his lot in life. Trench mortars were located far enough in reserve to be housed in deeper and more spacious dugouts, and in this new battery Stuart was out of the trenches and in French billets more often than he had been in his former infantry unit. In the following letter he managed a somewhat optimistic note about the war's progress, even in the aftermath of the heavy losses on the Somme and of Germany's November successes in Romania.

FRANCE, NOVEMBER 27, 1916

Dearest:—

You will be surprised to know that temporarily at least I have changed my berth and am now attached to the 6th Canadian Brigade Trench Mortar Battery. Of course when you get used to it abbreviations will do. I was given orders late night before last and came out yesterday afternoon—.... We are in very comfortable quarters here and I had a dandy sleep last night in a borrowed bed, not disturbed to any extent by the din of the guns. We had a good breakfast this morning and as the weather is glorious today I am feeling pleased with myself. I know I am going to like the work fine and am going to work hard at it. I have been quite disappointed about mail recently. Last night the mail was late, night before there was scarcely any, so I sent the batman across to the horse lines to get it if possible. I am hoping not only for letters but for a parcel.

I think I am quite fortunate in getting here. We are out of the trenches more and our billets are really good. Just now I am writing on what looks like a real walnut table and before a real grate fire. The officer whose place I am taking did not make good.

Now for news. On coming here I was introduced to a Mr. Watson... from Strathcona, ex-manager of Bank of Commerce. So I gently asked him if he knew you and gradually broke the news that we were married. Wasn't it strange. He was *really* delighted to meet me not for myself of course, recalled skating with you and asked about Dick Spilsted [a mutual friend]. So I was able to give him information. Watson came out last September was down on the Somme, so has seen more fighting than I. Of course he asked to be remembered to you.

Things don't look very bright these days do they. Of course I can't tell you of progress here but we are much better off than people realize. As soon as we choose to exert our full power, you just watch.

I wish people would write a little more. A letter from home never comes except about once a month. Philip never writes and all our friends back home have forgotten. I wish I could tell you of things out here but I must be careful. No I don't think leave will come my way at Christmas probably not till January or February. You never said what you thought about that Paris business. Well good bye honey. Look after yourself.

Your own
Stuart

During the war English women assumed roles previously denied them in industry, commerce, and agriculture. Stuart Tompkins, for one, saw it a patriotic sacrifice and he was pleased and proud that his wife contributed to the war effort by freeing a Canadian soldier from office duty to fight at the front. In the following somewhat pessimistic letter he touched on the matter of women workers and his growing concern about the abuse of alcohol.

FRANCE, NOVEMBER 28, 1916

Dearest:—

I believe I should have written this morning in order to ensure getting this off today but as it happened I was out this morning having my teeth attended to. Do you know they have been aching pretty constantly and I took the first opportunity that offered to visit a dentist. He assured me there was nothing wrong with the teeth, but the gums are affected.... One of the officers called it piereia [pyorrhea] or something of the kind. He cleaned my teeth and gave me some tablets for the purpose....

I was very much interested in the letters received from home. I presume that it will not be worth while to send the letters back as you have read them. I think I shall write a short letter to Harry. It tickles me to read your father's comment on the rivalry between Zeta and Harry. Your mother's letter made good reading. She certainly is as solicitous on our behalf as if we were her own children. I must find time to write them all before Christmas.

I have been thinking over the matter of presents and intended to go to town tomorrow and try to make some purchases. I think however I shall leave it in your hands to buy a few cards and send to our friends with greetings from both of us. If I get a chance to buy something really worth while I will but it is difficult and I don't wish to buy any rubbish. I hope the parcels the people from home have promised me don't all come at once or some of the contents are liable to be wasted.... If I am with the T.M.B. [Trench Mortar Battery] it will be all right, as we have our own billets and things do not have to be packed around. Do you know the mail has come and with it nothing from you....

I see by the papers that poor Dodsworth has been killed. You remember our tippling friend from Medicine Hat who got his whole platoon out one night when they were searching the camp for liquor. One of the last times I was in London, I met him at Charing Cross Station. He was drunk as could be, had lost his ticket and didn't know what to do with himself....

I see quite an appeal in this mornings Chronicle on the drink question. It was started apparently by the Toronto Globe and pretty well expresses the feeling of Canadians in this respect. Really the war must teach them some wholesome truths. When will they rise and throw out these brewery-ridden prelates and aristocrats. There are thousands of fine highminded Englishmen in the war but they are being sacrificed on the field of battle for the others. There is a long appeal in one of the recent Times for women workers. I hope it will lead them to investigate the whole question of women. I am glad you are doing something to release a man for the front. I could not be satisfied if you were not. Will they all buckle to now or have we got to go on another year carrying a useless load.

Well this is not as encouraging a letter as it ought to be. I am surely feeling fine and am more comfortable than in the trenches. Do you know the first night out I went to sleep before the fire in a chair.

Now little girl I can't tell you how much your letters buoy me up. I think of you all the time and what your trust and love mean to me. So cheer up. We have had a lot out of life and are seeing more in our few years than the average span of human life would be....

Well good night Honey, I am looking forward tonight to supper....

Your own
Stuart

FRANCE, NOVEMBER 29, 1916
[NO. 1]

Dearest:—

... I went this morning to the place where the battalion [the 31st] are in billets to collect a little money. I did not envy them I can tell you in their huts without fuel. On the way I called in at a British battery and met several of the artillery officers. Fine fellows they are, too. One of them sent an escort with me part way over to the billets. It made just a nice morning stroll; I was back in good time for lunch. It was very disagreeable for walking. There was no well defined road and the weather was wretched—a thick cold damp mist—almost impenetrable. I am not anxious to go out again.

Yesterday we bought some chestnuts and they are on the mantle ready to roast whenever we feel like one. I enjoy them very much. They are not unlike potatoes when roasted. They pop something like corn.

... I am sorry we are so hard up that you cannot take a rest. I know it has meant a lot of expense to have me over here. I am sorry that it has been so.... By the way you might let me know how finances stand. I really have not much idea. I wrote Harry quite a long letter last night. Someday I am going to try to get some souvenirs for him but until I know the ropes it will be difficult. I should like to buy some little things for your people, but in case I cannot get into town I wish you would do so. They have become very dear to me. . . .

I was quite touched by your mother's idea of the children praying for me. Without irreverence, I don't think that I will be left and others taken for any selfish reason on my part. Nor am I a fatalist. The other day when a few bombs came over as we were coming out, my batman said "I don't think there's much use in dodging them, if they have your number on." As a matter of fact that is wrong for in the case of the larger bombs you can actually get out of their way. Still I have confidence in an all wise Providence who is ready to receive us when we are tired of all this bloodshed and cruelty. I wonder if ever Christ will come again to turn our feet into the way of peace. How much longer are men at the bidding of a single man going to fly at one another's throats. It is distressing. . . . It is painful even to think of the future. If only the times would call forth what is best instead of what is worst. But lying, graft and other things are rampant. I have seen a lot and heard a lot since coming over here, and have been distressed beyond words at the standards our Canadian officers have set for themselves, though they know they may step off into eternity at any time. The sins of the old army are being perpetuated into the new on the plea that such things are justified in time of war. Truth to tell I think it is because they have found the English women easy conquests. There may have been a relaxing of old standards due to the influx, but when I hear the stories told it fills me with horror that women could be so easily seduced—pardon the word. When every woman you know is the soul of honour, it almost seems as though our world was tumbling about our ears and we were on the way back to the Oriental conceptions of women. Surely it is not so easy to betray them as some would lead you to believe, you know better than I. . . .

Well honey it is getting dark and I do not want to light the lamp. I should like to get a bath soon if that were possible but baths are scarce. . . .

Well, look after yourself. God bless you.

Stuart

FRANCE, NOVEMBER 30, 1916

Dearest:—

Now what do you think I was doing tonight. Mr. Watson and I have been sitting across from one another in our dugout preening and adorning our persons for the morrow. The Trench Mortar people have less time to themselves during the day than the infantry so I decided to do it tonight. One of the boys bought me some blades in town yesterday.

It is hardly possible to realize that tomorrow is the first of December, but such is the case and just a little over three weeks till Christmas. The boys have all got their "big pay" as they call it and will be sending little mementoes home. It is not very cold here, though the dampness is oppressive. Still we manage to get along all right.

Maxey [his batman] has just come in to say that there is no mail. I am going to put up a holler about that parcel. I am disappointed about it all right. I really do need one or two things and if they are lost in the mails it is pretty raw. Any one who would take such things is a rotter, but I suppose there must be somebody to do it. Tonight when Maxey was going out I sent a Field Post Card for fear I should not be able to send a letter. I am not in a mood for letter writing tonight as I am tired and cold and there is no letter for me.

I think I shall close just now. Good night good luck and God bless you.

Your own
Stuart

FRANCE, DECEMBER 1, 1916

Dearest:—

Just a line to let you know that all has gone well for the day and I am hoping soon to turn in to my downy cot. I had a good sleep last night in the dugout, cold and all as it was, but I rolled up in my blankets and stuck my head under them. Thank goodness we don't have to go out at night but can stay in till breakfast next morning. There was no mail last night and I guess I turned in pretty grumpy. We do not get our mail as regularly as they do in the infantry for obvious reasons, but I am hoping we get it tonight.

Watson is sitting across from me making a candlestick out of chalk. You see in these deep dugouts you have to burn artificial light all the time. Nearly all the dugouts have chalk candlesticks.

I think I made a find when I got Maxey. He came into the trenches with us and has been doing our cooking, steak and onions, stews, Welsh rarebit. It is mighty fine for us for my stomach feels about 100% better. I am really feeling fine now and hope it keeps up. The day has been very cold and foggy nothing much doing. I have not had to work very hard and work was done by four. Still I don't seem to have energy for letter writing. By the way, I need one or two things badly, my torch, ammunition.... You might send me a towel any time, a fresh pair of sox, a khaki handkerchief.... I should like a pen knife to keep my finger [nails] clean and a little nail brush convenient for carrying.

Watson and I get along famously. He knows nearly everyone that I do and he is such a fine fellow. The men and n.c.o.'s seem to like and trust him. We are going to town together one of these times and have a little jambouree—a very mild one....

This is a most disjointed and unsatisfactory letter.... [M]y mind does not concentrate when the others are talking. Believe me dear I love you and think of you constantly. Don't forget to write and give me all the news.

Goodbye Honey
Your own
Stuart

Stuart was pleased when Edna moved from the flat she had shared with Sergeant Williams's wife to live with Lottie Weir whose husband Norman was one of his closest friends serving in France.

FRANCE, DECEMBER 2, 1916

Dearest Honey:

I had three letters from you this morning dated I think the 23rd, 24th and 25th, all of them containing more or less reproaches. First as to the ammunition I did not know there was more than one kind myself. Ignoramus, I am. I know....

Before I finish the letter I will say that I have just had two more letters dated Nov. 26 and 27 and was glad to know you were getting my letters more regularly. Some of my epistles are not very good reading. Still, I certainly do not feel... that I can take liberties. I put my name on the outside of the envelope; if it means anything it means I have censored it.... [I]t is not playing the game to insert information which the men are not allowed to give.

Yes I think you are wise to go with Mrs. Weir.... I am glad you are going....

... We have had a quiet evening, shaving, reading, talking. The only drawback is my feet are cold. But I have managed to sleep very comfortably this tour in and am feeling fine. I think the good cooking has something to do with it. I am glad London life is agreeing with you. Why should you be thin and haggard.

Still no parcels. Of course they would hardly send any large ones in but I don't think there can be any. I am relieved that the ammunition is on the way. I shall be able to shoot rats. Do you want some skins? But when all those good eats come, won't we have a feed eh? I am not sorry you sent the shaving soap. I am always running short of it. The soap proposition is fairly easy to deal with. I got some Kerks medicated tar soap in town which was very good. The last day out I had a bath with it and it fixed my hair up fine.

Well good night dearest.

Your own,

Stuart

In the long letter that follows, Stuart once again wrote at length about the saintliness of good women and their impact on the character of a man. It is also a near classic expression of Edwardian values still present in the generation that fought World War I. Themes of much of the literature from the war are echoed by Stuart in such phrases as "our path to glory," their "sacrifice to honour, righteousness and peace," and their "playing a part in a great drama."

FRANCE, DECEMBER 4, 1916

Dear One:—

There was no mail for us tonight and I find it very hard to settle down to work. Wherefore the mood which is on me compels me to take up my pen to write to you. In some strange way tonight your personality is with me and I feel not myself alone but what I was, transformed by your influence. Every incident in our lives has been recurring with the greatest vividness and the power of your love, as Dante says, has been strong within me. Every time I look in the fire, I see you as you were on some occasion, either in your wedding gown or as you used to be at home, as you were when you joined me in England. Good Lord who am I that I should be merited such happiness. I some-

times tremble when I think of when you first let me take your hair
down. How softly I touched it, how sacred it seemed. What a difference in life love has made, how we all change under its influence. I remember with interest what my ideas of women used to be. I suppose I
have always been under the influence of good women—my mother,
my grandmother, my cousin Mrs. Ridgeway, a married friend in
Toronto [Mrs. Abbott]—all of whom more or less impressed me with
the saintliness of women. Though susceptible to wrong influences, it
was always with shame that I remember thoughts that should not have
been entertained. Poor Mrs. Abbott. What a brick she was. When I
was taken ill in Toronto she impulsively made a trip to the hospital
and smuggled in a book—the last thing on earth I should have had;
days afterwards when I was raving in delirium it was discovered carefully concealed in my bed. Before I left the hospital, she came to see
me and when she went she bent down and kissed my poor bony, hairy
face. How those influences and incidents keep you straight in after life
and leave ineffaceable imprints on your character. . . . I tell you these
things freely under a sort of compulsion because well I belong to you.
I don't know, it always seemed impossible to think wrongly of girls. I
appreciate now what it has meant and I shall certainly try to give my
son a chance should we have one. Of course I had never looked at a
girls charms and I remember when I first met you and was tempted to
fall in love with your hands, or the curve of your neck or your brown
eyes, I was always deterred by the thought that one should not trust
such things. I can't but admit that the attraction was there gathering
momentum but there was the other doubt to settle and I think I always
or rather consistently held myself in for that very reason, that the
physical should not dominate the mental. . . . You never made the
slightest effort to conciliate me. Why did you always show the thorns
alternately with the roses and drive me to despair. I often laugh when I
think how I put a limit on the number of times I should call and finally
by an admirable effort of self restraint actually succeeded in reducing it
to one call per week. Alas! . . . Oh I suffered at times but I suppose it
did not prevent me from worshipping you. And the wealth of devotion
you have poured out to me have long since erased the former
memories. It needed perseverance. How glad I am for it and how much
gladder that the woman to whom I was drawn dealt so scrupulously
with me. I was more or less at your mercy and yet after we became
engaged I knew that I had not only a lover but a friend and counsellor.
Listen to my secret, honey. I should never have been satisfied nor
would you to have found that this love of ours was built on the sands

of purely selfish desires. But to have found that over against the physical was set the moral and spiritual that... [we] also wanted that mutual aspiration and inspiration that can alone make love sacred that lift it up into those mysterious realms where body and soul meet. Little girl you always believe in keeping one foot on the ground and yet I find that to have known you and to have lived through three years of courtship and two imperishable years of wedded life has opened up new realms of thought and development and has given my mind and aspirations a cast which I hope preclude my doing what is base or wrong. How often do I think of your confidence and trust in me and pray that it may not be misplaced.

Pardon this long, prolix and impulsive letter. But my thoughts refused to be led to earth and have been soaring, dragging a flagging pen after them. You know me well enough to know that I speak truth and back of each written word is a hundred unexpressed thoughts and feelings. Our path of glory is indeed painful; yet it is lightened with great vistas that open into the unknown and teach us that we are greater than we know. I do not preach, honey I cannot. But I have tried to do my duty. I have come through with you, two of the greatest experiences of all time—a mutual devotion ending in marriage and the deliberate sacrifice to honour, righteousness, and peace of all that man holds dear. Already for me you have been apotheosized by that act of renunciation; you have passed out of girlhood into womanhood and in the years to come, be our fate what it may, you will know that in all the goings on of time, you have played your part in a great drama and that you in your own way have shed abroad an influence of selfless sacrifice which the world will not willingly let die. And our lives are one for time and eternity to react the one on the other and we hope to have each their small influence on the future of mankind.

Now this is a terribly long letter. Yet I find that it wrote itself under the dictation of some power I could not curb. It will explain a good many of the things I have been thinking. It has also brought me a feeling of content and happiness.

Now let me tell you little girl that writing so many letters is quite a drain on writing material which is practically exhausted. So if you can send more at once. I don't think there is anything else I need, at any rate not at present. . . . Good night honey. God bless you. Write soon.

Your own

Stuart

It was perhaps only natural that a man of Stuart Tompkins' sensitivity and integrity would be asked to seek information about men reported as missing as well as the circumstances surrounding the deaths of those killed in action and only natural also that he would feel an obligation to correspond with many who had lost sons or husbands. The status of Hugh Sharon, a friend from Alberta, was a matter of ongoing concern, and the following letter is one of many indicating that he took some pains to deal with Sharon's disappearance.

FRANCE, DECEMBER 5, 1916

Dearest:—

What do you think of five letters tonight, four from you. We had a double supply tonight as there was no mail yesterday. I got disgusted with myself after lunch today and decided to go into [censored]. We wanted to arrange for horses for tomorrow. I saw Yule at the horse lines... also Robinson, one of the officers who came over from England with us. We had not very good luck about the horses but we may get them.

Returning at six thirty I found supper and mail, letters dated Nov 28th, two Dec 1st and one Dec 2nd. The last one certainly made quick time. You mustn't talk about going back [to Canada]. It brought a lump into my throat right off. It may come in time. How your letters cheered me though, bridging the gap of time and leaping the months that separate us.... I am sending my watch back to be repaired.... [I]f it will cost too much or will take too long, buy me an Ingersoll. I will certainly appreciate the War Atlas. By the bye, some time not right away, if you get into a book store and can buy a small Russian Dictionary and a small cheap Russian novel, story or publication, you can send it for translation purposes but I must of course limit the amount I carry.

I don't know whether you acted on my suggestion but I am certainly glad you are going with Mrs. Weir. Did you thank the Williams for me for the cigarette case. I shall try to write them before going in. If you let me have Mrs. Sharon's address I shall try and write her. I spoke to a number of boys who saw Sharon on the 26th. He was last seen I believe one of a party bringing up bombs....

... I shall have more to tell you tomorrow. Tonight my thoughts are disturbed by the c-r-r-ump of the heaviest over my shoulder. This afternoon Fritz was putting 'em over quite near here, but on the whole we are quite free from shell fire.

Good night honey. God bless you
Your own,
Stuart

Dearest, Dearest Honey:—

After such a carnival of letter reading as I had yesterday, it is disappointing to return and find that there is no mail; but it did not come today hence I must fortify myself in other ways.

Well we went to town today, which means that after a very late start, we went to the horse lines and from there rode in. I chafed at all the delays; first the batmen did not get up till nearly eight which itself was bad and I did raise Cain about it. Then Watson was late getting up, took his time about getting breakfast and was very slow about dressing. Instead of getting to the horse lines at ten, it was ten before we left. My horse was brought up by the groom and taken back. We finally got our mounts and got away at 11:30. It was really ripping to be on a good horse once more and we slipped along at a good pace up and down hill reaching our destination in less than an hour. We stabled our horses with an English battalion (in fact there was no other place) and went into the nearest hotel. The concourse was not large but quite distinguished and as we sat a Brigadier came in and took a seat. The number of dinants [sic] increased and the speed of serving correspondingly decreased. Still it allowed our food to settle and gave us time to ruminate. Being ravenously hungry after our ride, I ate well to say the least. We then went about our shopping. I found an ordnance store and do you know in 5 minutes got everything I wanted. . . .

That left me with little to do and the rest of the time we wandered around the shops. Watson was anxious to buy some lace etc for lady friends. On the other hand, though I know my wife pretty well, I should hesitate to buy even lace for her. I will however give you prices and if they are not too dear I shall try to pick up something nice if you can tell me about what you want. Lace about 2 inches wide made in the Vosges (I suppose hand made) 6f.75 c per metre, other kinds from 4f [to] 8f. Collars, white like those you wear, with patterns worked by hand, according to the amount of work 5f [to] 15fr each. Handkerchief crepe de chine mostly with lace edges—5 [to] 50fr according to the amount and quality of the lace. They have various kinds of lace. I asked her but could not catch the names but wouldn't think of buying it except for a special purpose. . . . I hesitated to buy till I found out whether they were over-charging. Let me know about it. . . .

I am going to read all your letters over again tonight. Each time they give me a thrill of pride at the love that you have given me. The only question is—Will I be worthy of it and of the sacrifices you have made for me. And don't think that the criticisms you have made are lost on me. I am trying to make good I trust I will, even if I don't get the Victoria Cross as your mother suggests. . . .

. . . These letters are my only form of diary. I believe there is an order out forbidding diaries. Of course I can tell you a lot in these letters when I write every day, on the other hand I cannot tell you all that takes place in the front line. Of that a good deal is amusing—some sad, the greater part monotonous lightened by cheery optimism. Still it is the war as I see it and I should like to write down my thoughts about it. . . .

Now I really have no more news. Will I get my parcels in the morning or a letter.

Good night dear sweet dreams and may angels keep watch over you.

Your own
Stuart

FRANCE, DECEMBER 7, 1916
[NO. 1]

Dearest:—

. . . You will be interested to know that I had quite a bit of mail today—a package, a parcel of papers and two letters. . . . Needless to say I was quite relieved about the parcel. Apparently it was the one sent on November 16th. . . . I sampled the chocolate and put the other articles away, the edibles for taking up the line with us. I have some shaving soap but would have been out shortly. The other things are fine and I know are going to be much appreciated. I only fear you are spending all your savings on me. Is that the case? Eh.

. . . It seems so good to receive things here particularly when you are in the trenches. I only wish my ammunition were here. It is altogether probable we shall spend Christmas day in the trenches. We will probably have a few extras. In case you *do* send a pudding see if it is possible to send a sauce, in cans or something—merely a suggestion. . . .

. . . I am very delighted with that Atlas. I have wanted it you know for a long time and it certainly gives you a broad general idea of the country. Of course our military maps give more detail but you cannot get an idea of the whole front or theatre of war. It will certainly be fine for reference. . . .

This is a sort of a scrappy letter interrupted by visits to the fire place and around the room but it allows me to collect my thoughts. In fact I feel as though I were sort of carrying on a conversation with you while you were sitting in front of the fire. Let me offer you a bit of advice little girl. Don't allow yourself to think too much of the hour of my return. Lord knows how my thoughts will dwell on it in spite of me, but I am here to soldier and must not allow myself to be unnerved. . . . I should rather claim kinship with those martial ancestors of yours and to know that in that after world I could meet you and look into those clear eyes and receive the well done. Ah how I long to be worthy of you. . . .

I was cold for a while so I went and sat before the fire and thawed out while I read the Times. By the way I don't know what to say about the daily papers. When we are out we can get almost any of them. I usually get the Times. When we are in we get nothing so if you don't mind continuing it. Don't send every one just some of the more important and slip a weekly paper or some thing of the kind.

I do so enjoy writing letters to you. One needs to keep his spirits up here for it is fatal to let them slump. To sit down and chat for an hour is a great comfort and I always feel the better for it. Then I feel more or less uplifted and reconciled to what else would appear our hard lot. After all one lives and moves and has his being in the thoughts of those he loves, and you know that I do not live apart from you. Some force it seems over which I have no control draws me to you and makes you privy to my inmost thoughts. In fact by the same mysterious power are our souls brought into closest harmony.

I am sending this by one of our officers going on leave. Hope it gets to you all right.

Stuart

FRANCE, DECEMBER 7, 1916
[NO. 2]

Dearest:

You will probably get before this reaches you another also written today and sent down to Brigade HQ by an out going officer, Mr. Adams. I asked him to hunt you up when he gets to Blighty. I do hope he sees you. . . . He blew in from the trenches less than half an hour ago full of glee at his prospects of ten glorious days; by quick changes he got away a few minutes ago and if all is well, he will be into Blighty tomorrow night, lucky dog. I could not think of anything he could do beyond seeing you and telling you how I was etc.

My Russian is not getting on very fast these days. I fear I am lazy but as soon as I have cleared away some of the difficulties I am going to make it a rule to do a bit every day. I have unlimited time so do not need to worry how long it takes me. It seems essential to keep your mind occupied while you are here. I have a life of Napoleon in French, which I am reading also a magazine. I enjoy talking French very much like when we were in Bethune. . . .

I really must set about some Christmas letters. . . . I would also like to write to your father. By the way in case you do not hear otherwise, I got tonight the parcel mailed on the 16th, i.e. steak, chocolate etc. I thought it was well to tell you in case Adams does not see to my mail going.

Now I have already put a good deal of work on writing tonight so shall wind up. Be sure to write as often as possible and don't forget a little prayer at night.

As ever yours,
Stuart

FRANCE, DECEMBER 8, 1916

Dearest:—

Your long letter of the 4th came this afternoon also the copy of the Spectator both of which were very welcome. . . . The weather is very glum today and I think it is reflected in the temper of the household. We have been having more or less of a running fight today re batman, the maladministration of the past Government etc etc. We should feel somewhat better after the clouds have rolled by and the air has cleared. I sat down in front of the fire a few moments ago to think (which is our only consolation) but it just seemed as though my fingers itched for the pen since the spoken word is denied me. The words of endearment must come out in some way; they seem always to be a slow burning fire which will not be quenched and I must utter the feelings that surge up. I cannot tell you how near you are at all times to me both by day and in the silent watches of the night. It is only writing to you and receiving your cheery letters that give me ballast and keep me steady; so remember that as you get ready to crawl in at night and as you rise in the morning. . . .

I do hope that you see Adams. He will be able to tell you all about me that you want to know. He is a great lad. It will be a pleasure to see someone right from the front. He was quite fortunate. You see we are neither fowl nor flesh nor good red herring. We belong both to the Battalions and to the Battery. Consequently they don't know whether our leave is by battalion or battery. He arranged his through his battalion and in that way got it a little earlier. Lord knows when mine comes.

. . . You know there are serious complaints here of the men staying back home. I see numerous cases of men who have been here 15 months without leave. They should have some consideration. . . .

When I was in town day before yesterday I bought a very good life of Napoleon in French. I have enjoyed reading it very much. You take a good deal of comfort out of such things in this dugout life. The evenings are pretty long these days. It is interesting meeting the French people here and brushing up. Some day I am going to write re my impressions of France and her people. Any remarks probably will be unfair as the French people are at war. Unfortunately first impressions are I believe liable to be correct as I have found e.g. the present muddle in affairs in England.

Well supper is coming so I shall close with all good wishes.

God bless you dearest.

Your own
Stuart

FRANCE, DECEMBER 9, 1916

Dearest:—

Just a line from the trenches. The weather is cold and dismal outside and I think it would cheer me up to write a few lines, to write to you. Watson sits across from me writing his report. He is very thorough and very careful as I have found out and he is highly conscientious. . . .

I have a lot of very good advice which I shall hand out one of these days, say at the New Year. You are too unselfish and seem to spend your time thinking of nothing but doing something for me. . . . You never tell me anything of your London experiences. Do you never visit any place even on Sunday. Probably Mrs. Weir will help out along that line. You know Honey that you and your doings interest me more than anything else. I suppose it is because of the personality I have studied all along. We are probably both different from what we were two years ago. At increasingly frequent intervals I seem to grasp the meaning of the war and to rise above the sordidness and misery of it and feel that I have stepped out into a broader world. If one does achieve that, the war will not have been fought in vain. I often think of those who stay behind who are denied the exhilaration and who are called on for the sacrifices. What can there be for them. . . .

Referring to the war situation, in the midst of depression all we can do is to carry on. There is infinite relief at the appointment of Mr. Lloyd George. Everyone is prepared to stomach the present situation for that reason. Every fresh reverse strikes home the lesson afresh that national and social prejudices must go by the board. Please God, they have and a new order has been ushered in.

Now be sure to write me a good cheery newsy letter. I am doing my duty I think at least I hope along that line. News is of course hard to give; at least it is difficult to distinguish between legitimate and illegitimate. There is a certain amount of activity but of course you know our orders. Still every Tommy here is not interested in the war but in people at home. Do you know it is amusing to read some of them. I fear some of them are regular Lotharios. I'd like to have a go at some of them. Still there are a lot of them who are true. There were two chaps in the 31st, both sergeants, and brothers, who used to write the best letters. I think Pat's friendships were purely Platonic, such letters as he could write. I used to envy his gift. And they tell me that down on the Somme his sang froid was wonderful. Of course he was Scotch, didn't drink or smoke. What a combination.

Well, honey, goodnight. Let us hope there will be a letter tonight. I will try to be brighter tomorrow.

Your own
Stuart

When there was no time to write a letter, Stuart would on occasion send Field Service Post Cards, nicknamed "whizz bangs." The regulation printed card contained a variety of messages from which to select,

A.F.A. 2042.
114/Gen.No./5248.

FIELD SERVICE

POST CARD.

The address only to be written on this side. If anything else is added the post card will be destroyed.

[Crown Copyright Reserved.]

Mrs S R Tompkins
88 Stapleton Rd
Upper Tooting
London
SW

NOTHING is to be written on this side except the date and signature of the sender. Sentences not required may be erased. If anything else is added the post card will be destroyed.

I am quite well.

I ~~have been admitted into hospital~~

{ sick } ~~and am going on well.~~
{ wounded } ~~and hope to be discharged soon.~~

I am ~~being sent down to the base.~~

I have received your { letter dated ___13th___
{ ~~telegram~~ „ _____
{ parcel „ ___6th___

~~Letter follows at first opportunity.~~

~~I have received no letter from you~~
{ ~~lately.~~
{ ~~for a long time.~~

Signature } S R Tompkins Lieut
only }

Date 13/12/16

[Postage must be prepaid on any letter or post card addressed to the sender of this card.]

Wt W3497/293 29246. 600m. 9/16. C. & Co. Grange Mills, S.W

The Field Service Post Card was a staple of communication during the Great War, and it embodied near perfect censorship.

ranging from "I am quite well" to "I have been admitted into hospital—wounded," along with the stern warning that "NOTHING is to be written on this side except the date and signature of the sender... *If anything else is added the post card will be destroyed.*" One Field Service Post Card to Edna, dated 11 December 1916, postmarked 16 December, conveyed the following information:

I am quite well.
I have received your letter dated *5th Dec.*
Letter follows at first opportunity.
Signature: S. R. Tompkins Lieut.

FRANCE, DECEMBER 11, 1916

Dearest:—

I was very proud to get your letter of the 5th but also very humble because even your confidence cannot overcome my sense of my own short comings. It came at a time of some discouragement for we have our ups and downs in the trenches. Still I am sure that to have been thought worthy of your trust will bear me up in the midst of trials.

I know I have neglected you of late. Yesterday I got no time to write and by the runner tonight all I sent was a Field Service Post Card. Whether it brings any comfort you alone can tell. I consider they are a good stop-gap....

The little Bible you have given me has been a source of great consolation. My favourite authors bring one comfort and fills one with a sense of the "still sad music of humanity nor harsh nor grating but of ample power to chasten and subdue," and in the silent hours when the world is wrapped in peace and our friend Fritz is doing nothing more harmful than trying to catch someone in our trench with his machine gun, ones mind retires into itself and you get down to bed rock. I hope I shall come out of this better than I went in. I don't suppose that is the purpose of war any more than thrift is the purpose of poverty—only a by product....

No, things do not look over-promising in the war, but remember always, the darkest hour before the dawn. If one looks back on past wars that has been the case and the party that struggled through discouragement was the one that reaped the fruits of victory. There is no depression here, just quiet confidence and trust in the new leaders. Personally I breathe freely once more....

The weather continues very fair—a good deal of murky weather and a little sunshine. What will Christmas be like? We are wondering what will be doing.

I must get washed and shaved. Night is the only satisfactory time for doing that when we get abundance of hot water. It was later when we turned in last night, so I must to bed early.

Good night Honey dear.

Your own

Stuart

FRANCE, DECEMBER 13, 1916

Dearest:—

... I am glad you are at last settled and trust that you will enjoy life with Mrs. Weir. I cannot tell you how glad I am that you are together at this time.

I had a very long newsy letter from Alice last night. She announced that she was sending two parcels containing fruit cake, honey and mouth organ (incidentally also socks and a handkerchief). Also Mr. Yule is to get the Military Cross. There were two enclosures one of them a snap shot of the family taken in Edmonton the other a clipping announcing the death of George Sievwright. ... I think you will find Alice's letter good reading. I enjoyed it very much.

There was a nice letter reached me last night from you when the runner came in. Tonight I just sent out a whizz-bang. It seemed as though our day was very upset and I could not write. ... Say, when I opened your letter and found that dreaded word Hubby, I decided that I had indeed become a married man and really settled down. It made me feel old.

Now I am not going to write more. I must get warmed up, do some work and shave, then to bed to dream.

Well, sweetheart, good night. God bless you.

Your own

Stuart

FRANCE, DECEMBER 14, 1916

My Dearest:—

Do you know a letter from you dated October 16th turned up here last night. It was the one you wrote when you went back to London before I left and has been just a little under two months on the way. Perhaps I was not surprised. . . .

Well, I had my supper, finished my days work, read the paper and shaved. So I feel quite virtuous. Somehow, I seem to have annexed a lot of mud this tour. My breeches are covered with it. It is even in my hair. I expect to have some time getting it out.

We heard today for the first time of the peace talk. I am not putting any faith in it at all and I guess it is just our business to carry on as usual. There will be a little talk and then it will die out. After all as a good soldier, we should not have personal opinions at all.

I know you will feel neglected this week but I have tried to write when an opportunity offered. We are speculating on the arrival of Christmas presents. I see by the papers that 500,000 arrive daily at the Army P.O. in London while only 250,000 are distributed. Also that many are coming to grief through being insecurely packed. I have a good deal at stake in the matter so am naturally interested. Watson too is beginning to speculate. He has cousins and aunts in Scotland and is promised all sorts of things so I think we had better celebrate. I expect though that unless something unusual happens we will be getting our boxes about February 1st. . . .

Well honey, I must really go and sit by the fire and dry my feet so will close for tonight.

Good luck and good night.
Sweet dreams
Your own
Stuart

FRANCE, DECEMBER 15, 1916

Dearest:—

. . . Oh what a bunch of mail in the last two days—five letters and three parcels, two letters from you, one from Janet and two business letters, your parcel, containing coffee, ginger and socks, one from your mother and the ammunition. The ginger is really fine also the socks. I am tickled to death with the soup. You have no idea how good it tastes in the trenches. Your parcel was in good condition, so you do not need to worry. Your mother's parcel was fine. The only trouble was she sent some chewing gum spearmint and as it has a very penetrating flavour, I fear it has got into the cake. However, that does not affect the kindness that is contained in every morsel of the contents. It was accompanied by a Christmas card and a note that the contents were from the Christie family. So already Christmas is in the air and the rush is beginning. I had a very nice letter from Janet this evening. She complained of not having heard from me but really I have written consistently. They are sending me two parcels from home and have evidently gone to some considerable trouble. The girls really have been good about writing etc, are, I suppose, making up for mother.

I am going to try to write decent letters this time we are out. In the trenches it is [as] hard to concentrate as it is easy here. I have a lot of things to say if I could only express them. Ah how dear all the old memories, all the old friendships are! and how we resolve that none of the old narrow mindedness and sordidness will cling to us after the war is over. I think it will have an effect on me. I find myself looking into my own character and my own life as I never did before. . . . The dear old Bible gives me lots of comfort. How many throes has the human heart passed through in the past, into what valleys has it not descended. How prone to despair must they have been when all they valued was swallowed up by pagan tyrannies. At last I believe in England, they are realizing that selfishness and narrowness are a curse and that the war will not be won on the fields of France more than it will be at home. . . .

Poor Watson is asleep where I should be too. A nice warm grate fire has made us both sleepy. I think I shall close for tonight. I am beginning to look forward to another parcel. Will there be one before Christmas. You see we will be in [the trenches] by then. Goodnight Honey.

God bless you.
Your own,
Stuart

As the third Christmas of the war approached even the usually optimistic Stuart Tompkins showed an occasional sign of becoming dispirited. An air of resignation in the trenches matched one of anxiety in leadership circles, and in December radical changes took place in governments and commands, dictated in part by events on the Western Front. The state of things was such that any positive move, no matter how slight, was welcome, and the first day of a counter-offensive at Verdun was hailed as a victory, as the letter below indicates. The three-day offensive there regained some ground previously lost, at the cost of 550,000 French casualties.[1] The immediate beneficiary was General Robert Neville, who led the assault and replaced General Joffre as commander of French forces. He was to be the architect of Allied offensives the following spring. In Britain, meanwhile, the disastrous losses of the Somme had fueled demands for a change in government, and on 5 December, much to Stuart's delight, the government of the more militant Lloyd George replaced that of Herbert Asquith. Perhaps it was as much the determination and will to victory that accompanied Lloyd George as it was cynicism and distrust of Germany's motives that had prompted Stuart's 14 December observations about her peace proposal which many thought was floated primarily for consumption on the home front and in the United States rather than for serious consideration by the combatants.

FRANCE, DECEMBER 16, 1916

Dearest:—

I realize my deep guilt tonight when I think that although I have a letter written I have not sent one off today. The reasons therefor are not hard to seek. After rising fairly late and reading the papers in a lazy sort of way, we packed up our towels and soap and went for a wash. The bath house is in a town about a mile away. We had a real live bath. We had to make good time as I was due to attend a lecture at 3 p.m. at a place some ten miles away. We were late for lunch and had to really hustle believe me but we caught our bus very easily. . . . It was a real London bus, windows boarded up and all painted drab, but just the same as if it were driving down Piccadilly. The lecture was good. Its subject "Britain's Part in the War." The lecturer strove to give us a clear idea of the historical reasons for both Germany and England being involved. He told us nothing new but it was all told so lucidly and strikingly that it made quite an impression. About 400 British officers were present. Some senior officer made the announcement of the French victory at Verdun which was received with great enthusiasm. . . . On our way back I stopped at the 31st lines got my coat and some money but missed Watson and had to beat it off across the prairie alone. I got in about seven and Maxey had some supper and I found three letters from you. . . .

It was most disappointing that you did not get your shopping done. . . . Norman Weir is pretty lucky, has been away to a school for two or three weeks. . . .

Your letters gave me a great deal of comfort. I don't do any worrying about things. Sometimes things get on your nerves. I can't tell you how much it means to have you write me.

Well Honey I am just dropping to sleep over my letter so must close and go to bed. I have had quite a long day.

Goodnight

Your own

Stuart

[later]

Sunday, December 17, 1916

Just a few lines this morning to let you know I am thinking of you. We have had a lazy morning sitting before the fire. This afternoon though we are going to hear the Canadian Massed Band at present touring in France. We are going to do something every day. It gets very tiresome sitting around doing nothing.

It never rains but it pours. I heard this morning that one of the officers of the 31st got me some ammunition when he was last on leave so I guess the rats in the trenches will have a bad time next time in. By the way I got my new British warm from ordnance so I am well fitted out now. . . .

FRANCE, DECEMBER 17, 1916

Dearest, dearest Honey:—

I am heartbroken almost tonight. Watson got one letter, three parcels of papers and two Christmas parcels and I did not get anything. . . . I suppose I told you I had three letters last night, so the dearth is all the greater today.

Before I go further though, I want to tell you how I appreciated the parcel. . . . The soups are great, also the socks. I have managed to lose one or two pairs since coming here. These French washerwomen have to be looked after. They change your stuff otherwise.

Well this afternoon I went to hear the Canadian Massed Band, an aggregation of players (supposed to be 200 but really about 40) gathered from various units in England, now touring in France. They have been to Paris and are now making the rounds of various Canadian units. It was a rare treat and I tell you a great deal might be done along this line by the Government for the soldiers. . . .

I was very grateful for what you said in one of the recent letters. You overestimate me. . . . I can assure that what I am I owe to you and proud I am that you have thought me worthy of your love. If by my life and acts I can show how highly I hold that love and the personality behind, I shall indeed count myself most happy. Ah how women hold in their keeping the hearts of men and the future of the race. As I sat in that building full of soldiers today and looked around on the keen youthful and mostly noble faces, I could not help thinking what good could not be found in them. Brought under the right influence, they are capable of doing great deeds and leading good lives. Unfortunately the wrong influence too often creeps in.... I am finding out both the heights and depths of human character and beginning to understand much that was previously hidden from me. One thing though you are going to find is that young fellows who have seen life in France from the wrong side are going to take back with them a distorted view of womankind that will not find acceptance I believe in Canada.

Now that I have got started I know I cannot stop. There is that something in you that even across the seas that divide compels my mind and thought. Did you know you had that power, the power that Dante ascribes to Beatrice, the wondrous gift that enables one to bridge the physical gaps and come into touch with the soul when the body is absent.

I have been sitting staring into the fire for some minutes conjuring up your picture as I have seen you at times.... Ah, how can I put it into words... the courage and strength of character that lent courage to me....

... For I guess we are entering through this travail into a new realm of peace and content. May each and all of us who have suffered resolve that the suffering and sacrifice shall not have been in vain but that the deeds done, shall not be allowed to die. Do you know that only once in a while do I grow disheartened. I am acquiring a strange serenity that looks forward with confidence to the future, a firm belief that we labour not in vain....

Now honey I must close this little epistle. We expect to go to town tomorrow to get a few things for Christmas. I shall buy paper too as mine has now run out. I was very sorry you did not finish your shopping but cheer up you will have other opportunities. I got my automatic cleaned today ready to fire.

Good night dearest. God bless you. May all holy angels guard thee.

Stuart

By the way do you know that song of the exile from the Hebrides. It runs like this. "From the lone shieling and the misty island, Mountains divide us and a waste of seas." Hunt it up sometime will you. I always loved it. It expresses my thoughts re the Homeland.

Stuart frequently expressed shock and disgust when he encountered evidence of changing mores; he was appalled by much that he saw and he feared for the future of Canada. Such was the gist of his letter of 17 December, and, below, in response to some of Edna's observations, he carried his thoughts further.

FRANCE, DECEMBER 19, 1916

My Dearest:—

Can you imagine the pleasure I felt on coming in tonight to find five letters and a parcel awaiting me. The letters were dated the 12th, 13th, and 14th. I am not sure of the parcel but it contained towel, knife, diary and chocolate. But your letters particularly were welcome and eagerly devoured. Some of them like mine dashed off in the lull of work, but none the less interesting.

I must confess to a feeling of remorse that I have caused you to fuss so over me. Every want I have had has been met and it seems as though new wants are cropping up all the time. I know you like to do it and it certainly gives me pleasure, only I don't like you to spend all your money on me. I am going to look after my things so you won't need to be buying me stuff. . . .

Your observations re English girls came in very pat as you will see from another letter. One's mind cannot help dwelling on the contrast with Canadian life but my observations have been born out by those of more kindly critics of English ways, who assert that there has been a marked change in English girls of late years, though that is scarcely any compliment to them. I always dislike drawing conclusion on such matters. . . . But my belief is that the doctrine of having a good time has taken deep hold of all English life and unfortunately having a good time is being enlarged beyond bounds set for it in Canada. Those who pass such bounds out there can hardly do so with impunity. Here passions and desires seem to be cultivated if not for themselves yet too often in the guise of more lofty instincts. It has taken mankind a long time to discover that the baser passions cannot look after themselves. Why then after 2000 years teaching should a whole people condone such views regarding them. The poor may be to blame but there must be a strange callousness or coarseness in the better national fibre to permit such standards. The very ideas occurred to me as to you. We have succeeded in building up a standard on such matters and unless we are careful, we run grave danger of it crumbling.

How on earth do these girls regard themselves. They know they are despised and a man who finds he can use a girl for his own ends is not going to be faithful to her. Do they never think or are they so intoxicated with their ideas of love and gaiety that they don't stop to think. It beats me.

Now I haven't expressed half the gratitude for the nice things you sent me.... I am mighty well set up for Christmas.

The 31st are to have a big pow-wow at Christmas. Lucky dogs. I had a letter from Norman Weir at the Corps School tonight wanting to know what the plans are....

Well goodnight Honey. I feel contented tonight after so many letters.

Your own
Stuart

FRANCE, DECEMBER 23, 1916

Dearest Honey:—

Do you know I have just discovered the dreadfullest mistake. I found that the letter I wrote last night I did not send. So I have given it to the batman to see that it goes. I have the funniest batman. He is a redhead. Scotch Englishman who migrated to Winnipeg. He is only 17 years old but has already seen a bit of fighting. He writes to his mother that she is all he has in the world—no girl for him etc, and begins the next letter "my darling" a most ardent outpouring of affection. Poor chap. I sympathized with him.

... As you know, I am in the trenches so have not much leisure to write. You seem to be pretty hard worked in old London don't you. I feel guilty for though I am busy I am not over worked.

The weather has been very peculiar lately. It has done everything, but principally rain and wind today. A little rain goes a long way in the trenches everything caves in and they will get flooded in spite of you. Then they have to keep the pumps going to keep from drowning. What do they think at home—about the peace propositions. We don't think about them out here i.e. we don't take them seriously. Though everyone discusses them. The feeling is though that the Germans are fooling us and trying to bag the spoils. I have been surprised and pleased at the strong stand of the English papers and people. We should know our mind by now and Lloyd George is certainly the man to express it.

I think I am getting along all right with the Russian. Of course it is slow, but I am going to take time with the elementary stuff.

You said I would probably be disappointed with the last parcel because it had no eats in it. But honey, if you saw the amount of stuff we consume in here particularly at dinner you wouldn't send me more. Tonight steak, onions, mashed potatoes, bread, butter, pineapple, fruitcake, raisins, chocolate, cocoa. What do you think of that line up. Your mother's fruit cake was fine. And there is enough to do us nearly a week. Well I must not make your mouth water. I only wish I knew you fared as well, particularly when this food censor gets busy.

It is strange I have not had letters from home or Philip. I think we will get our parcels right up to Christmas day. The boys I think are going to have lots of eats. We are buying apples and oranges for them. I think they are being issued with plum puddings so they should fare not badly. I should have a parcel from Canada by then. Of course I shall not look for one from you as I have been spoiled in that direction. I am looking though for that photograph. I dream and think of nothing else day and night. I am sorry it turned out poorly.

Norman Weir will likely be back from the school tomorrow. I shall hardly see him though till after Christmas.

Well Honey dear I will close tonight. I hope you have a good time Christmas. Eat some extra turkey and plum pudding for me.

Thanks for the paper and things. I will be able to write a civilized letter. Well here goes for [censoring] my batman's letters. He has written three while I was doing this.

Your own
Stuart

THE TRENCHES
CHRISTMAS EVE, 1916

My Dearest:—

How can I write the thoughts that come over me tonight this night of all nights, in a hole underground. This morning it seemed as though nature had conspired to throw the mantle of peace over everything; when I went out the most glorious dawn had broken.... Hardly a cloud in the sky—that warm mellow light that we have out West, the air still and clear as the brook in Capilano. It seemed a hideous dream

The Trenches
Christmas Eve. 1916

My Dearest :-
How can I write the thoughts
that come over me tonight this night of
all nights, in a hole underground.
This morning it seemed as though
nature had conspired to throw the
mantle of peace over everything When
I went out the most glorious dawn had
broken — ροδο δακτυλος - rosy fingered,—
Hardly a cloud in the sky— that warm
mellow light that we have out West
the air still and clear as the brook
in Capilano. It seemed a hideous
dream that we were at war. that 100
yards away, burrowing underground
was a fellow man with hate in his
heart and cruel weapons in his hand
My heart swelled in triumphant exaltation over the sordidness of the
whole bad dream and pointed the
way towards peace. As the day wore

that we were at war, that 100 yards away, burrowing underground was a fellow man with hate in his heart and cruel weapons in his hand. My heart swelled in triumphant exaltation over the sordidness of the whole bad dream and pointed the way towards peace. As the day wore on and things warmed up, aeroplanes overhead, artillery booming, it might have seemed untrue. But during the bright winter afternoon it even seemed that Fritz could not resist the appeal. We had our daily strafe in which the trench mortars take part but Fritz's reply was half hearted. Ours was feeble too. It all seemed contrary to our thoughts and feelings. The only one who was vengeful was one corporal who got a nasty bump yesterday from a minnenwerfer. Finally it all died out and the solemn mystic night came. Such a night as nineteen hundred years ago looked down on the manger in which the child lay—the child who is to lead us out of this cursed land into the realm of peace and fellowship. And now our evening meal has come and gone—the last remnants of the fruitcake disappeared and the solemn influence of Christmas Eve has settled on all our hearts. What thoughts are they— of the Christ who has been wronged so oft, of the opportunities for love that have been wasted, of our fellow man contemned or condemned so easily—and ever that compelling power driving us or drawing us on and up to the nobler self to the wider vision to the purified and ennobled manhood. All the potent mysterious influences that stir in humanity's pulses from time immemorial till time is no more seem to throb and thrill through our very veins. Nowhere have I felt the call of such forces more powerfully than tonight in our poor dugout with the burst of shells heard as mere distant thuds. How near do all the powers of the universe feel tonight especially that quickening Power to whom we bend the knee in prayer and call "Abba" Father. Ah may suffering humanity find in this Christmas an earnest of others to come. We must find some solution for this horrible problem and make it impossible for all time to come.

Well, my own Honey you have been much in my thoughts today.... I seem to see you not so much as the warm hearted dearly beloved which you are as perfect womanhood. My own passionate admiration clarified and crystallized into that woman worship such as Dante felt. Poor old Dante how often I think of him. His adored Beatrice withdrawn became to him a guiding star, the realization of all his passionate religious aspirations, the woman clear eyed, clear brained as Diana, sensitive and tender as the angels that we dream of that stoop to touch our brows that beckon us onward to the vale of bliss, where withdrawn from earthly passions and ties we have company with the great spirits of the past. Ah what would we not give to know and have the friendship of the men and women, heroes and heroines of the past—... their wisdom, the wisdom of youth and enthusiasm, tempered by experience and contemplation. No wonder Socrates could exclaim if I am to be admitted to such a concourse, I count death as a great advantage.

Well truly Honey, my heart is ever yours as it has been since the first. In time of stress or strain I see those clear eyes resting on me asking for my best and I know that what I coveted selfishly as a constant joy has become by the process of time a power that draws me on that compels me to the best. Everything I have is yours, my life, my thoughts, my aspirations. In some strange way I seem to have found the rock on which to build.

I trust that your heart is as full of solemn joy tonight as mine and that you will have a joyous Christmas. We are not separated in spirit though we are in body.

We are going to have our Christmas dinner tomorrow night. Luck has not come our way. Something has delayed our mail—no letters today, no parcels no papers. We certainly hope they come tomorrow or we are out of luck. In addition to the parcel from you, there are two from Alice and one from Robertson Church. I appreciate the latter very much. It came in an official notification from J. S. Fry and Sons that at the request of Robertson Church Edmonton they were sending me a package of chocolates. This Christmas business is a severe tax on the transports. The 31st mail man told me there were sixty bags of mail one night. They simply cannot bring it up to the front line. There will be great doings among the battalions that are out for Christmas.

Well, honey, I have written a long letter but I am not through. . . . [The last page of the Christmas Eve letter is not among the surviving letters in the collection.]

FRANCE, DECEMBER 25, 1916

My Dearest:—

It is a very sleepy and tired boy that is attempting to write a letter. The day has passed quietly enough and we have done nothing, but Christmas dinner has left me lethargic and dull.

As you probably imagine our parcels have most of them been held up. As we nibbled the last pieces of Christmas cake last night, I involuntarily asked whether our Christmas parcels would materialize and sure enough the runner announced this morning—no mail. How-

ever, I did get this afternoon one of Alice's parcels which with a
Christmas pudding that Watson purchased rounded out our festive
board. We were a little short on meat rations. We had cold beef,
onions, mashed potatoes, Xmas pudding, rum sauce, candy etc, etc. By
the way I didn't tell you what was in Alice's parcel—devilled ham,
[illegible], home made candy (extra fine) a slab of Nelson's chocolate,
a box of shelled walnuts, almonds, and raisins, a tin of cocoa, a pair of
sox, a mouth organ, a tin of Sabadilla powder, tooth brush, toothpaste,
shaving cream, toilet powder, zam buk, can you think of anything
more to meet the soldier's needs. . . .

It has been a very quiet day. There was some stir last night down
the line. We went up to see shells and bombs bursting but all
quietened down shortly and we slept without a break till seven. The
day has been damp, and disappointing owing to the mail being late.
Still we made out fairly well and kept up our courage.

My batman has got his usual batch of letters tonight and is writing
as many more. The young monkey I know has half a dozen girls on a
string.

Well I wonder what kind of a Christmas you put in today—not
working I shall guarantee. You probably wrote letters. I am ashamed
that already the contents of two Christmas boxes are gone and I believe neither of them acknowledged. But we share things with the batman and they don't last long, but what does it matter if we enjoy
them. . . .

I have not much to write tonight beyond telling you the old story. I
trust you had a good Christmas not too lonely.

I think I shall shave now and get to bed. Sweet dreams.

> Your own
> *Stuart*

Edna finally had the photographs taken that Stuart had sought since
their parting in Calgary, and the proofs reached him just after Christmas. The following letter shows that the Trench Mortar Battalion's
billeting arrangements thrust Stuart into much closer contact with the
French whose property was often commandeered for British troops; it
shows also that conscription had by then become an issue of importance for the troops in the trenches as it would the following summer
for the politicians in London and Ottawa.

Edna Tompkins, 1916. When Stuart received this picture, he trimmed it to fit into his cigaret case to carry in his pocket when on a tour in the trenches.

FRANCE, DECEMBER 28, 1916

My Dearest:—

Your letters of the 20th, 21st and 22nd arrived yesterday afternoon and I do not need to say I was delighted with their perusal. The proofs were need I say it almost devoured. Of course the first thing I did was to show them to Mr. Watson.

Now before we go any further, I should tell you of the receipt of your Christmas parcel. I found it waiting for me at noon on the 27th, it having arrived on the 26th. . . . It was fine only I know you robbed your own parcel to fill it up. The short bread was I think the best I ever tasted. The Christmas cake. . . looks mighty good. The coffee we are enjoying as usual. The paper needless to say I am delighted with. It fills the bill best of any that I have had and I shall duly profit by my gift. Your mother's stuff was lovely but she came within an ace of spoiling it by putting in my parcel that spearmint gum. Fortunately the flavour did not penetrate the cake. I wonder who is perpetrating a practical joke on the soldiers by advising senders of parcels to send spearmint gum. It is cruel all right for it cannot help penetrating the other things but it appears to be done frequently. The makers of it should be hung. . . .

This morning we had a visit from the former owners and occupants of the billets we are inhabiting. There was madame and apparently two daughters, a young girl and "Madeleine." They came to look the house over and reclaim a few of the articles abandoned "il y a deux ans." I went around with them and did the honours. They had a small brewery in the rear and appear to be quite well-to-do. Madeleine is some girl. She chaffed a bit about the Canadian soldiers and of course had lots of nice things to say about them in general and my French in particular. I did get along fairly well. They were courtesy and good nature personified but were shrewd withal. I think they are the best class of Frenchwoman I have seen since coming. They brought a servant with them in the regulation blue of the French army. You should have seen how straight he stood and saluted. I was proud to return it. The one word that passed their lips oftenest was "triste" as they looked on the ruins of their former home. We helped them all we could and promised to look after one or two articles for them. But they never showed depression or discouragement.

When I got into deep water with my French, I had recourse to a little French Canadian working nearby. He was tickled to death to act as interpreter but it was as difficult to understand his English as her French.

I saw Norman Weir today as he passed the billets. He looked quite well and had had a good time. . . . Norman is disappointed at leave being postponed. He expected to get away January 15th. . . . We will be lucky if we get away Feb. 15th I believe.

Last night I spent my time cutting the proofs down to fit my cigarette case. Then I went and filled the case up so I shall have to get busy and smoke them up before I shall see you again. I am afraid if Watson had not been around when I got them I should have acted very foolishly.

I don't think I have done just right in the matter of writing. . . . I often lose a day going into or coming out of the trenches. . . .

Mr. Adams has now returned and stated that he did not see you. I am sorry. . . . Our O.C. Captain Pouncey is also on leave. I asked him to hunt you up if possible but have no idea whether he will or not. I certainly hope he does. . . .

. . . I will be interested in hearing how you like the battalion Christmas cards. I think they featured the O.C. a little too much but when you look at it it is reasonable. The personnel is changing so often. . . that before you could get the cards printed they would be out of date. They were very pretty I think, though and would be worth keeping.

Well, this letter has been dragging out tonight. I feel very lazy somehow tonight and it requires an effort. Watson is sitting next me with papers spread out in front of him carrying on as O.C. I am taking things more or less easy as becomes one of His Majesty's men.

I see that Sir Sam Hughes is beginning to spiel forth on compulsory service in Canada. As a private individual he is able to say things he could not as a Minister of the Crown. I hope the whole matter will be brought up for general discussion and settled. I think the British would like to see Canada adopt it, although they don't like to say anything. They feel the Canadians have done so well. I believe some of the Anzacs are sore that conscription did not carry in Australia, and well they might. I suppose the whole matter will be thrashed out at the next Imperial Conference. What dramatic things Lloyd George seems capable of doing. He does the bold and masterful things we would all like to see done and which appeal to the imagination. He certainly was a pretty safe bet for all concerned. How proud we should all be that Canada is to have a voice in framing peace. After all Canada's little contribution to the war is going to count after all. Not only her men but her munitions her money and her grain.

The weather has been quite mild lately, in fact really decent. I really suffered more from cold the first few days we were out than I have since then. Of course we get a bit of cold now and again, and a good bit of rain, but on the whole things are quite decent and I am feeling quite fit. Thank heavens I have been well supplied with sox. They pretty nearly save your life at times out here.

We are counting on making a bit of a spread here on New Years. Watson got a canned turkey. We have abundance of Christmas cake and can have another plum pudding. Then all the stuff the girls sent is practically intact so we can make out nicely.

Really do you know I sent away a lot of mail. Christmas. I wrote pretty steadily for two days I guess I wrote to some who won't write back. So do people in prosperity neglect their less fortunate neighbours. . . .

Now dearest this letter has taken up most of my evening so if I am going to get up tomorrow I must wind up. I did not sleep well last night so must try to make it up tonight. I hope you have now recovered from Christmas and are now able to resume your wonted duties.

Give my kindest regards to Mrs. Weir and tell her her husband is looking well and chirp. Don't forget to look after yourself.

Your own
Stuart

Cartoons by Bruce Bairnsfather did for the British or Canadian trench-dweller what those of Bill Mauldin did for the American G.I. in World War II. His best known character, Old Bill, was "chiefly remarkable as the antithesis of the immaculate regular soldier of pre-war days, an ironic comment on the common destiny of all troops consigned to the trenches."[2] A volume of Bairnsfather cartoons had obviously found its way into Stuart's hands.

FRANCE, DECEMBER 29, 1916

Dearest:—

Now that I am beginning to expiate my terrible offences of omission, I must start a wee bit letter this morning. We were up fairly early. After reading the papers my labours consisted in putting my house in order. I went through all my stuff. . . . I found my Christmas delicacies took up a bit of room. My treasured parcel from Alice was inspected by the rats last night, who took a nibble at the cake and the candy. No damage was done however, which is lucky. Things are now all packed up properly. . . .

I was looking at Captain Bairnsfather's pictures tonight and one of them struck me from a new angle. I think it is on page 35 . . . [showing] the explosion of a bomb which has buried [two] women. One asks "What was that?" Answer "Trench Mortar." Question, "Ours or theirs?" It is eloquent of the whole history of T. M.'s in which accuracy has only been gradually attained. At first your own were as dangerous as the other fellows.

I was looking over the atlas that you sent me. I was noticing on the map of the British front, you had Bapaume and Souchez underlined—

just why I don't know. It is a very interesting publication and I am mighty glad you sent it.

We had a very good supper tonight [and] invited the town major over. Our first course [was] tomato soup then hamburg steak and mashed potatoes, pudding (fig and raisin), fruit cake, figs, short bread, chocolates, home-made candy, cigars and cigarettes. No wonder I am feeling better tonight. It was really fit for the king—no indication of war time conditions eh?

It was disappointing that there was no mail tonight. It was the second day without letters too. But as I suppose I have been to blame for the same thing occurring myself. So I hold no grudge. Tomorrow I am going to a lecture so look out. I shall give you a full account of it and of my going and coming.

Now you must not expect more tonight after so long an epistle last night. . . .

> Goodnight sweetheart,
> Your lover ever
> *Stuart*

FRANCE, DECEMBER 30, 1916

Dearest:—

I am conscious that I have neglected you today but when I explain to you all we have had to do I am sure you will understand and forgive. Last night we were drowned out and as our billets were condemned anyway by the Brigade, we had to move. They were afraid they would topple down on us any time. Then the rain last night. How it came down. Fortunately I moved my bed and threw a tarpaulin over it as well so was fine but our dining room was in a fearful state. So we packed up and moved bag and baggage to the new quarters already selected. So we have not been exactly idle.

I feel I must tell you what was said about your pictures by Mr. Robertson of the 31st. At noon we were just finishing lunch when the door opened and in he walked. He was on his way from the front line to a school and was moving with his batman and Lares and Penates. We asked him to lunch. I showed him your pictures. . . I dare not put it even to you what he said but of course it was what I had always thought and I was glad to have someone bear me out especially when it was someone with the judgment and experience of Robertson. Do you know of the five officers who came over together to the 31st only

Mr. Weir is now with them. . . .

Well, honey, I do not believe there is any news. We are cut off from the world today. No paper no mail—rain, wind. You should have seen the streets of this little town. Say. We always have a sort of stream flowing down the side street and running in front of our billets, but this morning, it was nearly thigh deep. Horse wagons were splashing through. Today has been fine and it has more or less dried up.

Well good night sweetheart.

Your own

Stuart

7

New Year, Old War

❧ JANUARY, 1917 ❧

Stuart had thought many times of keeping a diary, but official disapproval of the practice left him content to have his letters to Edna serve as a record of his experiences. On 1 January 1917, he did start a diary proper on a very small scale, in a 3½ × 5½-inch address book. The first short entry began "This is to be a record of happenings in the life of a soldier in France."[1]

FRANCE, JANUARY 1, 1917

Dearest:—

First let me extend the season's greetings and wish you a Happy New Year. It seems almost too much to hope for and yet who knows. Tonight I am making my first entry in my diary for the year 1917. . . .

You will be interested in knowing that I went out to the horse lines today and was entertained at the 31st mess. Major Hewgill was on his way back to Canada on a three months leave. It appears his father has died and he is going back to fix things up. . . . My trip was more or less made in vain but I sponged on them for lunch. I was not a bit loath to do it as we are a sort of halfway house and often feed the stranger within our gates. I certainly like Major Hewgill. He certainly is fine. . . .

I enjoyed the walk very much and I think it did me a lot of good.

You get very tired sticking around the same old place too long. By the way. Janet wishes you would write oftener. Possibly she was sort of peeved at not having heard from me. I forgot to explain to her how little leisure you have for writing. They seem to have been anxious and over wrought. . . . They are beginning to feel the war over there now more than ever. These fogs in London have apparently been pretty bad. You will have to make arrangements about being accompanied. I should certainly feel worried if I thought of you wandering around London streets in the dark alone. And you must not forget to write and let me hear from you constantly. I worry and get depressed if I do not hear. ,

. . . Janet was telling me that Joe Clarke is again seeking election as Mayor!! Janet again asked re Mr. Bennett. It has become King Charles head, I fear. I think I shall have to write and ask you to convince them that he is all right. They have considerable confidence in your word.

Well honey, this is not satisfactory. . . . I trust I have reported all the parcels. The last one was the one containing the Christmas cake, candy etc from home. I certainly have been well treated.

Well goodnight. God bless you dearest.

Your own
Stuart

Stuart relished news of any sort from home, and although he complained occasionally about their neglect, his sisters kept him abreast of political events through their letters and the Edmonton newspapers. Joe Clarke, the labour politician mentioned in the letter above, did not win election as mayor of Edmonton until labour unrest after the war created the necessary climate. In anticipation, Stuart worried about post-war climate and in many of his letters, as in that below, he ruminated on the impact of war experiences on Canada's moral fibre.

FRANCE, JANUARY 2, 1917

Dearest:—

It seems strange to write 1917 already and I know it will take sometime to get used to it. However, that is the least of my troubles. Tonight, when the mail came in, there was nothing for me so I have got to starve for mental pabulum another twenty-four hours. I told you probably what a long interesting letter I had from Jentie and what a long reply I wrote. It nearly exhausted me, there seemed to be so much to write. I certainly hope you will take pains to write every day. I got hold of a paper this morning giving dire accounts of all the casualties due to the fog in London and I pictured all sorts of things happening to you. Of course they are extreme cases but I do hope you will be careful.

Your mother I wrote to night before last. It made me buck up to think that it should fall to my lot to cheer people up. I didn't feel exactly perky but I figured it was up to me to lead the way in the matter of cheeriness. As you know it is not exactly my fort, but I try to fill the role.

I fear my Russian has not been progressing, but we have been upset at Christmas and New Years. Do you know New Year's Eve I was prepared for almost anything and waited up till eleven or so when I thought indications would at any rate be forward if a strafe was on. There was very little firing however and I was relieved when I heard that the heavy batteries were at a New Year's banquet. So I dropped quietly off to sleep. Suddenly my dreams were disturbed by a deafening crash-bang-whang-bang. The noise just seemed to wrench me. Every battery in the neighbourhood I guess fired two salvos. Those in the trenches said that as the flash from our guns lit up the sky, there was an answering flash from the east and the projectiles from both sides practically crossed no mans land together. Fritz was apparently waiting for us. However, nothing further came of it... and I was left in peace. You have no idea how these guns get on your nerves at times.

New Year's was a dismal day. The country side has not yet got over its spree of Christmas week. I went for a walk as I told you to the horse lines and had lunch with the 31st officers mess there. Our New Year's dinner was not a brilliant success but we managed to rake up canned turkey and a plum pudding. By the way, you did not send me one did you. One turned up in the mess room but I have no idea where it came from. We ate it though with sugar, fruit juice and cream on it. I discovered also a box of dates, stuffed with nuts (sent by Jentie) so our little party was quite a success.

Your account of wandering in a fog reminds me of trying to find your way around a bad bit of the line on a dark night. I have had only one or two experiences of that, but they were bad enough. . . .

Parcels are coming through very slowly. I have still two to come. I hear that somewhere back of the lines there is a whole room full of parcels which they cannot move. I hope all things come to him that waits.

I wish I could write you a good long newsy and comforting letter just to make you feel that you can rely on me. I have begun to feel that you must move in a realm superior to events, if you are going to be halfway contented at this game. I know it is hard at times but we are all learning and I trust the lesson will be well learned. I so long to cheer you up and make you realize that things are all right and they certainly are. It is hard I know to go through the present but when it is over we will be glad we made good. When we go back we will be able to look everyone in the eye squarely. I believe also the end is coming more quickly than we know. I don't like to raise false hopes but those are my impressions. I can't tell you why. What a wonderful thing it has been to have Britons from all over the world gathered together like this in a common cause. What a broadening of ideas and outlook. There will be remarkable changes in the life and thought of the people when the boys go back. The only fly in the ointment is the exposure of our boys to the looser morals over here. Colonel Nasmyth told Father Fallon that the men from Canada should be sent to the front before they could be contaminated in England and I believe he is right. The normal man does not want to juggle with sin when he is face to face with danger every day. But in England, what a difference. I shudder when I think of those girls at midnight in Piccadilly. It hurts me to think of women being so. It jars sadly on one's sense of chivalry and the unfortunate thing is they do not typify a big city any more than they typify English life. When our boys get back, I fear we will have a popular idea of a soldier as a rake, or somewhat near that. The public will never discriminate between those who did and those who did not conduct themselves properly. Of course we will recover from it but it furnishes a sad commentary on English people.

Well honey we mustn't lose hope, must we, but plug ahead and try to make things come out right. Our own belief in our ideals and our love for one another will be some reward will it not.

Watson got a parcel tonight with a Christmas number of the *Sphere*, so we have the walls of our new quarters plastered up with fair dames. I never knew before what the Illustrated Supplement was for.

Well honey dear this must be goodnight as I must get up early. The wind is howling outside and the rain beating. Won't I enjoy my downy cot tonight.

Sweet dreams and God Bless you.
Stuart

While the mail service was unbelievably reliable most of the time, there were exceptions, and when they did occur they devastated Stuart's morale. The letter below explains the dearth of letters he had suffered in November.

FRANCE, JANUARY 4, 1917

Dearest:—

I know what you will be saying about me but I have had a good deal to do and no opportunity to write. Everything is fine. We are in now for our tour. Last night I received six letters from you dated Nov. 5th, 7th, 8th, 9th 10th and Dec. 25th. I often wondered why there was such a gap in your correspondence about that time. . . . Well this letter is not going to be up to much but as you got a Field card last night I must do better. Goodnight. God bless you.

Stuart

FRANCE, JANUARY 5, 1917

Dearest:—

These letters in the trenches at best are unsatisfactory. Somehow my mind fails to react correctly to obtain definite results. This morning brought no mail except a letter from Louise. . . .

The weather has been very delightful since we came in and everything has dried up quite nicely. We are not suffering from the cold which is one thing to be profoundly thankful for. My health is fine for which I am profoundly grateful. Watson is well too.

You must not expect much in the way of a letter tonight. In fact I am ashamed of these communications from the dug out. They are unsatisfactory. I do sincerely hope there will be a letter in the morning.

Goodnight and God bless you

Your own

Stuart

He often apologized for short and inadequate letters from the trenches but the following entries from his diary for 4 and 5 January shed light on the circumstances of those days:

Thursday, January 4
... We strafed Fritz 10 a.m. Retaliation severe. Everyone to dugouts. The artillery cooperated but support very poor. The afternoon was bright, aeroplanes overhead. Slight T.M. activity this p.m. ...
Friday, January 5
Beautifully bright. Great aeroplane activity. Hun strafe very severe this a.m., especially on right. Dugout crumped in—two officers wounded 4 men shell shock. Heard of 8 Hun casualties from Hun side, "Do you remember Herman? Well, the swine got him." The flying pigs—first days activity on this front.[2]

Communication between the opposing trenches was not uncommon, even at this later stage in the war. The "flying pigs" reference was to trench mortar bombs, which the Canadians were using for the first time in that locale.

FRANCE, JANUARY 6, 191[7]

Dearest:—
... This morning I received a letter containing what is the finest thing I have received for many a long day. Ah honey. Times like that I realize how much I love you and how dear to me that face is which has been withdrawn from me for so long. It is a very beautiful case without speaking of the face which it encloses. By the same mail I had a letter from your mother and a parcel from Canada. ...

Your mother wrote me such a comforting letter. I know she has an exaggerated idea of my goodness; but it is good to be overappreciated some times. Your mother thinks there is a religious meaning back of this turmoil and wretchedness. I do too but we seem to be entering on the almost impossible task of casting out sin with sin. The only real good that can come of this war is for England to see herself. The mere beating of Germany is pretty much incidental. ...

I am feeling well so do not worry about me. I wish you knew how much I think of that photograph. Then I have my cigarette case lined with your likeness.

Your mother pictures me coming home covered with glory like J. W. Tipton. Think of it. ... The letter also enclosed one from Harry; among other things he wanted souvenirs. I suppose he wouldn't object to anything in the way of a rifle, trench mortar or H. E. shell. Think of trying to cart around such luxuries. Perhaps sometime I can buy him something. Some of the boys have got dandy little Fritz revolvers and sold them. Most of the stuff is too bulky.

You do not say much about what you are doing or how you are feeling. Be sure to write everything. Now take care of yourself and don't work too hard. Be sure I love you more than ever.

Your own
Stuart

FRANCE, JANUARY 9, 1917

Dearest:—

... Fritz is stirring things up a bit this morning though in our neighbourhood it is quiet. There was no letter this morning by runner... worse luck. I hope I will get one tonight. I have now received all my Christmas parcels except the one from J. S. Fry and Sons from Robertson Church. It is now so late I think we will not get it now. However, I have been well treated, in fact more than well treated. I am glad you are taking the matter of leave philosophically. I have not seen any of the 31st officers lately to know how mine was coming through but I am not worrying. It will come all in good time.

That leather case with your photo is fine. I carry it in my breast pocket and I fear I make a good many excuses for opening it. But you don't blame me surely after three months away. Do you know the time has seemed quite long after all. The stay at the base and the trip across country are all in the distant past. Also my first view of the firing line by night. Well there are some weird sights here. Yesterday at dark there was a little strafe. Fritz big shells were going away back. We could hear them bursting away behind, a lurid flash like lightning and a peal like thunder. Every gun every shell has a different note. You get to realize how far off and what kind of a gun it is. Underground, you seem to hear sound much further off. We are never at a loss to know when something is doing. The strata seem to have something to do with the carrying of sound.

Well honey, there is nothing much to tell you today. I shall try to write a good long letter tonight God bless you.

Your own
Stuart

The intervals spent out of the forward line gave Stuart more time for long, contemplative, and thoughtful letters, such as that below in which he had some telling observations on England's educational system. It was written the day after a return to more comfortable billets in reserve. He reflected on experiences of the day before which his diary entry for 9 January notes as, "A long day. The Hun was very active on our right especially and even necessitated retaliation on our left." The company headquarters had been hit by heavy artillery, burying two officers, while "The mens dugout was crumped on, and both guns buried." Their relief had not been completed until early evening and they had not reached the billets until about 9:30 p.m.[3]

FRANCE, JANUARY 10, 1917

My Dear:—

Two letters of the 2nd and 4th reached me last night or rather were waiting for me when I got in. . . . I am sorry you are feeling tired as you must be after your strenuous four months, though you have said nothing as to how you are feeling. . . . I noted that you had just written to Janet in response I suppose to that tenderly worded appeal in that letter you forwarded. She put it more pointedly when she wrote to me. . . . Janet did not realize I suppose how hard you were working. . . .

Well, honey, dear, one cannot look ahead it is true. Except that one must have absolute confidence in the future and what it will bring forth. I think the people at home are beginning to feel worse than we do out here. Janet and Alice's letters betray quite a feeling of fed upness. Canada though has to some extent profited. I wish one could say the same of England. That has tired and disgusted me more than anything else. I suppose that Rome was not built in a day and the nature of the British Empire demands slow moving but thank heaven! Lloyd George is at the head of things. He ought to throw some punch into it.

The war is a perpetual puzzle to me. The writer has yet to be found to picture the soul of the Tommy in this war. He has been called on to go through incredible things and yet he has kept his poise and bearing. The coolness of men under fire astounds me; and their nerve. It is astounding what reserves of human power this cataclysm has unlocked. Yet some of these men are devils when they get to civilization and get booze. Nobility jostles laxity. I don't know which there is most of. Yet it has made a profound change on some characters, a change written too often in letters of blood.

No one complains of the sacrifice if it is not in vain. I am the last to preach a religious revival but I do think something must happen to change the heart of the people. What is the good of fighting for outraged virtue and oppression if our own women are content to fling the former away. There's no condoning it, it is criminal, useless and hypocritical. If people wish to interpret life in terms of pleasure, why fight for moral or spiritual things. You have already given all your hostages away. Why the dickens prate about national honour and all such high sounding names when you know that these meet no response in the average heart. There is too much "halfpenny paper" about the average Englishman today—combined of vulgarity, coarseness and cheap sentimentality. Everywhere the same. Somebody protests against amorous scenes in the parks and some fool comes out with a screed about harmless love making. Good heavens the love making can look after itself, only for goodness sake protect the honour and ideals. The love making will not suffer. Don't let the physical side dominate the other in such things other wise you lose the inspiration.

Well honey, I have written a lot but I have thought a lot about it. It pains me to find England dominated by cheap sentiment and shibboleths. It seems to have been so hard to get them out of their sloth and insularity. I think the wretched educational system has a lot do with it. Do you remember my becoming embroiled with that Mr. Beach and how warmly he defended it. Well whether it is good or not depends on what you wish to attain. If you wish to give some of the people the idea that they are superior and capable of governing others that is all right. But just now conditions in England have convinced nine tenths of the people that they will not be governed, the other tenth, the superior people, are out of a job. This wretched system only educates the few and not the many. The result is they imbibe ideals out of the halfpenny papers. Education even if just for useful trades would overcome half the trouble and England would not be cursed with such demagogues. Think of professional politicians running a country at a time like this. Good heavens if their sacrifice is not to be in vain it must give us a decent system of government and some form of international control that will make war an impossibility. It simply *must* be made impossible in the future.

Do you know the guns have been going all day. (mostly ours) A few minutes ago Fritz started putting some over off to our right apparently searching for a battery. You can always distinguish between the arrival and the departure of a shell. I really don't know which is more nerve wracking.

How would you like a couple of brass shell cases. The 18 pounders or A.A.s make very nice souvenirs and can be carved. Do you covet any such souvenir? Let me know if you do. . . .

. . . Now I have nearly run down. I had a lot to say and I said it. I suppose certain things keep burning themselves deeper into your soul all the time, and a fellow who has been out here I guess thinks he has the right to talk.

Well, dearest, I look for a letter tonight but do not expect one. Oh! I received the watch o.k. and it seems to be in good shape. Thanks for the trouble. I am very sorry dearest if I have been negligent in acknowledging anything.

It has been beastly cold today so cold that I would not have a bath though the bath house is but a step away. You feel the cold much more out of the trenches.

Goodnight sweetheart. God bless you.

Stuart

The rumour that wives who had come to England were going to be sent back to Canada recurred frequently, and it never failed to cause Stuart some worry. Food shortages were growing more critical, adding fuel to the rumours, but one condition on which a Canadian woman might be allowed to remain was that she have a job that contributed to the war effort. The apparent ease of transAtlantic travel for civilians had continued through the war, but by early 1917 increasing German submarine activity made the crossing more dangerous; reportedly the last ship on which women would be allowed to sail was scheduled to leave in January.[4]

FRANCE, JANUARY 11, 1917
[NO. 1]

My Dearest:—

My last letter may give you the idea that I have abundant energy, today's will be somnolent. After breakfast I visited the bath house and

had an oliver, now I am reposing before a coke fire and every moment
I am becoming drowsier. Otherwise I have a feeling of physical well
being. . . . I am more than pleased with the letters I get from home.
The girls apparently make quite an effort and they also put more heart
into it than they used to. I expect also they find Edmonton pretty dull
and their interests lie more across the water. They are beginning at
length to talk of national service in Canada. The young men who lurk
about in secret hiding places are being rounded up and told they will
have to [serve]. The School Board are threatening action. I cannot understand how the young male teachers could resist the example of the
men that went from the Edmonton schools. I consider it a high example of duty well done whatever I may think of the men themselves.
I have met I think all the surviving ones, Yule, Davies and Kennedy. . . . Little old Edmonton has done her bit. We were figuring out
a few nights ago and find that she has sent about 14000 [sic] men. Even
allowing for outside points there is at least 10% of the population. By
the way did you see that Frank Oliver's son had been killed. . . .

. . . The O.C. was asked last night for a return showing the names
of officers and others whose wives were residing in England. I do not
know the significance of the move. It may have none. I just thought I
would let you know. I was just wondering how having a job would affect the situation. Let me know if you hear anything.

Did I tell you it was snowing this morning. Our bedroom was
beastly cold all night and I crawled down low into the blankets, about
nine thirty it started to snow, the ground is half frozen. When I went
for my bath I nearly froze, particularly during the dressing process.
The bath man was very good and saw that I had lots of hot water but
the dressing room was fearfully cold. However I got back to a good
warm fire which did the trick. It seems to be clearing up now however.

Well, I have strung this letter out mighty well, I can tell you, seeing
that I had little to work on. Between this sentence and the last dinner
has intervened. Judge therefore of its merits.

I duly received the Spectator of December 30th which you forwarded, and it was mightily appreciated. The girls sent me a couple of
Saturday Evening Posts which I have not had time to peruse. . . . We
get the papers pretty regularly just now which is gratifying.

We have quite a bunch of pretty girl pictures in our mess room. I
wish you could see them. Still I have one which I carry in my pocket
that I prefer to all others, and withal she is goodness and modesty personified. How I long for the sight of your face. . . . You never said
whether you found Mrs. Weir good company or not. I cannot tell you

what a comfort it has been to me to know that you were with her and I dare say the same applies to Norman. . . .

Well, my own honey, I am going to drag this lengthy letter out to a close. I think next time I get any from home I shall forward them. They will save me writing. . . .

Now don't stay out late these winter nights. I worried about you during those foggy weeks. Goodbye Sweetheart. God bless you.

Stuart

FRANCE, JANUARY 11, 1917
[NO. 2]

Dearest:—

Now why, I wonder, should I be writing to a certain little girl tonight for at least the second and possibly the third time today. Why else than because I love her and cannot get her out of my thoughts day or night. Each day I thank God that I have known her and her love for me and each day I ask my self whether I am worthy of it. My own dear girl, if somebody had tried to picture to me in his most glowing terms what married life might be, it would not have even remotely approached the joy and blessedness that we have found in it. . . .

Well honey, three letters tonight, one from your little self, one from Louise and one a business letter. I wish I could refrain from criticizing Louise and her letters. In spite of the fact, that she is a bright girl, her letters always seemed frothy. . . .

. . . If there is one thing I would like to learn from this war, it is the greatness of soul to see evil and selfishness without allowing it to poison me. I do hope we will really learn how to live. People who have suffered can never be quite the same, no longer can they live and die unto themselves alone. In hours of loneliness, I turn to the Book you sent me. I hope you do too dear and try to live in the spirit of that faith we hold dear and which we hope will emerge triumphant out of the clash of arms.

I have several times wondered whether you and Mrs. Weir were congenial. You say very little about her except the common bond that you have. Will you be the same little girl when I get back I wonder. I think so, for you could never be anything other than your own self. I went for a long walk this afternoon. . . . It was a relief though to get away from my immediate surroundings though goodness knows the village streets in France are not very inspiring. I am inclined to dislike the French. They seem dirty and rather coarse. The people are shabbily dressed and live meanly; but their patience and courage are remarkable. It will be a wonderful thing to see France after the war and see what they have done. We could have done nothing had it not been for them. The agony through which France is passing is in some ways a terrible ordeal. The French leaders must know what they can count on and what their strength is. . . .

Tonight is a wild dismal night, a strong southerly wind was blowing when I came in and I tell you the outlook was not very cheerful. To make it worse our fire is not oversupplied with fuel, so it is early to bed for us. What simple pleasures should satisfy us after the war, a cosy fire, books, a few friends, reasonably hard work and regular hours. I tell you it will be hard to tear me from my fireside after this. . . .

Would you not like to see me clean tonight. I am from head to foot. The only drawback is, these Frenchwomen do not get your clothes clean. They only half wash. It may be that they cannot get clean water but I should like to give them lessons. They never seem clean themselves and their houses and surroundings are untidy. You see girls (pretty enough) get around in the morning with a morning after look, hair down etc etc. We have two sisters in the village to whom I am referring. They are characters, clever and good looking, they run a little canteen owned by their father. I fear it is the girls that draw the trade. They seem very nice girls and have the respect of all the soldiers. Think of keeping a store where you are at any time liable to have a shell fall on you. They don't seem to worry a bit. I suppose they take to the cellar when things get too warm. French cellars are much more substantial affairs than ours—are small and have stone or brick arches over them. I have taken cover in them more than once myself. Fritz doesn't care a hang about the civilian population I can tell you, and they expect no mercy.

Do you know we are having a regular snow storm tonight. It's bed for me as our fire is going out. It is a beastly dismal place here. I hope we get away from here.

Now good night honey,

Your own,

Stuart

In the letter above Stuart assessed the French harshly, but with some sympathy and admiration. There is irony in his assumption that the French leaders must have known what they could count on, coming as it did just three months before the mid-April mutinies in the French army. The focus of his criticism returns to the English in the letter that follows.

My own Honey:—

Your letter of the 7th came in tonight. You seem very tired and dispirited. In a way I am sorry you are looking forward to my leave for it will seem all too short. I know you are not well and it worries me. I guess you should not have taken that job or held it so long. You are a dear brave girl and I certainly honour you for your grit. . . . How little we know what is in store for us or what a day may bring forth. Sometimes you get disheartened when you think of things but cheer up, there is a good time coming.

I have been working hard at the Russian today so do not feel very keen on doing anything. My brain is in a kind of daze. I noticed one thing, I put on my specs to read Russian and find that they do not agree with my eyes. I have not been using them for weeks.

Sat. morning: What a wretched morning. It has been blowing and snowing all night and has continued on into the morning. I was cold in bed last night for the first time despite the fact that I had the furniture piled on top of me. This morning we have a good fire of wood and coke so are comfortable indoors but to go out would mean walking through oceans of mud. . . .

Studying Russian as I am, I am more or less interested in anything Russian. I noticed an article recently in either the Times or Chronicle severely criticizing English methods in trying to get Russian business. The same old story, trying to force English wares on the Russian, insisting on payment in sterling and as a result leaving the market open to the American and Swede. One British merchant replied complaining of being out of pocket by paying a tax and by being paid in roubles. Why a German would pay that cheerfully and make it up within six months. Why don't they willingly meet Russian requirements. The enormous business possibilities make it well worth while.

We hear all about the Council at Rome and the new War Loan, Lloyd George has certainly got the stride. And the Imperial Conference. Things are certainly doing these days. I suppose we are going through the dark days now and that things will brighten up gradually. . . .

You have never mentioned what your plans are when you leave the Pay and Records office. Are you. . . just going to rest. I really think you need one from the tone of your letters. Be sure to let me know what your plans are. I wonder what the [illegible] are re Canadian soldiers' wives residing in England. Have you any information on this point? . . .

I really think I shall have to apply myself seriously to study. It is really worse out of the trenches than it is in. Your mind is unoccupied and you get down in the dumps. When I get far enough on in the Russian to start reading I will be better off. As an old teacher used constantly to repeat, Nature abhors a vacuum. . . . It is a tremendous relief to write to you when I am out; in the trenches I am often either too busy or too tired at night to do very much.

Well honey I am worrying a lot about you. I want you to be happy and [the rest of this letter is not in the collection]

The cold Sunday of 14 January found Stuart thinking of friends at home in Alberta and feeling keenly the lack of mental stimulation. He mentions the Manleys (RWM and Velma), friends from Wetaskiwin whose new-born son he had admired on a visit in 1914, and this passage is a rare expression of his thoughts on children and parenthood. His estimate of British casualties for the year 1916 must be considered suspect.

FRANCE, JANUARY 14, [1917]

My Dearest:—

Yesterday's mail has not yet arrived so I am still in doubt as to whether there is a letter coming. However, I never miss a favourable opportunity to write. The abominable weather continues. Last night it was frosty and the whole earth is covered with an impenetrable mist this morning so you can hardly see one hundred yards—not as bad I will admit as a London fog but bad enough. The weather has been so beastly cold. I don't see how the men live.

Captain Pouncey, when he sees me writing, often asks what I find to talk about. I just smile in an indulgent sort of way. People who are essentially practical and always doing something with their hands do not understand I guess what reserves of mental power are. . . .

I shall be glad to be out of these billets. They are dark and cold and cheerless and so far from congenial company. Why I am getting out of the way of carrying on a conversation.

Do you know it is three months tonight since I bade goodbye to you at Sandgate, and that horrible lonely ride you had up to London. I worried a lot about it I can tell you and was mighty relieved when I heard you were all right. . . . A lot has happened in that time hasn't there?

Did I tell you Captain Pouncey has the Military Cross. He is an original 31st man and been here a long time. I was glad to see him get his decoration.

. . . I am to blame for not having written lately. Still I have so many to write to it is hard to get around to them all. If I were back in Blighty or Canada and had a friend out here I should write as a matter of duty. I think that is one thing this life should [do—] take all the selfishness out of one. Did I tell you of the scheme some of the girls in Canada have—getting the name of some friendless soldier and writing to him. I thought the idea very fine. I wish I had the last two years of life to live over. I should live it in a different spirit.

By the way, I wrote to RWM at Christmas. I don't know whether he would appreciate it but it was more for Velma's sake. I suppose she is very proud of that boy of hers. It is a way parents have I guess. What would I not give for the same. Parenthood is the crown of life. And the rest—somehow they seem to enter on its joys and responsibilities with the lightest of hearts. I think we are all careless in the way we regard child life. We are prone to regard the child as an intrusion instead of preparing the way for him. I noticed a statement in the paper this morning that in the United Kingdom there are 140,000 children lost annually and that before birth. What lamentable facts for medical science to contemplate. Why that is more I will guarantee than the British lost in killed last year. Well you will not appreciate my moralizing. It is said to be the mark of a dull mind but when your morning paper has not come and you are marooned "Somewhere in France" what are you to do?

I am much disappointed about the mail not arriving. I suppose the authorities have spoiled us so we chafe at any delays.

Thank heaven here is the morning paper coming so we shall have something to break the monotony. Do you know out here Sunday is the same as any other day. It is partly due to the French population and partly to conditions here. If you were to ask me in the line what day of the week it was I couldn't tell you without figuring it out.

Well I shall have to close,

Your own

Stuart

During January, the Canadian Second Division continued to hold the line in the Lens-Arras sector, where a pattern of limited action continued against the German lines. Patrols were maintained along with exchanges of mortar fire and occasional trench raids. Battalions of the 4th Brigade staged an exceptionally large raid on 17 January at 7:45 a.m., to "take prisoners and booty, and destroy enemy dug-outs three miles east of Lens."[5] On the day prior to that assault, Stuart's mortar battery provided covering fire for a smaller raid, which the following letter describes well.

There was a five-day gap in the correspondence at this juncture, and his diary entries enlarge a bit on the letter of the 19th in regard to their return to the front line after only four full days in reserve billets. Sunday 14 January: "In the afternoon... I took the battery in and relieved. Relief very quiet." Monday, 15 January: "The first day of our new tour. The expected did not transpire. Everyone sore at having to come back. Everything quiet as a rule. No activity. The night was pitch black. I had occasion to be out a good deal going to 28 Bn HQ and nearly broke my neck." Tuesday, 16 January: "The great event. Our division pulled off a raid at 4:30 p.m. . . . mines were exploded and a fierce artillery barrage put up. Our function was to distract his attention with Stokes bombs. At 4:30 prompt a battery of 18 pounders open then pandemonium. No casualties reported. Realized tonight I have not written to honey for 3 days." Wednesday, 17 January: "At 7:45 we were alarmed by the commencement of a violent canonading on our left... I called a stand to and hastened to the front line... was informed that the 4th Bde were going over.... The 4th got 100 prisoners... We were relieved at dark."[6] They moved to new billets on Thursday the 18th, and on the 19th he finally had time for a letter or two.

My Dearest Dear little Honey:—

I know that you are worrying your little head off and all on account of a no account specimen like myself. But when I tell you all of the things that have happened within the past three or four days you will understand though you may not forgive.

To begin with, we are out of the line in rest for a while so you will know that I am safe as far as the Hun goes for at least a while. I shall describe in greater detail, later, my present billet—a French farm. Meantime I shall go over the occurrences of the past few days.

You will probably have already seen in the papers of what the French call a coup de main, the British obscure its meaning by the term raid, carried out by the Canadians, in this case meaning us. I personally took no part in it except to direct covering fire. I think it no harm to tell you that the raid was conceived some time ago and postponed until favourable conditions developed. As a result of postponement, we were required for another tour in the trenches and in our tour the expected was pulled off at 4:30 p.m. on the 16th. At zero hour, a mine went up and hell was let loose. It was impossible to tell what was happening, save the explosion of bombs, shells. Everything was covered with a pall of smoke. The operation was only moderately successful. The German lines were entered and damaged. The attack was repeated the following morning shorty after it got light, this time we took no part. Everything went off brilliantly as you will have learned despite the snow that covered the ground. I shall tell you all about it when I see you.

Our battery left the line... [and] Watson and I got into our billets about 8:30 in the evening after the relief, almost played out. A good supper however revived us, and we made ready for our move at 8 the following morning. It was not a pleasant day to start, snow and slush over everything but we made it and got on the road. There was a great movement of troops that day. We met numbers of battalions and saw familiar faces just like ships that pass in the night. They flashed by with just a word. Our march was a long one, and as the day wore on, it began to snow—great wet flakes that turned into slush on the ground. Lunch was very light and when we reached our destination at 4 p.m. I was famished. However, I helped get the men fixed up before locating myself. There are always some French youngsters around selling chocolates and cakes. I purchased half a dozen cookies to stay me. Finally I got my own billet, got my baggage and changed my wet clothes. By this time, it was our supper hour and I joined Adams to go to mess. Imagine our disappointment to find our cook's stuff dumped in front of the building which was closed and silent. Madame had been away to [censored] buying for her store. She returned about 6:30 and we rustled up Maxey and tried to start a fire. Monsieur made frantic efforts to get it going but his mad rushes did not inject any energy into the fire which persisted in smoking. So we finally after an hours wait decided to take the meat to our several billets and get it cooked. Two of them came with me and my madame had one of her women do the necessary. I was famished when we sat down to our meal of steak, bread, butter, coffee about 8:30. Say we made a meal. The family sat around carrying on sporadic conversation while we devoured. So we stayed the evening, talked in halting French about anything and everything. Such pleasant people! At 9:30 I turned into a real bed between real sheets and slept, oh till 8 o'clock this morning. My batman was quartered with the cows and calves in the Etape, and he says he has not slept like it since being in France, so everyone feels "jake" this morning. All we need is a good lunch to round things off.

The place we are living is a French village—really a collection of farms. They have no isolated farms here. The farmers all live in villages. It consists of a courtyard surrounded on all sides by low brick buildings—the house is on the street side but the stables are simply a continuation of the house. We have all kinds of stock, horses, cows, pigs, sheep, chickens, ducks, geese, etc etc. The family consists of a couple and two "bebes." There are quite a few servants employed, who sit in the kitchen with the family and eat there too. The people are fine—madame kindness and generosity personified. She refused to take anything for our little spread last night. "Apres la guerre," she kept repeating. Monsieur is also very decent. They bring me coffee, hot water when I need it, dry my socks and boots.

Well, honey, you know I am in for a good time while here. Even if they work us sixteen hours a day, we can sleep in comfort and eat abundantly, eggs, milk, meat of all kinds. So here's hoping they won't pull us out for some time.

Now this is not much of a letter but it will be continued in our next.

Your own
Stuart

The winter of 1916–17, one of the coldest on record in Western Europe, presented a severe challenge to those charged with providing adequate billets for officers and men. The "Town Major," an officer permanently stationed in a town, had responsibility for finding billets for troops assigned in his area and even for parties of troops passing through. Once ensconced in acceptable quarters, all ranks could turn to preferred forms of recreation, and the *estaminet*, mentioned below, an establishment much like the "canteen" that Stuart wrote of on 11 January, was a favourite of the troops on the Western Front. Found in villages and small towns and combining attributes of pub, cafe, and restaurant, it sold such things as wine, cognac, beer, coffee, soup, and omelettes. Its owner usually "had a daughter or two, or nieces, or younger sisters who served at table and made no objection to tobacco smoke and ribald choruses in English and pidgin French. . . . [It] provided for the soldier off duty behind the line many and many a happy hour."[7]

FRANCE, JANUARY 19, 1917
[NO. 2]

My own Dearest:—

And now that I have got through the more urgent part of my letter I can settle down to the old familiar chatter. The day has gone pleasantly enough, solutus cura—and the mere relaxation of strain is a pleasure in itself. I had lunch at one. It seems impossible to get enough to eat. This afternoon I have been reading and thinking of you. We have made the men a little more comfortable. I guess the estaminets beckon to them with open arms.

As you probably know the weather has taken quite a change here— for better or for worse. Snow has come with lowered temperature and accompanied by wet and mud as before. When I think of Canada and the way we prepare for cold weather I cannot wonder that Europeans shudder at our cold. They make absolutely no provision against cold; the houses have cellars (not basements) the floors are tiled and clammy. My room at present is like an ice house and the sheets when I get into them!!! I know the men had rather be in the line. There they have dugouts warmed by braziers. We have a mess room hired which we expect to keep comfortable and cheery. And oh how I expect to sleep these nights. . . .

Say my French is getting on by leaps and bounds. I make all kinds of howlers but I expect to be able to carry on a conversation shortly. I can make myself understood and can understand fairly well. In fact I am never stuck. I should pretty nearly be a French scholar when I leave.

Now sweetheart, don't get too discouraged over me but forgive my delinquencies. . . .

Goodbye honey
Your own
Stuart

FRANCE, JANUARY 20, 1917

My own Dear Little Girl:—

Another day of clouds and cold with my feet almost numb. The weather has turned what must be very cold for this country, the roads are hard and slippery this morning. You could almost use sleighs today. I was up at 7:45 in the expectation of an early parade but it was called off for the day. We shall hardly start serious work before Monday.

This farm is a great place. The people are full of interest. Yesterday they killed a pig and for the task they brought in an octogenarian almost in his dotage. He was bent and wore glasses but he has a belt with a most fearful looking trio of knives. I did not see the initial operation but the second stage was piling over the carcase a heap of straw and burning off the bristles. Then came the hot water stage after which the entrails were drawn and his porcine majesty withdrew to the house. Here he was operated on by the chief surgeon and in a remarkably short time was reduced to hams, shoulders, pork chops, etc etc. It looked so good that I arranged to buy a piece for the mess at 2 francs per pound, not very cheap eh?

Last night after supper I visited one of the other billets where the girls were learning their lessons. How strange it all seemed, yet how homelike. I sat down and went over it with them. It was a written exercise consisting of a dissertation on metals. Vital words were left blank and from a list at the top the child had to select the one which would apply. This involved looking up the meaning of the words in the dictionary, a mighty good idea for teaching a child the significance of words. When I left, I came home and found the Captain and Carnegie talking to Adrienne, one of the farm girls here. A very fine type of girl she is—hard working, intelligent, good natured and kind. Carnegie my batman (a mere child) has taken quite a notion to help her with the chores. Last night she had to assist at the expected arrival of some little porkers so had to remain up late. We talked for an hour or so then I went to bed to dream.

. . . [W]e have heard that there is a lot of mail for us at the Brigade. I hope it is true for I have been very short on mail. Day before yesterday I had one from you, but none since and not a paper of any kind. We don't even know whether the war is still on.

Duty forbade my finishing this letter this morning, when I had my work done I came right on to the mess. Say we had one fine dinner today—roast beef, roasted potatoes, custard, toast and cheese. Oh my! I ate as I haven't for months. Things taste so good.

Well you don't wish me to ramble on about gastronomic delights. Still it is a joy almost to get back to civilized life once more and eat your dinner in courses etc. . . .

The Town Major from the place we just left has come in. He has removed here also and is looking for billets. We were lucky to get in first and get the pick.

As I told you, we are in a strictly farming community though it is a village. Consequently we can buy all sorts of things such as milk, eggs, butter, fresh meat, and can have them properly cooked. Next week we start training so we will have the appetites of horses I expect. Shouldn't we have great times, enough training and recreation to keep us in good condition, straighten us up, and comfortable billets. Do you know trench life leaves you in poor shape. You stoop so much in the trenches and the dug outs that you get round shouldered. Why the march here the other day left me stiff and sore. Poor old Watson, he doesn't usually complain but it has been one continuous grouch for the past week. Now he is complaining of his sore legs and stays in bed nearly all the time. I suspect he is sore at the calling down Adams handed out to him night before last. He lost his bed and his valise, in fact all his worldly goods. Mine, I kept my eye on and they turned up fine. I guess I have everything I started out with. My clothes are now dry and I have managed to escape a cold so far.

You should see the horses they have in this country, especially the draft horses. Why they all look like show animals. I looked in M. LaBroye's stable the other day; he has three teams and such splendid creatures—round and sleek and strong. They seem mostly to have Percheron blood or French coach horses. And of course they are all perfectly docile and quite intelligent. Their cattle I cannot say so much for. They seem to be scrub stock. It is a pleasure to see such thrift as they have here—without the grasping spirit that seems to characterize so many of the French. Madame here, that is at our mess, runs a little store. Her husband is a miner but she rules the roost and a little termagant she is. I believe he threw a plateful of potatoes at her this morning when she was scolding him. Then he beat it but very wisely he came back within half an hour and was last seen meekly splitting wood. The officers were all discussing the hardships of married life at the lunch table.

I just saw Maxey pouring hot custard over some cakes and innocently asked him what he called the dish. Do you know what he replied. "Trifle." Did you ever hear of it.

I think I shall go out for a walk this afternoon as soon as I have written to Alice. It is a pleasure to ramble along the roads without the chance of a shell dropping on your noodle to disturb your contemplations. . . .

Well little sweetheart, I have done pretty well I think. I must close now and get a letter off to Alice. I have not heard from Philip lately, have you?

God bless you dearest
Your own
Stuart

FRANCE, JANUARY 21, 1917
[NO. 1]

Dearest Little Honey:—

It is the Sabbath morn but lowering skies and the frigid air have robbed it of any pleasantness, though I must admit it seems more like Sunday than any since I arrived in this stricken land.

Your letters of the 14th and 15th reached me last night and very glad I was to learn that you had quit work, for I know it has been hard on you. . . .

Probably by the time this reaches you, you will be celebrating the second anniversary of your wedding and it is with a view partly to convey best wishes that I am writing this little note in what is practically a zero temperature. Still I guess my heart is not frigid at least I hope not. I wish I could have a fire. Still there is a warm kitchen handy so I need not complain, I guess. . . .

The other battalions are drifting into their quarters gradually. I hope to see all my friends in the 31st shortly although they are not in the same town. I think Norman just shot his bow at a venture writing as he did re leave. I am not sure when I come. Norman was looking well when I saw him. The day they moved out of the trenches I saw him for some time and made myself sick out of his Christmas box.

The men out here are pretty sore at such fellows like MacRae and Whittaker that stay over in England for staff courses and only come over here on Cooks Tours. I heard that Whittaker is going back to Canada. Do you know MacRae started out as a lieutenant and he has no more right to get out of doing his bit than I have. Domnie I believe... is musketry instructor somewhere in England. Well good luck go with. It's not soldiering though.

Well sweetheart this letter will be unsatisfactory. I shall take my material down to the mess room and write there. It is too beastly cold here. Goodbye dearest. I will write a good long letter next time, this p.m. if possible. Give my best regards to Mrs. Weir.

Your own
Stuart

Best wishes on your anniversary.

FRANCE, JANUARY 21, 1917
[NO. 2]

My Dearest Own:—

I have been constantly recollecting that I promised you the equivalent of three letters per day for a while—most rash I can assure you. If I am to be permitted to fill the pages full of my love for you, a dozen letters per day would not suffice. I don't think any of the old sweetness has departed from it nor the first morning flush of passion been even dulled. To look on your face is to kindle afresh every time the tender memories of our first love added to all that are the wondrous memories of our wedded life, the golden days passed together, our joys and sorrows and those heavenly moments when I could take you in my arms and feel that all of life was enclosed in that embrace. I fear honey I am an incorrigible lover and should never develop into a good husband. The only regret of these years is that there has never been any third. In a way I feel it is a distinct loss. Yet when I look ahead to the future, I suppose it is as it should be for we never know what is in store for us. But do you know it has been hard to give up everything a person holds dear to come out here. That is where the voluntary system will not hold water. Why should I do this and another avoid it simply because he dislikes it. Why should a man's predilection determine the service he shall give or with hold from his country. There is going to be a lot of questioning after the war now believe me. It should have been done during the war. Smug respectability will hardly count as a saving grace. . . .

Now let us see what wonderful experiences of the day I have to recount. I finished your other letter before lunch which happened at one. After which, being in a somnolent mood, I journeyed uphill to the billets turned in under the blankets and went to sleep undisturbed by even the barnyard noises. I had intended taking part in a little game of football. But it was over when I got up so I came down to the mess; the padre was here (he of the 31st) so we entertained him till supper. We had a good supper, too (just watch me getting fat) and saw him depart at seven. I am going over to see friends at the 31st some day soon. . . .

Well now for tin hats and ceremonial parades salutes orderly room and all the paraphernalia of tin soldiering. We are to brush off the mud of the trenches clean our boots hats buttons belts and become soldiers once more instead of fighters. I am going back to an officer's tunic once more and Sam Browne. At 9 a.m. and 2 p.m. Fall in. Bugle sounds officer's call and all that out of the far off distant past of Sarcee Camp. But it [is] to be all for the good of the cause, I suppose.

I see by the Bulletin there are to be no more battalions raised in Alberta. However they are ushering in this universal service idea. How it is to be hitched up to the present system or how to the object in view, I can't see. It is all balderdash I think. There is no use taking a census of people, if you have not got the authority behind to whip them in line. It is just playing at the game and the time has long since passed for that. We are in dead earnest now. I know the politicians are scared stiff of French Canada and they have one ear on the ground in good old hack politician style. So I suppose we are to drift along for a few more months till reenforcements begin to peter out.

I didn't intend this to degenerate into a diatribe as it is Sunday evening and I should be thinking of more peaceful things. But having been out here one has very decided ideas on things.

Now I should have liked to send you a little memento for January 27th but it is impossible in this little burg to do anything. Will you take the word for the deed? . . . I will think of you dearest when I go to bed and speak a little prayer for your safety. May le bon Dieu hold you in His protecting arms.

Your own sweetheart
Stuart

In the last two letters above, the fatigue, strain, and frustration felt by front line duty officers surfaced in Stuart's comments about men who remained either at home in Canada or in non-combat jobs in England. He maintained an early conviction that conscription was needed if the Canadian Corps was to remain at full strength, but he clearly foresaw the political, ethnic, and religious divisions that would mark the debate after introduction of the Military Service Act in Ottawa late in the following summer. One bright spot appeared for Stuart at this point in the arrival in the battery of William Reith, who proved to be a kindred soul with whom to share conversation and such civilized traditions as afternoon tea.

FRANCE, JANUARY 22, 1917
[NO. 1]

Dearest:—

... I am orderly officer today. That does not mean much work but it is significant that we are starting in to train and smarten the men up. Training started today. This afternoon I take the men for a short time in musketry.

Really this country is only about half civilized. Their houses are always cold and today when we went after coal, all we could get was a wretched little sand bag full. Of course, the product of the mines is restricted but people must keep warm during this awful weather. Then the people here are most crude or naive. I do not know which. There is certainly no prudery and I am not sure that there is much delicacy. But they are good hearted and agreeable, which counts a good deal.

I have all kinds of reading matter just now. The girls have been sending me Posts... though strange to say it is almost impossible to buy a London paper. All that we get is the continental edition of the Daily Mail. We assume that the war is still on though we do not know that such is the case.

One of the officers wounded at the Somme returned last night, so one of us will probably be leaving the Battery. I don't know who it will be. They endeavour to have one representative from each battalion, but it may be otherwise. Reith comes from the 27th the same as Watson so the latter may return.

Do you know I am developing chilblains. I felt them this morning when I put on my boots. I must not sit in this cold room. But even when you get out before the fire you do not get warmed up. They have the strangest stoves here... and such poor coal—not even as good as Edmonton.

Well I must go off and see if there is any mail, then see the men's dinner.

Goodbye dearest for the present
                    Your own
                        Stuart

FRANCE, JANUARY 22, 1917
[NO. 2]

My own Dear little Girl:—

Four letters tonight of the 16th, 17th, 18th telling of your various activities shopping and sewing. As for myself there is little to tell. This afternoon, Adams and I went shooting, he with his .45 and I with my little .38. I was more than pleased with its performances. . . . I am satisfied I should make it very unpleasant for a Hun at close range. It is a very neat, clean, straight shooting weapon and I am proud of it. It is the first time it has been shot at all. As I carry my own ammunition I should not be without at any time. We continued our walk out to a farm house and grove about a mile from town. France would indeed be a beautiful country if the weather were decent—such beautiful avenues of trees stretching away in the distance such carefully tended groves and fine chateaux. I begin to think after all it is La belle France, all the land intensely cultivated the country open and unfenced as the virgin prairie. This chateau is the scene of operations of a company of Canadian wood cutters, the farmer is an absentee land lord living in Armentieres. It really is a fine old place. I admired the beautiful trees. The birds we saw were quite typically Canadian—sparrows, crows and magpies—you know the black and white fellows with the long tails that we have in Alberta. We could also hear the drumming of partridges in the grain fields. After I came in I met Reith the officer who is just back and we came down to the mess for afternoon tea—a habit I think I should like to cultivate. Your letters meantime came and they were eagerly devoured, I can tell you. When I went back I found Carnegie helping with the operation of extracting the lacteal fluid. In the dairy room the hum of machinery told me they were separating so I went in. The machine in use is an R A Lister one made in Dursely, England. Adrienne poor girl is sick. Madam confided in me that clacking around in these wooden shoes they cannot keep themselves warm and they suffer from colds and chillblains. I know for I have suffered far more here than I ever did in the trenches. Dinner was a howling success tonight for we were all ravenously hungry.

I had a letter from Philip tonight. . . . He spoke of coming to France shortly. I do not know whether he really meant it or not. I suppose what you say about Emily is true enough. She struck me as being a very fine girl but true to type more or less of a man-worshipper. I wish you would do what you can to be good to her. . . .

I have before me a card (prepaid) to be returned to J. S. Fry and Sons acknowledging the receipt of a box of chocolates which I never received. I suppose some transport man collared it. . . . Doesn't it make you sore. If the man in the line got it you would not mind but the further back you go the greater the degree of comfort you find. . . .

I am going to try to make the raise of a bath shortly. I believe we are within walking distance of one but I have not yet gone. I am getting my washing done by Adrienne at the house so am hoping a better job will be done.

Don't work too hard. . . . You want to save a bit of energy for later. Now Goodnight dearest. God bless you.

Stuart

Stuart's letters of late January continued to reflect the front line soldier's disdain and resentment of the rear echelons, and they began to show his impatience with the United States. The following letter indicates an attitude toward Wilson's efforts at a negotiated peace that was held by men in the trenches, men who resented, among other things, admonitions from a man who had declared himself "too proud to fight."[8]

FRANCE, JANUARY 2[4], 1917

My Dearest Own little Honey:—

A whole day without writing to you. I did try to get a letter written yesterday but there was too much to occupy my time. To begin with in the morning, we had a nine o'clock parade. I escaped actually taking part in that drill but my little piece came on at eleven. I was just going into the mens billet to introduce them to the mysteries of musketry, when a staff officer appeared, wished to know what instruction we had under way and hauled me off to Captain Pouncey. . . . [H]e insisted on haranguing the men himself with the result that we had to break off without musketry instruction in order to get dinner. After lunch, two of us had intended walking into town and stocking up the mess with eatables, but at the last minute Adams backed out. I needed some articles very badly so decided to go myself on a bicycle. No time was wasted as the days are still short and I got away at two. It was a beautiful ride, crisp and cold, along one of the National roads which was in perfect shape. I spun along at a good clip I can tell you, passing everything except motors. The last half mile was down hill only I did not know it and I ran the risk of breaking my neck descending some of the streets of the town. Finally I spun through to Le "grande rue" and landed up at the B.E.F. canteen. These are great institutions. They stock nearly everything necessary to sustain life. My purchases included fruit, custard powder, sauce, baking powder etc. This part of my business was soon disposed of, but the other took longer—ransacking the town for oil cloth, steel plates and cups. It is the deuce of a job purchasing in a French town, where you are a stranger and your stock of French is limited. . . . It was two hours before I began the ascent of the hill. It was now getting dark and to make it worse, the brake which I had used on my arrival, quite generously, had set against the rim of the back wheel with the result that I could scarcely propel the wheel on the level let alone up a slope. . . . I thought I should never make it with the wind against me but finally, I got my second wind, the roads became level and the trees began to fly past. I gradually got used to the aches and pains in my leg. Now and again a motor whizzed by but I paid no attention. At last I realized by the descent down which I was going that I was near home so I coasted down into the village and alighted in front of the mess, tired and stiff and hungry. The boys were at supper and believe me I never had a more welcome repast. After supper. . . I decided to visit one of the other billets. Here I found four of the officers before the fire and the family gathered around the festive board making merry over beer and chestnuts. The French certainly know how to have a good time. It was the best stove I have seen in France and I just soaked the heat in for half an hour before going back to my billet and turning in.

This morning was the coldest day yet. It must have been nearly down to zero and I nearly froze my ears and fingers going to breakfast. . . . We were billed for a route march so I had to get on my tin lid and pack. (The latter I ditched on the first opportunity). Do you know, nothing reminded me so much of home as our little march this morning. As we climbed up out of the valley we caught the full effect of the biting north wind and it was just as though it had blown across 100 miles of prairie. There was about six inches of snow on the ground, not wet but dry and powdery and blowing up in hard little drifts like it does out home. The ground was frozen hard and the men's boots rang on the stony roads. Looking around, there was a magnificent panorama—rolling farm land reaching in all directions without fence or hedge as far as the eye could see. The country is covered with hay stacks, neat and trim and there were those magnificent avenues of trees. The sky clear, the whole world wrapped in snow—everything breathed peace. It was hard to realize we were in France. Even the distant boom of guns was for the moment stilled. I did not enjoy it at first as it seemed impossible to keep warm, but gradually the exertion got the blood pulsing into the extremities. We circled around, from south to east and came back over the trail I followed yesterday. We had the wind against us the last mile; all we could do was to put our heads down and smile. But even such things cannot last forever; we reached home just at noon. Our lunch hour is one o'clock but without any pre-arrangement everyone presented himself at the mess at 12:30. It was amusing how everyone seemed to do the same thing—so finding lunch ready we proceeded to appease our insatiable appetites. There is no more work today but we are going to a lecture at Brigade H.Q. this p.m. I am tired and stiff and suffering from a mild attack of chillblains; this continued cold with insufficient exercise and indifferently heated rooms has started my old complaint. It probably will be nothing serious.

Well, Watson has gone. With the arrival of Reith, the Battery had more than its complement of officers and the 27th Battalion two representatives. . . . Reith, the new arrival, is a particularly fine chap. I hope I shall be tied up with him. . . .

Last night, when I got home, I found waiting for me my last Christmas parcel—a package of chocolate from Fry and Sons, sent on behalf of Robertson Church, Edmonton. By a curious coincidence I had just written about it the night previous. I was getting sore at its non arrival, there is nothing peeves me quite so much as the thought of . . . transport drivers pinching Christmas gifts. . . .

. . . I can't understand President Wilson and his "peace without victory." The situation for us was well summed up by Reith, "I don't want to go back to the front line again, but I would rather go back and fight for six months more than see England make peace now."

So say we all.

Did you or did you not save the papers giving the account of the Canadian raid? I should much like to see them when I get to London. As we get hardly any papers here at all, the only account I have seen was that in a French paper two or three days ago.

Well, I have been very lazy this afternoon. It is... now three o'clock. At four, we have tea preparatory to walking up to Brigade H.Q. As we will be in the same town as the 31st I hope to see Norman Weir. If I do not see him before I should see him at the lecture any way. We will hardly get back before six thirty so this will be a strenuous day. The feeling of my legs and back would indicate that I have been working and the rubicun complexion I have worked up is ample evidence that I have been out in the fresh air. I have been feeling fine since we came out except for a cold in the head. And I have a voracious appetite. Watch out for me when I descend on London....

I wonder if there will be a letter today. There was none yesterday. Goodbye honey. God bless you.

Your own
Stuart

Stuart had remained optimistic about his chances of being granted a leave, and when he learned that his posting to the trench mortar battery did not negate his leave status with the 31st Battalion, he began to plan for a trip to England.

FRANCE, JANUARY 25, 1917

My Dearest:—

A short letter dated the 21st came from you yesterday. I think it is the promptest delivery I have seen in France. Just three days from Sunday evening to Wednesday afternoon.

Well I wrote you a good long letter yesterday so you must not expect much today. After I had finished writing, I went up to the orderly room with the letter, [and] came back to the mess where we had tea.... We then started for Brigade H.Q. to attend a lecture by the Brigadier on the duties of young officers. I met Norman just before we reached the hall, so I went back to his billet with him while he got his coat. He is quartered in a chateau. It sounds fine as he says, but it is really a great big barn. He is never warm except when in bed. There were upwards of a hundred officers at the lecture which was necessarily dry. Our G.O.C. Division [General Officer Commanding the Division] was there and spoke a few words. . . . I learned one thing, that I had been struck off the effective strength of the 31st; it disturbed me for I don't want to be ditched on the matter of leave. However the adjutant assured me that it would not. It was quite late when we got home but Maxey [his original batman] was ready with a welcome dish of hot soup and beef steak.

This morning, it is again cold and fine. The French here are all prostrated with colds. They are so ill protected against it that they all have chillblains and grippe. . . .

I am going to get my stuff fixed up here instead of waiting till I get to London. I am having everything washed that is possible, clothes pressed and boots repaired. . . . I will then have nothing to do but to loaf. . . .

The men are off to the Brigade H.Q. for a bath but I fear I shall not be able to get another oliver before I go on leave. All the bath houses around here are frozen up unless one goes to town. We were more fortunate when we were in the line as we had three bath houses within easy reach of us.

M. LaBroye, mine host, was up this morning for the first time in several days. I found him walking around the barn sizing things up. When he caught sight of me, he started to complain of the men burning some of his lumber. I denied it at first but when he took me around into the mow and showed me a plank hacked beyond recognition, I could not doubt it. The weather has been cold and it was the only available fuel and in a way I don't blame them but monsieur swears he will make us pay for it. That is the one characteristic of the French I do not like. I don't mind it here for the man has a reasonable complaint when good lumber is burnt but up at that tumble down village where we were where the walls were coming down every day with the concussion of the guns and where what was left of the village only stood on sufferance from Fritz, it was the height of absurdity for the people to claim compensation if timber or lumber of any kind were taken for fuel. Why some day the Germans will open up and there won't be one brick left standing on the other. But the British with their easy going ways prefer to be cheated rather than impose a hardship on the inhabitants.

We are going to have another lecture Sunday so I hope to go. I promised Norman I should have dinner with him.

Do you know in that company, the one I was in, there is not one officer who was there when I was with them.

Now sweetheart, I have done fairly well for today. . . . I really must leave something to talk of when I get home. . . .

Well, look after yourself. God bless you.

Stuart

FRANCE, JANUARY 27, 1917
[NO. 1]

My Dearest own little Wife:—

This is the day. To think that two years ago today I—well, had the nerve to marry the best little girl in all the wide world. Do you remember what you felt like two years ago today. I have very vivid recollections of my own feelings throughout that memorable day. They are treasured among the most sacred memories of my short span of life. These are the things that defy description that are among the things I suppose that eye hath not seen ear hath not heard. I lay and thought of you last night and of our married life. Try how one will, one does slip into the conventional way of regarding marriage. In this old world so few understand anything other and if at times I have sinned by secret thought or overt act in such manner I come to you for forgiveness. Ah just to sit at your feet and look into those dear eyes to feel the touch of that little hand to hear the soft accents of that voice to know that one is loved and that all his faults are overlooked and mistakes forgiven. That indeed is the joy given to few men to know.

The cold weather continues. I get up in the morning with patterns of ice on the window, my shaving brush frozen, boots cold. Wow. Today the sun has warmed things up a little and it is quite warm outside. The battery are taking part in a brigade route march and I am orderly officer. What a fortunate combination. My poor sore feet are being rested.

Yesterday we could not do any drilling so went for a march. The order was for no coats but I felt so cold, I got the captain's special permission to wear my British Warm. Steel helmets though were the order of the day. . . . They are about as much use as a block of ice on a cold day. The afternoon was devoted to a lecture. Then we had tea and at six supper. I had been promising myself all along that I should write you in the evening but after supper when we stoked up the fire and got a nice cigar lit up, oh, I became so drowsy. . . so my poor little honey was neglected. Still I shall have leisure today. . . .

Well sweetheart it is time I got away to attend to my duties as Orderly Officer. I shall have to bring this to a conclusion. I am hoping there will be a letter for me at noon. I missed yesterday.

Goodbye dearest. God bless you.

> Dinna forget.
> Your own
> *Stuart*

FRANCE, JANUARY 27, 1917
[NO. 2]

My Dearest:—

I have already written a short note today, but it seems as if before the day closes I might very well, indeed I should, like to write another. Every time I look at your picture I conjure up once more the days when we were together and am seized with a great yearning to clasp you in my arms once more. Ah to fly away to some forgotten planet where the sun always shines and one never knows want and there to spend the days telling of my love for you. But I presume that is not how one shows ones love for another. Greater love hath no man than this than that a man lay down his life for his friends. One thinks a great deal of life and death out here. The former, dear as it is, has become much less desirable and the other, if not an end devoutly to be wished for, to be at any rate awaited with calm and patience. Like St. Paul, daily we face death yet it is not the death of the body that is to be dreaded but that of the soul. I wish I could impress you with the greatness of the men out here. Men are essentially simple and they do not know how to phrase their emotions and sentiments. They express them in simple acts of heroism and duty. Never can the country repay them for the sacrifices made or the hardships endured. But these will surely be enrolled in the book of life to be summed up at the last day. And so, sweetheart, I am content and happy to be with such men. It is indeed a privilege nor do I grudge the things that must be foregone. My only doubt is, can this flood of patriotism and courage be crystallized into the national temper or when the war is over must we go over the same dull round. Must we be at the mercy of the predatory rich and the smooth politicians or are those who are left behind going to resolve that by virtue of the things endured, the race shall not be called on to enter again into the slough of materialism and greed. Is such poverty in England to be again tolerated. Are men naturally of a passionate nature to be encouraged yea tempted to indulge their nature or are they to be challenged to a higher passion for purity and strength and the protection of the weak. As for me I am not content to fight for the old England but for a new England—the England of our dreams.

These solemn thoughts have come to me on the second anniversary of our marriage and indeed how could I help telling you, the partner of all my thoughts, my joys and sorrows. Sometimes I think of you as my wife but in moments when I know the truth, you are to me infinitely more, the being in whom all my being is centred, my guardian angel and inspiration. Never did Dante pen truer words than when he portrayed Beatrice, not only Beatrice in the flesh but she who appeared to him in dreams as the inspiration of all his highest thoughts, who represented to him the entrance to the higher realm of feeling, the usher into the gates of heaven.

This sounds to practical you, perhaps, as an ebullition but indeed my whole being sets toward you and I know that I am yours body, mind and soul forever. In those realms of light beyond I know that I should never be content without you. I should long to hold converse with you always. . . .

. . . How little we seem to create our own destiny. The forces of the universe seem to sweep us on regardless of ourselves. . . . And so you came into my life, never to go out again. And all the joy and gladness anticipated in the flush of love's first confession has been realized a hundred fold. Not one jot of the sweetness has abated; not one promise unfulfilled. I some times think I should gladly die now if only to proclaim to the world that love is not in vain. It is not a tide that has an ebb to its flow but a river of life that grows with advancing years, that it brings on its bosom not only gladness and joy but inspiration for life and the courage to face the trials and the valley of the shadow.

If you like, you may burn this ebullition but I can no more refrain from saying it than the stars can cease to shine in the heavens. I want you to know right now all that you and your love has meant. Though I were to repeat it a million times I could not exaggerate. I want you also to know that I am here in great part not to win your love which I know I have but to establish it on a foundation from which I trust it can never be moved.

If I have spoken in epic terms dearest it is only because such is adapted to the two years through which I have lived. It beggars imagery and description but the fervour of my words only faintly conveys the thoughts. . . .

I shall hope and pray for a letter tomorrow. Till then God bless you.

Stuart

FRANCE, JANUARY 29, 1917

My Dearest:

Another day without a letter. None received or none written. . . . Indeed it was not the will that was wanting but the time. Yesterday was so busy it seemed impossible, in fact it was. In the morning we had just comfortable time to dress and get breakfast before going to a lecture on the German army by a Staff officer. I regretted going so early particularly as the S.O. was one half an hour late. The hall was cold. We employed our time clicking our heels together and seeing our friends. The lecture was most interesting. I shall tell you all about it later. Afterwards I went to lunch with Norman at B Company of the 31st Company Mess. They have a dandy place for which they pay nothing. It is the billet assigned them. I happened to meet Bennet and I asked him to call for me to accompany me back home. It was a snapping cold walk but I enjoyed it much more than I had in the morning. Poor chap, he is in a bad way, has been to hospital twice with rheumatism or something and is not at all well, though he has been discharged [from hospital]. He is looking for a bomb proof. If he can get it. I promised to do what I could for him. He stayed all evening. . . . I took him up to my billet and we parley-voused over coffee and chocolate. After he went I rolled into bed, had just closed my eyes, when a drunken soldier came in. I just opened my door. He was in the kitchen and I ordered him out. He kept coming back, so I got out of bed and turned him over to an n.c.o. I believe he afterwards went up and routed the captain out, so was up on a charge this morning. He was one of the 89th boys, had lost one brother on the Somme and had just heard of the death of another. I felt really sorry for him.

I had a long letter from mother last night—the first since I left home. It was not very sweet. She unbent a little but not very much. . . .

Now little honey, this is parade hours and I suppose strictly speaking I shouldn't be doing this. By the way, we move tomorrow so you will get no letter for that day. I shall try and write again tonight. It is hard to go two days without letters. I do it all the time.

No word yet of leave. Eh bien, all in good time. . . .

Well little sweetheart cheer up. I suppose you will be all fussed up when I get back, new clothes boots and hat.

Goodbye for the present.

Your own
Stuart

Bennet, mentioned above, was the friend of whom his sisters frequently inquired; the "bomb proof" he sought was a job back at a base or in the communications lines.[9] Stuart's hopes of leave upcoming soon faded and with another move they seemed all but dead. Perhaps as some consolation it appears as though each move brought an improvement in billets. Once again the entry in his diary provides additional details of the battery's latest move: "Tuesday, January 30—Today we moved. At 10:45 the brigade formed up on the route Nationale north of Divion, marched to Cauchy-a-la-Tour whence we separated, the 6th C.T.M.B. going through Rimbert to Burbure. Here we found comfortable quarters awaiting us. At the mess we had tea and later supper. Was much troubled by the long march and crippled feet."[10]

FRANCE, JANUARY 30, 1917

My Dear One:—

Just a few moments avant le soupe for a few words with you. I am utterly tired but am sitting before the cosiest fire in the most comfortable room I have seen in all France, and I am going back to bed after supper to the whitest sheets that were ever bleached.

To tell the truth I nearly froze to death in our last billets. Last night I went out to a nearby chateau whither I had been invited along with Adams. As he had gone away I really should have sent word that it was all off but I neglected it till too late so as things were slack for an hour or two I decided to go in person. It was a perfect winter evening and the sun was setting with a clear mellow light. As I left the village I started up a flock of partridges, then another. I carried my revolver but did not get a shot as they did not fly right. I had hardly gone a hundred yards further when I spied a good sized animal scurrying for cover. It was a real hare with long body and long legs—a real beauty. He scuttled for a patch of cabbages, then thought better of it and decided to put some distance between himself and my revolver. Just as he was making off I caught sight of his mate joining him in flight. They made a pretty pair galloping across the prairie—just like a deer or antelope. I did not get a shot so took it out on trees and piles of dirt at which I shot.

I got to the chateau about quarter after five. My [host] received me in his room where he had a fire lit. He pressed me to stay so we sat and chatted for an hour. Supper arrived at six and a dandy it was, too. Meat pie, potato, fruit, toast and biscuits. But nothing compensated for the cold. We were both shivering when we got up from the table and I was glad when an opportunity arrived of getting away. It took a two mile walk in the bracing air to warm me up.

Arrived at home, I was just going to start shaving and packing when company came. Of course that meant I had to stay especially as the said company included Agnes [a Belgian refugee who had fled to the village]. I had never before seen her on her good behaviour before. It was usually in the tom boy role. But say, she sat down beside me and entertained me in the most interesting way with an account of her school life and the arrival of the Germans, the flight of the refugees. How she bowed when madame drank to her health in the red wine they pass around in the evening. I took out my cigarette case and passed it around; of course included her. I gulped hard when she took one. When I questioned she explained that French women smoke when they are out for the evening. I certainly saw another side of French character. Of course she represents another (Supper intervened) type of French character.

Well our little fete postponed my packing and my going to bed but I did finally roll in at eleven with everything packed. I slept in my unaware [sic].

What it is to start on a march on a bright and frosty morning. Ah how I stepped out and sniffed the gale; only so long a column as we had involves endless delays—men, horses, transport, field kitchens and all the paraphernalia of military life. It was cold, too, and no stop for lunch—only [a] bit of chocolate nibbled at times or a sandwich from the haversack. But my feet were a bit sore when I got there and I was glad to slip into my slacks.

And our billets—but I think I should tell you about that tomorrow. For the first time in weeks I am warm sitting in the mess—lace curtains on the window. Maxey just poked his head in to say that Grandma starts the fire. He is in such clover here. The women folk help him out.

And my own room is a very neat little cottage owned by a Docteur pour les femmes or Sage femmes as she is called. Whitest of sheets. I only wish I were really clean but I shall get an Oliver tomorrow.

This seems to be a mining town. The people are kindness itself. Everything is fine and a letter tonight.

And wait till I tell you about madame who just came in to attend to the fire. She is a jewel and she wears a smile that won't come off. I am at rest tonight and content.

Well honey, don't fret for my return, all in good time.
Norman is in the same town I am.
Goodbye dearest.

> Your own
> *Stuart*

FRANCE, JANUARY 31, 1917
[NO. 1]

My Dearest:—

... Oh, honey, I am warm at last, no more chillblains, cold nights or chilly days. You don't know what it means. From the time we came in at two thirty till now I have not been cold. It has been great; and to cap it I had two letters from you, one last night after supper and one this morning containing one from Velma....

How much there will be to talk of when I get back.... Velma seems to take kindly to domestic life, still it is not an unmixed blessing even with a youngster. I have often wondered whether those who live through this war will be the happier with a background such as we have to bring up our youngsters in the light of the things we have learned. No dearest, I should not change places. We have set our hand to the plow, some day we will understand why so hard a task was set us. It does seem a hard road sometimes but I am convinced now it was the only road. And you know

> There are more things in heaven and earth, Horatio,
> Than are dreamt of in your philosophy.

If I had been content with a wife and with my own life it would have been different. But no one can stand aloof from a popular enthusiasm or refuse to do his bit without it reacting on himself and his happiness. This scheme of things we associate with life—home, friends, the round of duty, holidays etc are probably but a small part of life. Our religion teaches us that all our aspirations and ideals point that way.... With your hand in mine I would go anywhere; we could learn new things, think new thoughts and discover all the hidden meaning of life and love.

Do you know I am roasting here, so I think I shall have to take a turn outside or I shall go to sleep....

Goodbye honey. God bless you

> *Stuart*

My Dear One:—

This letter was started on the above date but it is now February 1st a.m., myself reposing in an arm chair before a comfortable fire.

I feel in a contemplative mood this morning thinking of Velma's letter and the picture of family life it contains. Honestly they are happy but I don't feel envious because we by our sacrifice are entering a new world. . . .

Well, honey, there is very little to say. I am orderly officer today, so time hangs heavily on my hands. Just now I hear madame and grandma trying to teach Maxey French. We have a dandy place here. I am tempted every time I sit down here to write to you.

Will there be a letter today. [illegible] I hear they are ordering the wives of all Canadians and Anzacs out of England. Is that so.

God bless you.

Stuart

Later—You're thinking not to hear from me again but I must break the news I have had a bath. Last night we discovered an estaminet which boasted a bath and we made arrangement with madame for a succession of baths from ten to twelve. I just soaked myself for an hour, dried myself leisurely and changed every single stitch. It is a disgrace how long I have gone but we simply could not get a bath though all my clothes were washed. . . .

Oh yes, I must tell you of a very heated argument in which we became embroiled last night. Something started it and I had occasion in the course of it to express my views as a Canadian on the motives that brought us over. I stated quite emphatically it was not danger to England but the Empire that roused us. Of course it all turned on what you meant by England, but in a moment I had the only two Englishmen we have down on my throat. They do not understand that appeals to love of England, English ways and customs, English life, fall on deaf ears when addressed to a Colonial and I maintained that if Canadians had been appealed to more on the principle of self preservation there would have been more instant response. I told them all the flag waving for the mother land was wasted effort. They were wild for a few minutes but of course good sense prevailed.

Yesterday, Carnegie my batman went back to our former billets to recover some article he had left. On returning he reported that an Imperial outfit had moved in. Madame sent her complements to me. She didn't like the officer who was billeted on her at all. When he came in he asked for his room in a haughty way she did not like. That is what the French around here keep repeatedly saying. The English are "fier" meaning overbearing. But the Canadians. I was just thinking how happy we have been since coming out, mixing with these people in their homes, men, n.c.o.'s and officers, no distinction. Our boys can certainly jolly these people along and I guess the French do like the Canadians all right. . . .

Well the next thing on the programme is a football match this afternoon in which I am to take part. Watch my smoke.

Well you will be tired with my screed so I guess I shall wind up for dinner. You need not worry about the chillblains. The swelling has gone down and now that I am in warm quarters, I shall be all right. The men get an issue of whale oil, a preventive of trench feet, which is quite similar, but lately I have not been able to get any. I think if I can stand putting it on it is the best.

Goodbye again.

Your own

Stuart

Stuart's pride in Canada and his conviction of the rightness of her actions were strong and clearly stated in the letter above, but letters and clippings from home evoked a sarcastic outburst from him when he compared men doing their duty at the front with those who stayed at home and enhanced their positions. Most of the people mentioned in the following letter were former associates in the Education Department.

Early in 1917 the National Service Board undertook a survey of Canadian manpower with the idea of using the findings to stimulate army recruitment. This was but the first move toward compulsory service that would come with passage of the Military Service Act later that summer and, as Stuart noted, the beginning of division in the country over conscription. The reference to Mrs. Murphy was to Emily Murphy, an Edmonton author who had been named a police magistrate in 1916 and who, in the twenties, was an outspoken and effective leader in the drive for women's rights.[11]

Dearest:—

... Well the mail came in and no letter but you see how magnanimous I am. I shall nevertheless write a good long letter provided of course I get the time.

First let me reassure you concerning my feet. They are almost better.... The cold I had has almost gone so you need have no worries on the score of my health.

I was quite interested in your mother's letter but I am going to take the time to read it again. Your mother is a great old warrior; fight to a finish. Mrs. Sharon's letter made me dread that she will look to me for fresh hope. All the information I have been able to gather is that Sharon was seen on the 26th either just before or just after the attack bringing up bombs with a carrying party. Missing under the circumstances can only mean one thing. He could not have been taken prisoner; for in an attack the prisoners are all on one side. ...

... Did I tell you that I have lately been receiving copies of the Bulletin? I also had a letter from Barron yesterday enclosing clippings from the Journal which would indicate that the inauguration of the National Service movement has pitched the fat in the fire and the country is divided into conscription and no conscription camps. Mrs. Murphy has mounted her war horse and pranced into the lists as the champion of the no-conscriptionists. Your mother feels very sorry for Elliott. I wonder what he gets his pay for? I suppose he has the regular New Year's volume of mail and is snowed under. Barron tells me that a reorganization is under way. A registrar is to be appointed. I wonder what that means and how it will affect me. I don't very much care. But if some slacker skips in there and picks up a fat job I shall have somewhat to say... I see Dr. Jas Collins [Miller] is still starring in the limelight and John Ross. Dr. Miller finds the war activities a sort of pleasant diversion. It enables him to appear in the press a little more often. Well I must not be sarcastic. One cannot help thinking of things once in a while but I am fed up on Dr. Miller acting a chairman of some committee with a long name going around talking of educating the soldier to some useful vocation as though he were some derelict of civilization instead of being good enough to wipe his shoes on the learned doctor.

And so the war goes on while the people at home argue and fight. But we do not need to worry I suppose....

... If I were you and the weather is good I should go and see some of the places we missed. There are some wonderful spots in Old London and it will be something you will not soon forget.

I have just been out for some drill this afternoon in the clear winter sunshine and my heart leaped with the joy of health and life. It seems very beautiful here even in winter and when one is feeling fine his perceptions are more acute. Then I thought of little Honey over in the fogs and smoke of London and wondered if she were depressed and down cast this afternoon, or whether her mind were healthily occupied. What a vast difference this war will make in the status of women. Why, I have before me a Chronicle of Jan 31st in which a resume is given of the deliberations of the Conference on Electoral Reform. It is recommended that women have the vote after they have passed the age of 30 (or 35) i.e., have grown up. Back home they have the vote and no one thinks anything of it. It is taken for granted. They work in munition factories and on farms, in fact do everything a man does, instead of performing the tasks assigned them by Mrs. Murphy of assuming the role of Joan of Arc, and riding where whirlwinds ride. Did you ever hear such pure unmitigated piffle. I must send you her speech. But women are not going to get their rights or their right status till they get (collectively) the respect of man, till the relations of the sexes are governed by mutual respect and true fidelity and it is reckoned a crime for either to exploit passion. I haven't words to express what I feel sometimes at the coarseness and selfishness we stand for. Alas old values have gone by the board. . . .

I have been surprised at the bad reputation the Anzacs seem to have out here. Whether there is anything in it I don't know. I hope there is not and I don't like to hear Canadians run them down. I trust and hope that the war will make us all one instead of emphasizing differences and distinctions.

I sometimes wonder how I find so much to talk about. In the trenches your topics are limited. You are wondering whether Fritz is going to put anything over, whether you have enough ammunition, whether you have anything for supper and there your mind stops in ghastly torpor. Here, however, it reacts to every slight incident and is turning everything over in spite of your self. I don't know whether my effusions interest you. They form outside of military details a fairly accurate account of my life here. With my diary it should be complete. My thoughts though all go in my letters. . . . My mind is a door open to you at all times.

Well sweetheart, I would not have it otherwise; nor would I unlive the last two years. By life we learn to live, by suffering enter into a new life, I trust where perfect understanding exists. . . .

Well, good bye, sweetheart. God bless you.

Your own

Stuart

Our mess has resolved itself into a debating club. Let one member cast into our midst any remark and it becomes a veritable apple of discord with each member ranging himself on one side or the other. You remember the discussion that was precipitated night before last. Why the two English-born Canadians thought I was well out side the pale to think that I would not come over to help England the mother land. Well it jarred them at any rate to know there were motives that might just as easily be appealed to that would in fact find readier response and are more in keeping with England's position as the head of a vast Empire. However, they all came around to my point of view.

8

Preparing the Spring Assault
Rehearsal for Vimy Ridge

❧ FEBRUARY—MARCH, 1917 ❧

Food shortages that had plagued England for some time grew worse in early 1917 when increased German submarine activity further hampered shipment of supplies. The fact of civilians living on a substandard diet and the reality of intense and bitter cold combined to increase Stuart's worry about Edna's physical and mental health.

FRANCE, FEBRUARY 3, 1917

My Dearest:—

Your letters of the 28th, 29th and 30th arrived tonight with one from John T. Ross. . . . I still think you are not feeling up to snuff when you are taking calomel and things. Your letters don't show the same poise they used to back in Canada. I am beginning to worry about things much more than I used to. It is hard when you don't know exactly what is wrong. If I could but surround you always with my love as an armour to shield you, to bear you up and guard you at all times I should be happy. I know you have sacrificed a lot and it is to girls like you who "have merited well of the state" that Canada owes a lot. We men sacrifice nothing. Our lives—why it is in the air here and it means nothing, no pain, but you who stay behind bear the whole burden. I should feel very badly if I thought you were getting into the slough of despond. Your cheerful letters have been a great help, and I was proud and in measure happy that you were so brave. To you and the inspiration I draw from you I owe everything and I am trying in my humble way to be true to the light I have. If I ever get out of this I am going to try to make you the happiest woman alive. . . .

We were on a route march today, full marching order. It was pretty stiff and we did not get back till 1:30. My legs and back were sore. We did not do much this afternoon. I was arranging a football match [for] tomorrow and while out I met Norman so he came down to dinner. Afterwards we went to a minstrel show put on by the 31st. I stayed only a short time. I had some business and then there were some letters in my pocket itching to be read.

Maxey just brought me in a cup of cafe noir. It is appetizing at times but awfully strong with chicory not much like we had at Hythe.

Last night I went down to Brigade H.Q. to a meeting re sports. It was moonlight coming back and quite cold. Major Piper and one or two other officers were with me and we enjoyed the walk. Only rolling into cold sheets in a cold room kind of takes the cream off. Then this morning my batman was late and I had to get up, break ice in my pitcher, pry the pitcher out of my bowl and try to thaw the ice on my toothbrush—say, talk of Canada!

But really I feel desperate tonight. I don't know why but my heart is rebellious tonight. . . . By some curious telepathy, I can maintain the even tenour of my way if I know you are fairly contented. Well I must not talk this way, but do the best I can.

I had a great letter from John T. Ross tonight. I shall send it on as soon as I can. Also had one from Janet announcing another parcel on the way. Think of it.

Can you imagine me eating hard tack at 10 p.m. Captain Pouncey came in and put me in the notion. Better for me than candy. . . .

Well honey sweetheart, I shall think of you all night and wonder how you are. Be sure to take good care of yourself.

I may get a chance to add to this in the morning before breakfast.

Your ownest own
Stuart

FRANCE, FEBRUARY 4, 1917
[NO. 1]

My Own Beloved:—

I am not expecting a letter today nor am I in a position to write one. My inspiration seems to have run out. I don't know that anything has occurred to depress me. . . . I am beginning to think all is not well with you. It seems as though your spirits have drooped. . . . This war seems to impose a strain on the heart in more ways than one and one needs a harbour in which to cast the anchor of his soul. You have been that at all times. . . and as you were to me I tried to be to you. I may not naturally be a strong man but each fulfills his destiny in his own way—I through terror and physical weakness but with my eyes on the goal. Sometimes the burden seems heavy; in the last analysis, it is the final weight in the balance that counts; with me it is what you would wish and in the months to come, I shall wear your favour on my heart O my beloved.

I was talking with Kennedy last night about the people back home and his words were borne out by the letter I had from John T. They are going about their business much as they were and those who have joined up have been forgotten. There is Dr. Miller and the inspectors Gorman, Boyce and others, teachers Fuller, Page, Barley. Then they are having a reorganization at the Department and Gorman is to go in as registrar. It amused me what your mother said about Elliott. Apparently Mrs. E has been telling her how hard worked he is and why. So he thinks he has more work than I used to do eh? and is telling everyone about it. Holy Smoke!!!! That gets my goat entirely. And I suppose he gets away with it. Poor old Kennedy has very decided opinions on his fellow teachers and about Dr. James Collins Miller. Well, I must not dwell on this strain. I should not change places with them.

This has been a lovely day. I was out most of the morning. We had a football match for which I had to arrange which we played on the 31st grounds. It was between our team and the 6th Canadian Machine Gun Company F. We were leading right till the last. Then they tied and in playing off they beat us by 2 points 3 to 1. Weren't we sore. Poor Major Durrand has a bet of 50 francs to pay.

A strange thing happened this afternoon. The French interpreter came around to take a list of our billets. When he enquired the price he said it was too much and told madame so. Say, such a torrent of French as ensued—all about the high cost of living, soap, water etc etc. I could follow her trail pretty well. Of course we can't do much; we're in for it now. But he says he will see that the next troops that come in he will billet men on them to teach her a lesson. His principle is that the people should not stick British officers and I think he is right. I have kicked once or twice about items but I have been overruled. Madame is very nice but she wants her money. My opinion of the French is that the women are much smarter than the men. They do all the work and the business, too. The men are either talking or sipping coffee or beer.

Sweetest heart, I cannot tell you tonight what my thoughts are. They will be with you all night even in my sleep. If I could project my presence over the water and be with you to guard you in your dreams, I should do so. My own best beloved. Good night. God bless you.

Your own
Stuart

In the two letters that he wrote on 4 February, Stuart appears to have lost a bit of his usual optimism, and he continued to worry about Edna. In the first letter he carped mildly about the men who had stayed behind in Canada, while in the second he again expressed his scepticism about the United States, a scepticism that would grow as the spring of 1917 wore on.

FRANCE, FEBRUARY 4, 1917
[NO. 2]

My Darling:—

I have already finished and sealed my letter but I must write and tell you how I love you. . . . How I look for every mail for a message of love, how my thoughts go homewards in spite of myself. How my whole being sets towards you—the star of my soul. No other being exists in the world for me; to you alone do I refer all my thoughts and ideals. If you could but understand how much and how great the longing is to be together. . . . No mail at all today. I really didn't expect any but had a sneaking idea there might be just a bit note—but nothing. Five yesterday will likely dry up the stream for a day or two.

Monday morning.—This is the first dull day we have had for nearly a week. The sky is overcast and it has been snowing. We were all crazy to get our English papers this morning to see what the States were doing but there was nothing new. What will Wilson do. He is in a corner all right but I believe he will wriggle. It is only the logical outcome of German-American relations. Germany has now no further use of the States so they cast them overboard. Well I think it will shorten the war. What will the States do to get out of it.

Tomorrow we have a big inspection and everything is to be shining. We hope to make a great impression on the powers that be. I shall appear in shining armour. . . .

Well, I should like to know what you are doing today. You must be getting a regular trousseau made up. I hope you have a real swell pair of boots and a nice hat when I get home. As for me, alas the shine will all be worn off what I have but that will be better I suppose. I will look like a real soldier. I do hope there is some mail to reassure me today. It is all very well to get letters from Janet and John Ross but you are the one from whom I want to get mail. It is indeed a blank day when it doesn't come. It seems to be feast or famine three or four one day and none the next.

When I was up at the 31st yesterday I asked the adjutant about their records of casualties and find that they have them with them. I will therefore look up the records with regards to Sharon and see what light they can throw on his disappearance. If worth while I shall send Mrs. Sharon a copy. Of course, the probability is that there is no hope.

Contrary to my expectations, I slept very well last night, i.e. once I got the sheets warmed up. Seven o'clock came too soon. Being orderly officer I had to get up and out to the men's breakfast at 7:30. That meant washing and shaving in cold water. You don't mind it after you get started but starting is the dickens. I am conscious that I dreamed last night—a weird succession of dreams in which the ocean played a prominent part. I remember a sail boat with a wonderful spread of sails driving along with her keel only occasionally touching the water, till her masts went by the board and the boat was almost overwhelmed by the sea. Almost at the same time, as I was watching the rescue, the sea drove over my point of vantage and swept me out. Then I was in an Observation Post in the line waiting for zero hour, when the great advance would begin. I remember waiting for the enemy barrage to come down in our lines. I think I must have awakened before it started. . . .

I look at the French girls around here and wonder if they are the same as our girls back home. They seem to lack all the graces, charm and good looks that one associates with young womanhood. Of course they are poor and live in straitened surroundings. Once in a while they dress up but they do lack the distinctive charm that Canadian or American girls have. But they are little more than peasants so there is some reason. . . .

I wish you could have been out with me yesterday. It was perfect.

The air keen but not cold. There were a few aeroplanes whirring around. They looked beautiful with their white wings shining in the sun. . . .

Now, honey, I must close as dinner hour is drawing near and there are duties. Don't lose heart about writing because I am delinquent at times. Take good care of yourself and don't worry.

Your own lover
Stuart

FRANCE, FEBRUARY 5, 1917

Dearest:—

I am going to start this letter with my pen and will write as long as the ink lasts. . . . There is of course not much in the way of news; in fact nothing. I went to a town down the line a piece, got a haircut and bought some trinkets. I wanted some stars for my British Warm. They wanted two francs a piece for gilt stars I came home without them. I got a few odds and ends at the B.E.F. canteens and then came home. It was a fine afternoon and the sun set in soft and warm colours of red and gold. Under other circumstances my heart would have leapt. Out here the beauty of nature seldom thrills. I recall well, the day before Christmas, what a wonderful day it was. How I enjoyed making my tour of the trenches. But to think that any particular spot like that can be turned into a hell in a short space of time sort of takes the joy out of life. . . .

Scoffield [a friend in Edmonton who had recently written] told me that his brother has been missing since September 15th. He gave me his number and unit and he wants me to get information. Of course, that is a kind of hopeless task. . . .

. . . By the way, Reith lent me the *Rhymes of a Red Cross Man* today. I shall read it and let you know what I think of it, whether you should read it. Do you never do any reading these days at all? Do you spend all your time sewing.

Let me tell you. Adams got a parcel tonight by mistake and as no parcels are returned through the Army P.O. we opened it. It was from a Miss Margaret Milne of North Bay. I suppose this young sub had made a catch at North Bay when the train stopped, sent his address and lo a parcel. It had raisins and nuts and cookies and candy, and cigarettes and cigars and Christmas cake. So we are going to write to the above Miss Milne thank her and ask for another. . . .

Well I can hear the youngster and Maxey droning out their respective lessons outside. The youngster is doing her home work and Maxey is learning French.

Oh yes the incident I was going to relate. I had occasion at my other billet to ask for a drink of cold water. Madame was at once alarmed and asked my batman what was the matter with me. She thought anyone who drank cold water must be sick.

Well, goodnight dearest. This is all you will get for twenty-four hours.

Your own
Stuart

During the lull in action, the Canadian Corps returned to such non-combat endeavours as inspection and drill. The inspection on 6 February was conducted by Major General Sir H. E. Burstall, commander of the Second Division. Throughout the winter, President Wilson's role as peace broker, which the belligerents had never wanted and had never made easy, grew increasingly difficult. On 31 January, Germany gave notice of intentions to launch unrestricted submarine warfare the following day. Faced with this challenge, but unwilling to relinquish his hopes for bringing about a "peace without victory," Wilson reluctantly decided on 3 February to break diplomatic relations with Germany; but in his speech to Congress that day announcing the break he maintained that he would not consider further measures unless Germany committed an "overt act" of hostility. This did not enhance his standing in the eyes of Stuart Tompkins, who noted in his diary on 3 February: "Today we heard for the first [time] of Germany's ultimatum to neutrals to cease trading with England. What will happen. Are the States going to crawl again."[1]

FRANCE, FEBRUARY 7, 1917

My Dearest:—

Sure enough I did not get time yesterday to write you and I fear the note I write this morning must be a hurried one. Well we had our inspection yesterday; both men and officers looked smart and were complimented by the G. O. C. I gave my batman considerable praise for the way he had things shined up. After lunch, I felt kind of on the rocks and very sleepy. I went up to the house, but there madame told me for the first time of the break between United States and Germany. We had not had any English papers giving full account of Wilson's speech to Congress. I no longer felt sleepy but went out instead and kicked the football.

This morning's papers confirm my surmise that Wilson's action does not mean war. I wonder if he can find a way to wriggle out. There were quite a number in last night at the mess and several of the officers were giving instances of treatment accorded Americans serving in the British Army by British (English) officers. I know Wilson has made Americans a laughing stock but English pride and snobbery can go too far. Why, one such was refused the use of regimental notepaper, was never addressed by his fellow officers and was generally treated as a rank outsider. I wonder if this will change it in any way.

I really must run up to the 31st and see some of the officers. I was up Sunday morning but they were just having church parade so I did not see many of them I also want to make further enquiries with regard to Sharon. The weather continues cold but my health is good. . . .

I got no mail yesterday at all so I guess I got my just reward. If this letter is to get off today I shall have to close. . . .

Well Honey shall we wish the States good luck in their new venture. As ever.

Your own
Stuart

FRANCE, FEBRUARY 8, 1917
[NO. 1]

Dearest:—

Though my fingers are so cold I can hardly write I'm going to try to dash—save the word—off a few lines. It is a beautiful morning but quite cold. . . . I am feeling fine this morning. Everything is lovely.

No mail came yesterday at all—i.e. for me. It is now nearly three days since I got any. I have not seen Norman Weir to know whether he has had a letter or not. . . .

What do you think of Wilson now. Even now after having broken off negotiations they don't seem to have tumbled to the fact that they are at war. They are still looking backward instead of forward. Too much like England in 1914.

When I came in I compromised on a cup of coffee which I am sipping between paragraphs while attempting to get this letter off to you this a.m. Maxey is pressing me for my breakfast so I shall have to wind up I guess.

Well Honey, write soon with all the news you can. . . .

Your own

Stuart

FRANCE, FEBRUARY 8, 1917

[NO. 2]

My Dearest:—

I am going to start this letter in the hope that one comes for me though I much doubt that one will come. We are more or less resting on our oars today. It is beastly cold and there is very little that we can do. Several of the officers are away today—only two being here.

. . . [T]hat blessed batman never got around till nearly nine I had to wash and shave in cold water. My big boots not being clean I had to put on my slacks and shoes. I sure was sore and used pretty severe language.

Well what do you think of Wilson. Is there any way for him to wriggle out now? I have eagerly bought every paper in sight but there is nothing definite. I suppose it must necessarily depend on the sinking of the first American vessel. I suppose it is a pretty solemn responsibility for him to have on his shoulders, but on the other hand it is up to the States just as much as it is up to us. I should like to be in New York, or even in Seattle for a day or two just now. Upon my word, in the light of announcements made by the German Government, I cannot see any way out of it but war. Still it is the unexpected that always happens in war and I will not believe the United States is coming in until I hear of an actual clash between them and the Huns. One thing is certain; Germany has definitely renounced the hope of reaching a decision on land. I believe that before that can be reached (by either side) Germany is going to starve and she is simply trying to turn the tables on England and starve her first. That means that the thing will be over in some way by August 1st. It is dreadful to think of the suffering to be endured by non-combatants and neutrals before that time. Thus will the German people suffer for the misdeeds of their rulers. I suppose it will be a terrible ordeal but it must be brought on in the hopes that better days will follow. . . .

I certainly wish we had the daily papers promptly. One cannot help but be excited about the prospects. The present developments throw a lurid light on the internal suffering of Germany. The question is, can the Navy deliver the goods?

Well, Honey, it is kind of hard to get along without a letter for so long. Yours are the only ones I really look for.

Goodbye and God bless you.

Stuart

FRANCE, FEBRUARY 9, 1917

Dearest:—

A few short lines today. I had five letters only yesterday, four from you. . . .

I am sorry you are getting fed up on flat life. It must be quite as bad as trench life, without of course, the excitement. . . . By the way, has there been anything further about going back to Canada. I have heard mutterings lately but you never mentioned anything about it. I have recalled lately the impressions we both gathered during our stay in England regarding the cropping of the land. You probably remember one of us mentioning that despite two years of war practically nothing had been done to increase the area of land under cultivation and how surprised we were to find it so small. . . . Well, now a panic has started over the food problem and they have appointed a Minister of Agriculture with the idea of breaking up a great many parks and pastures. Well I know enough about farming to know that you can't expect to get a good crop the first year. Why on earth they never got after it before is more than I can tell. It makes me tired. I don't mind people failing to see things but I protest against them shutting their eyes to the truth and then crying when they get caught.

Well I trust the new National Service Movement will have some results. It will probably have more in England than Canada, though why they have shut out the women. [sic] The men who can should all go to the front. I suppose it is the British way of doing things.

Well Honey do you know I have missed a day this week. I was quite convinced it was Saturday and tomorrow Sunday. Out in this part of the Field Sunday is the only milestone we have. In the line even that is forgotten and it is just a succession of days. . . .

Well dearest, Good bye. God bless you.

Your own

Stuart

Rumours that wives would be sent back to Canada again abounded. Worsening food shortages, together with the threat of even greater deprivations posed by the German submarine "blockade," lent them credibility and caused Stuart renewed worry. At the same time his battery were being sent to the front near Arras, where they would remain while training for the April assault on Vimy Ridge. As he mentioned in the short note below, the trench mortar people made the march in company with his old 31st Battalion. On 8 February he had reported that several of the officers were away; his diary entry elaborates on their whereabouts and traces the ensuing route of march: Thursday, 8 February—"Today Pouncy, Reith and Adams left for Mont St Eloi to look over new front. . . . " Saturday 10 February—"Today we left bright and early rendezvousing with the 31st at 9:00 o'clock for Houdain. . . . We had a fine but a hard march and got to H. about 3 p.m. . . . We saw when passing through Bruay a German n.c.o. give 'Eyes right' when passing Pouncey!" Sunday, February 11—"Today we continued were off early and reached Mt. St Eloi and Ecoivres at 2:30 p.m. Took over our billet and got supper."[2]

FRANCE, FEBRUARY 10, 1917

Dearest:—

Just a few lines before we turn in tonight. We are on the move once more and are resting tonight in a French town some miles from our former place. I met Fred Shouldice on the march today. He afterwards came back with Norman and was with us for supper. I may say I am with the battalion for the march. My feet were bad today and I want to give them a chance so must to bed early. Goodnight.

God bless you.

Stuart

FRANCE, FEBRUARY 12, 1917

Dearest:—

In the line again. The same old round in the same old way, I am going to have a few spare minutes while dinner is getting. I have not had mail from you—it seems for weeks, it is probably only days. . . . We had yesterday's papers. Still nothing about the States, beyond the fact that Germany wanted to parlay, while of course she continued her devilish plan of sinking unarmed and helpless neutral ships. But apparently Germany is in no hurry to start things and in the meantime, submarine commanders have their instructions.

You see I have very little to talk about when I get on such an unimportant matter as the intervention of the U.S. As a matter of fact, as Major Durrand said to me some days ago, the Americans are scared stiff at going to war and are not going to if they can help it. Mighty good policy I guess if yourself only is concerned.

By the way, I wish you could send us a Times now and again. We don't get anything here except the Daily Mail and that is poor fodder. . . .

Down in our last billet I picked up a travel worn copy of Daddy Long Legs which I proceeded to pinch without delay. I am going to read it and let you know the results. I have read nothing more exciting than the Daily Mail for some weeks now. I think I will end this little screed. Gee I am getting hungry and we don't have dinner till 8:30— two hours away.

Stuart

The trench mortar battery returned in mid-February to the trenches and to the pattern of rotation from front line to reserve. By that time Stuart had realized that there would be no leave and no trip to London.

FRANCE, FEBRUARY 14, 1917

Dearest:—

. . . Your last letter filled me with a great peace. For weeks back your letters were more or less of a puzzle. . . . Your last letter though was more natural and I tell you I feel content with my lot for the first time in weeks. This thing is not hard to put up with as long as you are reconciled to your lot. When you are not it is pretty bad.

Now as to leave, I have been greatly disappointed. I really did not think of it until it seemed to be almost within reach, and now it is getting pretty problematical. So you will have to go ahead and make your plans without reference to me and take things as you find them. . . .

As usual there is no news I can give you. The weather is still cold but in the trenches you do not mind it. In fact it is really better than if it were warm for it keeps the mud frozen. . . .

I shall not write more except to say that we have good quarters, a real comfy dugout and very pleasurable companions. . . . Reith is a cracking fine fellow and I count myself lucky to be with him.

Well good night sweetheart. God bless you.

Stuart

FRANCE, FEBRUARY 16, 1917

My Dearest:—

Are you aware that four months ago today I landed in France. It is indeed hard to realize that so long a time has elapsed since that memorable day but "Time rolls his ceaseless course" as we are told. . . .

I have been feeling much better since coming into the line. The work has been pretty hard and I have been on the jump. I guess it has done me good; my appetite certainly is tremendous. The only thing that bothers us is a shortage of rations. Somehow we seem unable to keep up with the demand. There are three officers and as many batmen. The medium T.M.'s share the dugout with us, we have very commodious quarters and have a good time together.

It is great on a clear day like this to see the aeroplanes circling overhead and the constant pounding of the archies as the anti aircraft guns are known. They are certainly (our aircraft) the wonders of the war and one never ceases to be astonished at what has been accomplished. We have very few aerial combats though; the Hun does not venture much over our lines. . . .

I really must bring myself to write to Philip telling him the leave stuff is all off. . . . I wonder what news I can give you. I have just finished *Daddy Long Legs*. What bright, entertaining letters but she was [a] somewhat nervy and disrespectful young lady I thought. I don't know what your ideas were on the subject.

You never said anything about being ordered back to Canada although there are constant rumours here to that effect. Of course I am not sure you would go even if you were ordered. . . .

Well sweetheart, I haven't really much to tell, I regret to state that I only sent a whizz bang today but I put the letter off till too late. I want to get to bed right after dinner, so am writing before. You see we do things "comme il faut" have tea in the afternoon and dinner at night. The latter is a matter of necessity as the rations do not come up till late.

Goodnight dearest, God bless you.

Stuart

FRANCE, FEBRUARY 18, 1917

My Dearest:—

Just a few lines tonight from a very tired individual... As the mail goes first thing in the morning, I thought I should get a note off.

I have not had a letter for some days now. Last night's mail brought me a letter from Jentie and one from your mother. I was of course glad to get them but they did not count and I left them unread till after supper....

We have been getting papers very irregularly lately and news is about four days old when it reaches us....

My digestive apparatus is sadly over worked tonight. I came in about four with Reith; we had a cup of tea and bread then supper came at six with steak and onions and all kinds of etceteras so I feel rather full fed. I have had a terrific appetite since coming back to the line.

The weather as you know has broken and the frost is coming out of the ground. Did you say "trenches"—no just channels of mud and water. It is a relief to change into dry sox. My supply has lasted well but I am beginning to poke my toes through. I had quite a letter from Jentie last night. As you remember I heard from Scoffield a few days ago asking re his brother. Same old tale—missing, and I have to convey the harrowing news. Why should I be picked. By the way I can add nothing to what Fred Shouldice learned of Sharon's death. I had picked up a little among the men myself and the orderly room information was little more. It seems as though an effort should be made immediately after an action to get all available information re missing men. Something is done but it is not done systematically enough. Do you wish me to write Mrs. Sharon....

I am afraid one of these times I am going to get "crumby." We have been shifted around so lately, sleeping everywhere. However I am close to a bath house so tomorrow I shall patronize it, change my clothes and sprinkle a little powder around.

Well good night dearest.

Stuart

Stuart had so far escaped an infestation of lice, but the letter above indicates that he feared his luck would not hold. The evacuation of an old friend and comrade to a London hospital for treatment of syphilis pitted Stuart's senses of loyalty and moral rectitude against one another, and in the following letter he wrestled with what should have been a simple matter of absolute right and wrong for him. He found solace in his friendship with Reith, and pride in his Scottish roots.

FRANCE, FEBRUARY 22, 1917

My Own Dearest Honey:—

Your two letters of the 18th reached me this morning and it was with horror I heard the news of Bob. . . . Now I am going to tell you something. . . . I have hesitated to tell you for you like Bob and I always thought a good deal of him. A man always has a sense of loyalty towards his fellows that he does not like to violate. But I think it wiser so that you may know how things lie. Last summer Bob did a lot of running around. . . [and] on our last leave in London when we came back to Shorncliffe together. . . he gave me an inkling of the sort of thing he was doing. On the way over to France. . . from Bob's talk I gathered that he had been treading the primrose path rather freely. Two others of the occupants of our tent waxed very voluble on the subject of the women in London. It made me pretty sick. . . . I felt sorry about it. Bob was an awfully likeable fellow. . . . I will not tell what he did on his last trip to London. I did not know that vice could wear such a respectable face. Well, Bob went into the trenches, was in support the first tour, the second tour he was in the front line. I saw him I think the day he went out and he gave me an inkling what the trouble was. The doctor was reticent but from the speed with which he was evacuated, I surmised that the trouble was more serious than he told me. Norman of course had the same idea. . . . Of course, I would not say what the trouble is. What Ike Mooney told you may be the case. But of its origin there can be no doubt. You will probably understand the nurses lack of sympathy. I shall write to him as you request. I have been inclined to be sore at the men who in such manner get out of doing their bit, but on second thought, they are also sinned against. . . . To think that vice would be so organized to catch the young colonial officer and soldier. I am fed up on the flapper and the toff of English life, the hypocrisy and cant that cloak their easy virtue. . . . The English (and more so the French) think that sensuality in moderation is compatible with civilized society. Probably if you know the ropes it is, but I maintain that immunity from disease is not the only object of morality. . . . I hope you will understand why I have told you this. It is not solely to tell a secret because I should not do that but rather to explain what might be an awkward situation.

Now little Honey, bear in mind what I said about leave. If I am not to get it, that's all there is to it. It must be borne.

By the way I have not told you much of Reith, with whom I am associated. He is a *Canadian of Scotch* extraction—a good start eh? and one of the finest fellows I ever knew. He is also a dandy soldier and I am lucky to be with him. Some time when you are sending me something send *two*. He knew I wanted a muffler and when he had an extra one from home he insisted on my accepting it—. . . .

Now I must close this crotchety pessimistic letter. I am feeling a great deal better this morning and will be able to take my three squares a day. Bob Pearson dropped in to see me last night, is coming around to dinner tonight.

Goodbye dearest.

Your own
Stuart

FRANCE, FEBRUARY 26, 1917

Dearest:—

Shall I call this good morning. We got up pretty late, and I am now waiting for breakfast. [Later] As a matter of fact I didn't have to wait hence a stretch of four hours between these two starts on my letter.

It is really a fine day but the trenches are still in a bad condition. I was out for two and three hours. Do you know our men are incorrigible the way they wander about overland. They just invite sniping but I am sure it is a bit of bravado. I met some imperial officers this morning on my rounds. "Your fellows must have a streak of Indian in them" one of them said referring to our raids I presume. Canadians are given the credit for making the first trench raids on this western front. Which in turn reminds me that I got a whole slew of papers last night, the Bulletin, a parcel of magazines from Jentie, and two parcels of Edmonton, Calgary and Toronto newspapers from the Department of Education. . . .

We heard this morning that the British had taken Miraumont, the

Hun having retired his line a mile or more. I trust we will have more good news.

Well this is not much of a letter but I shall add to it if I get a chance. I have a bit of head ache just now and think I shall lie down.

Well good bye Honey dear.

Your own as ever

Stuart

On 26 February Stuart noted the British occupation of the village of Miraumont in the Somme sector; this was part of the movement leading to the German strategic "scorched earth" withdrawal to newly fortified entrenchments that came to be known as the Hindenburg Line. The strategic retreat aimed in part to delay action on the Western Front pending results of unrestricted submarine warfare as well as to strengthen defences in anticipation of the Allies' spring offensive.[3]

Even as the Canadian Corps prepared for that offensive, there were instances of officers being rotated back to England on leave from their units at the front. Some of Stuart's colleagues enjoyed such good fortune, but his luck did not extend that far. At this point a tired and somewhat dispirited Edna Tompkins had left her job in the Army Pay and Records Office, and Stuart now worried lest she find nothing to occupy her mind and her time.

FRANCE, FEBRUARY 27, 1917

My own Dearest little Girl:—

Your letters of 21st and 22nd reached me last night and glad I was to get them. After a day's plodding around in the mud and slush it is fine to get them in the evening when I have time to peruse them. Reith is always green with envy when letters turn up regularly and indeed I am very fortunate to have so faithful and loyal a little girl. It was good of you to send me your own red toque for my poor old head. As I told you I now have a muffler contributed by Reith. I will be very glad to get the other things not least of all the chocolate and other eatables. . . .

We had an incident happened not far from here. Some of our observation planes were attacked by a German battle plane and one machine brought to earth. The pilot was badly wounded and died. It was quite exciting while it lasted.

Now little honey I want you to take this leave business right. Frankly I hope you will get down to something to keep your mind busy. It is war time and one must not look for the impossible. Everything will come all right in time. I am glad you hit it off with Mrs. Weir better. Norman is such a fine fellow I should not like you to part. . . . Well I have work to do so must get away and finish this later. I cannot tell how much I love you dearest.

Your own
Stuart

Stuart remained optimistic that Lloyd George would "deliver the goods," but he still had the trench soldier's disdain for those who sought exemptions from service. "M and M," in the letter below, refers to William Mackenzie and Donald Mann, the railroad magnates whose transcontinental Canadian Northern Railway, together with the Grand Trunk Pacific, emerged from bankruptcy in a government salvage operation to form the Canadian National Railway.[4]

Edna and Lottie Weir moved from their flat to a boarding house on Woburn Place, improving their situation and easing Stuart's anxiety over her living arrangements.

FRANCE, FEBRUARY 28, 1917

My Dearest:—

It is now morning and I am going to write a few short lines before breakfast. . . . I suppose I may begin addressing your letters to the new location. It strikes me I remember Woburn Place on my wanderings in the neighbourhood of Russell Square. You did not tell me much about the boarding house what kind or description it is. How is it that yours and Mrs. Weir's taste in boarding houses manage to agree. I should have thought she would have demanded something rather more pretentious. Well I suppose we are all getting down more or less to hard tack. I read in the papers every day of some innovations, some restriction in the sale of alcohol, some reduction in luxury, the deprivation of some time honoured privilege and I wonder if England is really changing or if these changes are just on the surface and the abiding qualities most of which I abhor are the same. It is more than an expression of opinion to me. It hurts me I can tell you to think that I have come over here for that—that England might be protected in all her smug hypocrisy. . . . What a hide bound lot that Asquith Government was. Thank heavens we have a red blooded man in the saddle now. We will probably see more changes in the next month than in the previous 18. Lloyd George is down to hard pan on this submarine issue and I believe he will deliver the goods. . . . England can yet surprise the world, if only she will. The exemptions scandal is the sorest touch to men out here. Nearly everyone knows someone that is slinking back—somebody's gardener or perhaps a trusted employee on whom the business depends who is making about three quid a week. I suppose England needed this awakening. I trust she will profit by it. Poor old Canada. I get the Bulletin and Journal. They are still hammering away on new subjects of course but in the same old strain getting after M and M for wanting to tear up some 200 miles of track to send over to France or knocking the National Service Movement. They should come over to the trenches for a while. Then they would change their tune. It is a great corrective and the men who are here will have impressions that will abide till their dying day.

Well, Honey, I have no news as you know. I love you dear as ever and long for the sight of your face. God bless you and keep you, through these dark days.

Your own
Stuart

While the Germans continued their retreat to the Hindenburg Line from the territory of the Somme, the Canadian Corps remained north of there during the winter to train and build strength for the planned spring offensives, and units of the Corps continued to make occasional raids of varying magnitude and importance against enemy lines. The most elaborate assault went in the early morning of 1 March, when units of the 4th Division staged what was to have been a surprise attack involving tear gas and chlorine. Preliminary release of the tear gas alerted the Germans, and while a shift in the wind ruled out using the chlorine, German shells hit some of the gas cylinders and released the contents in the midst of Canadian troops. The raid was assessed as virtually a complete failure; losses were high, and in the days immediately afterward the Germans allowed and even assisted in the recovery of the dead.[5] The 6th Trench Mortar Battery was out of the front line at the time of that raid, and while Stuart makes only casual mention of its accompanying bombardment in the following letter, his diary shows a concerned interest that he did not share with Edna:

Thursday, March 1—A terrific bombardment about day break indicated an attack of considerable size. I peeked through a hole in the wall but could see little. All the batteries around us for miles were going. . . .

Friday, March 2—. . . Heard disquieting rumours of the 4th Div. Said numerous casualties reported from gas and Machine Gun fire. . . .

Saturday, March 3—. . . Still bad rumours of the raid, hundreds of casualties. The cause not known but apparently the gas never reached the German lines. . . .

Sunday, March 4—. . . It was said there was an armistice this a.m. on the IV Division front to enable the Canadians to recover dead and wounded. Promptly at its expiration the Hun started firing.[6]

FRANCE, MARCH 1, 1917

My own Dearest:—

March is indeed coming in like a lamb whether the old proverb holds good in France I do not know. But this morning during the pounding of the guns the birds were singing in a bewildered sort of way and now the sun is shining and I can hear the skirl of the pipes down in the valley below.

This morning the booming of the guns. I do not know what started it but for nearly two hours they kept up a deafening roar. There must have been hundreds at it. Sublime you might almost call it. Only it disturbed my sleep to too great an extent.

I was very fortunate in the matter of mail yesterday—one from Alice, one from Macgregor, one from Zeta and the boys and last but not least one from your little self. Somehow I seem to have mislaid them all except Zeta's. . . . I remember now Macgregor speaking of his appointment and complaining that no extra pay went with his promotion. Pro deos immortales. I read both his and Alice's letter in such a hurry that I cannot recall much of what was in them. . . .

Well my own honey, what do you think of [the] British army now and the new dent in the German line. Isn't it fine? . . .

I have found that Atlas you sent me very interesting particularly when things are developing as they are now. Needless to say the parcel has not arrived yet but I am looking for it any day.

... I was going to ask you to get a holster for my automatic but on second thought I shall get my present one cut down. It is a good fit and a little alteration would make it o.k.

Well I shall close for the present.

Your own as ever
Stuart

MacGregor, mentioned above, was a former colleague in the Education Department who had recently returned to civilian life. Further reference to mail from home in the following letter shows that Stuart still doubted the politicians in the crucial matter of conscription. Life at the front continued in a round of tours in and out of the trenches, changes of billets, mud, rats and a fear of lice.

FRANCE, MARCH 2, 1917

My Dearest:—

I had another letter from you last night in which you enclosed letters from Zeta and the boys. I enjoyed reading them very much. The mail also brought one from your father. I felt very proud and happy when I read his. . . . I am indeed glad that I wrote him at Christmas as I did.

He spoke of the fine weather they had had in the mountains but the cold weather was on them and he recounted one bitter experience of that day. I was surprised to hear him say that conscription would come with the spring. I hope it is the case but I don't think it will have much effect on the war. But I don't think there is a single politician in Canada with the courage necessary to carry it through.

Well we changed our billets today not much of a change for the better though, we are very warm but the difficulty is to get a stove to cook on. We have been very fortunate lately but are now out of luck.

Guess what happened. I got your parcel last night. It was a dandy. First the dates which are nearly gone, the chocolate, the short bread and all the toilet things. They are great. It is a great satisfaction to have these things. . . .

It has been very hard to write. Every one is talking and as there are four of us it is interesting. By the way, I had a bath this morning. I needed one. I am awfully afraid I am getting lice. I was very foolish to sleep in borrowed blankets but I am going to take every precaution to rid of them if I can. Well I have been very fortunate so far.

It has been quite a nice day. I rambled around this afternoon and met Cruikshanks whom I knew at the University.... Well I really cannot write more, everyone is talking. I shall finish in the morning. [next morning]

I feel awfully guilty. Here I had three letters this morning from you, two dated the 26th and 27th and I have not finished this one to you. I rather regret some indiscretions in writing to you. I don't want to prejudice you against Bob.... I am beginning to think some of our fellows are more sinned against than sinning. However, I don't feel inclined to think the matter out. It will have to wait till after the war....

Dearest your letters have been such a source of comfort to me. You do look after me well.... You have been a brick and I had no business to load all my troubles on you. If I lived to be a thousand years old I could never repay you for what you have done and all the love you have given me....

Don't worry about leave. I am not thinking of it. With best love

> Your own
> *Stuart*

It is obvious from the letter below that the nature of the German retreat on the Western Front had become apparent. Stuart notes British success in the recapture of Kut-el-Amara, which they had lost to the Turks a year earlier. The British then began an advance on Baghdad, whose fall on 11 March Stuart hailed in a later letter.

FRANCE, MARCH 3, 1917

My own Dear little Girl:—

... No mail today except a paper from Edmonton—several Bulletins and a World Wide. I can see that they are still fighting over the same old things back home. I have just come from a call on Bob Pearson—.... He told me that Fred Shouldice had gone over to England on leave. I wonder how he worked it. He was certainly lucky.

It has been a very lazy day and I really must stir myself tomorrow to get some things done. I have got to get my breeches mended.... I think I shall take them down to the 31st tailor and get them repaired. I shall not need then to get a new pair. I took that holster down to the cobbler and he can fix it up. . . .

I haven't yet recovered from the satisfaction that that last box gave me. We finished the dates today and had some of the short bread. The chocolate I think I shall keep, at least part of it, as an iron ration if you know what that is. It is [a] mighty good thing for an emergency. . . .

Well, Honey, you have been mighty solicitous on my behalf. I wish I could begin to repay you for all your thoughtfulness. I love you, dearest, more than I can tell you and am trying to be worthy of you. . . .

What a great victory the British have had in Mesopotamia. It thrills us all through and through. The advance on the Ancre is not nearly so much of a triumph. I think Fritz is taking his own good time and is skinning the country absolutely bare. I suppose even the civilians are moving with him. Still it all helps and it is significant. . . .

. . . Good night dearest.

Your own
Stuart

FRANCE, MARCH 4, 1917

My Dear Little Girl:—

I can not refrain from writing you a few lines this morning. It is a beautiful day, but cold. I have been out once but have no desire to go out again. It is much better to sit here and write letters. . . . I have been thinking a lot of you lately and of the golden memories. Not that I grudge them past but everything is sort of clarified as it becomes more distant. Oh what a change [the war] has made in life. How it has lifted us out of the mundane humdrum things about which we used to concern ourselves in the old days. I suppose that is as it should be. In the years to come it will steady us and give us a broader outlook on life and best of all it will consecrate life more [than] anything else could have. The worst is that it will be hard for the soldiers to settle down to civilian life. Not that they will not be glad to get back but I imagine there will be a restlessness in the blood that will be hard to eradicate.

I am clean out of writing paper and envelopes. Reith and I are going to a nearby town where there is a B.E.F. canteen and try to buy some, also some other things. I seem to have written quite a bunch of letters in the last three or four months. . . .

It is [a] very windy day but it is wonderful to see the aeroplanes away up, nearly 10,000 feet. Nothing whatever appears to daunt them—neither weather nor archies nor machine guns. They have surely stood up to it. . . .

What do you think of the latest German retirements? Strategic retreats. I wish they could keep them going. It seems to be easier to do that than to start them on their way. However I have do doubt that when we do start them, we can keep them going.

I feel kind of sleepy today, whatever the reason is. We are just now leading a really lazy life. Do you know, I never recollected till just now that it was Sunday afternoon. I always remember the day of the month but never of the week It is always a surprise to me to know when a Sunday comes. . . .

Don't forget to write. . . .

Stuart

FRANCE MAR 5/17

Dearest:—

. . . Well we went into town today [Aubigny]. The trip in was not so bad. We picked up a motor lorry which landed us there about twelve. We located a nice place for lunch and fared very well for 4 francs. When they brought in the hors d'oeuvres Reith got very anxious and asked me to enquire whether there was anything else coming. We visited a B.E.F. Canteen and bought some odds and ends, gloves, paper. What do you think of my paper. Not bad eh, but it will not last long. It was as good as I could do. We had to walk back and believe me I was tired. Had a good supper, steak and chips. Also met an old college friend Meegan. Do you remember that lad Miller whose girl was very ill when the battalion was confined to barracks last winter in Calgary. He dropped in on me tonight still keen as mustard but a little more sober than formerly. . . .

You should see the transports moving on the roads here. It is a wonderful sight to see. One who has never seen it cannot realize what it is. I know I should not have.

I hope my scrappy letters will not give you the idea that I don't like to write. We all live in one room and it nearly always happens that when I have an opportunity it is hard to write. Tonight I am sleepy and my mind will not concentrate. By the way, Macgregor spoke of compulsory service as a probability. Quite a number have spoken in the same strain. I wonder if it is true. This National Service System seems to have balled things up pretty badly. It is time something was done.

Well little Honey, I shall not write more tonight. God bless you and keep you and don't forget to write.

Your own
Stuart

FRANCE, MARCH 8, 1917

My Dear Little Girl:—

At last we have a measure of quiet about the place and I am going to sit down for a quiet talk with you. This morning, it has been snowing; what do you think of that. I plucked up courage to go over to the bath house but found it frozen up. We have fared very well for baths lately but I like to take every advantage of it; one never knows how long you will be able to get them.

I have somewhat regretted giving expression to my feelings in recent letters. You have enough to put up with apart from that. And after the war we shall not want these petty things to intrude on our relations. Life is just as much a puzzle to me as ever but I am not going to worry nearly so much about things or people. I am going on my own way and let others go on theirs—trying to live up to those principles which I hold dear. If I could only sit down and talk these things over with you, feel the touch of those hands and read the light in those eyes. . . .

As to writing to Bob. . . . I have no objection. You see I knew all along so my feelings have in no wise changed. I feel sorry for him and indignant at the creatures who were his undoing. But more than that, I loathe the society that tolerates and encourages that sort of thing, flaunting loose chorus girls and actresses in the magazines. Love should be a clean thing and not other. His own sins have been visited on Bob. It is not for me to cast any blame.

Well the States is staying out. I can hear you say, "Thank heaven." I should hate to be an American now. They are cowards, and worse still hypocrites—staying out of the fight because afraid but pretending it is for humanity's sake. Heaven help them if they ever have to deal with Germany themselves.

There is one thing I always intended to ask you to send out and this is the rod for cleaning my revolver. I think it is in the trunk. . . . My batman has lost my brush. I am very pleased with my little revolver. It is sure a straight shooting gun. . . .

Nobody will ever be able to tell me about Sunny France again or the vine clad hills. Just now the ground is covered with snow and it is fearfully cold. I am glad I got gloves the other day. All mine have disappeared.

By the way, I think I am not going to be bothered with vermin. I had a good wash and sprinkled my blankets with Sabadilla powder. Well I am going out to try for a bath again. God bless you dearest.

Your own
Stuart

Reversion of officers to a lower rank, which Stuart mentions below in connection with his friend Fred Shouldice, stemmed from the Canadian method of handling reinforcements. Units stationed in England, such as the 89th Alberta Overseas which was virtually absorbed into the 31st Battalion, were tapped for replacement drafts for other battalions at the front, depleting them of junior officers and noncommissioned ranks and leaving them top-heavy with senior officers. By May 1917, policy required surplus officers of rank higher than lieutenant either to revert to that rank or return to Canada.[7]

FRANCE, MARCH 10, 1917

My Dear Little Girl:—
Your letter of the 6th reached me this morning but there are still gaps in the correspondence. Somehow or other I seem cut off from the world as I never used to. Mail is somewhat irregular and we have suffered as a result.

This wretched weather will be the death of me. Not a sight of blue sky or sun today—just a damp heavy fog that beclouds the brain as well as obscuring the landscape. The effect it has on the temperament is even worse. This afternoon we went out and had a tramp across country. It must have been four or five miles. My heel got sore as well as my legs getting tired so I am glad to be back. I am going to settle down and do a bit of letter writing tonight. I must write to Louise. It is a shame but I have not answered her Christmas letter.

Norman wanted me to go up to dinner tonight. I wish I could get out of it. I should rather go tomorrow. It was lucky for Fred S. that he managed to make his leave. I don't believe he was on any raid between you and me. How did he break the news of his reversion. When I saw him on the road down here it was the first thing he said to me, not to tell you about his third star. So I could do no other than promise. . . . Better men than he have reverted. If his wife sets so much store by such things, well so much the worse. Norman is so much more sensible. . . . Norman is making good out here, there is no doubt. In fact, I think most of the 89th boys are. I was thinking particularly of Millican, Andrew and Rossie. I do not know anything about the others.

What would I not give for a couple of weeks back in dear old Alberta with you. This whole blessed country is not worth fighting for I think, with the climate and people. The only real aims are of course not material but moral—otherwise the whole thing would be a wretched failure. But when I think of the fresh air and the sunshine and the kindly people, I almost get homesick. One never sees a really clean attractive woman, or a cosy home. Their ideas of home is just something tacked on to a barn, where the children are housed. Thank you, the first boat for Canada will do me nicely, straight through to Edmonton, Alberta. What do you think about it eh? What a vast change in our ideas and living this war will make. We will never be the same again. Indeed the old world will never be the same.

Well if I am going out to dinner I shall have to hustle. Goodnight dearest be good and God bless you.

Your own
Stuart

In the following letter Stuart reminded Edna of a debate they had in 1915 regarding the wisdom of the action in the Dardanelles, when Britain had launched an unsuccessful Naval attack in February in an attempt to force the straits and link up directly with the Russians. In April British troops had landed on the Gallipoli Peninsula where trench warfare lasted until they evacuated the peninsula at the end of the year after sustaining 205,000 casualties.[8] In March of 1917, the Dardanelles commission published its report determining blame for the disastrous fiasco and it mirrored Edna's earlier assessment.

FRANCE, MARCH 12, 1917

My Dearest:—

... Well, dearest, the news is decidedly heartening lately despite the report on the Dardanelles. I thought of you when reading the report, and our discussions of the project at the time. I took the part of the military and naval authorities, they had more information, had made careful reconnaissances of the ground and had much better means of judgment than the civilian; therefore they should be trusted. You said no, they had gone into it with their eyes shut, had failed to get information as to the difficulties and the men and means available and was just a muddle. Well it turns out that you were right again. Was that womanly intuition. You seem to have a faculty of being right, I don't know how or why. I suppose the Mesopotamian business was not much better but it has been brilliantly retrieved and I think Baghdad will fall. Turks na pas—fini. Everyone out here is tremendously enthusiastic. I suppose a soldier becomes in time a confirmed optimist. Well you are always happier and healthier anyway but I think we have reasonable grounds for optimism. The present Government and the fact that we now have a General Staff to formulate plans for a campaign give me grounds for believing that things will be all right.

Well, the papers we had this morning set me thinking and I have made several clippings for your information and promulgation. This Dardanelles business put in the language of the Daily Mail assumes a most terrible aspect. ... When I stop to think of this all, it fills me with sadness. Is all this sacrifice in vain? The Englishman is asleep mentally and morally. I think nine men out of ten in England before the war were content with their own little sphere and never worried about moral questions. "It has always been so and always will." I think even the leaders were reconciled to the state of affairs and thanked Heaven they were not as other men were. The things I saw in England bore ample evidence of the callousness of public conscience. It has required a crisis such as the present... [to make] people begin to realize their collective and individual responsibility. I see around me the men who are the product of past generations and I know their weaknesses. I have the same and yet. ... I don't thank Heaven that I am not as other men. I know I am made of the same clay and have the same possibilities. The only thing that keeps me right are the influences on me of good women. After all they hold in their hand the secret of the future. Don't you think so. ... The trouble has been in England that women have too long taken man's standards and the result is as you see it. England has surely got to buck up if she is going to avoid national extinction or degeneracy. And the women have got to do it. They can't bury their heads in the sand or wring their hands. They've got to face the issue at once or suffer the consequences.

Well Honey I don't want to discourage you; but I see these things in a different light from what I used to; I also feel that the sacrifices made by those who have gone have laid on the men and women left a burden they cannot escape from; and I hope to heaven they don't shuffle it off as they have in the past.

This isn't a sermon, though you might think so. I find it hard to settle my mind on anything. I guess after being here for a while your mind gets torpid. . . . It seems sometimes as though all we have left is our memories and they seem more or less indistinct at times. Still we don't get down hearted. There is lots to encourage one here and we are satisfied with things. I often think the people at home could learn optimism from the men out here.

Your experience re Canadian mail is like mine. I have not had a scratch from home for two weeks or more. . . .

Say I wish you could send me a weekly paper. I long for some intellectual provender at times. I left all my reading matter at our last place.

Be sure to write and let me know how you are.

God bless you

Your own
Stuart

FRANCE, MARCH 14, 1917

Dearest:—

I don't know that I should write this letter except that I found this paper and decided to use it—quite a good motive isn't it. . . . I had your letter of the 10th yesterday so I know better than to expect another. As to the [ammunition] clips, they are worth the price. I feel about them as I did about the automatic. I simply wouldn't take chances. I may tell you now that I was without a weapon at all the first tour in the trenches. I did not feel a bit nervous and I suppose it was all right at the time. The troops we were opposed to were war-warn troops from the Somme and as anxious for a quiet time as we were. But I decided it was taking a chance and I should not do it again. You never know when you need your weapon.

So Baghdad has fallen. We had the papers announcing it this morning. . . . The great city of the Caliphs, of good Haroun-Al Raschid as all the papers are quoting just now. What a pity it did not occur a year ago. It would have saved that mortifying surrender of General Townshend. Do you remember how upset you were about it that day you came home in South Calgary. How far off all that life seems and it was barely a year ago. Will we ever get back to it. Who can tell?

So Miss Calvert has pulled up and left the old Department. She showed lots of spunk. I think it would pay some of the rest of us. . . . I wonder if things will run along the same old way after the war, if people will still be jealous of one another and petty. The soldier well disciplined as he is will hardly stand being brow beaten I think. I often picture myself going back and meeting all the people there. But of course that is too far to look ahead. . . .

I have not heard from Philip for nearly a month nor from the people at home. . . . I have a splendid opportunity just now to write letters and should like to take advantage of it. . . .

I have not had any papers from Canada recently—neither the Bulletins nor the Globes. I suppose they are still fighting over enlistment and National Service. How far off they are still from reality.

The weather continues to be dull and depressing. Nothing but rain and fog—more rain and fog. The only decent part of France is I guess the south.

I think Norman and I will take a hike into town this afternoon, at least we will try it once more and possibly get a meal there. I don't care for these French meals except once in a while.

Well I am really rambling and not writing. What I really want to tell you is that I love you, more than ever, my own dear little girl.

Goodbye. God Bless you.

Stuart

While out of the trenches, Stuart and his fellow officers could travel over a fairly wide area behind the lines. In the trip described in the following letter, according to his diary, their destination was Hersin and he was describing the spires of Lens.[9]

My Dearest:—

As you will see by tangible proof, I have now received your parcel containing writing paper and reading matter, for all of which I am duly thankful. . . .

Yesterday turned out a very beautiful day. Adams and I decided to go into town. I wish I could tell you the name of it. The walk did not take long. We kept along the main road for a half mile then took a short cut across the fields. Another four hundred yards brought us to the edge of an escarpment from where we could look down on the world below. I am sure I do not know how many towns I could see. Not only our objective but far off to the north and east half a dozen others, some behind the German lines—great patches of red tiles. Away to the east we could catch the distant spires of a town whose name you have often seen. Some bright object on the sky line caught the afternoon sun and flashed it back across seven or eight miles. Now and again we could catch the flash of our guns away off and after a long interval would come the report. Now and again we could hear the drone of aeroplanes sometimes high in the zenith sometimes far over the German lines. A number of our observation balloons were up taking advantage of the clear day. There did not seem to be a great deal of shelling. Once or twice we heard the explosion of a woolly bear, a very heavy shrapnel shell. It broke over the distant woods and hung outlined against the clear sky like a great balloon, the gentle breeze scarcely disintegrating the smoke. We did not purchase much in town, as I am not anxious to spend my pennies. It was about five thirty when we got home. I had asked Norman and Sawley to supper but Sawley did not turn up. After supper we fell to discussing matters and Norman got started on the efficiency of the Army. He certainly was strong on it and I guess we all agreed with him. A lot of improvement might take place without hurting any one. We talked uninterruptedly till ten o'clock. . . .

I have not had a letter from you for several days whatever the reason. I had one from Philip yesterday the first in several weeks. There is nothing of any particular importance to record, as you probably know. I hope the English get into Bapaume before long. It should be quite a crushing blow to the Hun. . . . That reading matter you sent will come in mighty handy. I enjoyed the Spectator. I always meant to tell you, what good time my watch is keeping, good time since it was repaired. It has been a great satisfaction to me.

Well this will do for this morning. I will try and write later. God bless and keep you.

Your own
Stuart

FRANCE, MARCH 16, 1917

Dearest:—

I have come in tired after a hard day but it seems impossible to turn in without saying something to you. My heart is filled with thoughts of you tonight and a great tenderness. What you have been to me and what you have done is more than I could have anticipated or expected. I know it is hard sometimes to express these things; the tongue halts and the words sometimes stick but you know dearest how much I love you.

. . . I was very disappointed not hearing from you today. As a matter of fact, I did get your parcel with the clips, the socks and the fruit cake. I was mighty glad to get the clips I can tell you. Two is hardly enough for an emergency; they are worth the 5/6. Today was rather a fine day though a bit hazy. France is a wonderfully beautiful country when the sun is shining and it is half way decent. I don't wonder that Frenchmen love it, though I never could have such feelings towards any other place than Canada.

I wish I could usher you into our little billet here. We have two beds, two tables a stove with a fine coke fire and abundant candles and light. And above all we are contented and tired. These places aren't so bad, if you forget the mud and the cold. But I would like to see a decent clean girl once more. I have just forgotten that there is such a thing as feminine society. What a strange thing war is. It upsets all our life and habits and turns things upside down. It would seem strange to go back to our old ways. . . .

Somehow we have gathered quite a bit of reading matter lately. I have been lying on my bed reading by the light of a candle. The Times and a copy of the Strand which we bought in town. It does seem good to get the things of civilization once more.

Well goodnight, God bless you.

Your own
Stuart

In late March Stuart wrote of stepped up training, cancelled leave, and Canadians moving out of England—all hints of the big Canadian push that was to come in April. The German retreat continued, and Stuart referred to such events as the retaking of Bapaume, which had been a pivotal town in fighting on the Somme the previous autumn. He shared the early optimism of much of the world that saw the Russian revolution aligning the "three great democracies" against autocracy, yet he was apprehensive about Russia's willingness to continue in the war.

FRANCE, MARCH 18, 1917

My Dear Little Girl:—

I wish you knew what an effort of will it required to get up this morning to write this letter. But your letters of the 11th and 12th which came yesterday gave me a picture of a very lonely little girl over there in London to whom there is coming some love and letters. And indeed my conscience has pricked me more than once of late for my neglect to make connections with the mail in the morning. It was not a good time to turn over a new leaf as I was pretty well tired out after a strenuous day, yesterday. Norman, Carter and myself went to town yesterday. In the morning we were out training. I tramped from Dan to Beersheba. . . . It was a most glorious morning—much the finest day I have seen since I came to France—a light breeze a clear sky and sun and breeze both helping to dry the ground. The views we got of the surrounding country were most impressive. Smooth outlines of rolling country, for all the world like the stretch of country around Calgary with deep green woods crowning the summit of the slopes. I got a kind of spring feeling in my bones so could not stay still. As Norman was going into town with Carter, I decided to go along. To say we had a fine trip would be to put it mildly. It was gorgeous. . . . It was fairly late when we got back but we certainly enjoyed the trip to the utmost. There always is on bright days much aerial activity and yesterday was no exception. Both Fritz's and our own planes were circling overhead and the Archies were busy.

We were all astounded to hear yesterday of the revolution in Russia. It certainly took my breath away. I had anticipated trouble but I must admit I was not prepared for anything so sensational. My first thought was what a pity it had not occurred 12 years ago when the trouble arose just after the Russo-Japanese war. The present is certainly a most critical time. I only hope the country and the Allies can breast the present storm. I shall certainly be anxious until I hear the effect of this on the continuance of the war.

Well, little sweetheart, I wish I could fly over to you for just a few hours. But you know I am a soldier now and that means that I must not allow my feelings play. I am trying to do what I think right and what will make me worthy of you. . . . Pray God the time may soon come, when we shall be reunited. There is so much to talk over so many things to tell. I think it would take weeks. . . .

Goodbye dearest.

God bless you

Stuart

FRANCE, MARCH 18/19, 1917

Dear Little Girl:—

The first three words of my letter were written last night. . . . [A]bout supper time we had a message about the fall of Bapaume; naturally that occurrence and its consequences had to be discussed rather fully despite the fact that there were only two of us to do it, Adams and Pouncey being away. That took up most of the evening and when the time came, I was tired and crawled into bed.

Yesterday was Sunday. I was up early to write your letter. After breakfast there was little to do but read. Bennet came around during the morning and we went off for a stroll. It was very nice, although not nearly so fine a day as Saturday. I did not go out after lunch, resolved to devote the afternoon to my neglected letters. Alas for the plans of mice and men.

We have had a lot of trouble re our mess. Out here in billets we have a stove and every convenience but we don't seem to fare a bit better than we did. Maxey seems content to dope us out anything, showing no initiative. . . . Truth to tell batmen and cooks get lazy behind the line. Norman Weir tackled the problem in B Company. I think he solved it pretty well. Norman is certainly a capable officer.

I am going to have an Oliver today if possible. I believe a bath house is running in the village so I am going to try it. I got my washing yesterday. I had my old sweater washed so I feel half way clean. It has certainly been a comfort to me.

We have just got the morning papers announcing a Zepp raid in Kent on Friday night. England has had quite an intermission but they will not be able to operate much during the short nights. I hope they leave London alone. I suppose it is more or less of a try out to see whether their machinery is running all right.

Well, what of this revolution in Russia. It certainly is a very grave time for us all. I hope the Russians are not fools enough to allow Germany to profit by such. I wish the whole thing had occurred six months ago instead of the present. However the only thing to do is to take things as they come. Sufficient unto the day is the evil thereof.

I suppose you are now back at work. I hope the conditions under which you work are better than they were.

I very much enjoyed the Spectator and the Times you sent. The weekly papers are especially enjoyable. When you have time to read. . . .

Well this is all I can write just now. I must get shaved etc for breakfast. Look after yourself Honey and write.

Your own
Stuart

As the following letter indicates, Edna had returned to work in the Army Pay Office, to Stuart's great relief. It was during the short time away from her job that she and Lottie Weir had moved to a boarding house that was more convenient to the office.

FRANCE, MARCH 19, 1917

My Dear Little Girl:—

On coming in this morning I found awaiting me both a letter and a parcel. I had not previously been advised of the dispatch of the latter so it came as something of a surprise. I had not even made away with the other one, in fact was hoarding it up for the trenches so that we can look forward to the two of them now. Cakes taste mighty good out here I can tell you, better than almost anything else.

I hope you will like it in the Pay Office. Although the idea of your working does not inspire me with enthusiasm, I am mighty glad your mind is occupied and that you are doing your bit. . . .

I have always meant to tell you how much I have enjoyed that Atlas—of late especially when there is something to see on the map. It is the only Atlas around that gives all the battle fronts and everyone goes to it. In fact the men used to ask permission to borrow it when they had an argument to settle. There certainly have been a lot of things to stir the imagination. Russia is of course one of the main topics of conversation, but we are naturally more excited about the German withdrawal to the Hindenburg line. All kinds of theories are propounded as you can see in the papers. Of late we have traced out each evening the places occupied by the British and French troops. Each day, the line has moved a bit further forward. It looks as though we might be winning the war.

Of course the revolution in Russia is the most world shaking phenomenon of all. I am glad now it has occurred. It will range three great democracies together; it will become an out and out struggle of democracy against autocracy. It will certainly make the issues stand out more clearly to both our own countrymen and neutrals. If Russia rallies, her strength will be irresistible. She will be like France was during the revolution. Of course everyone here is extremely confident as I have told you before and we're not worrying over our ability to keep track of the Hun.

Well, little Honey, I hope you are reconciled to my loss of leave. Perhaps it won't be so long after all. I am not worrying over it. When it's all over, the disappointment will all be forgotten. I am pretty steady now—much more reconciled than I would have been three months ago. . . .

. . . There is a rumour that Colonel Robinson is coming over. The circumstances make me very doubtful. . . . He is a mighty fine soldier and a good fellow. I guess they will pretty well be cleaning England out of Canadians for the season's campaign.

Well I am going to drop off to bed. I suppose you go to bed early and rise late these days eh. Be sure to write and let me know how everything is. Goodnight. God bless you. I cannot tell you, dear, how much I love you.

Your own
Stuart

FRANCE, MARCH 20, 1917

Dearest:—

This was a black day for me. No letter came at all and while I tried to comfort myself with excuses it was difficult. To make it worse the weather has been nothing short of abominable. There was very little doing today. This afternoon some of us went out revolver shooting. I was real proud of my achievements. It was snowing and blowing all the time. I was wet and cold so we went and had a cup of cocoa afterwards.

I suppose all England is excited about the German retirement on the Somme. I am not a bit. It must have been long premeditated and it was well carried out. There seem to be few prisoners taken although a German convoy was captured today. I am wondering how long it will keep up. The French are pretty headlong when they get started. Needless to say, it was not altogether unexpected.

I am wondering how you are getting on back at your job once more. You will probably find the trip much easier by the tube than where you were before. Don't let them work you too hard. By the way, what shift did Fred Shouldice make when he went home; did he take off the star or did he tell his wife?

Well, little honey, I wonder if this war will ever be finished. I very seldom allow myself to think of the future. One cannot help wondering what it will bring forth. All the old things seem to be gone irrevocably. Oh to have a few weeks of leisure with you just to love you and talk to you as in the old days. There would be so much to tell. Life is nothing but a dreary wilderness without you. Of course it may have done me good but it seems a precious waste of time. If love is the greatest thing in the world and life and joy mean anything—why all this prodigal waste—.... Why should the human body be considered a thing to be marred and maimed, solely in the interest of the insane ambition of a few men. I hope the Russian revolution marks the end of such things. The human soul will know no master but itself. I pray that Russia, England and France, the three greatest democracies will always be found fighting together as they are now for right and freedom. That is one good result the present turmoil may bring forth. It looks as though Turkey, Germany and Austria, the three greatest curses in the world today, were certainly doomed.

I was mighty glad to see the French brought down one of the Zeppelins that tried to raid Paris. If only the English could do the same. I think these raids were just feelers and if successful will be followed up. They say the Germans always pull off an air raid when they have bad news to break to their people. If they don't watch out they will have worse news one of these times. The British army has reached maturity now—so look out.

Well I don't like appearing in the role of prophet. Such stupendous things are happening that the mind stands aghast. I should like to be in something big some time before the war ends.

Well, goodnight dearest.

Your own
Stuart

My Dearest:—

Your letter of the 15th came this morning. It welcomed me when I came in to lunch. . . .

We have been getting a deluge of papers recently all hysterical about the recent German retirement. It is ridiculous. The British knew all about the "Hindenburg line" long ago and all that it means. It is not a great victory or anything like that. It does mark a step ahead and I do rejoice with the French from whom the territory was so long ago ravished and the civil population who are now returned to the French side of the line. They will know what unrestrained joy means in welcoming back the relieving troops. I sure wish I were there. It would certainly be the experience of a life time. But here we are tied down to the part of the line that is not moving, so we are having no excitement at all. You speak about a humdrum existence. What is a humdrum existence. How quietly things used to go with us in Edmonton, yet we had hundreds of things to discuss and never lacked for interest. . . . War seems to create a vast desert in one's mind—perhaps more imaginary than real. But one cannot afford to react so quickly to experiences as in civil life. I sometimes think I won't know how to act in civil life especially in the presence of women and I have been here only five months. What a change it has brought about. Yet I have no doubt that before we know it a fairer day will dawn for humanity. The Russian revolution may very well be the determining factor. Here's hoping that it will.

How quietly the French take all the excitement. You have got to hand it to them. When they decide to go they get there. The celerity of their following up of the Hun is proof. I believe they will rush him off his feet this year. If they do, then he's got to beat it hot foot. The French are primitive but I admire their method and directness. . . .

Well Honey I am like yourself, not much to write about. But I do long to see you again. I love you so. However there is no use worrying over things. Everything will come all right in time.

Goodbye and God bless you

Stuart

FRANCE, MARCH 28, 1917

My Dearest Little Girl:—

... The weather is perfect today and as you can imagine, the guns and the aeroplanes are taking advantage of it to liven things up. But the trenches are in abominable shape. Thank heavens I manage to get dry at night but I manage to annex a whole lot of mud during the day and it seems to stick unless forcibly separated.

I had the most delightful letter last night from your mother; it quite bucked me up. She appears to be feeling better and is facing things somewhat more bravely. She certainly is a brick. She quoted some poetry which I must remember. It was written by Robert Service on the war; but in spite of that it is good. It seemed to suit my mood some how and I went to bed feeling very much better. I must find time to write her, though it is not easy. ...

I wish I could write you an interesting letter but one feels very much cut off from the world some how. I don't know why it is. I have had no papers for four or five days so in a way I don't know whether the war is still on or not. However I suppose I can trust my senses for that.

... I have certainly enjoyed the parcels you have sent lately. Your two cakes which came to me when we were out; whether selfishly or not I did not pass them around but kept them for my trip in. One doesn't really need them. There are so many other things to get, so I brought them in and have shared them with the batman and runner and we have enjoyed them, I can tell you. ...

Well, Honey sweetheart, there is very little for me to tell as you can imagine. I only wish I had time to answer all my letters but the correspondence has sure got ahead of me for the present.

I am glad you are liking your work and hope that you find the people congenial. I will get this letter off by the runner tonight.

Goodbye and God bless you.

Your own

Stuart

My Dear Little Honey:—

... It is beastly cold and wretched today and there is no mail in yet. It has just come as I finished the previous sentence but no letter from my darling Honey. ... I have got stacks of papers and magazines from Canada—two more parcels this morning in addition to four or five the other day—also an enormous package of papers... so I am hardly neglected.

Last night I went down to see Rossie and Moore, my old sergeant now Lieutenant. ... Reith and I came back in the rain and it was raining, too, believe me. The roads were just covered with that thin slimy mud and I had on only my slacks and low boots. There was all kinds of transport on the road too so I fell in with his suggestion that we should stop in an officers' club. We had a cup of hot coffee—cafe noir—real hot and it went fine. I felt like a new man. Then home and to bed. Wasn't it jake? This morning I went down to get some money. I dropped in the Field Ambulance to have my ear attended to. You'll laugh when you hear what happened to it. The other night I got up when a little show was on—by show I mean a raid. I climbed to the top of the trench and looked over at the flares, bursting shells, bombs on our right. Suddenly I heard a shell coming so I ducked for the dug out, got my leg tangled up in the signalling wire and went down head first. I did not know I had scratched my ear till the next day, when I noticed it bleeding. However, the M.O. didn't do anything except to give me an injection and tell me not to work for 24 hours, which precaution was superfluous.

Well Reith is a good soul, just got a parcel now and allowed or rather insisted on my sampling everything. He is absolutely a brick, never loses his head or anything like that.

... I think I shall sleep all afternoon I just feel in the mood for that today. Today is Sunday though it is hard to believe it. The peace that we associate with the Sabbath is not abroad by any means. Well, darling, my heart is with you today. I can assure you. Don't worry over our being separated. Your mother's last letter gave me to understand you were getting despondent—never do, you know.

Well I shall wind this up for the present and get my lunch. Believe me dearest, I love you more than ever a hundred times.

As ever your own

Stuart

9

Over the Top and Return to "Blighty"

⟡ APRIL 1917 TO MARCH 1918 ⟡

As time drew near for the Canadian offensive, Stuart's letters grew shorter and fewer, and the Field Service Post Card came into its own. Edna received a barrage of "whizz bangs," and she kept the parcels flowing in return.

FRANCE, APRIL 2, 1917
[NO. 1]

My Own Darling Little Girl:—

Your letter of March 28th reached me last night when I was in bed. As a matter of fact I went early. . . .

This morning it is beastly cold. I got up a little early in order to write this but really it is just like a January morning. The guns are going and the airmen are out but they must be frozen to death. It is always my luck to be out of the line when things are frozen. Really the last time in, the mud was bad, I haven't got it all off yet.

You spoke of a Mrs. Young who was going home. Who is the lady. I don't think you had mentioned her before. At least I don't remember. Are they sending all the soldiers' wives home at last.

Do you know I have before me a letter started to Alice on the 28th which I have never finished. I am ashamed but it seems almost impossible to write letters these days except to you. . . .

Well I must close for the present I shall add a little postscript after breakfast if I can.

Good bye, best love, dearest

Your own
Stuart

FRANCE, APRIL 2, 1917
[NO. 2]

My Own dear little sweetheart:—

I am so happy tonight I can hardly contain myself. To begin with I went to town today.... [Aubigny]. It was a soppy, juicy morning, that is under foot, and as cold as Greenland. I was really glad to get away. Our billets were so beastly cold. I warmed up to the walk and when I got to town was feeling fine. I visited the canteen and made some of my purchases—then went back to the eating house where I had luncheon. Just as I was going out, whom should I meet but Captain Ritchie of the 137th. He seemed glad to see me and we went around while I "shopped." We then went and had tea and tried my best to spoil my digestion. We ruminated and chatted over our tea then I finished my "shopping" and we went about our several businesses—he down basewards and I homeward. Say, I was discouraged at the prospect. It was snowing—great big wet flakes that made a splash as they lit and oh! how wet it was. I could hardly see a hundred yards ahead. Fortunately I was overtaken by a motor ambulance which
[Later]   (Alas for the plans of mice and men. I was in the midst of this when Moore came in and insisted on being entertained, to continue) was coming close to here. I finally got home in a flurry of snow and a splash of sopping feet to find Reith anxious to make advance cause—two fat parcels—one from you and one from Alice and Jentie. We were just like school kids and fairly danced with delight.... Oh say listen to what I got—a cake, a box of cookies, a box of shortbread, a box of candy, soap, tooth paste, a tooth brush, then a pair of socks another box of candy, figs.... So we sat down and proceeded to make our selves sick. I know Reith enjoyed it every bit as much as I did. We sure had one great time....

Well sweetheart, I wish I could write you more but time is short. I love you, dear, a thousand times more than I used to. God bless you.

Your own
Stuart

FRANCE, APRIL [3], 1917

My Dear Little Girl:—

... I am going down to the 31st to see Norman but meantime I thought I should write and tell you I am well and so forth. ...

I had a letter from you yesterday (last night). Oh it seemed good to hear from you. I have not heard from anyone else lately. I reread your mother's letter and wrote to her, though I had little to tell. I have mislaid Philip's last letter but I must write to him. He has some Quixotic notion about coming out here again. ... We have enjoyed that last box splendidly. Reith particularly. He is sure fond of chocolates and cake. He is without doubt one of the finest fellows I ever met. He is a prince and best of all a thorough going Canadian. I often tell him how we used to argue about Englishmen and English ways. He feels about as you do. We have great times discussing the war etc. ...

We are still wondering whether the States have declared war on Germany, also whether St. Quentin is taken. We hear rumours say sixteen times a day. However, we only believe what we actually see with our eyes. I think things are going all right though from what we know.

Well I must hurry away and get something done. I am trying to arrange to get a new batman from the 31st. I need one badly enough. Goodbye sweetheart.

Your own
Stuart

Stuart's admiration and affection for J.W. Reith endured long after their sharing of trench and billet. On reading Reith's obituary in the Calgary *Herald* in 1954, he wrote a letter to the editor saying in part: "I should like to add a personal tribute to an old comrade in arms. ... He was one of those self-effacing, reliable, stout-hearted people who bore in their humble way, the burden of the war and who were the backbone of the Canadian Corps through the hard fighting of 1916–1917. ... [H]e assumed more than his fair share of the dangers and toil imposed on his command. His courage, his optimism and his consideration for others kept up the morale of his unit and won the respect and gratitude of men and officers. I would, therefore, salute his memory which will always be an inspiration to me."[1]

My Dear Little Girl:—

No letter yesterday, but after the avalanche I have had lately I did not expect one. The weather has been abominable, yesterday broke with an inch of snow on the ground and a gale blowing. Gradually it cleared and by noon it was fine. I had been so cold sitting around that I decided to go for a walk, so I started on a cross country hike with a vague idea that I might land up in town. However it was so fine that I just kept tramping—went on one road and came back by another. The latter was one of those beautiful wide main roads, lined with stately trees, crowded with traffic and transport of all kinds [the Arras-St.Pol Road]. You really have no idea the amount of transport to be seen moving in the war zone. At times two continuous streams travelling in opposite directions. As you can imagine the poor pedestrian gets little consideration. And the poor infantryman having no horse is jostled unmercifully. As I came back I stopped at one point from which you could catch a distant view of the German lines. It was so far, you could just faintly distinguish the burst of shells and hear the rumble of the guns. Nearer were observation balloons and aeroplanes. The whole scene was very wonderful. I had a tremendous appetite I can assure you and that fruitcake nearly vanished. Reith had a friend in and we three did good work. . . .

I haven't really much to write of this morning and I am beastly cold. If I were wise, I should write you a long letter at night when it is warm and I am feeling more cumfy. . . .

Well sweetheart, I love you more than ever. I go to sleep at night thinking of you and you are with me in my dreams. I shall try to write again today but want to get this off with the mail.

Goodbye Dearest. God bless you.

Your own
Stuart

They had been preparing for the assault on Vimy Ridge for weeks, and the date of the attack was now imminent. In accordance with his word to the wise given above, Stuart chose to write the following "last" letter that same night when it was warm and he was comfortable enough for introspection. The desire he expresses that such a calamity as the Great War not be repeated is one of several early indications that Stuart may have entertained an interest in pacifism.

FRANCE, APRIL 4, 1917

My Own Dear Little Girl:—

I have had it in mind for some time to write you this letter to be held for sometime and posted on the eve of a certain event of which you will hear in time. For before this reaches you, no doubt, the Canadians will have "gone over the top" and many a heart in Canada and in England will be torn with grief. I know that the future must needs be uncertain for each and all of us; I have seen enough of life at the front to realize what such an attack will mean. I want you to know however that I went through it all with a glad heart, eager in some way to show myself worthy of you.

It is superfluous, I guess, to pass in review the years we have lived since we knew one another both before and since we were married. It is scarcely five years since our love was sealed and promises given and received that changed our life. You already know how I loved you even in those days of our first acquaintance and you must know that it has never faltered. But I should like to tell you once more of something that strikes far deeper than passion and words and that is an adoration, almost, of the tender womanhood of you and a devotion that is called forth by your unselfish nature. Your father, when last writing said that from merest infancy your strongest trait was your solicitude for the happiness of others and in voicing his sentiments that there were not many like you, he echoed something that was in my own heart. Dearest, if in days of courtship I spoke fervently of my love to you, ten thousand times more has it grown and been cemented by our two years of married life. My only regret is that so noble and pure a life should have so little reward.

Now, sweetheart, I do not wish to be sombre. I shall need all the help human and other, that it is possible to obtain, for the ordeal before me. But deep down in my heart, I know I have nothing to regret, nothing to complain of. I have lived my life. I have tasted the greatest joy of life, the consciousness of the love of one of the best women that ever drew breath. And in this ordeal which we face, I am fulfilling my destiny and contributing I trust my bit towards the development of mankind and the bringing of the Kingdom of Heaven to earth. The realm of darkness can have no terrors, for Another has gone before and banished them all by the Light of His presence and I believe that "beyond the vale" we shall see face to face.

If there is one hope I might express, which I shall put into practice if ever I get home, it is that those left behind, men and women, should labour to prevent the recurrence of so great a calamity and to bring into play such principles of justice and righteousness as will secure all, rich and poor, the fruits of their heritage—no more booze, no more social evil, nor more oppression. Such an end can be secured if enough people will it. And I trust and hope that those who have been through this hell will be enough interested to do their bit, after the war also.

I don't think there is more I need say sweetheart. In writing this I am thinking only of you and your loneliness. I shall write again I trust as I get opportunities, but the occasions will not now be many when I can send a letter. So goodbye. God bless you and keep you. I trust Him absolutely for the future.

Your own true lover and husband.
Stuart

FRANCE, APRIL 6, 1917

My Own Dear Little Girl:—

. . . This is really a perfect morning. All the rain and mud and slush of the past week is forgotten in a most glorious burst of spring sunshine. What a sin war is to mar the beauty of nature. I have really enjoyed the weather of late, have been outside a good deal and am feeling better though I can't claim to have put on any flesh. I have done a great deal of walking. I only hope the weather in England would break so that you would be able to get out and enjoy a little fresh air.

I had a letter from Philip last night reproaching me for not having written. As a matter of fact I mislaid his last and could not answer it. . . .

Norman is not yet back from the school though he is expected back today or tomorrow. I shall probably go up again today. The battalion are just now out of the line for a few days. Their quarters would not impress you, a combination of tents, dug-outs and bivouacs all glued together with mud. I "bummed" a couple of meals from my old company yesterday when I was up, coming back in the evening. The moon was shining and the air was very soft. Every minute of it was a pleasure, though I was jostled right and left by the traffic on the road. . . .

There is a fairly steep grade in front of the house and when the traffic is passing at night we often have "incidents." The other night I was wakened from a deep sleep by a roar of some kind. I sat up looked around and finally in a stupid way called Reith. "Was that a shell?" He must have chuckled to himself. Gradually it dawned on me it was a mule team and a General Service wagon that got started down the road and couldn't stop. Whatever happened to the mules I do not know. This is repeated nearly every night.

Yes, dear, Sunny Alberta would look pretty good to all of us just now, wouldn't it. Think of the crocuses eh, and the wild roses.

Well sweetheart I must get off a note to Philip this morning. God bless you and keep you.

Your own
Stuart

When the United States declared war on Germany, 6 April 1917, Stuart reacted with much less fervour than might have been expected considering his previous exasperation with "the States."

FRANCE, APRIL 7, 1917

My Dear Little Girl:—

No letter yesterday and as I did pretty well myself, I almost feel aggrieved. I was up yesterday to see the 31st again. Norman was still away. . . . Bob Pearson dropped around during the day and I went down with him to supper. He is living in a wee bit canvas shack at a quite important road junction. I had to leave right away and it sure was raining. I finally got a lorry going part way home and as usual the roads were crowded. I got home at eight sharp and turned in for a good sleep.

This morning I should have finished this letter but I wanted to go to town so I left it unfinished and beat it. I am mighty sorry I did for this should have gone. However as I did not get any letters today I suppose I am not such a delinquent after all. It has been really quite a fine day, cold and windy but quite clear.

I got a lorry in most of the way but was not so fortunate in getting back. However, it only took me four hours to go and come and have a cup of tea as well. I did not have much luck buying stuff though. I went to the canteen.

Well, Honey dear, I am not in much of a mood to write very much this afternoon, so I shall write a postscript after supper. Goodbye dearest.

Your own
Stuart

April 8, 1917

Here goes for a finish. It is a most glorious morning as fine as you could imagine in Sunny Alberta with such a soft fresh air. It is really too fine a day for a war. I hope to see Norman this morning all being well. I only hope there is some mail for me. I have not had any for two days.

Well dearest, the States is in the war I guess. Everyone here is sorry but I think it is for the best. I have never been so reconciled as now seeing the inevitability of the struggle between the right and wrong, good and evil. It is all right.

Well, Honey, good bye. God bless you.

Your own
Stuart

The British launched the long-awaited Allied spring offensive on 9 April. The opening phase, known as the Battle of Arras, began with both the First Battle of the Scarpe, in which the British 3rd Army attacked on an eight-mile front, and the Battle of Vimy Ridge, in which the Canadian Corps simultaneously attacked on a four-mile front adjoining the British on the north. The presence of the Canadians had been intended as a strong defensive flank for the British, "but the Vimy operation was significant in its own right," in that the ridge dominated the high ground between the Scarpe and Souchez Rivers, forming a nine-mile barrier on the west side of the Douai plain. Vimy Ridge, "was tactically one of the most important features on the entire Western Front" because it was a keystone in the German defences that linked the new Hindenburg line with their main lines to the north and the Belgian coast.[2]

The ridge had fallen to the Germans in October 1914, and while the

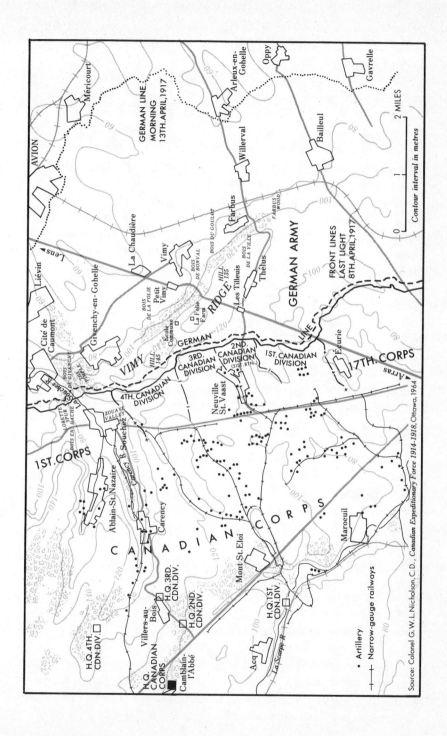

Source: Colonel G. W. L. Nicholson, C.D., *Canadian Expeditionary Force 1914-1918*, Ottawa, 1964.

French had retaken much of the surrounding area, including a temporary foothold on the ridge, the Germans had held the high ground, improved their positions, and undermined the French at the bottom of its western slope. The British replaced the French in that sector in March 1916, and two months later lost 1,500 yards of forward and support line trenches. By April 1917, the Germans had fortified the ridge, whose slopes afforded them an excellent field of fire, and they held three main defensive lines which the Canadians were to attack along a front of 7,000 yards. The German front line, 500–700 yards deep, consisted of three rows of trenches, deep dugouts, and concrete machine gun emplacements, all linked by communication trenches and tunnels. The second defensive line, in places two miles deep, lay behind heavy barbed wire barricades, and some of its dugouts were large enough to accommodate an entire battalion. The third line extended as much as five miles from the front line, and its heavy fortifications included those in the villages of Farbus and Thelus.

The Canadians had prepared thoroughly for their part in the operation. Behind their lines they had laid out a full-scale replica of the attack area, with enemy trenches and fortifications well marked, and while in reserve all units had rehearsed their roles over and over on this model. By the time of the attack everyone knew what he was to do and when and where to do it. High command made no secret that an attack was coming, keeping only the exact day and hour from the participants.

An artillery bombardment pounded German defences for two weeks prior to the infantry attack, and at 5:30 A.M. on Easter Monday, 9 April, the artillery began the assault with a rolling barrage that stayed ahead of the advancing infantry. The Canadian Second Division, including the 6th Trench Mortar Battery, attacked at the Corps' right centre along a 1,400 yard front, and by mid-afternoon it had reached its objectives on schedule. The Battle of Vimy Ridge lasted until 14 April, with fighting continuing on the highest and most heavily fortified ground at the Corps' left or north. When it ended, the Canadian Corps had advanced 4,500 yards and inflicted heavy losses on the enemy, while suffering 10,602 casualties of its own, including 3,598 killed.[3] The ridge did not change hands again.

Success at Vimy Ridge stood as one of Canada's most significant achievements in the war, a victory in which the entire nation took justifiable pride. Stuart Tompkins' descriptions of the battle and its aftermath provide an excellent soldier's view of the events.

My Dearest Little Girl:—

I know that you are saying all sorts of things of me today for neglect in writing but I have been feeling so tired that it was all I could do to get off a whizz-bang to you. Now, however, I am at my leisure sprawled out in bed and am going to try to get off at least a short letter.

The sun is shining this morning and a soft spring breeze blowing and somehow the events of the last few days seem like a dream to me. As you have been aware for some days, last Monday morning the Canadians took the Vimy Ridge, including the villages of Thelus and Farbus, and as I was a participant in these events you will expect a more or less connected account of such proceedings. That is not a very easy thing to do, as I saw only a small part of what was really a gigantic battle you may not get the right perspective.

Last Sunday night, about ten p.m., I left our quarters here with two guns and reported to my own battalion with whom I proceeded to the assembly trenches. It was a severe task. The trenches were familiar but it was pitch black and the carrying party for our ammunition were all green men and could hardly keep up. We finally reached our position after no more serious adventure than a little shelling. I served the men their rum and we proceeded to dig ourselves funk holes and wait for dawn. I made my bed with the corporal and another man but could not sleep for the cold. I got up about four thirty when a shell landed near, we started in to deepen our shelter. We had just finished when it began to get light. Of a sudden one of our batteries opened up; I looked at my watch, it was zero hour and in a moment the battle awoke with the flash and reverberations of thousands of guns.

We crouched low while the shells and bullets whistled overhead. I tried to keep the men down but even I could not resist taking periodical glimpses over the parapet. Suddenly over the low ridge, about 300 yards in front, I saw a disordered crowd of figures stumbling back into our lines. My heart was in my mouth; my first thought was "Our attack has failed; it is our men coming back." But as they got nearer and dropped into our lines, I saw they were Germans who had given themselves up. Apparently, they followed our communication trenches for some distance but as they came back a sentry turned them out and made them go overland. They came across our trenches in twos and threes, dirty, unkempt, pale and emaciated, the most pitiful sight I have seen, some of them wounded, stumbling along with the assistance of their comrades. Our men became wildly excited and would not keep down. Just then, the tanks were making their appearance, nosing their way forward across the squudgy [sic] ground. There were at least six, a few hundred yards to our left. Fritz' artillery was now waking up and he began to turn one battery loose on His Majesty's Land Ships while his barrage came down on our front line.

At eight o'clock it came our turn to move, we climbed out of the trenches and formed up in artillery formation i.e. small columns in single file. I was busy picking out the weak spot in the German barrage; the horrible crumps they were throwing were very demoralizing so I edged over to the left towards the tanks. Soon we were in the barrage, making our way slowly forward. Big shells fell on both sides of us and we could see men falling around us, but gradually we drew clear without a single casualty. It was funny to go over our old front line. Things look much different on top from what they do in the trenches. No man's land was easily negotiated. The wire was blown to smithereens. Then Fritz' front line, resting from time to time in shell holes. In fact that is about all there was. The trenches were almost obliterated. In less than an hour we reached the point from which we extended to open order and in this formation crossed Fritz' strong second line about 1200 yards in rear of his first. Here a stronger resistance was shown and one of our battalions was held up here by a machine gun. I found the gun and the crew. They had succeeded in getting the gun over the parapet when the barrage lifted and rattling off a dozen or so belts before a shell put an end to gun crew and everything. They lay huddled up in all sorts of postures where they died. From this point on, I was up with the first waves of the attack, the troops who had taken the first objectives remaining behind. We lay in shell holes, while the artillery pounded the Hun defences to bits and advanced as the [rolling] barrage crept forward, I shall never forget the sight of the division on our left slowly creeping up the slope as if on review with their barrage licking up the ground in front of them. It was magnificent. In less than half an hour, we reached our next objective then the next on schedule time. Here I saw Norman and was mighty glad to see he had come through. I believe he got some prisoners though I myself had seen very few Boches.

However, I and my crews had to keep going, this time with the leading company. But there was no longer any resistance. The trenches now becoming fewer and fewer were even more badly battered. Houses, streets, dugouts, everything absolutely demolished, the earth a series of craters, here and there a vast hole made by our 12″ and 15″ howitzers. A snow squall that intervened did not hamper the advance; we kept right on as we all knew our bit. Before noon we were pretty well clear of the trenches and in sight of our objective—a broad belt of wire on the ridge. We were now on the crest of the Vimy ridge, walking around in broad daylight as though it belonged to us. It was great! There was no shelling from Fritz. He was beginning to get nervous about his guns and being under the ridge, had no observation.

There was another battalion to go through us and it looked fine to see them advance in extended order through the barbed wire and disappear down the far side of the ridge. We proceeded to "dig in" just this side. Everyone worked like niggers. My carrying parties went back for more ammunition and by four o'clock we were all set. I found a group of houses with a cellar under one, recently vacated by the Huns and we took shelter here, munched our beef and biscuits.

Here we remained all that night, the next day and the next night. We were shelled from time to time but no one minded it somehow. Both my guns were blown up and one of the crew killed so it wasn't all sunshine. I had little leisure but I managed to explore some of the dugouts in the village. You probably know the name. [The village was Thelus, according to his diary.] Stacks of ammunition, bombs, flares, shells all sorts of things in dugouts fifty feet underground. There was very little in the way of souvenirs. I got a chunk of German bread to eke out my vanishing supplies.

But it was the cold I suffered from more than anything else especially at night. Our cellar was draughty and I never could sleep more than an hour or two at a time, but of course we were not long in the line. The second night we were to be relieved. I waited till nearly midnight, then went down into the village to hunt up my relief. I got down into one of the deep dugouts hunting up the battalion officers. It was so far down when I got there that I had not the strength to go up so my runner and I lay down a hundred feet below the surface with all kinds of explosives around us and slept on a bench in peace. I got up about 3 a.m. . . . no word yet of relief so I lay down on the floor and slept. As day was breaking someone stumbled to the door. By chance, it was the officers of the relief so in half an hour I was off with my men.

We returned to our old front line [in front of Neuville St.Vaast] where there were congregated in a few hundred yards the whole brigade. I took a tumble that there would be congestion, so as soon as we drew our rations we went on a hunt. My old dugout was occupied so I struck back towards our supports. I came on an old bomb store now deserted in the advance which I remembered. Here were two bunks, kindling, coke, a brazier. Near by my men found another dugout and oh say, didn't we settle down for the day. I had a fire and made out my first decent meal—a whole tin of beans, 4 hard tacks. My corporal stayed with me and weren't we cumfy that night, despite the snow outside. Next morning we returned to our H.Q.

It was most stimulating to see the guns moving (or attempting to move up) despite the snow and mud across our old lines and no man's land, digging in in the open, men walking around everywhere, where formerly you would see nobody, the ground pitted and torn with shells—one vast wilderness. Enthusiasm was in the air and though they were tired my men held their heads high as we swung back on the homeward trail.

Well, honey, I have told you in brief all that has happened. I may think of something else later. Our optimism was of course doubled last night by the news that the Hun was further retiring. I was played out but couldn't help taking a round out of Reith. Everything is moving ahead, transport, artillery. This place which used to be shelled a week ago is now out of range and we walk about every where. As you know our cavalry have been in action. I have not seen them but they were busy the first day for we smashed Fritz whole system of defences and got right into the open.

We have seen none of the papers giving an account of the attack, so if you can get them, save them and send them to me. It will be worth keeping. I will try and get some maps also; it will be worth keeping won't it.

As you know, casualties were light. By the way, though, Bothwell (of the 66th) was killed, Clarke was telling me yesterday.

Well goodbye Honey dear. I am sorry if you were worried. I hope for a letter today.

Your own
Stuart

During this time of combat and dislocation, Stuart relied on Field Service Post Cards to avoid a gap in his correspondence. Those that have survived all bear the same markings, to the effect that he was "quite well," had received her letter, and "letter follows at first opportunity."

FRANCE, APRIL 16, 1917

My Own Dearly Beloved:—

I have had a very indolent day but somehow felt in the mood for writing tonight; I know I am in a better position to sum up the events of the past week. When you are going through them, you feel only cold or hunger or fatigue; when it is over a great weariness seizes you in which your faculties are more or less benumbed. Fortunately outside of a cold, I had no ill effects from the exposure beyond a cold; it worried me at first but today I am feeling fine almost happy and contented.

Will the censor object to my telling you that we are occupying part of Fritz' old line and at this very moment living in a German dugout that barely ten days ago sheltered its Hunnish occupant. Mementoes of Fritz lie all around but no one cares; everyone is sated with things German. By day we can walk about where formerly we dare not show our head over a parapet. How things change. Only at times do we hear the sullen whine of Fritz's shells in the distance, grudging us what we have gained in the sweat of our brows.

Well it was a great experience that I should not have missed for a good deal. Men who were on the Somme say that they never saw anything to compare with the artillery fire here. It was wonderful; and the men they were great the way they walked right into it. Why we were over the rear lines before Germans in the dugouts knew an attack was on. And everything went like clock work. I think it gave the Hun a bad jar and I don't think it's a patch on what we can do.

I was mighty relieved when I met Norman after the worst was over and they had gained their objective. He had a grin on his face—had taken some prisoners I think. Old Watson came through all right. I had a chat with him in a shell hole on the top of the ridge. Really it seemed like a picnic. As soon as I got my guns in position I got out my bully beef and biscuits and had lunch. I really felt fine all the time though awfully tired; when I tell you I ate my breakfast in bed three successive mornings, you will know I have gone a long way to recuperate. . . .

By the way, I heard that Fred Shouldice had been wounded. Of course you know we will not get papers from now on likely. I wish you would keep me posted. Also don't forget about those papers giving an account of the doings. I should certainly like to see them. By the way, in case I have not before acknowledged it, I may say I got your parcel with the tinned meat, cake [and] chocolate. It has simply been splendid, living this camping life as we do. Nothing could have been better. We all enjoyed the cake immensely. I have a little piece left.

Now I must close and write a little letter to Jentie. We had no mail today but look for it tomorrow.

Goodnight Dear
God Bless you
Stuart

FRANCE, APRIL 17, 1917

My Dear Little Girl:—

Your letters of the 11th and 12th came today. I was sorry you were so cast down over my participation in the fight a week ago Monday and that I could not get you out word before I did. . . .

Well we heard tonight that the French took another round out of Fritz so he will be feeling pretty sore tonight I guess. I do wish I could see a paper now and again to know what was happening. I wish I could tell you how much we all enjoyed that Spectator and Nation. It was like a breath of fresh air and caused endless discussions. You should have heard Mr. Reith's expressions when I told him about the fudge. Boxes and letters are our sole comforts of life these days.

I was wondering who started the story that we were not going to be in the scrap. There never was the least foundation for it—not one iota. It makes me tired having people spread rumours on matters of which they absolutely know nothing. . . .

This dugout life is not agreeing with me. We have over 80 men in this one and in our particular 6 × 6 there are four. Consequently the air is very bad. Just now after a nights sleep it is very bad. I went up for a walk around the shell holes but it is wet and snowing so I did not stay long. When will this wretched weather end.

I am wondering when that parcel will be along. Last night the boys told me there was a parcel. I had my mouth all fixed but it was just the ammunition. Of course I was glad to get it but you don't get any gustatory joys out of .38 ammunition. It amuses me the frantic way I sent for that ammunition. The only thing I saw to shoot at was a hare. (There were numbers of them around the battlefield.) I pulled a trick to pull my gun on him but it wouldn't come. It was comical to see one fellow in the thick of the fighting packing around a hare he had killed. Apparently he was saving it for his dinner.

Well little Honey I shall close now. I must go out and get some fresh air. I hope Norman is all right. I have not seen him for several days. Goodbye. God bless you.

Your own
Stuart

A span of four days with no letter may have alarmed Edna, or it may have prepared her to receive a long-dreaded telegram announcing, in this instance, that Stuart had been hospitalized. The events of those few days that led to his eventual return to England are noted in his diary. Tuesday, 17 April: "... cold began to get much worse. Went down to Aux Rietz to Dressing Station and was told to come back in morning and go to C.R.S. [Corps Rest Station]." Thursday, 19 April: "Reported at Dressing station at Aux Rietz at 10 but did not leave for a couple of hours... caught an ambulance for Fresne Court where I was shortly installed in clean linen and a cheerful hut with a dozen or so other officers. Temp. 102°." Friday, 20 April: "... feeling sick and weak. Did not get out of bed all day. Examined by doctor this p.m. and marked out for C.C.S. [Casualty Clearing Station]." Saturday, 21 April: "Left this p.m. for C.C.S. at LaPugnoy which we reached about 4:30, had a delicious tea and saw a WOMAN—the matron. She put some of us to bed at once—nice soft blankets, fine pyjamas and a hot water bottle. Delightful."[4]

FRANCE, APRIL 21, 1917

My Own Darling Honey:—

Now don't laugh when I tell you but do you know I am actually lying between sheets in the most cumfy place I have been in in France. As a matter of fact I am at the Canadian Corps Rest Station. To tell the truth I could have come down after the show but I thought that if we were going to be out for a few days I would be all right so I decided to stick it. When we went back after about two days, we were in the old Hun dugouts with half our battery. The grub, the stuffy air and wet weather didn't give me a chance. So little Willie had to beat it down country. So you don't need to do any worrying. It is just a little bronchial trouble. It wouldn't have bothered me at all, only I was about all in after the show.

I know I have neglected you most shamefully of late. You have had a profusion of whizz bangs but letters have been as hard to write as could be but I shall have lots of leisure in the next day or two and shall use it for writing. I am mighty sorry I am going to miss that swell parcel you sent me, but the others will enjoy it. They are a generous lot; the only one I grudge is the O.C. He appropriates everything in an offhand manner, is absolutely selfish, but the rest—say they would give you their last hard tack. I am sure that Muirhead doesn't eat one tenth of the contents of his packages and Reith is the same. He got a parcel with the swellest fruitcake from Edmonton the night before I came out. I knew I shouldn't but I had two pieces and would have eaten another. My temperature was down next morning so it was not fatal.

I have not seen anything of Norman for nearly two weeks. I don't really know where or how he is. I trust he is all right. There was an impressive list of casualties among Canadian officers in day before yesterday's paper. It makes me think we got off pretty lightly after all. I am not kicking. Fred S is certainly lucky to be home for the second time in six months. He'll see very little of the war now I imagine. Well of course I have no news. My temperature is down to about normal this morning. I don't think there is any chance of my being taken off solid food. I should hate to see good eggs and butter going to waste around here.

Well good bye for the present. I don't think it worth while to address mail here. I shall be here only a couple of days.

God bless you

Your own

Stuart

I see Rossie is wounded. You want to hunt him up if you ever get a chance. I was just rereading the list and see that Lieutenant J. J. Moore previously reported wounded (I heard that) now reported killed. He was my platoon sergeant. You remember the night he sang Mother Machree. I saw him only two weeks ago.

Again, the diary provides details that the letters do not. Sunday, 22 April: "Felt rotten this morning. Entrained about 8 a.m. for Boulogne. The morning passed all right but very sick in the afternoon. Could not sit up so got a stretcher to be on, reached Boulogne about seven, washed and put in bed—light supper then to sleep." Monday, 23 April:

"Was kept on liquids today—quite a temperature... Hospital over-looks harbour. Red Cross ships coming and going all the time, also leave boats. Weather clearing very nice."[5]

Had Stuart truly wanted to allay any fears Edna may have had, he should have relied on Field Post Cards. No matter the message, the handwriting in the following letter was unsteady, obviously the effort of a very sick man.

FRANCE, APRIL 23, 1917

Dear Little Girl:—

This is to let you know that I am at present an inmate of No 7. Stationary Hospital Boulogne, having been despatched hither yesterday through the Casualty Clearing Station. You do not need to be alarmed; it is just a bad attack of bronchitis and I can assure you I am in good hands. The nurses are very good to us and I do not think I shall lack anything. Unfortunately I left my kit up country when I came out and am hard up for a razor. If you get this within reasonable time you might get me one, no better not. I don't know how long I'll be here and shall take [a] chance. I shall let you know as soon as my address is fairly permanent.

I had a very uneventful trip down country, felt weak and sick but a good night's rest has revived me. I am sorry I missed the box—am writing to Reith to divide it up. I suppose I shall get no mail at all from you now.

There was an officer of the 31st Battalion on the train, a Mr. Carson from Medicine Hat. He was the only one I knew.

Well Good bye dearest

Your own

Stuart

Will you write to the folks at home and tell them. It is quite an effort to write. I sent letters to Janet and your mother after the show.

FRANCE, APRIL 24, 1917

Dearest Little Girl:—

Once again I sit up in bed to get off a few lines to you. Let me tell you, it comes with less effort today than it did yesterday. I am feeling a good deal better.

There is very little that I can tell you beyond the fact that it has been an ideal day, and I have revelled in looking out across the water at the ships going and coming. I wonder if I shall ever get a letter from you here.

Everyone here is very nice and I am fed pretty well considering. I have certainly had a good rest. What they are going to do with me I do not know.

Goodbye for the present
Your own
Stuart

FRANCE, APRIL 26, 1917

My Dear Little Honey:—

Just a wee bit note before I turn in for the night to let you know I am feeling fine. It is the first decent day I have had. I was rather all in when I got down here.

I have not had any mail from any where not even from you. I was wondering whether it would be a good idea to wire mother. I suppose my name will be in the lists worse luck. However if you write home telling them it will probably be all right.

Today has been a most gorgeous day, we lay and watched the water shimmering and the ships moving about in the harbour.

Well I must not attempt more tonight.

Goodnight
God bless you
Stuart

The letter above is the last that survived from France. The day before it was written Stuart finally had that glimpse of a proper Canadian female that he had so nearly despaired of ever having again; the diary recounts his trip to "Blighty." Wednesday, 25 April: "A streak of sunshine slew in in the shape of a Canadian girl... a peach, very proud of her. Gradually mending, M.O. says nothing. Others going to Blighty." Saturday, 28 April: "Doctor definite. Tells me I am going to Blighty. Temperature normal all day." Sunday, 29 April: "Most beautiful day, crawl around ward a little and look out of window. About 3 p.m. warned for Blighty. Pack comes up and get ready. Taken to boat about 7 p.m. Many wounded on board." Monday, 30 April: "On boat all night. About 9 a.m. cast anchor and after a couple of hours run tie up in Dover harbour. . . . Taken to Chatham, Fort Pitt Hospital. Dropped Honey a card."[6]

The stay at Fort Pitt Hospital was short. On 3 May he moved by ambulance to a convalescent home that was in a farm house on an estate about four miles from Sevenoaks. This was Combe Bank, the estate of Robert Mond, an heir to the Mond Nickel empire, who invited Edna to stay in his house while Stuart convalesced there. She remembered those weeks fondly, saying "So I went down and I slept in his house and had breakfast there and then I would go up to the hospital and help the matron there . . . [she and I] became very good friends. . . . I'd been starving in London . . . the people across the road, Lady Plender and Sir William, used to send the meals over . . . for the men and for the matron and me from their place. And of course they had gardens and all sorts of things, so I just naturally bloomed out with all the cream and butter and fresh vegetables that I was getting."[7] The matron, Cara Hall Hall, left Combe Bank at about the same time that the Tompkins did, she to join the nursing staff of Queen Mary's Hospital at Roehampton in London, a facility dedicated solely to the care of amputees. Edna later joined her there as a Voluntary Aid Detachment [V.A.D.] after a three-week holiday that she and Stuart spent in and around London and on a memorable trip to Scotland.

Following the holiday, Stuart was assigned to the Alberta Regimental Depot at Bramshott. Edna left the Army Pay Office to work at Queen Mary's Hospital during that time. She was able to go from London for an occasional week-end, and he, in turn, made trips into the city whenever he was granted leave. He filled his letters with expressions of concern, impatience, and frustration at being somewhat in limbo and they reflect the difficulty of readjusting to life after combat. In the following rare instance he talks of how the war in the trenches affected him, and, in discussing the exploits of others, a wry bitterness creeps into the words of a man who had always been much too modest and unwilling to push his own cause.

ALBERTA REGIMENTAL DEPOT,
BRAMSHOTT
JUNE 23RD 1917

My own Dear little Girl:—

Here I am sprawled out at a six foot table with a blanket on it writing to the best little girl in the world. At last I have my own room, my own bed (save the mark) and am squaring myself away. Needless to say I have both consciously and unconsciously been taking stock of my surroundings and will give you the net result.

After leaving you, I got a fairly cumfy abode in the train, although two other officers joined we were not crowded. There were few stops on the run down till we got to the camp area. . . . We reached Liphook about three and after claiming my luggage and galvanizing a taxi driver into life, I got away for camp with two others. When I reached the Depot, the first man I saw was Major Seaton. . . . I was duly entered up and taken to quarters. Owing to congestion I suggested a change to a vacant room which was granted and this morning I got moved.

At dinner last night I met Major Hewgill, Cox and others that I knew. After dinner I wandered around camp and seemed to be running into someone I knew at every turn. First I met Harold Riley, who was anxious to hear all about the great war so I discoursed on it for an hour in his room. Later I met Richards now a Major. I talked forestry and ate maple sugar at his expense. . . . It makes me laugh, the deference paid you by those who have not been out to the front, that is they seem to think you should know all about every thing. Their ideas look funny after six months in the trenches. I am just wondering if I was like that six months ago.

On the other hand, it is funny how much they "know" about things over there. You will notice the inverted commas. Some of them can tell you more of what happened at Vimy than I can. For instance McGregor (formerly of the 137th) got the Military Cross for the Vimy show for no other reason I believe than because he was the only officer wounded in the 31st. . . . The idea here is that he performed some peculiarly gallant deed. Ditto Ainliffe also of the 137th. I was with Ainliffe most of the day on April 9th. I know I kept urging him to fill in the gap between us and the 1st Division. I finally filled it in with my own men and now Ainliffe has the M.C.

It is amusing to hear them discourse on the construction of deep dugouts as taught at the "Trench Warfare School." All about the bursting layer, resisting layer, etc etc. They are as wise as owls but really don't understand the first thing about it. How men hope to understand the first thing about trench warfare without going over to France beats me. . . .

I have been particularly warned that I am not to do any work here. That is emphasized by everyone. The Lord alone knows how I am to put in the time here. I am devising ways and means of arranging that.

There are of course lots of friends here and time should not hang too heavily on my hands. . . . Now as to what is nearest to my heart. What about coming down? I shall not urge you, much as I want you. I know I could get accommodation (Major Blair put me wise last night) quite handy. But if it does not seem feasible to come down altogether what about week-ends. Write at once and let me know.

You will laugh when I tell you I am planning to get my little stove into action once more. But they do not serve tea in the afternoon. Dinner is early (i.e. 5:30 pm) so I expect there will be times when a snack will come in handy so I am going to ask you some day *soon* to send down a few biscuits and some tea or coffee. The milk I can buy. My needs are not large you see. . . . There is a canteen here where I hope to buy fresh fruit once in a while. There were strawberries around this morning large beauties but they were very soft. That was a fine apple you bought for me. . . .

You will be interested in knowing that the arrangements with the Royal Automobile Club were made by Sir Francis Lloyd commanding the London area. So that one is scarcely sponging when he accepts their hospitality. They are required as I see by a notice to provide officers with rooms or to see that they are so provided.

Well now I think I have done very well, considering I had nothing to say.

Still there is one thing not yet said. If I just had a good opportunity without distraction for instance I could tell you how I love you. You are the same dear little girl who so held my heart in thrall years ago and you hold it still. And oh I love you and am so happy in our love. Neither the lapse of time or the limitations of the English tongue can dim the memories or take from the sheer delight, dear one, of having your love. I really have no words to express myself.

Goodbye Honey, Write soon,
Stuart

By this time, senior Canadian officers stationed in England either reverted to lesser rank or returned home. While Stuart had assurance that he could remain, there was little or no chance for promotion, and future plans were uncertain. At the Regimental Depot old associations were renewed as the paths of former battery and battalion mates crossed every day, but Stuart chafed at having his mind inactive and unchallenged, and the letter below may represent the point at which he began to think of pursuing an academic career after the war. In his assignment at Bramshott he served on various rating boards and courts martial. He later said the purpose of those boards was "to judge men that were battle fit and those that weren't battle fit and [to decide] which had to go back to Canada" and which were to go back to France.[8] The following letters indicate that he really lived for weekends and the possibility of spending them with Edna.

ALBERTA REGIMENTAL DEPOT,
BRAMSHOTT
JUNE 28, 1917

Dearest:—

I must just dash off a few lines to you before I settle down to do nothing. There is nothing much happening at the office so I beat it till I was wanted. Do you know I am in demand now. Major Hewgill of the 21st is wanting me for the permanent cadre but Major Seaton is also anxious to keep me at the Depot. It's funny to be popular. But it also is a great temptation not to think of going back to France. I don't know what to think about it.

The bolt has fallen now. I know you are not coming down. I got your letter of the 26th this a.m. telling me. Do you know your letters are two days old by the time they get here. How stale are mine. I believe letters posted in London in time for the evening mail get here the following evening. . . .

. . . I have no word yet of my leave, don't know whether it is through or refused. I am not sure just how things are developing but Major Seaton is trying to keep me on the staff. . . . I should like to have something to say in the matter as I want promotion if I stick around, wouldn't you. It's apparent I am here indefinitely but I am afraid I shall die of dry rot if I stay with a reserve battalion.

I am afraid I simply can't write, my thoughts seem clogged. . . . I really don't know what I shall do to avoid vegetating here because I must keep myself alive. I think I shall have to indulge in some books or something. There are a lot of things I should like to know. In other words I should like to become educated. This is really a wonderful world if people would only open their eyes to it.

It is strange there is no mail for me from Canada or France. Old Reith I guess has forgotten me. I believe Pouncey has been trying to get back to Canada. I believe he has been swinging the lead a bit. He told some one about being buried and severely injured but all he is in the hospital with is sickness, probably boils which were beginning to trouble him when I left.... I think I shall have to send this pen to Sloans. It is leaking like fun....

Well I am going to wind up this very unsatisfactory letter till a more fitting season. My inspiration seems to have departed. Goodbye Honey.

Your own
Stuart

The surplus of officers continued to thwart Stuart's hopes for promotion, and as the letter below shows, no promotions were likely unless the total Canadian strength in England was increased considerably. The general election campaign of 1917 would soon be underway, with conscription a leading issue, and Stuart tried to garner what support he could for the popular Colonel Hewgill.

[BRAMSHOTT], JULY 10, 1917

Dearest:—

We are all on edge tonight because of reports of a great air raid on London tonight. Surely it can't be true. I shall be waiting anxiously for papers in the morning.

Norman and I went out for a long walk tonight up to Grayshott and Hindhead, did not get back till 9:30....

Well now, you will be interested in knowing that I approached Major Seaton on the subjects mentioned. Things are in a state of flux and he really could promise me nothing but he is trying to get several of his officers made captains. This can only be done (I understand) if the establishment is increased. He promised to let me know but unless he can give me something when my board comes along I shall ask to be passed to the 21st. He is trying to do something for me I know but I shall look further afield.

Also Colonel Hewgill is going to stand for Alberta Representative and I want you to boost for him. Major Seaton promised me leave to London if I would do some work for him, but in the meantime, you might just corral a few votes yourself. I am more than delighted that the Colonel is running....

Now it is nearly 11 pm and I must to bed. My batman bought me some things today but was not able to get a coffee pot. He got me some nice apples. He is a jewel....

Well Honey I must close. I am anxious tonight. I hope tomorrow will bring reassuring news.

Your own
Stuart

[next day]
... I am feeling fine this a.m. (Wednesday). The papers contain no particulars of an air raid....

In the letter below, Stuart once again wrote with premature optimism about the end of the war. The chaotic situation within Russia and her army was, at best, unclear to the Allies. A Russian attack had begun in May in Romania even as the Russian army's disintegration began. A renewed offensive, launched on 1 July, probably accounts for Stuart's observation that the Germans would have to make peace, but a German counterattack ten days after this letter was written drove the Russians back. Peace talks were not to take place until 22 December when negotiations began at Brest-Litovsk, and these were certainly not solace for the Allies.

[BRAMSHOTT], JULY 14, 1917
My own Darling:—

Life is a great big empty void this afternoon. I quit work about 1:30 and was expecting to go out for a wee bit walk with Norman... [but] he has his transportation and instructions to report to Shorncliffe and just half an hour ago he went off in a taxi....

It hasn't been a very satisfactory afternoon. I lay down after coming back from the office and was just dropping off to sleep when the batman came in and woke me up. Then some one was packing next door and that prevented me from going to sleep.

Did you hear about the captains. They all got instructions this morning to report to London preparatory to sailing to Canada. They are to be discharged and I believe there is a special provision in the new conscription act that leaves them liable to military service unless they are over age or medically unfit. That strikes me as being pretty fair. Then there are to be no commissions granted in Canada. I tell you I shouldn't want to be an eligible over there now. Think what they will have to go through. I can just hug myself that I came over when I did.

I imagine there are big events pending in Germany now. If the Russian offensive is maintained—they will have to make peace or court disaster. It may not be this month or next month but the end is drawing near. What momentous changes the war has brought; what vicissitudes. . . . War defies all calculation. Who could have prophesied the Russians' revolution or the revolution achieved could have foretold Russia's recovery. The case is now clear between democracy and autocracy and the scales are loaded against the former. [sic]

We will have fighting yet but every step from now on Germany will go backward. The great crisis for her is the undeceiving her people as to the real nature of the situation and the reconciling of them to the role of vanquished. But you have heard all this before; it appears daily in the papers but it is nevertheless true. . . .

Well good bye Honey. I just got a letter written on the 13th. . . .

Stuart

[later]

Well, dearest, here I am at it again. . . . I feel quite contented tonight having had a bath and a haircut, and the wind blowing fresh and cool.

I can't tell when I have been so happy as I have been since I came back from France. I suppose I have sized life up for what it means grasped at the substance instead of the shadow. I often look back in wonder at the strange creature I was five years ago. What is the reason, what has changed the face of the universe for me, has made life a bounding rushing glorious stream instead of a dried up watercourse. I sit mixing with men and the world; is it soldiering. The only rational cause that I can see is the fact that life has been touched by love. . . .

I remember well those far off days of diffidence and courtship. How solemnly you and how reluctantly you admitted that you love me, counselling me that life was a long time and that it was full of reefs. How we have sailed over them all and how glad and joyous life has become.

You mustn't reproach me for writing this way for it is the sole comfort of a lonesome heart tonight. I so wish I were with you. Never mind, the war is coming to an end so cheer up.

Colonel Hewgill reiterated what he told me before that none of the overseas casualties were going back [to France] until the others had been over. The subject came up when I met Major Gillespie (you remember him Doctor Gillespie's son). He was here this afternoon and I shook hands with him. He guaranteed me a good long rest. I think he was rubbing it in a little.

Well sweetest heart good night....

Stuart

In December 1917, Stuart received a transfer to Mytchett, a Canadian Musketry School near Aldershot, for a brief stint as instructor, and it was possible for him to live in London during part of that assignment. He had continued to study Russian, and while at the Musketry School he attended a series of evening classes in Russian language at King's College, London. He remembered that the instructor "was not a bit enthusiastic," making it a "dreary, dreary, dreary business," and he confessed having difficulty with the Russian alphabet which he considered "in a class by itself" and getting it "mixed up with the Greek."[9]

He returned to Bramshott in early spring 1918, by which time food shortages in Britain had become critical, and the army returned all expendable personnel and their wives to Canada. On 12 March 1918, Stuart received the order that he was "being returned to Canada, AT THE PUBLIC EXPENSE, by the next available sailing," with the added warning that "It is an offence under the Defence of the Realm act to mention names of transports or other ships, ports or date of sailing." Hence there is no record of sailing date or port of embarkation.[10]

Edna, too, was given passage home, and they made the return trip together on the *Mauritania*, which had been outfitted as a troop transport. She recalled that they landed at Halifax where devastation from the December 1917 explosion of a French munitions ship was a severe shock to them. They proceeded on to Montreal by train, encountering an April blizzard, and "then of course we wended our way across the prairies to Edmonton." Stuart received his release from the army on 16 May, 1918.[11]

C.E.F. Siberia

Whatever the date of their departure from England, Stuart never forgot one date from that voyage aboard the *Mauritania*—22 April 1918—when a chance encounter with Major J. Macintosh Bell, late of the Canadian 73rd Black Watch Battalion, very likely changed the course of his life.[1] Bell had worked as a mining engineer in western Siberia before the war, and his knowledge of Russian won him an appointment to the British intelligence mission in Russia. In July 1917, he was appointed Allied Passport Control Officer in Vladivostok. He returned to Canada in January 1918, and his activities early that year took him to England. In April he was enroute, via Canada, back to Vladivostok where he again served with British military intelligence.[2]

Edna met Bell first, when she was writing a letter at a double writing desk in the ship's lounge, and he came and sat opposite her. He took something from his brief case, put it on the floor beside him, then reached down and picked it up, and then returned it to the floor. He repeated that several times and finally said to her, "I must apologize for being so noisy, but I'm writing a letter in Russian and I do have to consult the dictionary to get the right word." She later recalled being young and brash at the time and saying to him "Oh, my husband is studying Russian." This news stirred his interest, and when Stuart joined her, she saw to it that he met Bell. Stuart, in turn, showed intense interest when Bell told him that a proposal then under discussion in London had every prospect of culminating in a force being sent from Canada to Siberia.[3]

By the time Stuart left England, what had begun as an intellectual diversion stemming from both a love of languages and the challenge of mastering a difficult one had grown to a serious interest in all things Russian and in the events that had dramatically brought Russia to the world's attention. The meeting with Major Bell not only intensified that interest, it presented the very real possibility of his actually visiting one part of that little known country, and by the time he returned to Canada, he was intent on being a part of the force that would be sent to Vladivostok.

Knowing of the Siberian expedition considerably in advance of the order-in-council that authorized it on 12 August may have worked in Stuart's favour. He was able to plan, make a decision, and put his affairs in order early enough to secure military reappointment to the 260th Infantry Battalion on 16 August, and he was named 13th Military District recruiting officer for Edmonton later that month. He maintained a recruiting office at the armoury and kept daily hours at the Great War Veteran's club rooms to sign up "veterans who desire to top off their 'bit' by doing 'another bit'"; veterans of the war in France were given preference, and conscripts could opt for assignment to the C.E.F. Siberia.[4]

The Allies' intervention in Siberia was a tangled and complex affair. Quite apart from its opinion of the Bolshevik regime and fear of the spread of radicalism, each Allied nation harboured its own set of motives and objectives as it weighed the decision to intervene. Canada's route to the intervention was especially tortuous.

Russia's withdrawal from World War I, cemented in the spring of 1918 by the Treaty of Brest-Litovsk, left her former allies fearful of being overwhelmed in the West by German armies reinforced by troops no longer needed on the Eastern Front. Strong German offensives mounted that spring on the Somme and the Aisne and at Lys lent credence to their pessimistic view that the war was still far from over.

The Allies had shipped enormous stores of war materiel to Russian ports, and in March 1918, Allied troops landed at the port of Murmansk and soon afterward at Archangel with the avowed intent of preventing the supplies from falling into German hands. Protecting supplies at Vladivostok constituted part of the rationale for moving into Siberia.

A third and volatile factor in the various decisions to intervene was the presence within Russia of the Czechoslovak Legion, 70,000 strong, which had fought with the Allies on the Eastern Front. In March the Czechs entered into an agreement with the Bolshevik government that granted them freedom of travel to Vladivostok enroute to join Allied forces on the Western Front. A violent incident between the Czechs and some former Hungarian prisoners of war in the railroad station at Cheliabinsk led to a directive from Trotsky that the Czechs be disarmed. The Czechs resisted, and armed skirmishes between them and the Bolsheviks ensued along the length of the Trans-Siberian Railway as they made their way to Vladivostok. Part of the Czech force occupied that city on 29 June 1918.[5]

President Wilson had resolutely refused British efforts to obtain his approval of intervention by the Allies as a means of bringing pressure on Germany in the west. He saw no need for intervention, and he adamantly opposed committing American troops anywhere other than on the Western Front. However, his fear that Japan, the only Allied power with sufficient troop strength in the Far East to move with any force, might make a unilateral thrust into Siberia caused him to at least study the feasibility of joining the Japanese in a Siberian enterprise. With an apparent crisis in Siberia and the reported possible destruction of the Czech Legion by some 30,000 former German and Austrian prisoners of war now free inside Russia, the British moved without American approval, and in the first week of July ordered a regiment in Hong Kong to sail for Vladivostok. The supposition that the Czechs were in danger served also to convince Wilson and Secretary of State Robert Lansing that intervention was necessary, and on 6 July 1918, the United States agreed to a joint move into Siberia with Japan.[6]

In the meantime, the British War Office had looked elsewhere for troops for an independent British intervention and found the idea of sending Canadian units to Siberia directly from British Columbia an attractive possibility. When the Imperial War Cabinet met in London in June 1918, the British made a great effort to persuade Sir Robert Borden that intervention in Siberia would ease pressure on Allied troops on the Western Front. Borden himself favoured the idea of sending a Canadian force, but he felt it necessary to consult with his cabinet back in Ottawa. There ensued a five-month exchange of transAtlantic cables in which the cabinet continued to show Canadian independence, wanting to know what command the troops would be under and, given the politically explosive issue of conscription, how the force would be recruited. Whatever the military considerations, the popular assumption that Canada and Siberia would become trading partners after the war helped to tip the scales toward intervention. Canadian trade commissioner C. F. Just had returned from Russia that summer to promote sending a trade mission to Siberia; he tied military and economic interests together with a suggestion that officers and NCO's in the C.E.F. Siberia be trained in searching out "new markets for Canadian manufacturers."[7]

Both the readily accepted idea of sending a Canadian economic mission and Wilson's decision in July that the United States would intervene eased Canada's mid-August decision in favour of a Siberian military expedition. All Canadian troops bound for Siberia assembled at the Willows Camp in Victoria for final training and embarkation, and the first units of the C.E.F. arrived in Vladivostok on 27 October 1918.

The British War Office had conceded to Canada control of its own forces, and with the signing of the Armistice on 11 November, the cabinet in Ottawa showed reluctance to continue with the military intervention. Again the cables flew between the cabinet and Prime Minister Borden with the result that Canadians were restrained from taking part in military operations and from venturing beyond Vladivostok without the consent of the cabinet.[8] Future troop shipments seemed in doubt, and it was against a backdrop of political vacillating in November and December that Stuart Tompkins saw his military reinstatement and his passage to Siberia in jeopardy.

As the letters attest, his actually going to Siberia remained in question virtually until the 260th sailed from Victoria. An overwhelming number of officers applied for the C.E.F., far more than could possibly have been included. Stuart felt that political manoeuvring, resulting partly from this surplus, put him at a disadvantage. Colonel F. C. Jamieson commanded the 260th, and, in addition to Stuart Tompkins, its other officers, who figure in the letters to Edna, included Major W. J. Shortreed, Captain Henry Sawley, and Lieutenant Earl Hardisty.[9]

Stuart and Edna spent the summer of 1918 in Edmonton; she once again worked in the Education Ministry while he recruited troops for the Siberian Expeditionary Force. During that summer the people of Alberta began to learn more about Siberia from press coverage that gradually shifted some of its emphasis from the Western Front to the chaotic events inside Russia. In addition to details of military considerations, some articles presented historical and geographical background. These often made comparisons between Canada and Siberia, and one such appeared under the heading "Dominion Sending Troops to Land Which Is Much Like Canada in Some Ways," with a photograph of Vladivostok harbour and a subheading that said the soil and natural wealth of the two areas were almost the same, "But the Country Is Not So Far Advanced As Our Own."[10]

The catastrophic influenza epidemic reached Alberta in late September, and by mid-October all schools and public gathering places had been ordered closed. Inevitably, the disease hit C.E.F. members bound either for Siberia or the Western Front. On 21 October, 57 cases, one of which proved fatal, had been hospitalized off trains passing through Edmonton enroute to the west coast, and two days later four flu victims were taken from a troop train from Vancouver headed east for embarkation to England. On 4 November, provincial health authorities reported a total of 8,563 cases for Alberta with 138 deaths, and although reports of the epidemic's decline appeared the next day, the death rate remained high.[11] Both Stuart and Edna Tompkins contracted the disease and suffered fairly severe cases.

Although Edna had entertained no great enthusiasm for Stuart's return to the Army and a projected absence from home of indeterminate length, she did not stand in the way of his plans. His letters from the early days of the Siberian adventure indicate stress in their relationship, and he is at pains to promise better things after his return. They lived apart for part of the summer and when both became victims of the influenza epidemic Stuart lived with his mother while Edna shared an apartment with her friend Lydia Lawlor. It was from this arrangement that he departed for Willows Camp, Victoria, on 21 November, still wearing the gauze mask dictated by public health officials.

C.P.R. [ENROUTE TO CALGARY]
NOVEMBER 21, 1918
[NO. 1]

Sweetheart:—

Here we are at Lacombe. . . . I am sitting in the observation or rather cafe parlour car looking out across the snow covered landscape and waiting for dinner for I am really beginning to get very hungry. The car is cold but we have one compensation—there are very few people in it—only six at present. But I am really quite comfortable and feel fine. I am dutifully wearing my mask in an effort to protect other people.

Well little sweetheart—this is the first letter I have written you for many and many a long day but really a letter is a pleasant thing to write when you are the recipient. There are so many things that go unsaid in the wear and tear of daily life. . . . Dearest I often wonder why I have been allowed to live so near you and know you so intimately— you who are so far above me in loving unselfishness and tenderness. If I lived to be a thousand I could never overtake you; I only pray that I may somehow sometime give proof that it has not all been lost on me but that I am really more of a man.

Well dearest—I wonder what the future has in store for us and what part I shall be called on to play in the drama overseas in the East. It will be a strange and I hope thrilling experience. I shall write you good long letters about things and you can keep them if you like for future generations. It is a vast and tragic puzzle for which no one has yet found the answer.

Gee it is cold in here. . . . The company must be saving fuel all right.

Well dear I haven't anything to write about except my love for you. It dominates and thrills me in spite of the unsatisfactory conditions under which we have lived. I only regret that I have been so impatient but never mind, when I came back we will have a real home and then I shall show you how good I can be to you and we will forget the years of work and separation.

Well it is most unsatisfactory writing here as the train is swaying badly. I have never travelled with so few people in my life. Now look after yourself as I am doing and don't over do it. I really am feeling fine today and hope it keeps up.

With best love,

Your own

Stuart

With his sense of history and adventure, Stuart anticipated the drama to come, but his most immediate concern was to obtain absolute confirmation of his appointment to the Siberian force. A short stopover in Calgary enabled him to check on his military status and to visit with Edna's family whose home was there at that time.

Dearest darling Honey:—

Just a few lines to tell you of all the the things that have happened since I reached this delightful burg. First of all they don't wear masks as I discovered first go off when we pulled in here so I stuck mine in my pocket—Oh I hope for good and all. Well as soon as we pulled in I started down to Headquarters of Military District #13. Lo and behold [they are] now at the armouries so I made tracks for there. . . . I had to walk most of the way which didn't please me. But fortunately I . . . got my expense account through—you will get the cheque addressed to me at the Parkview. Better open all official mail. As to my appointment. They absolutely know nothing i.e. "officially" but recommend it privately. What do you know of about that for red tape. They have instructions to hold me and while they believe my appointment is through will not take it on themselves.

Being near your father's I went over and introduced myself—but had to tear myself away and go down town to secure my berth and ticket which I did—then had a hair cut. For supper I went into a little sort of tea room and do you know I met one of the interesting fellows—a life insurance fellow I guess—a native of Oban—named Robertson. . . . His father was at one time a minister in Oban but was professor of history also at (I think) the University of Berlin and one of the Scottish Universities. Robertson himself is extremely well read in Scottish history, especially the West Coast—knows all the country—has sailed all the lochs in the neighbourhood and can talk by the hour. . . .

After supper, I went up to see the folks and had a most pleasant evening—we had coffee and toast at 10 o'clock. The last thing your mother said was to try and get off going if I could. But your father who came out to the car with me thinks I am fortunate. He is very sorry now—you didn't take that job at the Normal [School]. He would like to have you in Calgary. Zeta has had the flu. Looks a little thinner—I guess she had a hard time. Well honey I have had a busy day so must get to rest. Goodnight sweetest heart. God bless you.

Stuart

Regardless of instructions that he be held at Calgary, he did go on to the Coast, and in the following letters he shared the beauty and wonder of the Canadian Rockies.

CANADIAN PACIFIC RAILWAY
[ENROUTE] NOVEMBER 22, 1918

My Ever-dearest Honey:—

To think that for days and days, weeks and weeks I shall long for your presence when I have had you now for six months without perhaps realizing how blessed I was. And now I shall dream of you by night and yearn by day and my only relief will be in writing to you.

Nevertheless apart from missing you, I have had a glorious day. We are now within a few miles of Revelstoke; it is nearly five o'clock. Since eleven o'clock our eyes have rested on an unbroken procession of lofty mountains, deep gorges and tumbling rivers. I really was scarcely prepared for the stupendous nature of the scenery. We ambled along after passing Banff quite peacefully. I was talking to my neighbours reading or otherwise engaged—when suddenly after passing Stephen we swung around a curve and saw the valley of the Kicking Horse stretching away hundreds of feet below us—with the famous spiral turrets and loops just under us. It was a wonderful and bewildering panorama as we circled, came back on our tracks then plunged into the mountain. I worked my camera overtime and of course used up all my films before I got into Field [British Columbia]. . . .

We have had a most charming lot of people on—many of them Americans—and not the talking kind either. I have enjoyed the trip very much—talking to all the nice married ladies and not bothering with the single ones. I must be losing my interest in girls. Honey it is getting dark and looking out the little window at my side and cricking my neck I can just manage to see the top of a mountain that stands just over us.

You probably know that the Selkirk range is now pierced by a five mile tunnel (it took us 18 minutes to go through it). As we pulled away from the western end there was a most wonderful sight. The pass is very narrow and very gloomy. High up on its sides, we could see the old grade and snow sheds—of the line now abandoned, while above everything and seeming to block the whole valley towered the whole range—its peaks sharp and clear against the sky and glowing in the evening sky—a most wonderful sight.

We must be coming into Revelstoke where I shall try to post this. I have no more news except that I have been feeling well—extraordinarily well all day. There is a good deal of snow in the Selkirks but the air is somewhat milder than it was this morning. The temperature was around zero at Field this morning. Well goodnight dearest. Sweet dreams and don't forget your own

Stuart

NOVEMBER 22, 1918
[FRAGMENT]

Dearest:—

If I were not so tired tonight I should like to talk for a long time— not to say anything but just to think on paper and have you listen. We are now somewhere near Kamloops but I am in bed tucked in for the night. I have been reading and thinking and talking and my mind is alive. All the magazines (American) I have read today have dealt with the Russian situation and have been most discouraging. The Americans don't want to intervene in Siberia. What they want the Lord only knows—they don't.

CANADIAN PACIFIC RAILWAY
EN ROUTE, NOVEMBER 23, 1918
[NO. 1]

Dearest:—

I thought up all sorts of things last night to tell you but we are now running into Vancouver and I haven't time to tell them. I went to bed early, started you a letter then my ink ran out, so I put it off till morning. . . . I woke up as we were running into Kamloops and I lay awake until we passed Ashcroft. Our route followed the Thompson river on its south bank. The country was all great rolling hills absolutely bare except here and there for a few big spruce. Across the river were great cut banks, a hundred feet high or more. At one point we swung around a great bend in the river. . . . Just to the west of us a mountain towered over the track while over all shone the stars and the moon, its beams turning the river into gleaming silver—a wonderful sight. I lay back with a great peace. Whenever I woke the stars shining with a wonderful light brought me a great peace such as I have not known for days and weeks. About 5:00 my upper berth comrade, an old Calgary rancher, tumbled out of bed and woke me up but I was glad to be awake and gaze at the passing hills bathed in soft moonlight. Finally came the dawn, so I got up, shaved and dressed and had breakfast. An old gentleman came in and sat down opposite me and on beginning conversation found that he was one of the economic mission going to Siberia. At once we had a common ground. I have never had such interesting conversations with people. We are now rattling along the lower Fraser and will soon be into Vancouver. The scenery latterly has not been as fine as along the lower Skeena—still it is beautiful and the day is lovely. We missed the best scenery during the night along the gorge of the Fraser. My bunk was on the wrong side of the train.

Well, Honey, of all the things I could tell you. I thought with a great thankfulness of our love. My love for you is the one bright spot in my life—all that lifts it above the common place. . . . I shall write as often as I can and tell you my thoughts. Not simply tell my love but of the inspiration I get from it. Now write often dearest. I need your letters— More as soon as I can.

Stuart

While he was in Vancouver, and later in Victoria, Stuart had the opportunity to renew friendships that dated from before the war. Both cities were beginning to stir socially for the first time in four years, and men in uniform were deluged with invitations to dinner, dances, and other social events and outings.

HOTEL VANCOUVER,
VANCOUVER, B.C.
NOVEMBER 24, 1918

Dearest:—

I am strangely outrageously ecstatically happy. To begin with, I have washed shaved and had breakfast in bed. But that is not the reason. I am in love, and last night Love lay next my heart like a warm cheerful fire. When I awoke I was conscious of its grateful warmth and I went to sleep with thoughts of you. Now why should I feel that way on leaving home; I should by all rights be most wretched. But I suppose it takes separation and detachment to really show us what our life is and . . . to make me conscious of the strong sweep in our lives of the current of love—. . . .

... Well Honey I may not be perfect or all you fondly imagined me but [your] trust, those confidences and your real purity of heart have done one thing, they have erected an unassailable wall between me and temptation. I will admit there are times when evil comes before me with siren beckonings. I have lived much among men of all classes, and though wicked men are not so numerous, they make more stir than the others and unfortunately more impression at least superficially. Their stories and innuendoes, how I wish I could get them out of my life. Their hateful and subtle poison cannot be eradicated altogether. But your presence and love brings a great calm to my life. . . . When I was in France—after the first pangs of separation—I settled down into a calm—a pride and satisfaction at our life together— a real effort to be worthy of you. Your love and presence were a charm against danger and wrong thoughts and I can safely say that at no time was I less subject to temptation. Love shielded me through all.

I don't suppose you will ever answer this letter. Perhaps there is nothing to answer. You can destroy it if you like, but I could not help writing it. It is only about a tenth of my thoughts last night. . . . I could never forgive myself if I found at any time that I had failed to understand you or that you had not found satisfaction in your life with me.

. . . Pardon this horrible scrawl. The words forced themselves out so fast that I could not keep up. I shall tell you of my experiences later. I was at the Nicholson's last night, am lying in bed now, where I have been writing. . . .

Oh—wonderful peace and joy. I plunge eagerly ahead into life because I have within me a perpetual source of comfort. A love unquenchable.

Stuart

Later

. . . [Y]ou will want to know what I did yesterday. I ordered a tunic, foolishly, now I think, for the material has to be wired for and I shant have a fit but so be it, and I almost bought you a waist—a beautiful Georgette but I knew it was too big for you and if you had to alter it you might just as easily buy the material and make it. Also there might be other things you would rather have. So I resisted temptation. At six o'clock I started for Nicholson's—after foolishly refusing an offer for Neilson to come for me in his car. I got there about 7 after devious wanderings. Mrs. N was cordiality itself. We had a good dinner. Steak etc etc. Neilson did most of the talking. You would think it was he who had been to the war. However I did not mind. I am a good listener. But he is a great fine healthy boy who has been spoiled. After a lot of monkeying around, after the Military Service Act came into force he was found A2—then his father butted in—brought pressure to bear through the family doctor and he was covered and finally discharged. I really think the man in him wanted to go but his people have just spoiled him. He is as much A2 as I am. However he brought me back to the [Hotel] Vancouver where I had engaged a room and after buying and eating a couple of snow apples I rolled in. This morning I woke at 8 o'clock; to find it raining; got up at 8:30, washed and shaved. Then after enquiring and finding that there was a boat going [to Victoria] tonight decided not to go till then. So I ordered breakfast in bed—horrible extravagance. . . . After breakfast I lay in bed and wrote. How much I had to tell you—things unsaid for weeks—through living with other people. . . . Shall we get back to the old days when our love was sufficient though [we] were separated. I think we shall. If you don't write to me I shall die. Similarly you must not record simply happenings but tell me your thoughts.

. . . [I will] take the boat tonight. I hear we are liable to move the 5th. I am not in a hurry now as Vancouver is full of members of the Siberian force. Vancouver is much livelier than when we last saw it—more evidences of life.

Now sweetheart—don't forget to write and take care of yourself. I must write to Alice so good bye.

Stuart

VICTORIA, NOVEMBER 25, 1918

Sweetheart:—

You broke my heart; there was no mail for me today at all and here I am lonesome and cast down in a strange land. Of all that has happened today—I could write reams but I really have not time tonight except to tell you a little. First of all I reached Victoria at 4 a.m. I rolled out at 6:30 and got away at 7:30—left my luggage with a transfer company and went and got breakfast. I didn't go to the Empress [Hotel] but to a restaurant up town and got a very good meal for 40 cents which surprised me but I needed to economize after my stay in Vancouver. Then after buying one or two things I found my way out to camp on a street car—saw Colonel Jamieson and sundry others—everyone in fact I knew. Then got busy and have been going ever since. I drew $200 worth of stuff nearly from the Q.M.—listen, a fur cap, sheepskin lined coat, two very heavy woolen shirts, a woolen scarf, a toque, sweater, pair of goggles; two pair lumber man's socks, two pair ordinary socks, pair shoe packs, pair of mocassins and am still to draw an eiderdown sleeping bag. In addition I bought a bed roll to roll the bag in and stow some stuff—then I chased up the Paymaster but why narrate all my troubles. I can't get outfit allowance or pay till I go through orders. I am chasing it up but it may be days or a week before I get it. I have a lot of messy things to clean up but my appointment is the crucial thing. I got the loan of a batman and got a tent up—drew beds, blankets, canteen, stove and got it all fired up. This afternoon Cresswell and I went into town and bought some more things—my money gave out but I managed to get back though we had tea at the Empress. You remember seeing Cresswell's name. He is a political appointee—just got a commission and has never had service—was private secretary to J. S. Dennis—nuff said. I am senior subaltern in the company. I was told today. How about it?

Why ramble on so fast when I can't tell you the half or quarter. I want to talk about yourself. What else is worth while. I have worried that you have been so extremely—what shall we say—bored in the last few months. We must have a home of our own when I go back. What's the use of pretending to be contented hanging on the edge of existence when I live only for you and long to see you happy and going on from grace to grace... to see you absolutely contented.... Tell Mrs. Lawlor I never before thought a woman competent to judge cigars—those she sent are *fine*. Gee this tent is getting cold so I won't continue much further.

You know I love you so what use in saying it. . . .

Goodnight sweetest.

Your own

Stuart

That the Siberian expedition was rife with politics never did sit well with Stuart Tompkins, and a commission politically arranged for a man with no military experience and clearly less qualified than he obviously rankled. J. S. Dennis, mentioned above, was Colonel John Dennis, a member of the Canadian economic mission to Siberia that was authorized in October 1918. Dennis had been a surveyor and engineer for both the Hudson's Bay Company and the Canadian Pacific Railroad and was considered qualified to evaluate Siberia's economic potential. He had already been assigned to the general staff for Siberia as head of the Canadian Red Cross operations there. He and his entourage sailed for Vladivostok on the *Madras* in late January 1919, thus avoiding the rough passage of those aboard *Protesilaus* that is described in some of the following letters.[12]

VICTORIA, NOVEMBER 27, 1918
[NO. 1]

Dearest:—

I didn't write last night and I am not going to write again until I hear from you. Think of it, six days since I left home and no word yet. Why it seems as though the earth had swallowed everyone up.

Well the worst has come. Instructions came through that all men were to be asked whether they wanted their discharge. Result about one third are quitting. So we are likely to be hung up here waiting for reenforcements for another month or so. It is discouraging.... Well we are going to sit tight here and wait.

Say it is cold here. It froze last night and really I was beastly cold in bed even with everything piled on but I am feeling fine, really great. We have a pretty good mess everything considered. I am going to find out my fate today—get them to wire to Ottawa to learn whether there is any authority for taking me on. I guess there will be lots of chance to go....

Well goodbye. Officers' call has gone

Stuart

With the signing of the Armistice, the C.E.F. Siberia had entered a limbo of domestic and international politics, and individual officers and men found themselves in situations of uncertainty as to their own involvement. Stuart Tompkins badly wanted to be a part of the expedition, and he spent the weeks in Victoria in near agony of suspense.

VICTORIA, NOVEMBER 27, 1918
[NO. 2]

Dearest:—

Your first letter came today and reassured me. I expected to hear before then but better late—No word yet of my appointment and I can draw no pay. Chances are the battalion leaves next week. I should know in a day or two whether I go. I am getting sore all right. Am working hard, though enjoying it. I do so want to go. I believe there are to be NO discharges. At least we were told so today. I think Jamieson is sorry he stirred up all this trouble. He wants me to go.

Let me hear from you often. Oh I wish you were here.

Goodnight dearest.

Stuart

VICTORIA, NOVEMBER 28, 1918

Dearest:—

I was delighted to get your letter today. . . . It nearly succeeded in cheering me up but not quite. Things are all wrong—no word yet of my appointment—no money—nothing. Then to make it worse there was a dance I wanted to go to and I couldn't. My uniform was dirty—and I was tired and I couldn't afford it and it was contrary to [regulations] for officers [not] in uniform to attend and there you are—so I shall just have to forget I guess.

There is a route march on tomorrow which I want to avoid—but I am Company 7 Orderly Officer tomorrow and Battalion O.O. Saturday so there you are and if we go Wednesday—time will be short enough. There isn't very much to talk of, everything is so upset. However ordinarily I am happy and feel well. The weather is beastly but not so cold tonight as it has been.

Oh dear. I have nothing to tell you except that I love you more and more but it drives me to despair that I can't write an interesting letter at all at all. . . .

Well sweetheart I am going to say goodnight and roll in. . . .

Your own

Stuart

Dearest:—

I have a few leisure moments this morning as I did not go on the route march, having no men for that purpose. I was disappointed about going to that dance but I had compensations. Out of all the turmoil and confusion of my thoughts emerged things that brought me a great peace and hope. I suppose it takes the anguish of separation to let us know what we mean to one another. I am glad now for that for I have caught a vision of what our life really is. I know the past six months have been topsy turvy with nothing ahead and little pleasure. . . . I know we are poor and that things seem in a way dark and yet I am better off than the average soldier and all our discontent and anxiety I suppose obscure the fact that we are living and fulfilling our destiny from day to day. Oh I know this is a strange lecture but truth is my love for you makes me want to see you happy. . . . Oh dearest let us make something of life—let us cultivate friendships and learn to live. I long to grow old with you and make life worth while.

You may destroy these tedious homilies. . . . Perhaps you don't understand me. I am discouraged sometimes when I think that all I ask is that you love me and love me more and more. Sometimes life seems poor and cheap and I am discouraged but I have got away from that mood now and see it as a glorious struggle and a real tasting of the wine of life. And I sit and write my thought to you. You are all I have—but ah more precious than gold. My beloved. My darling—far away but ever near.

By the way, we have a problem in mittens. There are no decent mittens issued. Do you suppose you could pick out a good pair of fur mitts, not too dear.

Your own
Stuart

VICTORIA, DECEMBER 1, 1918

My Dearest:—

It is no effort at all to write a letter now at night as I have a new haversack which has a special compartment for my portfolio and as it hangs at the head of my bed I can reach in any time, haul out my paper and start to write.

Yesterday at noon, I found no letter waiting for me . . . but a nice long one came at night. In the afternoon Sawley and Hardisty asked me out to tea. I was orderly officer but as I wanted to go in and see the chief paymaster I was relieved and worked in tea at the Empress very nicely. Both appeared with girls—so imagine my confusion. It was a dansante but I sat and looked on. It was a very fine sight. The girls were fine girls but I was roped in before I knew it for two evenings next week—woe is me! I hope we are away before they come off. The people here have been shut in since the flu epidemic started and now that the ban is off are anxious for festivities and they particularly fall for Sam Brownes. How I scheme to get out of this week's festivities I shall let you know.

You cannot imagine how overjoyed I was to get back to camp and find a letter awaiting me. I have perused it many times already and it has given me much food for thought.

Last night I played bridge for an hour and won—10 cents. There really is so much going around here, it is hard to keep out of it and get letters written. I had staff parade at 10:45 so did not get to bed till nearly midnight. I slept in till nearly 9 a.m.—was late for church parade, which I didn't mind. After lunch I went into town for the Thanksgiving service which was to be held in front of the Government buildings; there was some confusion as it was understood that it would be held in one of the theatres in case it rained. Instead they tried to hold it in the legislative chambers; as a result the corridors were jammed and no one outside could hear a word that was said. The music was good—our own battalion band provided the music. The service seemed very short [and] I was surprised when God Save the King was struck up. I went over to the Empress, bumped into my tent mate who introduced me to friends whom I joined at tea. One of them a young Russian I stayed and had dinner with. I do not know his name but we had a delightful time. He is going as interpreter to Colonel Dennis. . . . I came out at 10 o'clock just in time for a letter before turning in.

My mind is full of all sorts of unuttered thoughts tonight. You will have to dream what they are. I should indeed like to see you tonight if just for a few minutes.

I was surprised when I looked in the mirror tonight to see that I looked so well—so you see I am coming on. I feel very much better I can assure you and have put on weight.

Well goodnight sweetheart. God bless you.

Stuart

Dearest:—

It is now 11:30 a.m. and as I have a few moments I shall sit down and find comfort in writing a few lines to you. It has been raining all night and all morning but in spite of everything I am cheerful as my appointment I believe has gone through. At any rate, a wire came through this morning and I shall know my fate definitely at noon. So I guess I shall go down town after lunch and get fixed up. My tunic also is coming today so I shall have the wherewithal. Things are looking up and we shall be away from here tout de suite. I only hope I have time to get everything fixed up. We are in an agony of packing now and getting ready.

I had a good sleep this morning, did not get up till eight and missed breakfast otherwise I feel o.k. I have practically cut out tea, coffee just once a day before breakfast.

Evening: I just reach down into my haversack and there is my portfolio and letter started. It has rained all day and I have done nothing. You really must not look for long letters now as I shall be busy as can be. I devoted the whole day to my own affairs and have not much now to do. This afternoon I got my money matters straightened up. My appointment came through this morning so I have interviewed both the PM [Pay Master, Regimental] and C.P.M. [Company Pay Master]—result, I now have over $250 on me. The Regimental Pay master gave me an advance of $100 and when I got down town I found a cheque from Calgary paying me up to November 30th—of course I shall probably have to return the $100 advance as I am paid up to date. But I am still to get my outfit allowance and expenses from Edmonton—tres bien—eh. So I think as soon as I figure out my needs I shall send the balance home.

My tunic came today but I haven't seen it as my batman has it away having the badges etc put on. I have nearly everything complete—have my trunk fixed up, a new tray in it etc. We think we will go Sunday. I am all ready now except a few extras. . . .

I was amazed to get two letters today, one at noon and one tonight. I don't know who brought the latter into my tent but it was a most delightful surprise.

I got my black ties this p.m. You know being a rifle regiment we wear black ties. I was able to purchase beautiful poplin for 50 cents each whereas they are charging $2.50 for knitted ones.

There is a boxing bout on in the gymnasium tonight—at least something to keep the troops engaged.

Would I not like to see you for a few minutes tonight or just to hold you in my arms. Well sweetheart, I must get to sleep early as I have been late lately.

Goodnight and God bless you.

Stuart

Whatever cheer accompanied Stuart's appointment to C.E.F. Siberia when it finally came was short lived; bad weather, constant rumours of departure dates, and the tedium of waiting all combined to produce the negative frame of mind reflected in some of the letters below. They also indicate that he felt somewhat guilty about his plunge into Victoria's social whirl.

VICTORIA, DECEMBER 4, 1918
[NO. 1]

Dearest:—

I hadn't the heart to write a letter last night. Do you know it rained all day yesterday. In fact it has rained almost continuously for three days, only yesterday more so. There were practically no parades and I got away from camp about 4 o'clock. I had my business practically finished at 5:30 but I stood in vain on the corner waiting for a car. As dinner is a parade, and as I wouldn't get out to camp in time, I decided to stay in to dinner. I went to the Dominion Hotel and had a bang up dinner. As I was going down towards the Empress, the pay master told me that some one was looking for me. This some [one] I found to be Perelstruss, Russian interpreter to J. S. Dennis who is going to give me Russian lessons. With a friend he was bound for Charlie Chaplin so we went together with the idea partly of drying out—vain hope! We came out about 9:30 so I decided to come right out to camp. I found our tent in a swamp—or rather a lake but managed to get in. . . . Everything was wet in the tent; my great coat absolutely saturated— the leather buttons almost ruined. However we were fairly comfortable when we rolled in. The rain rather subsided in the night and our tent was not quite so deep in water. However, it has started again so this will probably be a day off.

I don't know that there is any special news today. We hear all sorts of rumours about moving but no one knows anything. We are still here. . . .

My tunic fits very well and looks well but of course is not the tunic the other was.

Goodbye. God bless you.

Stuart

VICTORIA, DECEMBER 4, 1918
[NO. 2]

Dearest:—

Just a few lines tonight before getting ready for the dance. Yes I am a great big fool. I am going to a dance and two of us are going to take three girls. Isn't it terrible. The brigade is giving a dance tonight and of course everyone is going so yours truly got roped in also.

Well I am reduced to living on hopes once more. No mail came through for me. The reason of course I know well enough as you explained it but it did not make it any the more welcome. I am not in a very good mood tonight to talk somehow. We had a drink of hot coffee before we went to bed [last night] and it made me wakeful. I thought of all the things I wanted to tell you. But after all, what is the use of moralizing about love and analyzing it. All I am conscious of tonight is a great tenderness and longing for you I would like to sit before a cheery fire and have you come and sit on my lap and whisper nice things to me. I don't want to go to a dance tonight and meet a lot of silly girls. . . .

I suppose really my disquisitions on the subject are due to a desire to control our fate and make love something more than an ephemeral passion. But after all this is a matter of character more than mere thinking.

The weather has cleared beautifully today and things are drying out. But, oh, I should like to roll into my downy cot instead of going down town. I sent you a little parcel today—the cap badge of the battalion gold plated. I meant to have it made into a brooch but of course forgot. If you would like it so I hope you won't hesitate to have it altered. I kicked myself afterward. Your remarks about Xmas presents rather took my wind away. I shall tell you later. Well it is now 7:30 and I must get busy and shave. My water is boiling. My little Primus stove is a veritable godsend.

> Well goodby sweetheart,
> Your own,
> *Stuart*

VICTORIA, DECEMBER 6, 1918

Dearest:—

I was very tired last night and rolled in without doing any writing whatever. The weather was very decent yesterday not only that but we moved our tent and got a better one so we were fairly comfortable last night. Still the sky is almost always overcast and it is wet under foot always. It was naturally a great disappointment that there was no letter yesterday. I suppose though I shall have to get used to that. We hear now that we are not going till the 15th which is a week from Sunday. But I presume we can console ourselves. I am going out to another dance tonight—that is if I feel well. If I don't I certainly shall not. It was certainly a disappointment to me what you said about Xmas presents but I shall abide by it and send instead the money. You can then do what seemeth best with it.

Do you know Hardisty is on pins and needles these days. . . . He had another unfortunate experience. He is secretary of the mess and while making a final levy had collected about $400. This he left in the mess and night before last it was stolen. There was only about $175 in cash and the cheques were returned. I can't help believing it was an officer. There have been some heavy card losses lately. Jamieson has taken steps to end that state of affairs. I know of course you won't speak of that. So poor Hardisty is upset. He is not a bad fellow and seems quite reconciled to my being senior. They are all very nice fellows at least those in the company and we all get along fine.

There was a route march today. I was all ready for it—booted and spurred—but was told to stay in camp and look after some new men. So I am playing hookey from duty.

I must not write more.

By the way. I forgot to tell you how I got on at the dance. Well, I danced about six numbers mostly waltzes and had a fine time. I was induced there to by a young girl, a Miss Neroutsos, a very fine girl who has taken quite an interest in Sawley—save the mark. However she is a good sport and insisted on taking me around and she can sure manage it—she is so big and strong. It was a very nice party they were with—it may have been politeness but they seemed only too glad to pilot my blundering footsteps—well more tonight.

Your own
Stuart

Just as she had earlier sent goods and equipment across the Channel to France, Edna responded to his report of a "problem in mittens," but the inadequacy of the pair she had shipped added another irritant to those stemming from continuing uncertainty and the politics surrounding his inclusion in the Siberia force. In the following letter Stuart shares with her his conclusions as to the root of the problems surrounding his appointment.

VICTORIA, DECEMBER 9, 1918

Dearest:—

What a long account I have to square with you. No letter written yesterday and all sorts of explanations to give. Now first of all re the gloves—I hope you won't feel hurt but I blame myself for not being more definite and the Hudson's Bay Company for selling you the gloves. I really meant fur gauntlets—of racoon, preferably meant for real outdoor life. I have now just six pairs of gloves more or less heavy. But the opinion of Stefanson who was [t]here a few weeks ago is that even the heaviest are far too light for service in a northern winter. It seems to me the H.B.Co should take those gloves back; they should not have sold so light a pair for Siberia. Now I hope you won't feel hurt about this. I might have kept them and said nothing but I really didn't think the expense would be justified. If you can't get a pair of heavy gauntlets such as I had in mind—why don't bother—I can get along. I really don't think you should pay more than $15. I don't think I could get anything here and if I did I should have to pay $25.00 which is too much. We have been stung on our caps and collars I know.

I was disappointed at not getting a letter yesterday but as I didn't write one I suppose it is tit for tat. Friday was my red letter day. I got 3 letters in the morning. In the afternoon I found a Times and a Round Table awaiting me at the mess—a parcel also came in the afternoon. In the evening I got a registered parcel and letter. The cake certainly looks good. I may sample it one of these days. I enjoy the coffee in the morning before breakfast—the only stimulant I have during the day as I take milk at every meal. Now, honey, I know. I put you out too much. I must not really ask for things so casually for it means a lot of trouble to you, I know. The same about the gloves. The sleeping cap is jake also just what I have needed these many moons. I have not slept cold lately, my blankets are drying out now fine and we keep an oil stove burning all the time.

Well I have another story to tell you—Orders have come through for no supernumerary subalterns to be taken. I have nothing official about it but so it is. I think the colonel will fight for me and try to get me on. Now I am going to tell you the rest of it as far as I have it doped out.

You remember recommendation for my appointment was forwarded by Colonel MacDonald to Ottawa about September 1st. Now it appears that Colonel MacDonald was ordered to submit the name of Cresswell who had been private secretary to J. S. Dennis and you will remember Cresswell's name appeared in Routine Orders about September 19th when I was first made aware that things were not as they should be. It was about one week later that I saw Colonel Jamieson who told me about my [medical status] being unsatisfactory. I cannot figure out yet whether or not it is a case of "post hoc ergo propter hoc" whether there was any causal connection between the one or the other. I imagine not as the medical difficulty was overcome. The real stumbling block is Cresswell, recently a cadet of the Royal School of Infantry at Esquimault, formerly attached to the British recruiting mission with no experience in soldiering. He is my roommate so it is a delicate matter to raise but I am beginning to feel sore at the way I have been badgered. Of course I am appointed to the C.E.S. so will draw pay and get all expenses, but the question is whether I go. I have some good friends in the battalion and I think they want me, so I may get along all right. Meantime I am not going to kick or ask for anything.

Now I am going to tell you of some more dissipation. Friday night and yesterday. Friday night I went out to [a] dance, fell in with a party and danced nearly every dance. Wasn't it scandalous. And yesterday I was out to a dansante at the Empress, too. Now you mustn't really blame me. You know it is so disagreeable around camp and this is our last week. We are almost sure to be going Sunday, that is, next. I have felt sort of lost lately don't know what to do with myself. Although I had a couple of lessons in Russian this week I am not making much progress. I am rather fed up with Perelstruss who was instructing me. He is a sergeant attached to us but is really Dennis' interpreter—is a free lance, goes around in civilian clothes and lives at the Empress, very well educated but a typical Russian, so I don't suppose I shall see much more of him. . . .

I was hoping for some pictures this afternoon. The day broke beautiful with the sun shining on the Olympic mountains but the sky is overcast now. Well I must toddle along to lunch. Goodby dearest.

Your own
Stuart

VICTORIA, DECEMBER 11, 1918

Dearest, dearest Sweetheart:—

Just a few minutes while I am free this morning to tell you of the events of the past two days. Did I tell you I was out to Sunday afternoon tea and supper at Captain Neroutsos'. It is his daughter that Captain Sawley has taken out to tea etc. I went over to Foul Bay in the afternoon to hunt up Tom Cook. . . . He drove me down to the Empress where I met Sawley and started out for tea. I thought we should stay till about six but on the other hand we stayed till ten. They [the Neroutsos family] are most interesting and hospitable people—though they are English. We talked of everything from the army to juvenile literature. After we left Sawley wanted to write to his wife so we went down to the club and I waited for him then we went in (it was now eleven o'clock) and had a hot drink—after which home. Next day in the afternoon I felt pretty tough so I. . . went to bed early. However shortly after midnight the water began to heave and the weather to moan. I was up three times in the night to fasten down my tent which threatened to go. . . . I did not sleep much after midnight but lay listening to my tent straining and threatening to go any minute. Several of the large tents went but ours held. I got up about ten and after shaving went to the mess and read. After lunch I had a lesson in Russian, then went down town and had tea at the Empress.

Now I bought money orders totaling $300 which I am going to send home though I admit I shall have to do some close figuring to get on till the first of the month. Now what I want to ask is this. Would you like to come down to Victoria for a week or so. We are not leaving any way till the 20th and possibly later. If we are to be here for Xmas of course there would be no two ways about it, but I don't like to urge you. However in view of your urgent request, I did not buy you that present and I consider you are entitled to the trip, of course I have been somewhat uncertain about going and am yet. What do you think about it.

Last night I went for a skate. I took Miss Neroutsos or rather we made up a party. She is a very nice girl but a poor skater. It was raining when we started but the ice (which was artificial) was all right and we had a fine evening. I was fortunate in getting tube skates.

Today is a beast snowing raining and blowing.

Now Good bye dearest. God bless you.

Your own
Stuart

VICTORIA, DECEMBER 16, 1918
[NO. 1]

Dearest:—

My suspense was ended this morning by a sheaf of letters from Edmonton. I really did expect you this morning and met the boat but was disappointed. I am going to town this afternoon and will wire you not to come. The time is now getting so short that it would be a waste of money. It struck me first on Wednesday that the trip might do you good and seeing that I was not going to send you anything for Christmas, we might very well afford a little holiday. I wrote you I believe to that effect and that evening decided to wire in the hope that you could get off at once. Your reply was most unsatisfactory and left me waiting for letters which of course did not come till this morning. In the meantime I have not written as I was on pins and needles all the time. Yesterday I was feeling pretty tired and sleepy. We had a long church parade, marched into the Cathedral and back, so after lunch I lay down and before I knew it it was supper time so I didn't get much done after that. It was my intention to go down to a labour meeting in the evening but our Company Commander grabbed me and made me orderly officer so I stayed in. Our fellows went down nearly in a body and broke it up and cleared the house. I should like to have been there. You will probably read about it in the papers.

Our camp is very disagreeable these days. Today and yesterday have been clear and cold but the place has been saturated with rain. I have been thinking of sleeping down town a few nights. I thought if you came and I got a couple of days leave it would be a good arrangement. However I can carry on I guess till we sail. My cold is better though I cough a little. I have put on flesh and am generally feeling fine, manage to eat like a horse.

You probably were surprised to get that $300. I sent it before I thought of your coming down and really I took a long chance but I think I can make it all right and I felt if I kept too much money here I should just spend it. I have decided not to get a sword at all. The colonel will not insist on it. You are a brick about those gauntlets. That is $10 cheaper than I could have bought them here. I am really well set up except that I need another suit of underwear.

Well we are to go on or about the 21st, so a week from today will find us on the broad Pacific.

Good bye dearest
Your own
Stuart

A confused exchange of letters and telegrams had led Stuart to expect Edna to join him in Victoria for the last days of his stay there, and in letters that followed he elaborated on his disappointment that she had not come. The labour meeting that Stuart mentioned above was one of several that caused unrest and provoked violent response. The previous Sunday the Federated Labor Party had sponsored a meeting that filled a theatre with an audience holding a large number of soldiers from the Siberian forces, who listened to speakers who "railed against the sending of Canadian troops to Siberia."[14]

VICTORIA, DECEMBER 22, 1918

Dearest:—

This is the first honest-to-goodness letter I have written you for two weeks, and there is so much to say that I do not know where to start. Of course it all has reference to your not coming to Victoria. I originally gave way to the impulse to wire you as I thought it would do you good and I wired you on Tuesday because I thought it would be unsatisfactory coming for so short a time as it then seemed we should be here. Whether I was right or wrong it is hard to say but the fact remains that we are going to be here over Christmas and I shall be without you. All I can do is to forget it and carry on.

There is just one other consideration and on that I don't know whether I dare make a suggestion. Of course when a man's wife is working he has only half a claim on her but you always have one thing to face and that is that in her absence he may seek consolation in other ways. Now when I came here it was after the let up in the flu epidemic and everything was loosening up and I was grabbed by Hardisty and Sawley and dragged into their bunch. Now they are without exception a fine lot of girls and officers and I have had a very nice time. We were entertained most cordially and I think, well, no thinking, I know there was perfect frankness and propriety in the "understanding." There are about five of us who travel together and three of us are married. Now it is nice and all that but I have straight laced notions about such things. It is about the first time we have not been together in any pleasure and I know perfectly well [it] is a danger. Of course Hardisty says he has a perfect understanding with his wife and Sawley well he doesn't worry, but I am different because I gave myself body mind and soul to one girl and I know without talking of divided affections that pleasure hunting dulls the edge of devoted love. Now you have been a brick and undergone sacrifices like a dear. . . .

Now I don't think my dissipation has spoiled me in any way. It is the first time I have ever gone in for a good time and it certainly was not sought. But it has left me quite untouched. There is a good deal of sham and sometimes just a little that is sordid and I could search not only Victoria and Vancouver Island but the whole of the province to find one girl like you. Your love is the most precious treasure that I have and I guess I have not appreciated it. I would give anything just to take you into my arms again.

Well I am not fessing up dear but just clearing the air. You can take it and think it over and write or not of it just as you like. Life isn't the simple thing we imagine in our youth and yet we can be simple and true and play the game. Personally I would not give all the good times and money and friends in the world for one little wife.

Well I have an invite out for Xmas in case we are here. At Capt. Neroutsos—marine superintendent. They are very English but very nice and have been good to us.

Well did you see discharged soldiers and officers were to get six months double pay on discharge. We should get a good start in that case should we not. At the present rates that would be $1500. It seems too good almost to be true. Well the country should do something for us.

You may not know that we have had quite a lot of trouble here. This is strictly "sub rosa" and is not to be repeated. There has been a lot of socialistic agitation here and two weeks ago there was a meeting here largely attended by 259th men—French Canadians. At this meeting the Siberian Expedition was discussed and a strong resolution taken against it. Last Sunday night our fellows went down and broke up the meeting but the harm was done. When two companies of the 259th were marching down town yesterday to embark some of the men egged on by agitators refused to go on. They were [forcibly] escorted.

Well I went into mess and had supper but as I am going out now for exercise I must ring off. There is another labour meeting on tonight so there may be something doing.

So Goodnight Sweetest.

Stuart

WILLOWS CAMP, VICTORIA
DECEMBER 26, 1918
[NO. 1]

Dearest:—

Well we are leaving today and life is one mad scramble to get things ready. I have just had five hours sleep but of course duty must be done.

There is no use telling you again I suppose how badly I felt that you were not here yesterday. We had a stirring time but I was almost sorry I had to go out for dinner; but it kept me from thinking.

I suppose this thing will wear off but the disappointment has made me very bitter. I felt that you didn't treat my request with proper consideration. It was either a case of come then or not come at all. When you said you were coming later I assumed you would get ready and come in a day or two. There was no likelihood of us being here any length of time and then of course the inevitable occurred and we were delayed and had to spend Christmas here. I wanted it more for your sake than [my] own. I have had many bitter hours since then.

Well I shall close now and try to write later.

Stuart

ON BOARD S.S. PROTESILAUS
DECEMBER 26, 1918
[NO. 2]

Dearest:—

I suppose I wrote you a very blue letter today but what could be expected. This last four days has been very hard on me and I suppose I haven't pulled myself together. Now I suppose you will think very ill of me for sulking in my tent but I couldn't without being a hypocrite sit down and write letters feeling as I did. However Christmas has come and gone and I have looked into my own heart and found things unchanged and life coming to meet me with something of a smile on her face. As I came down town today my heart beat a chant—I love her, I love her, and I thrilled at the thought. So I suppose that the pain will wear off and things be as before.

Well the boats' sirens have blown and we will be off shortly so I think I shall post this.

God bless you dearest—
Stuart

Miss Neroutsos wired you for me.

Across the North Pacific
260th Rifles Reach Vladivostok

❧ JANUARY–FEBRUARY, 1919 ☙

When the men of the 260th Battalion boarded the *Protesilaus*, they were headed for what was perhaps the roughest crossing made by any of the Siberia-bound Canadians. The ship was a British Blue Funnel Line freighter that had been converted into a troop carrier. It was foul-smelling and "decidedly not a comfortable ship in which to cross the north Pacific in mid winter. . . [it] had closely packed hammocks for the troops, only one small galley, and latrines over the ships's sides."[1] It carried a Chinese crew to whom Stuart applied the ethnic label "Chink," and racial indifference, or bias, common at the time marks a letter that mentions the loss of a crew member.

They encountered storms virtually from the beginning of the trip, but, while he admitted that it was terrifying, Stuart seems to have revelled in the awesome power and beauty of the sea. While he reported grim events of the voyage, Stuart kept to his practice of displaying a comparatively light tone in his letters; his account did indicate, however, that conditions could well have warranted the reported instructions that "if the ship foundered the men would be better to forget their lifejackets; without them they would drown more quickly in the freezing sea."[2]

ON BOARD PROTESILAUS
DECEMBER 27, 1918

My dearest:—

Now that the rush and confusion are all over we can settle down I suppose for the voyage. I am going to write a little every day and send you a good long letter from Japan.

We are now out on the wide waste of the Pacific having set sail yesterday evening about six thirty. We got the men shaken down into their quarters and fed about seven o'clock, though it was a great agony. I had dinner, a cold one, about eight. I rolled into bed at nine or thereabouts. During the night and this morning the ship has pitched considerably so that there was no great rush for breakfast. I was up and fussing over the men this morning so that I was pretty hungry. I made out pretty well and am feeling all right.

Well honey I have so much to say I don't know where to start. I have had a strenuous time the last three weeks but must now settle down to serious business. We had a pretty good time in Victoria but I am glad it is over. There was an air of hysterical unreality about it all. The girls there have had little fun for the last two years and this gave them an opportunity for a fling. I suppose you know more of girls than I do but even I can see the fly in the ointment. I can't find any fun in anything sham and when girls, many of them engaged, chase around with officers who are married there can be nothing real about it. The silver stars and Sam Browne seem to have a fatal attraction. However maybe I am doing an unnecessary amount of worrying. Perhaps the girls can look after themselves; not all of them however. Well you can be assured that I did not break any hearts.

Sawley is a great source of amusement. A couple of days before Xmas he wired his wife to come but it was too late and you have no idea how relieved he was. His duty had been done. Poor old Hardisty felt bad but he had consolation. I felt badly enough but managed to keep from showing it. But you are not anxious to hear about this. I shall tell you what we did Christmas.

Up till Sunday we expected to sail on December 24th—but on that day we were told it would be the 26th so arrangements were at once made for Xmas dinner. The IODE [Imperial Order Daughters of the Empire] took the thing in hand and engaged the manager of the Empress to run the thing. They bought turkey and all the trimmings and the night previous everybody at the Empress and the camp were working. That morning a lot of IODE girls came out from town to serve. It was necessarily slow at first but every man was fed before one thirty. It was a great experience you would have enjoyed. After dinner there was a dance. I... had just time to get to Neroutsos's at six, in fact I was late. We had a pleasant evening. I had a room at the club down town which I was glad to roll into at midnight but I was up at six for the great day. I shall tell you later about leaving. That was the one indulgence I have permitted myself lately, that last night in town. Unfortunately we had to be out to camp at reveille so I had to go half in hiring a car. However after breakfast I came back to town on business and managed to get another hour's sleep. I then went down to the dock and left my haversack. I went back to camp in a car but found the battalion had left. I evidently missed them en route. We had a great send off—all Victoria I think turned out. At any rate we had a bunch of girls to say farewell, i.e. Sawley and Hardisty, no one came to see me off but it was very cheerful at any rate.

Well I feel pretty well everything considered. I have been sick off and on today but missed no meals. In fact I really feel exceptionally well. I only hope it keeps up. Meals are not much. The boat in fact is a freighter—just fitted up for trooping. We have a few very crowded staterooms between decks and a smoking room above on deck. But things are rough and ready. The crew are all chinks and none too clean.

But really I am more at peace with the world than I have been for a long time. I am more myself. I think my sojourn in Victoria must have upset me and Oh I feel more and more that you are with me and I get more time to think of you. Well goodnight dearie. I am for bed.

December 28, 1918
The evening of the second day out. Although I have not felt well today I have no ground for complaint. The pain I had wore away and I am feeling pretty jake now. It has been a glorious day. The weather cleared although there is quite a sea running and we have enjoyed it immensely.

I feel so much better than when at Victoria. I feel quite contented. Thoughts of you have filled my mind all day and have brought me a great peace. When will we be reunited I wonder. All the thousand memories that unite us kept crowding on me insistently.

Tomorrow I am going to read all your recent letters and answer any questions not dealt with. . . .

I think I shall establish a connection with T. Eaton [Eaton's Department Store]. There are so many things I need that it would be an imposition to ask any body to get them. I want to thank you once more for the gauntlets. They really are one of the finest things I got and I was mightily elated to get them. They really are beauties.

Well, I am going to bed as it is after 10 o'clock and I am sleepy.

December 30th

Well Honey I skipped you last night. This is the fourth day out and we have covered ¼ of the distance. There is not much to record except that we buried a poor chap at sea today. He was killed on deck while the ship was rolling. A huge case of ice and meat slewed and crushed him against a hatch. I was there and helped get him out. It was sickening. We have had a bad day. The ship right now is rolling fearfully. Just while I was writing the foregoing line I was spilled out of my chair. Many humorous things happen. Last night at dinner the chairs broke under two officers and they shot across the floor as though shot out of a gun. Still we are fairly contented. I am well.

The experience described above remained indelibly etched in Stuart's mind. He recaptured the scene and added to the details some fifty years later when he noted on the original letter that the following be inserted in the unpublished edition of his letters:

I omitted my own experience. I was orderly officer for the day and was down in the hold. . . . I had just completed my rounds and was on the point of going up on deck when the ship gave a mighty roll. Fearing that the ship would go right over, I grabbed the nearest upright I could find and clung to it, while there slipped past me tables, chairs, men, dishes. The ship righted itself and rolled in the opposite direction, the heterogeneous mass sliding back with it. Hearing. . . running feet on deck, I decided to hasten "top side." Here I found a great confusion the cause of which I soon saw. In the absence of refrigeration, a makeshift was designed. . . a sort of enormous packing case containing alternate layers of meat and ice. . . . [It was] bolted to the deck. When the ship rolled to utmost extent, everything gave way and the whole began to slew across the deck in a crazy way. It caught and knocked down two men, one of whom got away, while the other was caught and. . . it pinned the unfortunate man against the hatch. Unfortunately, the cable for the rudder ran along the hatch and as it moved it tore the flesh of the poor wretch. It took some time for the pilot to bring the ship around and into the wind and so stop this torture. . . . The victim was far gone when released and was taken to the sick bay where he died that afternoon.[3]

Thursday, January 2nd

Well we had New Year's on the Pacific and a wild day it was. Tuesday evening we ran into a storm about dusk and we most assuredly had a shaking up that night. I simply could not get to sleep at all. The rolling and pitching was certainly bad. We lost one of the chinese crew overboard—but of course no attention was paid to it. It quieted down towards morning and the afternoon was not really too bad. Today has been really fine. We should have seen the Aleutian Islands yesterday only the storm blew us out of our course and we are too far south. Tomorrow or Saturday we cross the 180th degree of longitude where we lose a day. Today has been really fine and there was more life about the ship than at any other time. But always the men are cheerful. It makes no difference what the weather is. Even on the first day when everyone was sick it was impossible to repress their good feelings.

Our good weather seems to have broken. It is blowing and raining tonight and the rain is coming in. I hope we are not in for more bad weather.

Yesterday morning we started a class in Russian and we are going to have it every day till we land. Englehart an ex officer in the Russian army is taking it. He is very good and we are getting along fine.

Sunday, January 5th

Though the date is the 5th I have really missed only one day as we dropped a day last night. Yesterday the weather cleared towards afternoon and was rather fine but today has been very blustery and during the last half hour we have run into a hurricane. It is snowing and the waves are breaking over the bow pretty constantly. We are now over half way and with good luck should be in Vladivostok a week from tomorrow or Tuesday. Our Russian is getting along fairly well though we have not had a class today at all. Things have been very quiet on ship board. . . .

Monday, Jan 6th.

Our wild weather lasted for several hours last night and it certainly was a dandy. I felt wretched and sick all evening with biliousness. All I ate was a couple of oranges. This morning I felt better and was able to eat but a kind of bilious feeling still hangs over me. The weather is getting cold and disagreeable on deck so one does not stay out long.

One certainly gets lots of time to think on a trip like this. We have been out now 10 days and have covered about 2500 miles. We expected to be in port in one week's time. There is a good deal of discontent about the accommodation we are getting. This is entirely a cargo boat and the few staterooms there are are given up to the brigadier, the colonel and some of the staff. For the rest of the officers they have simply taken one hatchway and filled it with bunks. The whole space between decks is not more than 30 feet square in one case and about 20 in the other case where the senior officers are quartered. After the dining room is taken off there is very limited space left [for] bunks. Results—we are herded in like cattle. There is no deck space and to crown all there is a Chinese crew which does not add to the pleasure of life. Fortunately I have been well but for the poor chaps who have been under the weather it has been a severe ordeal. The food is not too bad if we only knew it was clean.

I have been very sorry that I was so cross about your not being down at Christmas. Of course I felt very badly but in view of the sacrifices you are making I suppose it was pretty small. I would hate to think I made you feel badly for I love you so. I wish I were back with you for a while. There is so much I should like to tell you. I am not however in a contemplative mood and cannot really express my thoughts. The old life seems so far away now I really seem to be living in another world. I am really contented except when I think how happy we used to be. Well we are going to be happy again I trust when I come back.

We had another Russian class this morning and made very good progress. The colonel took a hand for the first time and did very well. Since I organized the class everyone is learning Russian. Several of the officers have dug Russians out of their platoons. There are quite a number of real educated chaps.

Well I think I have written enough for today and will ring off. I am feeling much better since I had my tea.

WEDNESDAY JANUARY 8TH!
[ON BOARD PROTESILAUS]

Well this has been an eventful 36 hours. Yesterday morning I was up fairly early. . . . Just before breakfast the wind sprang up and by ten o'clock was a gale. Such a sight I never saw—the sea lashed into foam, the scud driving like snow across the prairie and the waves rolling in tremendous volume. I watched it for a long time fascinated. It was marvelous the way the ship behaved—climbing up those immense waves and sliding down a sickening distance into the trough. For all the tremendous size and power, we rode them well though waves broke over the deck incessantly. About 11 a.m. a wave larger than usual lifted us up and as the boat turned on its crest the propellers cleaving the water roared like a giant aeroplane. As they struck the water one of them snapped off ten feet up the shaft. Fortunately the other one held and we rode out the storm which dropped towards evening. But now we are alone on the broad Pacific with one propeller only and incapable of doing more than 8 knots per hour. We will not make port for another ten days. We are just moving along and we are beginning to wonder how we shall put in the time and whether we can stand one another's company for so long a time. . . . [W]hen the storm was on I was up on the poop deck where you could see it all and believe me it was terrifying. I expect there will be great rumours afloat about us tomorrow, or probably by now. I wish I could reassure you. Fortunately no one is ill, at least very few.

So here we are and nothing to do but read Russian and Greek or anything else. I wish I had some more reading matter. . . .

Well sweetheart I be awake and think of you at night and wish I were with you. Oh I haven't half appreciated you. I am more in love with you than ever and you seem so far away. But when I get back— oh we will have some time and a good holiday and we are going to have a home of our own and I am going to do nothing but live for you and to make you happy. But how can I tell you more. I have written reams about our love and I no more understand it than you. It is just there—a driving force against which no one can strive—it is life, it is everything. I bow before it. . . .

And now I must get down to more practical things. I want to thank you a hundred times for those gloves—they are fine and from the feel of the air in this part of the world will be needed. They are fine and I am the envy of all my friends. Now as to what I need, there are so many things I think a mail order house is what I need. I shall make out a list and send to you and you can at least relay it on to T. Eaton's. Of course I really don't yet know what I lack but there are a lot of things that would come in handy. Clean clothes will be at a premium when this voyage is over. You can bear in mind that almost everything I have will have to be replaced in six months or less. Pajamas, underwear, flannel khaki shirts, collars, handkerchiefs, ties (black). But the list is so long, I will not attempt it. I shall go into that again. Well goodnight sweetheart,

Your own
Stuart

OFF THE COAST OF JAPAN
JANUARY 12, 1919

Dearest:—

I know I should have written yestreen. . . . [It] was really a wonderful day and we slipped along at a good rate. . . . We had a Russian lesson in the afternoon and I did very well.

Today has been quite a wonderful day. This morning I was awakened by the ships siren and when we went on deck found a blinding snow storm raging. It let up during the morning. I . . . kept on deck so far as possible. About 11 a.m. a party of us went down through the engine room. It was quite interesting and gave me a great respect for the ship. When we came out, the engineer told us when the snow lifted we should be able to see land. Sure enough in half an hour we caught sight of shore about 8 or 10 miles distant—the southern coast of Hakashu. As we went on, bold cliffs and headlands showed up and shortly after coming out from lunch we saw a town with ships lying at anchor. It seemed hard to realize that was Japan—that rocky snow covered desolate coast. Everyone was on deck most of the day and it was real exciting. I really feel as though our great adventure were beginning. Tomorrow morning early we go through the straits at Hakodate and then it will be straight away for Vladivostok. Everyone feels more cheerful than before. We made wonderful time yesterday, 274 miles with one propeller. Wednesday sees us at our destination 19 days out from Victoria.

Monday, January 13th

Well Honey, I have had a most interesting morning. From the time when I went on deck for my bath until now the last rocky islands are slipping eastward, we have been passing through what must be in summer most entrancing scenery and is even now most picturesque. We have been passing through the straits between the northern and southern islands of Japan. On one of my maps the straits are called Gruyara on another Sangara. I think the latter includes the smaller or more Western Strait. I presume that at the narrowest they are 10 miles wide. We have now slipped out into the Sea of Japan and are just leaving behind us the last rocky outposts—far in the east rise the main ranges—rising like giant icebergs sheer from the ocean.

Today we made a run of 288 miles—the best yet on our one leg. If we make the same rate for the rest of our journey we shall reach Vladivostok tomorrow night or early Wednesday morning. Already all preparations are being made for landing. . . . Now I haven't very much in the way of news but I shall indicate in a rough way what my requirements are likely to be. I fear I shall have to ask you to send some things. The easiest way would be to order through Eaton's. I appear to have a plentiful supply of clothes, underwear and sox, also most toilet articles and necessaries of daily life. But there are lots of little things that I believe we will have difficulty in getting so I shall take a slip of paper and try to indicate in a general way what my needs will be.

Stuart later noted on the original of the following letter that they had arrived at Vladivostok on 14 January; in that letter he had described his first venture into town. The railway station in Vladivostok, the eastern terminus of the Trans-Siberian Railway, provided shelter for countless refugees every night during the winter of 1918–19 when the city's normal population was swollen with the addition of 150,000 refugees who had fled to Vladivostok and its immediate vicinity.[4]

VLADIVOSTOK, SIBERIA
JANUARY 18, 1919

Dearest Honey:—

Well here we are at last, dearest, at the beginning is it? or at the end of our long journey. On the day when I last wrote you I had a hunch it would be the last before we landed. That letter was posted to you yesterday and I hope is now on the way to Canada. I am not sure where I left off but believe it was the night after we sailed through the straits. That night it turned cold. I was ship's orderly officer and when I went on deck at seven everything was frozen up and the deck was covered with ice and snow. I nearly froze during the hour I stood in the aft galley waiting for the men's breakfast to be served. All that day my duties were decidedly unpleasant with that icy wind blowing from the north. I got out my furs and kept them out. I was the envy of all the officers.

That night we all went to bed early. Oh yes, I forgot to tell you, we sighted the coast of Siberia about 10 a.m.—a long line of ice clad mountains stretching far to the north—truly an earnest and a symbol of this great silent land.

Everyone was expectant in the morning and about 5 a.m. I was on deck to see what was to be seen. We lay at anchor in the harbour with ice all around us and about a mile away on all sides could be seen the hills on which the city stands, the lights shining brilliantly through the cold winter atmosphere. About 7:30 it was light and when I went on deck, it was to see a truly fine sight—a regular winter morning—everything snapping with the frost, with the city spread before us all over the hills. The smoke rising from the chimneys and over all could be seen the hills crowned with the forts that make Vladivostok a regular fortress. About 10 o'clock the ice breakers came out and made a way for us into our berth and we moved slowly in. It was quite a struggle, for the ice persisted in blocking our passage and at last the ships officers gave it up and made fast to shore with a gap of fifteen feet of ice between us and shore. This did not materially hinder disembarkation though. That day only half our troops disembarked, two companies of the 260th staying behind. I got leave that afternoon and evening and went out through the town. Say did I see anything. I never saw in a few short hours so many outlandish things.

To begin with Vladivostok is in the East and was apparently stolen from the Manchurians by the Russians. The streets were crowded with the former and their funny little ponies and dog carts—a most picturesque combination. It is a long, long walk up to town but about three-fourths of the way up we came to the railway station, quite a fine building for a frontier town—and the sights it contained. Russians, Czechs, Japs, Americans, English etc etc. Everyone in uniform—whether rightly or wrongly. They may have been Russian deserters or Czechs as the latter wear the Russian uniform—a motley picturesque crew that stared hard at us—and of course emitted a characteristic odour. One individual of hard visage approached us and claimed to have been prisoner in Germany for over two years and a half. He spoke a little French [and] German but when I tried my Russian on him—govorite li vy po russkii?—you should have heard the volume of conversation he emitted, and finally he invited, nay pressed, me to a drink of vodka—at my own expense of course. I got away as best I could. That night as we walked down the streets, we saw the young gallants with their sweethearts. The Russians are not [illegible] untidy but there is no use talking, there is a certain swank to their clothes and

S.S. Protesilaus *in Vladivostok Harbor, January 1919. Troops are from the 260th Rifle Battalion, recently disembarked following their somewhat perilous crossing of the North Pacific.*

Men of the 260th Rifles leaving the boxcars that transported them from Vladivostok to barracks at Second River, Siberia.

their tall hats and long boots. When we went back to the ship following the road along the harbour, it was a most glorious sight. The moon at the full, shining through the crisp winter air on the hills and harbour. I slept like a top that night but was up early and we were ready to move by 8 a.m. As a matter of fact we did not leave until nearly ten when we marched to the ordnance shed for our issue of rum. I was personally opposed to the issue on a cold morning when the troops were to be exposed to the cold for some hours—I took the coffee myself and from my observation of one or two officers all would have been better to have done the same. We entrained about noon, not in 2nd, 3rd or 4th class cars but in the 8 hommes 4 chevaux kind—in other words, ordinary box cars, officers and all. Our run of about 12 miles occupied about 3½ hours at the end of which time we reached our destination—Vtoraya Ryecha or Second River. There is a town of that name but the station is just dumped down on the prairie along the sea shore, if you can imagine the combination. A walk from there of a mile or more brought us to our barracks up on the hill.

So here we are. As we came around the shores of this great bay and gazed across its frozen windswept surface at the mountains beyond, toward which were struggling in the far distance the teams of the Manchurians, it seemed as though we sensed for the first time the vast loneliness of this country—the oldest and youngest of all the continents—its frozen wastes repelling the imagination with its sense of unmeasured distances and dreadful isolation and yet drawing with its magic spell the adventurous of all lands. We are indeed encamped on the shores of Asia—we breath its air, we move with its people—a treasure house of antiquity that carries locked in its bosom vast stores of material wealth for generations yet unborn.

Our quarters here were formerly barracks occupied by Russian imperial troops built at great expense between 1905–14, but now abandoned to refugees and the allies. They are large and commodious and represent a part of a vast outlay undertaken by the Czar's Government to make it a great fortress—now, alas, a dead loss—all abandoned and running into the ground. The hills crowned with forts, trenches, galleries, etc, now forgotten and grass-grown and so on with the end of the chapter. Many of the numerous buildings were occupied by Russian refugees and Czecho-Slovaks, but some of them have been taken by the Japs. They are next door to [us] now; I have been observing them today. They strike you as comic opera soldiers but on close observation you see they are better equipped than we are and just as smart but I will tell you more of them later.

These fortress-like barracks occupied by Canadian troops at Second River, Siberia, were built by the Czar's government between 1905 and 1914.

Well today I was skating. Being Saturday, it was the wish of the O.C. that some of the men should get a chance to go down so I went down with them. So we were down on the bay. It was a strange experience, skating in this godforsaken land. The natives stared at us, particularly the Manchurians and Japanese, and nudged one another though the Russians seemed in no wise put out. But it certainly was unique.

Strange to say, this country is different from what I expected. I thought it would be like Vancouver or Victoria but instead it is like Southern Alberta—all bare rolling hills with a light growth of scrub, and the climate is quite dry and not at all maritime—quite bracing and not unpleasant.

I may tell you that I was laid up yesterday—the day after we arrived I was all in and my feet were swollen with chillblains so I stayed in and had a good rest. My batman, i.e. my new one whom I just selected, looked after me and I had a real good time. Our mess is now running and now we are getting very good meals—a welcome change from the chinks.

Well I must close now. Tomorrow is Sunday. More then.

Stuart

Second River Jan 21-19.

Dearest :-

It is now Tuesday evening and
I have not written since Sunday night. So
before I lay my little head down to rest
I shall indite a few lines. We have
had beautiful weather so far and
has been a little milder. Everyone
is enjoying things here to the limit.
Today we got paid for the first time
in 20 & 40 rouble notes. For some
reason it is Bolshevik money
but our Government sees fit to
issue it. They say it is turned out
by the bales in Petrograd & Moscow
I have not had an opportunity
to spend any money yet but
hope to go into town tomorrow
so watch my smoke. I should

Perhaps Stuart's choice of coffee over rum can account for his having survived the trip to Second River with nothing worse than chillblains; several cases of severe frostbite resulted from the long confinement in the box cars.[5] In the following letter Stuart announced another attempt to start a series of Russian lessons, and this round of tutoring would prove to be the most beneficial and profitable of any of the language study to date. He also mentioned that he was keeping a diary, however there is no trace or memory of it and once again, as they had from France, his letters to Edna constitute what would be considered a diary.

260TH BATTALION,
CANADIAN RIFLES
CANADIAN EXPEDITIONARY FORCE
IN SIBERIA
SECOND RIVER, JANUARY 21, 1919

Dearest:—

It is now Tuesday evening and I have not written since Sunday night. So before I lay my little head down to rest I shall indite a few lines. We have had beautiful weather so far and [it] has been a little milder. Everyone is enjoying things here to the limit. Today we got paid for the first time in 20 and 40 rouble notes. For some reason it is Bolshevik money but our Government sees fit to issue it. They say it is turned out by the bales in Petrograd and Moscow. I have not had an opportunity to spend any money yet but hope to go into town tomorrow so watch my smoke. I should have something to tell about then.

Things have been going along nicely for the last couple of days. We are now getting down to work and are enjoying it in the cool fresh weather.

Well I really have very little to tell you tonight. I was sorry I forgot to ask you if you could send me over some films. I have two or three yet but they won't last long.

However I shall close for tonight.

Your own
Stuart

I am much ashamed of the letters I have been writing but it seems so hard to settle down to work of any kind. However I am mastering myself and I am going to see all sorts of interesting things within the next few days to tell you. I have put in for leave today for town but am not yet sure of going as Hardisty cannot go.

I am wondering, wondering when we will be united again. I live only for that—We hear rumours of all kinds—none of them true probably. I certainly am anxious to learn how things are here, though probably I cannot tell much about things. I am keeping a diary. We are all asking one another when we will get mail. There are rumours that there is some here now but I have not seen any. What are [you] doing with yourself these days. Are you well. All these things I am wondering about. I am fed up on wandering and should like to settle down and have a home of my own.

You will be interested in knowing that we are starting Russian lessons again. Englehart, our official interpreter, has discovered a little Russian girl who will give us lessons. She is the daughter of a Russian colonel, now I believe a prisoner in Germany—one of the innumerable refugees living near here. I shall write and tell you how we get on or whether we get on at all. Today is really a lovely day. We have most wonderful sunsets here. Particularly over the Bay—the Bay of Amur it is called. It just makes your heart leap to see the wonderful colouring.

Well Honey I have not more to tell you this morning. It is now nearly 9:30 and I must get to work. Be sure to look after yourself and be a good girl. I love you all the time, sweetheart.

$\qquad$ *Stuart*

> 260TH BATTALION,
> CANADIAN RIFLES
> CANADIAN EXPEDITIONARY FORCE
> IN SIBERIA
> JANUARY 25, 1919

Honey Darling:—

Of all the interesting topsy-turvy days, yesterday takes the lead. It was to be "our day" i.e. Hardisty and me. . . . We did not do much work in the morning as we were dolling up—hair cut etc. About 11:30 we left for the train but just after leaving barracks a couple of army trucks came along so we commandeered a ride into town. It was a glorious but cold morning and we soon were out to the fine military road that runs almost in to Vladivostok. The first few miles was through the open country. We could see the immense stretch of the Bay of Amur on our right and the hills that overlook Vladivostok in front of us. There was very little snow but it was cold. About 12 o'clock we climbed the last hill and there below sprawled the city. One prominent feature was a Russian church which you will see on the cards I am sending. It was a wonderful sight down, down, down through the most bewildering scenes, catching a glimpse down side streets full of Japanese shops where Manchurian coolies jostled with pig-tailed dignified Mongols to the accompaniment of street cries wrangling and a perfect bedlam of sounds. Suddenly we came out on the harbour front and the main street of the city—the Svyatlanskaya and here we left our transport. At first we could just stand and gape at the sights—the hurrying crowds, coolies, fashionably dressed women, smart officers, soldiers of all nationalities, droshkas, street cars. We soon gave up trying to salute or look our part and just drifted along in the crowd jostling and being jostled. Our first destination was a restaurant to which we had been directed. It is called "Cawkins" but I imagine that is just an English corruption of a Russian name. It was a queer scene as we went in—several rows of hat racks, presided over by a fat looking commissionaire who whisked away our coats etc. We were then ushered into the dining room, quite a large bright room abutting on the street—with small tables bare of any cloth—a sort of white lunch. It was full of soldiers—Russians, Czechs, French, Americans, Canadians, smoking, chatting and generally having a good time; there were also civilians, Jews, Russians, Mongols, also dressed in their characteristic garb and dining in their characteristic ways. One of our officers met us as we came in and ventured some advice which we found to be wrong. An English (?) menu was put in our hand—which we intended to pinch but were unable. The English on the card was almost unintelligible as was our Russian so we experienced a delicious thrill of suspense as to what each new course was to be. Hardisty drew clear consomme in a glass. My first assortment was a consomme in a gravy bowl into which some one had plopped a hard boiled egg, also a bowl full of a mess consisting of soup, vegetables and chicken. I drained off the liquid with my soup spoon and then fell to on the solid portions with my knife and fork. It was "tres bien." Then fried fish. . . heads and all. There were three or four of them. So by the end of the fish course [my hunger was pretty well satisfied]. After this came French pastry and tea—served hot in a glass with a lemon—fine! Our bill for everything was 19 roubles. Just about 10 apiece.

After satisfying our curiosity staring at the crowd we left. Our next visit was to the American YMCA down on the water front to change money etc, etc. From there we went shopping. It would be very difficult to go into detail as to the shops—one large department store in particular is worthy of note. Its shelves however were almost empty so outside of a roll of films and post cards I made no purchases. Another interesting place was a Japanese bazaar where all sorts of Japanese goods were sold quite cheap. For tea we went to the *Zolotoi-rok*, or as our fellows say, the solitary dog. It means "golden horn" and refers to the bay of that name which forms Vladivostok's harbour. Here we met some C.A.M.C. [Canadian Army Medical Corps] officers and we sat down with them to compare notes and drink tea. They brought us more tea and lemon and what they call toast, which is a kind of zwiebak—very nice. When we got up about five, many Russians were just finishing their lunch. After buying a few more articles we went for a bath at the Central Bath House. After paying for a ticket at the "kassa" we went up stairs into a sort of ante room where we waited amid a crowd of citizens. When our turn was called by a chink we were ushered into our suite consisting of a dressing room with a lounge and a bath room. In the latter we found an oblong marble bath, a shower bath with hot and cold water and a long marble slab either for massage purposes or to make steam by pouring on water. We did not bother with it anyway. We sweated and lathered and stewed for half an hour then came out feeling much better but very tired. We were not hungry so after dressing decided to go to a movie. It was something of a walk and when we did get there we couldn't read the Russian legends but we could laugh at the funny parts and cheer the hero when he finally overcame all obstacles and married the unfortunate heroine who was born an heiress.

But don't get impatient—the best was yet to be. We were ravenously hungry by this time (it was ten o'clock) and we had to eat. We hesitated for sometime, whether we should go to the Solitary Dog or the Aquarium. Before deciding we went up the street to give the latter the "once over." We found it to be a very nice place but there was nothing doing till eleven. Finally we compromised by going up to the station to buy our tickets. I have described the station before so you know something about it. The same applied last night—it was crowded with refugees, the poor flotsam and jetsam of humanity—stretched everywhere in all postures—asleep—so weary that not even the hard floor or the lack of pillows made any impression on them. We bought our tickets and went back to the Aquarium. It was beginning to show signs of life, so we paid our roubles and went in. We entered a long hall—very high galleries around both ends and one side while a part of the other side was taken up by a stage. In the body or the pit as it might be called the tables were arranged where at the audience dined. We took our place in the centre and after settling ourselves looked around at the crowds—a large number of officers, mostly Czechs and Russians, were present with ladies. There were some civilians including a considerable number of girls who seemed to have no particular claim on any one. Some of them were beautifully dressed. In one corner of the room a lady presided at a booth. Whether she dispensed drinks or whether flowers and bons bons I could not see. Before the stage sat the orchestra who caused sweet music to sound for the epicures. When it came to ordering we dispensed with hors-d'oeuvres, soups, entrees and other trifles and proceeded at once to our final objective—a course of roast pheasant, French fried potatoes, bread and butter. It was some time in coming but before it arrived the curtain went up and we were entertained by a company with some violent melodrama, fierce invective, tender passages, brawling, and finally a murder scene—the sort of drama to add zest and enthusiasm to your attack on the main piece de resistance. Well finally it came; we saw and conquered—a wonderful bird, the kind Dickens wrote of—all boned and sliced with rich gravy. Say I can taste it yet. We were a good part of an hour at it; our next course, tea with lemon and cakes. Meanwhile when we tired eating, we could look across at a party of men who ate through the menu apparently, or rather who made their final objective by easy stages, stopping to browse among all the by paths of the menu and sipping vodka copiously. It is wonderful the capacity these Russians have, but come to think of it we didn't do so bad by ourselves.

Over my left shoulder I could see another party of three—two young men and a very pretty girl with a doll's face. At the close of their meal they did as several others and ordered tea in a samovar, a large silver urn heated by spirits.

The other parts of the programme followed in due course consisting mostly of songs such as you would hear in a London music hall but of course we couldn't judge as they were all written in Russian and we caught only a word here and there. But twelve o'clock came too soon and I had some to do to get Hank away after paying the damage. The latter was some 40 roubles.

Then came our tramp back to the station through streets as dark as Erebus. Once or twice we passed a dark object huddled in a corner which we took to be a Manchurian coolie. At the station everything was still; we descended to the tracks and found a train in semi darkness. We fumbled around it and finally Hank conceived the bright idea of inquiring of the driver where his train was going. "Vtoraya Ryech-kaka?" (Second River). "Yes da yes yes" was the reply of the Slav who acted as chauffeur. He was so delighted at his success that he shouted out *spichka* (matches) instead of *spasibo* (thank you). I burst out laughing and probably the engine driver had a quiet laugh himself. We don't know for we plunged into the darkness of a car where we ensconced ourselves comfortably in upholstered seats. Only a few people were on the train—an amourous swain or two who made love quietly in the corner and a drunken peasant who insisted on coming through repeatedly to look over his fellow passengers and leered drunkenly through the gloom into our faces.

But Second River was soon reached and then again into the night and the cold; but it was short and at 1:30 a.m. two tired but happy warriors laid their heads on their pillows to dream of hold ups, refugees, Chinese coolies, roast pheasant, Russian money and a weird reproduction of their day of fantastic experiences.

Well, this is all I can write tonight as it is now one o'clock. I am for guard tomorrow so must get to bed tout de suite.

I have lots more to write but enough for tonight. You will catch echoes of my experiences in my letters for the next month. Goodnight, Honey.

Your own

Stuart

... I am afraid in my last letters I haven't found much time to say any words of love, but it isn't that I lacked the inclination. In fact it is the other way. Perhaps more in my next. Meanwhile we are promised mail in the next day or two. "Hurrah!"

Goodnight again, dearest,

Yours

Stuart

SECOND RIVER, SIBERIA

JANUARY 27, 1919

My Dearest Sweetheart:—

Do you know what day this is that my guard has just ushered in. It is the anniversary of our wedding day—of the day that ushered in four years of uninterrupted happiness, and it finds me in far off Siberia. I have been on guard all night, the bugler has just blown reveille and I am waiting for the time to elapse before I go to breakfast.

It was a strange night. When the vitality is low and the customary sounds are stilled one is alone with ones self and the imagination runs riot, over the past the present and the future. Now that the day has come, night's shadows seem to have vanished. A new moon casts its pale glow over the hills though in the east the sun is already lighting up the sky. Across the valley the cottage lights can still be seen in the semi-gloom.

I had my bed down here [at the guard post] but slept only an hour or so. The batman brought down my primus stove and the sergeant (Sergeant McAlpine) and I had a cup of coffee at midnight. Well do you wish to hear more of Vladivostok. Honey I could write volumes. By the way, two of our chaps had an experience day before yesterday. Suddenly a limber with four horses dashed around the bend. The driver had fallen from his saddle and was trying to regain his control by climbing into the wagon. Suddenly he fell and the wagon passed over him. However, as it passed Hart he grabbed the reins and though dragged for some distance he stopped them. The driver was badly hurt and had to be taken in to the base hospital so they accompanied him. Having got into Vladivostok thus surreptitiously so to speak, they decided to make a day of it and went to dinner at a restaurant. They met one of the 259th officers who speaks Russian and he... introduced them all around; he was invited to a concert and ball. It would have been a wonderful time for them, only they had shoepacks on and had to pass up the beautiful ladies. So they stood and looked on. They said they had a fine time though the Russian ladies must have laughed at their attire, which was anything but elegant. Which leads me to remark that the Russians seem to enjoy themselves and dress well despite the fact that their country is going to the dogs. Perhaps it is just on the surface, but one can't help but think it.

Oh I wish I could give you a real description of the things we saw; why it was just a regular picture book. A restaurant when full is a sight and the queues at the station. But I know you could not stand the smell of garlic and foul air. But those pathetic homeless refugees. What stories they could tell. I saw one couple apparently elderly lying on the hard floor, one shawl drawn over both their heads—a most pathetic picture. The other night a Russian officer with his family arrived from no-man's land. They were richly dressed, apparently had money, but were exhausted—dead beat and no place to go in this big town. If even the wealthy suffer hardships, what of the poor.

Well sweetheart I have just three quarters of an hour before breakfast so will close for this time.

Stuart

260TH BATTALION,
CANADIAN RIFLES
CANADIAN EXPEDITIONARY FORCE
IN SIBERIA
JANUARY 28, 1919

Dearest Honey:—

I promised myself I would write you a letter tonight and though I have spent most of my evening at Russian I feel I still have the strength and inclination left. Today has been a very beautiful day—in fact nearly every day is the same—clear cloudless sky with only a slight wind stirring. We have had a number of inspections and owing to the reorganization of the battalion my platoon has disappeared. As I had nothing to do I went for a walk over the hills with my compass and binoculars. I enjoyed every minute of the walk—first I went north through the light undergrowth along a half beaten path, then swung east until finally [I] struck a road which brought me back to camp. I wish I had had a camera to take a picture. Away to the west lay the great bay (some call it the Bay of Amur) while all around me were hills—almost bare. I guess it is typical Manchurian scenery. I guess I won't be giving away any military information when I tell you that it is all very strongly fortified—not by actual guns but by the building of roads, covered approaches etc., absolutely wonderful and I take off my hat to the Government that did it. The walks are really beyond description and my only hope is that we will be here for the summer. If we stay for the summer I should get some fine views. Don't I wish you were here. In the afternoon we were to have a little company inspection so though I have no men I turned out with the company and did my bit. When we were marching off to our ground we passed the Japanese parade ground and found the Japanese formed up in a hollow square facing a stand on which was unfurled a Japanese flag. The ceremony we could not see much of, though we heard the fan fare of trumpets. On coming back we found the ceremony almost over but we saw the finest of all, the present-arms-to-the colours. It really was fine. The Japanese seem very sloppy personally but are wonderfully steady on parade. I should have liked to get a photograph of it.

This afternoon three of us officers went down to a place near here to get a lesson in Russian—two of us to take from a girl and the other from a Russian officer. None of them know English and our Russian was limited but we got on. I was in great demand to make the necessary arrangement. Really everyone talked and gesticulated as hard as he could, while mama stood off in the corner and laughed at us. Five pupils and five teachers, each one trying to teach some one else his own language—but it was very good natured and very amusing. We had a good time.

Well sweetheart, it is getting cold in this room so I must close and get to bed. I just remembered that I forgot to mail the letter I wrote the night I was on guard but I shall do so tomorrow. Still no mail from Canada. Everyone is getting sick.

Well goodnight, dear.

Your own

Stuart

260TH BATTALION

CANADIAN RIFLES

CANADIAN EXPEDITIONARY FORCE

IN SIBERIA

JANUARY 31, 1919

Dearest:—

I am going to start a good long letter to you as you have been quite neglected for the past two or three days. Things have gone on pretty much as usual during the past few days—beautiful bright clear weather without exception. The only break in our routine has been an inspection by the brigadier which has been in progress all week. Our company came out with flying colours and every one is proud and happy; if we can only keep up the good work!

February 1st

This poor old letter of mine hasn't been getting on very well. It was interrupted for the day by my second visit to town. Hank H., Sawley and I made the trip. Leaving in the morning about 11:30 we walked to the station and from there across the ice of the bay to town. It was a bright cold day but fortunately the wind was in our backs all the way. A walk of about three quarters of an hour brought us to the point on which stands the power plant from where we struck off through the lower part of the town. But say, we soon discovered there were sewers or something worse around. We had to hold our nose going through the first quarter of a mile. We emerged in the Chinese quarter and turning to the right we suddenly came into an open market crammed with jostling Russian peasants, Manchurians, Mongolians, Chinese,

Japanese and numerous other races. We were as much a curiosity to them as they were to us, and when I started to take a snap of them there was a free-for-all fight to get in, I can tell you. But the other fellows wanted to get away for lunch so I couldn't take many. Our walk took us around the Japanese bazaar and out into the Svyatlanskaya, the main street of the town where we were to get dinner. Do you know I just thrilled in the same old way to the extraordinary sights we saw. But I have described them before. Oh, how I wish you could see it all: the swank of the officers, the crouching coolies, the ladies dolled up with furs etc, and the hills across the bay standing out in the clear frosty air. We had lunch and after finishing wandered through the town buying things or rather I should use the accepted term, "shopping," as we often found we could shop without buying. An officers clothing store was filled with the swankiest looking swords, gold braid, and decorative material, but when it came down to such useful things as a lanyard or a whistle—it simply was not. We made another discovery yesterday and that was a real departmental store just as good though not quite so large as the Hudson's Bay Company's in Calgary. But their stock—well they still dress their windows and display goods on the counter, but when it comes to sales, I imagine they are running sort of an old folks home to save them pensioning off their staff. We bought some paper and incidentally got short changed. We then wandered into some book stores, wretched parodies on the term. We found nothing except magazines months old and wretched cheap Russian books. There were no maps of any kind. For tea, we tried a new place but on entering it we discovered we were in the wrong pew, so after ordering just tea, we beat it out. Not, however, before being approached by... the Provost sergeant major whose business it is to keep the Canadians straight while on leave in town. We did not ask for it but he certainly volunteered all sorts of useful information about the city and its disturbing element. The Canadians have been very well behaved since coming, for which we are all very thankful. For our real tea we went to the Olympia known as Cawkins where we ordered tea and cakes. The cakes were a dream and Hank would not be satisfied with one helping. We had to have two. I could not persuade the boys to go for a bath as the baths are at the other end of the Svyatlanskaya, so we went to a movie show. It lasted nearly two hours. Do you know we could both read the little explanatory things much better than we could a week ago. I could at any rate follow most of them, and I really enjoyed the play. From there we went to dinner at the Solitary Dog. This consisted of crab, beef steak, French fried potatoes, bread, butter, and the inevitable tea. It was an interesting meal to say the least of it. We had to wait for half an hour while the first course was being prepared so that we had lots of time to look around on our fellow diners. There was quite a sprinkling of Canadian officers. One officer had dug up a little American Red Cross girl and was having a nice little dinner for two in the corner. An old Russian officer came in, was bowed to by the management and took his seat at the far end, where he spent the rest of the evening, alternately eating and staring at the rest of the company. Finally one individual came in and caused quite a stir of excitement. As he passed our table Hank whispered, "This must be Moses." He was a most fierce looking individual, short, stocky, dark—dressed in a dark blue uniform—a very short tunic, baggy breeches with red facing, top boots. He had a formidable mustache and bushy eyebrows and stared like a Cossack, which he possibly was. Incidentally I might point out that when one's senior officer comes into the same restaurant as you in Russia you are supposed to rise and bow—all sorts of quaint ceremonies obtain here, dating back I suppose to the middle ages. . . . Well supper over, we hied us to the station where we bought our tickets and boarded a train. There was as far as our own volition could carry us on the way home, and do you know that that train did not stir from 10:30 p.m. till 12:30 a.m. Sawley and I went up and got tea in the cafe in the hopes that it would go while we were away, but you know it was still there when we came back in an hour. The crowd got impatient and restive. An altercation developed into a fight. Two women and one man were the centre of activities. There were no hat pins used, but say the way those women stood up to the offending man was good. Dog was one of the mildest expressions used. Do you know the women here are the back bone of the country. I understand now all about the Battalions of Death. I was tired I can tell you when we got in at 2:30 and rolled into bed.

Well as I am going out for a while, this afternoon, I must wind up this epistle for the present—I shall continue it later.

Your own

Stuart

You will be interested to know that I will probably be able to get all the films I need from Shanghai, will certainly be able to get my pictures developed and printed; so one of these days I shall send along some views.

Did I tell you about the furs I saw in Vladivostok. Every occasion I have been in, I have looked up some kind of a fur house, in fact it was the fur department of the departmental store. We saw three things—a simply wonderful red fox stole, price $80.00, a lovely lynx skin $30.00. That really was lovely. But I am sure there are furs coming into Vladivostok every day I am going to keep on the look out for one. I wish you could have seen these furs.

Well Honey, my Russian is getting along fine. I can carry on a limited conversation already—so I think another month or two should see me well under way. I do wish we would get some mail or papers. We get nothing these days but scraps of communiques. We hear there will be a boat in soon.

Before I close I want to say something about things here. I can't say much, but there is undoubtedly the greatest distress, especially up country. If you can do anything by your influence or by getting Red Cross work organized and getting things sent over here, not to the troops as much as civilians, you will be helping a whole lot. I feel very seriously about the thing and do what you can, dearest.

Your own,
Stuart

Stuart later wrote that in his Siberia correspondence, "The tone of the letters is light... but no normal person could be insensitive to the vast misery spread over Russia... [and] an utter dislocation of all social life."[6] The letters all reflect the chaos that was Vladivostok, and they indicate that Stuart was deeply affected by the suffering he observed as he came to know individual Russians and to visit in their homes, and to sense "some new, terrible force pulsing everywhere."

SIBERIA, FEBRUARY 4, 1919

Dearest:—

I started a letter to you yesterday but I didn't like the tone of it so I tore it up. This morning I am orderly officer and... I still have some few minutes left before breakfast is ready. I think the last letter I wrote was on the occasion of our last visit to town on Friday. Saturday we had arranged for a Russian lesson but [Hardisty] was orderly officer so I had to go alone. It lasted nearly three hours. I am afraid I get wound up when I am learning Russian. Did I tell you about our teacher. She is a young Russian girl of the Intelligentsia class who lives with her mother in what was formerly part of the married quarters. The father was prisoner in Germany for a long time—left or escaped but has not been seen or heard of since. There is quite a colony apparently of former Russian officers and their wives around there. We were introduced to them by Englehart, one of the Russian officers in the 259th. I have been taking lessons for about ten days and my progress has been I consider quite satisfactory. Still it is most horribly difficult and I am sometimes discouraged. Well we went over and in addition to the young lady whose name I will not give you, in fact I cannot spell it, there was her mother who considers she is in duty bound to assist. Later came in a Mr.___, a Russian officer who is learning English, and his landlady. So we all sat and "gassed" and as a result were late for dinner. I wish I could tell you more about things here. I suppose it isn't so much that you see anything out of the way, but somehow you seem to feel some new, terrible force pulsing everywhere.

Yesterday at four o'clock before we went for our lesson we had a visit from three French officers—most interesting fellows they were. Everyone at once began to jabber French—much to the amusement of our allies. I admired them very greatly. They are so smart and business like.

Everyone is much agitated today over the anticipated arrival of mail. Of course we have had rumours of it for the past two days but it seems to be a reasonably sure possibility. Won't there be rejoicing in Canada town tonight if that is the case. The fellows are all getting fed up. If I stop to think of it I sure get heartsick. It seems so long to look back on the last time we were together and so long to look forward to when we will be reunited. I hope you will begin to get letters from me in a few days. My first films are to be done tonight so I should at least have one or two pictures to send you. I wish I could think of all the things I see. There is so much of interest; if you don't get it down right away one is so prone to forget. When I write the account of a trip to town, I have to skip some things with the idea that I can come back again to them but I forget them. There is one thing around here that is an inestimable blessing, a healing balm to the soul, and that is the sunrise and sunset. We have not had one cloudy day since coming here. I wish I could describe to you the scene we saw last night of the sun setting over the bay—the purple hills in the distance—while the hills on our side of the bay were all lit up with the softest warmest colours. It was a great comfort. Sunday night I went down to take a picture of the church. . . . I fear, though, the picture will be a failure as the light was getting poor and the tower is so high that it is very awkward to get in. Sunday the paymaster was down, there is a service. It was really two services—a christening and and a wedding and was exceedingly quaint. He says the church is quite clean and very pretty inside—perhaps I shall get a picture of it. I was quite amused the other night, the wife or widow of a general—as they call her, the generalsha—approached me on a curious subject. She has been after me several times about our transport, so Sunday night it came out what she wanted. The Woman's Auxiliary or some organization has bought an ikon or some ikons for the church but have no means of getting them out from Vladivostok on account of the excessive cost of hauling—so they thought that it could be arranged through us. Fortunately I was able to decline without hurting her feelings.

I have probably told you that I am to become mess secretary. How I want the honour you probably know from my experience at Westenhanger. However, it is the O.C.'s orders so I suppose I must take it but, I certainly hate the idea—but duty must be done.

Now I haven't anything more that is very exciting to tell you—not that I can think of for the moment. . . .

We get almost no news these days. There is an English paper published in Tokyo which we get—also a French paper from Peking, but they are days old when we get them.

Well Goodbye, Sweetheart

Your own

Stuart

While Stuart was not happy to be mess secretary, the assignment may well have given him a rare opportunity to see the city and the countryside from a perspective that he might not otherwise have had. He later discussed that job and how it had come about:

> *Jamieson, who commanded the 260th, had to write me in as a supernumerary. That was a disgrace, because I was senior to all. . . . the officers. I was senior. I had had four years of war. I knew something about it. I was taken on as supernumerary, that is the fact of the matter, and as a result they gave me a job to keep mess accounts for the officers.*
>
> *So I had to provide the meals and drinks for the officers from week to week. That entailed trips into Vladivostok to buy them. . . . The country was ideal*

for game and you could get various birds . . . ducks and geese the natives
brought in to the market—there was no use going to the real stores because
their shelves were empty. . . . But the markets [were] set up in every commu-
nity and there we would do the buying of the goods that were necessary.
Ducks and geese were easy and there was some venison to be obtained and
consequently we lived respectably at the mess.[7]

12

Breaking the Language Barrier
Living Among Russians

❧ FEBRUARY—MARCH, 1919 ❧

In the following instance a letter from home may have been a mixed blessing. While Stuart was overjoyed to hear from Edna, he suffered pangs of remorse and probably regretted ever having shared with her the details of his Victoria social life. But the enormity of what he was observing around him far overshadowed any personal pain and he did not dwell long on his past transgressions.

SIBERIA, FEBRUARY 6, 1919

Dearest, dearest sweetheart:—

The mail is in and what a flood of letters—five spread from December 23rd to January 5th. I read them twice in the first hour then talked about them all night. . . . And now that I come to write, it is very difficult. I pitched and tossed night before last thinking of things and, oh well, remorseful. I felt awfully bad—worse than if you had given me a calling down. I can't say anything bad enough about myself for even entertaining a harsh thought of you. I am a fool a dozen different kinds of one for ever saying anything.

Now as to what I said, of course it was all very childish, but I assure you it was said not because I did not love you or was disappointed in you, but for the very opposite reasons. I was drawn into gaiety in Victory for the first time in my life and it seemed so unfair to be enjoying

Stuart had great sympathy for the Russian civilians and refugees living at Second River in the winter of 1919; he frequently visited in their homes, and on one occasion he took this snapshot of a little girl.

it all by myself that I wanted you along. When you couldn't come I was all cut up and sore—sulked and moped and all that and you get the rest. Shall I ever recover my standing or will you sit in judgment on me for the rest of life.

I think a kind of mad fever gets in the blood out here. The far East outdoes the far West. Sickness, disease, poverty, squalor, wealth, luxury, licence, callous indifference, frivolity all jostling one another on the streets of Vladivostok and under all a great, passionate, world wide movement that is sweeping all our old land marks away. I never so had the feeling that nothing matters before. I was in town yesterday and the sights we saw were indescribable. If only the people of the Western world knew of it—that it was up to them to do something in the name of humanity.

As company mess secretary, Stuart regularly shopped the markets for provisions. He labeled this picture: "Semenoffskaya Market. I consider this to be a very good picture. The individual in the foreground I take to be Corean [sic] in his typical white coat."

Well I have just read all my letters a third time. . . .

Now let me tell you something. Every time I have gone into town I have worried around trying to get something for you. There are quite a number of things—one is a pair of the little Symukas the ladies wear—a sort of overshoe, but very fancy with fur tops and sides. Hank laughs at me but I covet a pair for you and the ladies here all have small feet so they should fit you. But there are two things against—one is the cost, 100 to 150 roubles $10 to $15 and as they are probably all made in America that seems ridiculous to buy them here. Then there were furs. Made up furs are quite scarce but there are raw furs drifting in all the time. We saw some in a large departmental store. One was a beautiful red fox stole—a really magnificent thing, 800 roubles. That is of course cheap. Then there was a very fine lynx robe which I shall probably kick myself some time for not buying. These were both gone when I was in yesterday. There seems to be lots of otter and mink and a good deal of ermine. I think eventually I shall get something worth while.

I did not tell you about our shopping yesterday. We visited the

Chinese market and bought game—venison and pheasants. The pheasants I consider a remarkable buy—9 roubles a pair, 90 cents. They each weighed about 4 pounds, really beautiful birds. The venison came to 1.80 per pound, that is about 18 cents. I don't know where they get all this stuff but there seems to be no end of it.

Well I must not write more now. Good bye for the present. God bless you.

Stuart

SIBERIA, FEBRUARY 7, 1919

My Dearest:—

I wrote yesterday but I presume another letter is in order today. . . . The topic of greatest interest just now is our removal from our present barracks to one south east of the city—Gornostoi (or Ermine) Bay. We will probably be leaving the first of the week. Whether the change is for better or worse is rather doubtful. I shall not bother repeating rumours as to what it is likely to be but shall wait till we get there when we will know.

I have been under the weather today. I don't know just what the trouble—will probably be all right in the morning. Hank is very good at looking after me. So is my batman, Todd. He had a lapse the day I was in town and I tramped on him pretty hard. I felt very badly about it. He has been such a good boy and we think so much of one another. He was very penitent about [it] and I do hope he keeps himself better in hand. This week he was working in the mess i.e. waiting on table, he won't have much time for me. Still, he cooked me some lunch—scrambled eggs and toast. He really is most efficient—a thoroughly good rustler. I hope he will stay with me. If you are sending any sox, could you send him a pair. I have given him one or two pairs myself.

Last night was mess night and though I was not there I believe they had a good meal—venison. I was telling you I suppose about our shopping and getting the venison and pheasant. The pheasants are beautiful birds and we should have a good feed on Sunday. . . .

I felt rather hurt that you did not receive any word from your folks at Christmas. Perhaps your mother is sore at me but she should take it out on me. Of course, the children are growing up and absorbing all her energy and no doubt the flu is bad. We hear terrible reports about its prevalence in Western Canada. If only we would get papers we would not get so agitated but we are dependent for news on the semi weekly communique and the local papers. There are several Russian papers published here and at Harbin, but what everyone reads here is the Japan Advertiser—a daily English paper published in Tokyo. In that we get snatches of world gossip, but really we feel a long way from the heart of things here.

Oh honey, I wish you were here. I could talk to you about our misunderstanding and explain things as I cannot do on paper. Believe me, though, dear, I love you all the time. Be sure to write often.

Your own
Stuart

SECOND RIVER, SIBERIA
FEBRUARY 8, 1919

Dearest:—

Think of it. Two more letters today. I relieved the orderly officer this morning and was around the orderly room when the mail came in. Imagine the grins and when it was sorted two for yours truly. I fairly fell on it and devoured it. . . . I am very sorry you did not get down to Calgary for Xmas. Your people would have been glad to see you.

Today has been a most beautiful day. Just a faint haze in the air, but quite warm. They say our winter will shortly be over. As to the other question you raise about my staying in Siberia—that will be more difficult to decide. It altogether depends on whether I would be of any use, for no one will be tolerated here who is not of some use. I am looking around and will probably know shortly what are the chances.

Sunday morning, February 9th

Here I am at this letter again. Last night I did a lot of Russian and did not get away to a start until after ten. I could write volumes on the problem of Russia and Siberia and on our remaining here. Hank and I were talking it over the other night. You know perhaps how he feels that he has not done very much in this war and he did hope to get a chance here. If there is no chance to do anything any other way, we will try for relief work. Heaven knows it is needed. So I shouldn't be surprised if we did something like that—if we can travel together. Of course, if we have to go back we will neither of us be broken hearted.

This morning, the major wished me to go on church parade but as I had my packing to do I begged off. After getting my packing done I went down to the canteen and got my films. Oh, Honey dear, there were only two any good, I was very much disappointed. I shall send them all home and if you want any of those printed which he declined you may. One that I was much disappointed in was that showing the coast of Japan—at a distance of a couple of miles. The detail is good but I have taken too much sky. It is taken with the sun shining on the mountains and should have been an excellent picture. Another one which I should like to print is one showing the coast of Siberia—as we saw it on the afternoon of January 14th. It is much further away than the former. The cloud effect is very good and I should like you to get it printed—for sentimental reasons. I will keep the prints I have. I think I found the mistakes I made and shall not repeat them. The atmosphere here is perfect for taking pictures and I should have got better results. I hope however to improve. The only really good picture is the group of peasants taken in the market at Vladivostok. If I only get the chance I should send some really interesting ones—different characters and uniforms. . . . I may of course be able to buy some but they would not have the same interest attached.

Well here I am rambling on and on indefinitely without saying anything, Sweetheart, though I love you dearly and want to see you so much. I shall tell you more of our move in my next letter. Good bye dearest.

Your own
Stuart

By the time Stuart's unit of the C.E.F. Siberia reached Vladivostok, the decision had been made that it would not go inland, and it did in fact return to Canada within six months. As the letter above indicates, some of the officers and men entertained the idea of volunteering for relief work in order to see service on a wider front in Russia. Stuart ventured beyond Vladivostok to visit his sister and brother-in-law at the Presbyterian Mission in Honan, China, but at the time of the following letter that trip had not yet reached the planning stage.

SIBERIA, FEBRUARY 11, 1919

Dearest:—

Your letter written Christmas Day reached me yesterday and never did I receive a more satisfactory letter. I get so blue sometimes thinking of things and wonder whether life is really what we think it to be. Your letter was really like a breath of wind from the mountains.

I am on guard tonight and have just finished my midnight supper of sandwiches, pie and coffee. My batman rustled them (stole them I guess) from the kitchen. He is on duty there this week but hard worked as he is, he finds time to look after me. He is certainly a brick.

I do not know what to do about going down to see Louise. I have not heard from them and I do not like to make any move until I do. I should hear from them one of these days. I fear this letter will not be very interesting as I have been talking to Hank all evening, and my ideas have all been exhausted.

Well my long night's vigil is ended and... I am going to write a few lines. I went out after my midnight supper; the night tempted me so. The moon was almost full, there was no wind and the stars in heaven fairly came down to meet you. The peace of nature that broods over this silent land seems strangely at variance with its human sorrow. I came in and crawled into bed half dressed and dozed for an hour or so then I woke up hot and unable to sleep. I lay staring at the walls and the ceiling, thinking of every subject under heaven. Then I got up and—whisper it not in Gath—undressed. I only slept for half an hour or so, then I awoke and did some more thinking. A runner called me at 5:00 and I got up in time for reveille. The moon had gone down and it was quite cold, but I enjoyed the walk around the buildings.

Later:

Although I slept so little last night, I don't feel a bit sleepy today. I have just been relieved from guard and while waiting for dinner will write you a few more lines. . . .

The mail that brought your letter of Christmas brought one from Alice written January 7th. It was full of Christmas and New Years, flu and school. . . . I must write to the girls but really after writing you a full account of everything it seems like unnecessary repetition to tell it again to them.

I am getting my second lot of films today or rather hope to. They were taken on an Ansco roll so should be better than the others.

Now I really haven't any more to tell just now, and as I am beginning to feel sleepy I shall roll in. . . . Good by dearest.

Stuart

The following letter shows a presentiment of a theme which Stuart later incorporated into his interpretation of Russian history. The role of national tradition and national character assumed a primacy in his view, and the somewhat casual connecting of character flaw with the roots of the revolution that he made below in 1919 was argued in fuller and more sophisticated fashion in 1967 in his final scholarly publication, *The Triumph of Bolshevism.*

My Dearest little Girl:—

For once the sun is not shining when we get up; it has been snowing during the night but now the air is quite still and fresh. I was orderly officer for the company and quite enjoyed the walk down to the barracks. The hills stood out so clear with their new covering of snow.

Hank complains that the material for letter writing is becoming exhausted but I do not find it so as yet. I manage to fill my days and certainly Russian takes up a lot of my time and I am certainly gathering a bunch of useful information. This Russian revolution is the most stupendous spectacle of all time, a vast tragedy in which a great people are driving themselves to destruction. It all has its roots in the weakness of the Slav character, and one feels a great sadness for them.

I have got to know quite well a family here of the military or perhaps rather just semi-military class. They call themselves "intelligentsia" which is intended to distinguish them as university people. In our conversations are revealed in bold relief the divergent ideas and ideals of two peoples. As I probably told you before, they live in some of the married quarters of the old barracks here. The father was a prisoner in Germany but escaped some time ago; nothing has since been heard of him. The son—I haven't the heart to talk of; they speak of him a good deal; they must have thought the world of him—was an officer also and educated at some of the cadet schools; the daughter a very fine girl about 18 years of age had the equivalent of a very good High School course—here the Gymnasium—and knows French and German. I do not yet know why they are living where they are in really wretched quarters but I imagine it was for mutual protection. There is a small colony of defenceless women with a sprinkling of ex-Russian officers and their wives. The rooms are fitted up comfortably enough but without luxury at all. They still retain a *prisluga*, a man servant of former times. Their days are passed apparently in a monotonous round of eating and sleeping varied by trips to town in the wretched packed little train that runs in a dozen times a day. I have been going over for Russian lessons four of five times a week. Mother sort of does the chaperoning and when the formal lesson of reading and writing is finished we sit around and *razgovoryvat* which means just "gas." Say, a book could be written about our sessions there, I talking about Canada in my broken Russian, answering their hundred questions as fast as I can and getting all sorts of interesting side lights on Russia and Siberia. These rambling talks arise out of our conversation on everyday topics. For instance the other day mamma offered to go into town to help me do some shopping. That seemed fine; so I suggested that both she and Miss Olga should go in and that afterwards we should go to a restaurant for lunch. "Nyet Nyet." I felt rather confused at first and she saw it so she explained the proprieties as they exist in Russia— you may only enter a restaurant with your husband. So we had a fine session. She gave me the Russian equivalent for doing as the Romans do. When you run with the wolves you must howl like a wolf. Miss Olga took exception to this—you know the young girl idea that it's nobody's business [what you do], which is our Canadian way, but Russians are great talkers. I guess I am sowing the seeds of Canada here all right and giving these people an idea of what a decent country is. Their eyes stuck out last night when I told them of the comfort we have in Canadian homes. Oh, a hundred questions came up which I cannot now remember, but I am certainly getting my money's worth out of my knowledge of Russian.

I have just got some post cards giving views of our arrival at Vladivostok and our trip out here. I hope you will find them of interest for the future. I shall make a memo on each one.

Good bye dearest

Your own

Stuart

Thursday evening February 13th:

I have already finished my letter today, but I thought I would add a few lines. I was going to tell you about the other day when I was down for my Russian lesson when the generalsha came in, that is the general's widow, an old body of about sixty years, as interested and as curious a person as you ever saw. She heard I was married and wanted to see a picture of my wife. So I trotted out your picture. Oh my "Oichen Krasivyi, Krasivyi" [Stuart's later translation: how very beautiful, beautiful] and were you a brunette and what large eyes and what lovely hair. All of which I knew to be true but of course I couldn't say it myself, and I must persuade you to come to Russia and you would learn Russian, Olga would teach you herself. My goodness, I had to tell all about you. I blush to think of it now. How lonely you must be without me, and how long had I been away. Now what those people don't know about me and Canada won't be worth knowing by the time I get away from here. These people are not so poor as I at first thought them. They used to have a summer home up the bay from here and of course their standard of living is much higher than that of the people around here. But to think of them riding in these trains. It is a corker.

Hank and I were out for a long walk tonight down to the station, up the railway and doubling back to camp. So we are tired. We are going into town tomorrow so must be up betimes.

Now be sure to look after yourself and write lots of letters.

Your own
Stuart

SECOND RIVER, SIBERIA
FEBRUARY 15, 1919

My Dearest little Girl:

I did so want to start this letter while things were sizzling hot inside me. But it was impossible as we were tired when I got home and I wanted a bath. Then this morning when I might have had an hour or so to myself, I was ordered into town to a meeting and had to chase in in hot haste. Well more of this again.

We left about 9 am yesterday and as it was a beautiful day, we decided to walk in across the ice. We followed a slightly different route than on our other walk, taking the main military road for the first mile and then striking out to the bay. We have had a real January thaw and it was positively delightful. Our route took us through an immense engineering dump—full of all kinds of rolling stock for a narrow gauge railway and engineering material ad infinitum; then through a culvert and out to the bay. We made town in an hour and a half and all but kept our appointments for ten thirty. My banking business kept me till after eleven. We then had very little time before lunch but we made an appearance at the Chinese market; but it seemed to be an off day and we could not get what we wanted so we went off down town. At the departmental store I nearly had a row with one of the clerks. You see they close the stores from 12 to 2 and no clerk likes to have his sacred rights infringed on. We then went to "Cawkins" for lunch, where we had a very nice lunch—this time without the fish and soup. We had rather an unpleasant aftermath. I had the mess corporal with me and it seemed almost impossible to get our business done; he could not make up his mind. However I made it up for him, bought the stuff and then we got away. We were climbing the hill up into the Chinese quarter when we passed a bunch of coolies, one of them smoking a pipe. We have both rather fancied one of these pipes so Hank asked one of them where they could be bought. He waved his hand up the street and we fondly imagined that direction enough but we did not meet with any success. So nothing would do Hank but that he should go back and get one of these coolies to guide him. I waited for him and a few minutes later I caught sight of Mr. Coolie hiking along as fast as his legs would carry him, holding his long whip in front of him as though to clear the way, while behind him about half a block panted Hank, trying his best to keep up. Just as I caught up, he dived down into an alley full of Orientals, dirty and noisy. We jostled Japs and Chinamen, Mongolians and Manchurians, then around a vile corner and down a flight of steps into a dark shed. Here were a group of shops with goods displayed on either hand, partitions running down the length of the shed screened off an inner shop, the shop keeper doing his business through a hole in the wall. Here we found our pipes—two roubles. An interested crowd of coolies gathered around and I was nervous the way they kept looking over my shoulder at my wad of money. We bought our pipes but I demurred when Hank suggested going on. I was glad to get back on the street, even if it was just the street of Chinatown. But our adventures were not yet over. We wanted to get some skins so we proceeded along the street, every once in a while turning under an archway into one of those terrible courtyards, but as many times coming back nauseated and discouraged. I could hardly describe some of the things I saw. We got into one shop and asked for furs. The Mongolian shop keeper hauled down some little brown pelts, much affected by his countrymen. We examined them closely and found them patched. Just at this juncture in came another pig-tailed individual, leered over our shoulders and mumbled something in broken English. I was trying to make out whether he was describing the skin or telling us to "Take care," when Hank said, "He's drunk." His drunken reel then showed his condition and we decided it was about time to beat it. He followed us out to the street and called after us to know where we were going. But we were well on our way back to the bazaar.

It was the first chance we ever had to loaf around the bazaar and we really did enjoy it. The sun had dismissed the morning fog and was lighting up the hills and the forest to the east. I could not resist the temptation to try a snap or two which you may see some day. I noticed a French officer doing the same thing so I went over and spoke to him. He had just come out from France. Strange to say after talking with him in French for several minutes, I discovered he talked perfect English. We fooled around for half an hour pretending to look for samovars, but without any serious quest in view. After we had seen enough we went off to the fruit, vegetable and fish stands and then down town—by down I mean the business portion of the city, headed in the general direction of some "eats." I was anxious to go to the Canadian Economic Mission offices on the Svyatlanskaya. We passed it earlier in the day and were at once attracted by the map of Canada in the window. The young lady behind the counter assured me that while we might see and admire we might not take them away, so we went back on the odd chance that I might get some literature. Sure enough the man in charge was my old friend whom I met on the CPR when I came down to Victoria. He was very glad to see me but what is more gave me the literature, so we went away happy to the Canadian Y.M.C.A. to eat. This place has just been started on the Svyatlanskaya. They took over a [motion] picture house and have put in a cafeteria. All the home dishes are to be introduced. We got only coffee and cakes but as the coffee was made in an urn and the Russians make beautiful cakes any way we were well set up. It was full of boys from the 260th, also Americans, French, Czechs, Russians. However they drew the line at coolies and one fellow was chased out into the street.

I omitted to mention that the rent paid by the Y.M.C.A. for this building is 20,000 roubles per month.

This practically closes my day's proceedings as we went back to the station and then home.

Next morning, I was asked to go into the city to represent the canteen at a meeting called to discuss the purchase and sale of some light beer. The chaplains service is behind it and I was surprised to find the senior chaplain in the chair. Their idea is to keep the men away from the vodka, a great deal of which is being made and sold secretly to our men. It comes in little flat tins, square like the top of a biscuit tin, but very shallow, so that the tin can easily be slipped into the pocket. Although the sale of liquor is controlled by the state, bootlegging and blind pigging cannot be prevented.

I had a great to do to catch the train but Captain O'Grady and I climbed in a practically vacant box car and made ourselves very comfortable. It was a most pleasant ride into Vladivostok and I was sorry when the trip was over. I walked down the Svyatlanskaya to Canadian Headquarters. It was fairly early but I was surprised to see none of the shops open. I discovered later it was a "prasnik" or Russian fete day. I believe they call it the New Year, the 2nd of February and if weather has anything to do with it, it certainly seemed to mark the birth of a new year. Everything bathed in glorious spring sunshine. I should like to be able to describe the crowd I saw on the street yesterday morning. Everyone seemed to have on his gayest. Do you know despite the penchant for uniforms these peoples show more originality and eccentricity in their clothes than any other people. I should give anything to stand on the street corner and snap the people as they go by. I saw one old fellow with a rough sheepskin hat and an immense long cowhide mantle with no sleeves which he wrapped around him as he stalked majestically along. One apparently quite wealthy old top with a rich black and brown fur coat on created a most startling effect by a brilliant yellow crown to his fur hat. A third old johnny that I noticed was clad in brown with quite natty boots, a long sash confining, or attempting to, his generous paunch. Then the ladies with their little boutiques of fur. There was certainly lots to see.

A description of my business would bore you; it was tedious, as H.Q. are not known for expediting matters. Another call down town delayed me so that I was late when I arrived at the *Zolotoi-rok* for lunch with Captain O'Grady. He had already ordered pheasant and had started on crab so I followed suit. There was quite an interesting crowd present including some Italian officers. There were quite a number of women but Captain O'Grady lost interest as soon as he saw them begin to eat. Our lunch was good but I ate too much. I had intended coming out on the 1:15 train but Capt O'G assured me that train was off. However I did stroll down that way to find out. I was assured the train would go right away which means anytime in an hour, so I was soon aboard. The 2nd class carriage was jammed with a rabble who were talking their heads off. I had to stand in the corridors so did not much enjoy the trip. I gathered though that they were excited at what one man was reading out of a paper. We were soon home and I got fixed up to go down for a Russian lesson. It was a great success. I took over my Canadian Atlas and pamphlets and mama and the generalsha and another old lady gathered around while I told them about the greatest land under heaven. Then they insisted on going and getting the padre who was domiciled near. He knows book English quite well so I drew him out and talked to him—one of the finest types of Russians I have seen. I liked him very much. He shortly excused himself as he had another service. Really enjoyed my call very much.

Well this is a long letter. Next time I shall tell you about the Russian service I attended this morning. Good bye dearest. Oh, I hear there is mail coming in on the Monteagle.

Your own

Stuart

I forgot to tell you about a Japanese funeral party I saw yesterday when coming back from town. It consisted of about a dozen files carrying flags and pennants. An officer rode on horseback; behind was a rough carriage with the body in a box. I suppose they were sending the body back to its ancestral abode.

TUESDAY, FEBRUARY 18, 1919

Dearest:—

I may tell you in opening that the censorship regulations have been lifted. There are however certain rules laid down for us to which we must conform. Apart from that however it is a great relief as having to keep in mind the censorship was always sort of a drag. I will now be enabled to go somewhat more into detail than heretofore with regard to things in Siberia.

I believe I have not written you since Sunday when I brought things up to Saturday night. Sunday morning I went down to the little Greek Church in the village to service. I got in about ten. As I entered the building I was suddenly forcibly reminded that in a Greek church everyone stands. There were about twenty people of all ages and both sexes standing stolidly throughout the little building. They were mostly of the lower class and were dressed quite in contrast to the rich ornamentation of the far end and of both sides of the building. There was a partition about three quarters of the way down the building screening off the altar where the priest and the choir chanted. At times two large doors swung open for the priest to come out on a little platform in front of the partition and again they closed it behind him when he went in. Behind it also the choir ministered throughout the service. This partition which really closed our view was most richly ornamented in gold and silver, amidst which stood out prominently figures of the apostles and saints and numerous ikons. The pillars, too, held numerous ikons and paintings and everywhere there was an ikon there seemed to be a series of tapers.

The service was not unique, consisted for the most part of chants, the music of which was very fine. After a while though one of the pages or waiting boys or whatever you call them came out and set up a little pulpit. From this he read I think a lesson and then preached what was apparently a sermon for little children. I understood quite a bit of it. The priest was rather a handsome figure in his rich green and gold vestments and he had a deep melodious voice pronouncing his words slowly and distinctly. I thought that perhaps he was doing it for my sake. His words were addressed in every day Russian, whereas the greater part of the service was in Church Slavonic. After the service proper closed there were two christenings and what looked like a sort of confirmation service. At any rate the priest stood in front of the altar and seemed to be dividing bread among the children. This bread which looked like tea cakes could be bought, as well as the tapers, at a little counter just to the right of where I stood at the back of the church. Quite a business was done with the people as they came in. After everything was over the people crowded around and kissed the crucifix. During the service Madame Krasnopol'skaya, whom we know here, had come in and I walked part way home with her afterwards. It was a beautiful morning and as I got on top of the hill that overlooks our camp I heard our band playing the battalion back from church. It was a fine sight to stand and look down on the men half a mile away marching along.

In the afternoon I called on the Russian colony here and spent the afternoon with the generalshaya who was most interesting and interested herself particularly in you. I have spoken of her before. During the afternoon the padre or batoochka as they call him came in and we spent a pleasant hour. He mentioned having been at two weddings where he had partaken of whiskey and apologized in a jocular way for being in a merry mood. Well I had a pleasant afternoon and was almost sorry to leave.

Next morning I went into town for the mess. It was a most strenuous day and as it was devoted entirely to business would not interest you. One thing only. A woman fell off our train just as we were pulling into Vladivostok station and was killed. It was a ghastly sight and temporarily unnerved me. The train was horribly crowded and such might occur any time.

Well, I got my second lot of films tonight and am very pleased with myself. They were all good but one. I shall send some home as soon as I get a chance. I also got [your] letters postmarked January 13th and 14th. The letters were so unsatisfactory, I am sorry to say, though it was nice to get them. . . .

Well Honey, you may not believe it but I have had a hard time today. The battalion is moving to Gornostai Bay tomorrow. I leave on Friday. It is now eleven o'clock. I must close dear. Goodnight. Sweet dreams.

Your own
Stuart

The 260th Battalion transferred from Second River to a similar barracks compound at Gornostai Bay; Stuart later theorized that since Gornostai Bay was not on the railway the purpose of the move was to deter the men from going into Vladivostok.[1] He was willing to label her letters unsatisfactory at times, but it can only be imagined what she thought of letters such as the following in which he seemed compelled to confess his near surrender to temptations in the Far East.

GORNOSTAI BAY, SIBERIA
FEBRUARY 22, 1919

My Own Darling:—

The finest batch of letters was awaiting me when I reached here yesterday afternoon and though I was hungry and lunch had to be prepared and eaten, I sat up on a table and read all the letters. It set up a train of thought that has been running all night and I am going to talk to you right now just as if you were here and were in my arms. I started in once before and then tore up my letter thinking that you might not understand or care. You know you are very downright in your opinions and don't make much allowance for differences of temperament. That would not affect the situation if we weren't very near and dear to one another, in fact we are more than that. I am what you have made me.

Now for my plain unvarnished tale. Shortly after coming here, Englehart one of the Russian officers came to me and asked me if I wanted to take Russian lessons. My answer was prompt, so we arranged that the following day three or four of us would go down with him to the village and meet a young lady and see if we were mutually agreeable. We went down. For some strange reason we climbed over a very steep high hill and dropped down into the excavated back yard of one of the innumerable barracks around here. It looked very uninviting particularly as we went in the back entrance. Englehart passed through several doors into the kitchen and when he knocked at the next door some one said something Russian; we entered a passage where we laid off our wraps from which were ushered into the dining room—the only bright clean place we had seen—a large dining table with white cloth in the centre of the table, a huge Russian upright stove in the corner—against the window a writing desk covered with writing and sewing material and to the right of this a book case. But what surprised me most of all was a tall nice looking girl with very fine features and dressed in very good taste bowing to us and giving us a formal salutation in Russian. We sat down. Englehart and she carried on a conversation for some minutes in Russian; he then proceeded to show her how he had been instructing us. Finally we were each asked in turn some questions in Russian. I was about the star performer, which was to say the least not much. It was decided to continue the lessons but owing to the uncertainty of our several hours we had to set different times. I came the following day at 4:30 I think, and before I left, I met the mother, a tall fine looking matron, and we really got on well together. My French helped me out wonderfully and I could always fall back on it. Now perhaps I shouldn't have gone over alone; still it was the only way to carry on. The third day I think it was, "mother" was in town. I did not know it until after we had been working for some time. Now I guess I know how to behave when alone with a girl but I am afraid the East had begun to instil its subtle poison into my mind. It seemed so far back to the old life and the mad life of Russia and the East was all around me. In the twinkling of an eye I was overboard in a wild storm. I am ashamed when I look back on it but I did the only thing that I could which I thought at least partly rational. I ran away from temptation. I don't know whether the girl understood it but she seemed sorry to see me so distressed. I tossed all night on my bunk and wondered whether my anchors would hold; but they did. I didn't get over it for two or three days and finally your face and all the gold memories came back and joy and gladness reigned on the earth once more.

Now please don't think the worst of me at once and think that my mind and impulses were all evil. At the worst I *could* not have followed the promptings of my lower nature. You surely cannot think that but what gave me most pain the following night was that I might have snapped the spell by some rash act. It seemed so easy and harmless to venture a word or caress. But—well I guess I sobbed in relief when I found the storm had abated.

Well that does not end the story but it ended that phase. I found that things got straightened out. Next time mother was there and I had a fine time and we have got on better every day. They have almost adopted me. They want you to come out. Of course I showed them your picture. . . . They ask questions about our life, in fact about everything. Now you may not be a bit interested in this tale. But it gives me an immense satisfaction to write about it. I have learned a vast deal since coming out here. The East and Russian life is so different and so interesting—the passions, the emotion and the sordidness all mixed up together. But to have fallen down on the upward path you and I have been treading would have been a great shame and humiliation. You know how we have often talked it over and said that love is not love of one person only, it must over flow on to the rest of the world. It is you of course who are the source and fountain of all my love, but if we make it narrow and selfish and mix it up with passion we kill it. Instance Anna Karenina, and that is the tragedy of Russia today. Had I added one whit to that tragedy I should never have forgiven myself.

Now don't think that the young lady has any designs on me. She is a brick, a real good sport, and I think that why we are such welcome guests is that neither of us (though I have been there much more than Hank) has shown anything except the greatest respect and I think they appreciate it. Really the Canadians, though they have waited a long time for recognition, have come home to the hearts of the people here. The Vladivostok papers have been full of nice things about the Canadians and I think they deserve it. I hope the reputation the officers leave behind is as good.

Well my lessons came to an end on Thursday and I paid. But this was an awful task. Neither she nor her mother would talk money at all. They are the most stubborn people in the world. They will not talk about money but they leave it to you. So I had to slip it in an envelope with a note and slip it surreptitiously under a book.

Of course what really stirs me deeply is the great uncertainty as to future events. The Vladivostok papers published a story the other night foreshadowing the immediate withdrawal of all British and allied troops. If that is the case, the future of these people is indeed dark; the day I left them madame was in tears. They fear that if the Canadians go, their days are numbered. But more of this later. Good bye dearest. God bless you. I am enclosing some snaps.

Stuart

Stuart felt great affection for the Russian family with whom he had spent a great deal of time; he was concerned for the future when the allies would have withdrawn from Siberia and obviously had sympathy for their plight. He returned to Second River to visit them at his first opportunity, and in the following letter he describes that trip.

GORNOSTAI BAY, SIBERIA
FEBRUARY 25, 1919

Dearest:—

It is a most glorious morning. The sun is flooding the whole valley beneath us and on the far hills every tree and every rock stands out in bold relief. Were it not that I am homesick this morning, I could be very happy. But my mind persists in leading back across the six thousand miles and picturing all the foolish joyful things I will do when I get back—waking every morning to a day when you will be with me and all the things we will do together. I think we will be very happy.

Well now I have so much to tell you I do not know where to start. Sunday was a red letter day in our lives—mine and Hank's. We were to Second River for the day; left at quarter to nine. It was not a nice day, the weather was foggy and threatening when we left, the clouds hanging persistently over the tops of the hills. But we travelled light trusting that it would change for the better. We travelled by the road we marched in on Friday, striking straight northwest across the valley to the road running into First River, following that west for several miles and then striking off across a divide to the valley of Second River. We made the village about 11 a.m. found everyone coming from church. As we entered the house we encountered a full blown Russian lieutenant-colonel but he entered the next suite, that occupied by the generalsha. The daughter of the house, Miss Olga, had been out gathering what looked like pussy willows but is I think a species of poplar or a sallow. I forget the Russian name. However, we were ushered in, found mamma and a strange lady whom I had not met before. So we had to discuss all that had happened since we left, about 48 hours, how tame life was since we had gone, how much better they like our battalion than the "cavaleria" as they call the Mounted Police. All of which we were much pleased to hear. We sat and talked for a while, then somebody suggested cards. I wasn't a bit anxious to play as it was a game I didn't know (called 66) and I was not very familiar with the Russian names. However I had to sit in while Hank was entertained by Lola with the family collection of photographs. I gritted my teeth and tried to get interested but the others persisted in nudging me when their Russian and English got tangled up. So I was much relieved when the game ended even though I was defeated. About one [o'clock] Nicolai showed up—a young cadet from Russian Island to whom Lola is engaged. About two o'clock lunch made its appearance. I was prepared for anything so was not surprised when we sat down to a table spread with cold fish (you know how I like it). One platter consisted of a small fish something like sardines, covered with onions, another huge platter was apparently something like herring covered with a very thick jelly-like sauce with onions and other vegetables in. Then there was a plate of smoked salmon shaved off into large flakes. I drew some of the second; took a large slice of black bread shut my eyes and waded in, determined not to taste anything. I made such progress that when I finished it I must have some of the raw onion variety. Hank seemed to side step all the encores so I was it. After I began to feel satisfied the plates were removed and we had a huge bowl of soup—with large pieces of potato in and floating on top of which was what looked like cream. It was really delicious. I did very well by the soup and another slice of bread but imagine my dismay when the course was removed and a smoking dish heaped with pheasant and roast potatoes came in. I groaned inwardly when madame passed me a plate with a drum stick, an enormous chunk of bread, a dill pickle about a foot long and a helping of cold slaw or sauer kraut. I just nibbled. Then came rice pudding. I felt like the proverbial poisoned pup. Everyone ate well except the girl, but as Hank says, they are well dug out inside.

When we had finished dinner instead of having tea at home we were invited into the generalsha's house where we met the old colonel, his wife and the other well remembered faces. The colonel was a nice old man with a row of medals but his wife was an old shrew. The generalsha had a decanter of Caucasian wine which she had brought out. We filled our glasses—little things like communion cups—and the general toasted prosperity to the allies. Then we had tea and chatted on. The cadet insisted on telling me all about explosives and things and the dear old ladies told us how much we should be missed. Hank brought out his pictures of Edmonton which much interested them.

We did not get away till five. The youngsters came with us part way but it was nearly dark when we left them and began the long hard journey home. However we made good time. About 6:30 we reached the Czech hospital, about half way. A young Czech n.c.o. overtook us and when we asked him where we could get a drink he insisted on taking us in to their quarters. Say such an hour and a half session I never had. His friends all came in to welcome us and we sat in their room eating and drinking till we were stuffed. They gave us some delicious buns which had a filling of something very tasty. I could not make out what it was. Well we left about 8 o'clock and reached home about 9:30. It was pitch black and it was only my torch that kept us from breaking our necks. I was good and tired when we dropped into bed.

Well, dearest, I have brought our narrative up to date so will close. I am getting some more pictures printed; they will be along immediately.

Stuart

Stuart later wrote what in 1919 he had not thought "prudent to reveal to a wife of tender years" about the return trip to Gornostai Bay:

> *[W]hen we stepped out of the hospital I was as near being drunk as four or five rounds of beer could make me. But repeatedly, every time I rose to leave, our host protested, "Nein. Trinken sie mein Herr" and forthwith another bottle was produced from the case under the bed. . . I had a hard time keeping control of the ground with my feet. It seemed to keep falling away while the stars wove crazy patterns in the sky. . . .*
>
> *One thing I got from my host which I well remember; when I asked him how the Czechs got on with the Bolsheviks, he opened a drawer, revealing a hand grenade, which we knew as the Mills bomb. This was his answer.*[2]

Stuart's first letters from Siberia did not arrive in Edmonton until February 20, and in the letters from Edna to him that survive from this period it is obvious that she was lonely, that she missed him, and that letters to him were difficult "to write against silence." Stuart refers below to her account of the visit of J. W. Reith, his friend from the trenches; she had written, "Your esteemed Captain Reith came and went and left quite a thrill of excitement in his wake." The accusation of matchmaking stemmed from her saying, "I think Janet and he would make a fine pair. Don't you?"[3]

My Dearest:—

When I got home from town last night I found the finest bunch of letters waiting for me. I was beastly tired but I had to sit up and read them all through twice before I turned in. Really they were I think the most comforting letters I ever read. I wish I could answer them all individually. Indeed I will if I get the chance. To think that you had Reith up to dinner. It seems hardly possible that he is back after all that he has been through. Well as to my opinion of him he will have to speak for himself. But you are a naughty little match maker to be thinking as you are. I used to think of that in France when I thought over Janet and friends but I never allowed myself to dwell on it.

It is now two days since I started this letter and for this I am very very sorry but it could not be helped as I have been very busy with the mess. There is a good deal to tell and I am afraid I shall forget some things. Friday Hank and I went into town. Transport was ordered for us, but as usual it fell down and we had to take a chance ride in on the Y.M.C.A. car. As a matter of fact when I found there was a car going in, I sent up for Hank and we went in. Imagine our disappointment when I found the stores closed. However, I went into Kunst and Albert's office to arrange about buying supplies. I was, however, again disappointed as they did not do business of that kind. Instead they sent me down to a Chinese contractor and I fixed my business up with him. However it required a second trip down but when we had finished we went on a pleasure expedition taking photos. It was most interesting. We finally landed up at Father John's house just around from the cathedral. We had a very short but enjoyable stay. His wife was a very nice little thing and he had some nice kiddies. However, we had to leave so we peeled out for Gornostai Bay. It was a beast of a long walk and I was played out when I got here but I was cheered by the arrival of mail. It was fine. . . .

Now darling look here. I wonder how you will like that last letter of mine. I wish I knew. I wrote as I did because partly of what you said in a recent letter and partly what I resolved to do when we were married. . . . Now I don't wish to pose as a saint or anything else but I believe I have got down to realities and it fills me with a joy sweeter than I can tell you that such is the case. . . . Is love a reality on which you can build or is it an evanescent passion that ebbs with the lapse of time? The answer is given not by the guarded years of those who live together for an uneventful lifetime but by the sudden turn in the road that reveals life, as it were, like the flash of a searchlight, a stab in the dark. I have lived with you and been spoiled as every selfish husband can be. I have lived away from you in the long months of service when your face came to me in my sleep and in the long watches of the night. I have gone pleasure hunting with other girls I confess to my shame. But Honey I will admit that there is some tie or chord that is stronger and more insistent than all others; and I surrender my soul to the call of a love that is stronger than all else. Your love... speaks to me of something more permanent that transcends the temporal or physical temptation and that we trust will survive for all time and for eternity.

I am telling you everything. I trust I have builded for eternity.

I am enclosing the snaps.

Stuart

GORNOSTAI

MARCH 7, 1919

Dearest:—

My writing has been most unsatisfactory of late. My days have been so hurried and broken. But I am going to take a couple of days off and as a start I climbed into bed at seven thirty and read. But I had it in mind to write you a note, for I have felt very guilty lately but what could I do.

I know I did not even write a narrative of last week's events—of the Czech officer for instance who strolled into our mess and was wished onto me because I spoke German and later entertained us with the exploits of the Czechs. The days Saturday, Sunday and Monday were filled in with lying in bed—I felt wretched and done up. Tuesday I had to go into town as we had an order.

This letter which was started on Thursday or rather Friday last is just being resumed. The reasons therefore I shall give elsewhere.

Well imagine my dismay when I got into town to find the shops again closed. It was Shrove Tuesday. Well I at least picked up the order and feeling too tired to walk back to Gornostai decided to sleep in town that night. The afternoon I devoted to going out to Second River to see the people there. I got back about ten, coming back with the Russian padre. West Barracks welcomed me and I made my bed on a couch for the night. Next morning having considerable business to do I left early, visited the bank and started shopping. I decided to hire another coolie cart and send another load out. I shall not overwhelm you with the details. They are too painful. I did get the coolie cart away and devoted the remainder of the afternoon to making some much

A squad of Czech Legionnaires march through the streets of Vladivostok, 1919

needed purchases. I ran into some officers of the machine gun battalion and together we went to tea to the Solitary Dog. We hadn't much of a tea but it cost the five of us 86 roubles—imagine our dismay. We left there about five, hired a car and drove out. It was a most glorious ride—as we swung east out of the town the hills took on the colours of sunset which deepened to a most wonderful purple as the night descended. Really this is a glorious country. We reached home about six and there I was informed that I was to go into town again. There was a big dinner on and we had to make some additional purchases. So next morning I was up bright and early, ready to leave at nine. I was to have a horse and at 9:45 it was brought to my door. I took the First River road as I was to pick up my transport there. The day was very cold but I enjoyed the ride. The battalion had gone ahead of me and in about half an hour I overtook them. A squad of Czechs had fallen in behind them and were singing a marching song, wild but very sweet, with perfect chording. As I was in a hurry I decided to pass the battalion. I saluted and spoke to the colonel who advised me to hold my mount in well. I was just passing by the leading company when our little white dog—the mother of the six odd pups born on the boat—rushed up and barked. That was enough. Before I could pull up the slack of the reins we were away—but I said to myself "I can go

Two members of the Czechoslovak Legion, the future safety of which had figured heavily in Allied decisions to intervene in Siberia.

anywhere this animal does." I was preparing myself for a mad ten mile run but fortunately the dog dropped behind and we settled down to a steady canter and then a trot. You can bet that the next time a dog barked at us I had him well in hand.

Well I did my business and got away from town without further incident, reaching home at six just ahead of the transport. We had a wonderful dinner only a little too much booze, but no one suffered much.

Friday was very quiet as I was all in and wanted sleep, but that night there was a party next to us and I couldn't sleep. Saturday I started seriously in the mess books and that is what I have been working on ever since. That is why there has been no letter. I am very sorry about this seeming neglect sweetheart. . . . You know how much you mean to me, don't you. I really have so much to tell you I am going to take a whole letter to [do] it. . . .

Stuart

GORNOSTAI BAY

MARCH 13, 1919

Dearest:—

You have had a hard time of it lately but no harder than I. I have been really just working all the time trying to get my books in shape. However that job is done and I have quit. There is nothing in the way of news except rumours and stories. Meanwhile of course we know nothing. This much seems assured, that we are going [home] in a month or six weeks.

Now for the real story however. Colonel Dennis is going back to Canada to urge the Canadian authorities to undertake Red Cross work in Siberia. He has likewise asked for the names of officers who are willing to stay for the work and who will be seconded to the Red Cross. Of course my mind was made up right away and my name went in but I haven't hopes that anything will come of it. Now you know the worst so if I don't come home you will know the reason.

But if we come home I want you to come to Victoria (or Vancouver) and meet us. I don't know what our fate there will be but I shall have some time and we may be able to go back together. I may cable to you; it will be dependent on the circumstances at the time.

I have applied for leave to go down to Peking but it may not go through. In fact I don't expect it and really am not prepared financially, but Louise wants me to go. However I may have more to tell later. I should know tomorrow.

I went out for a walk just now. We went down the valley to the sea and then climbed to the hills overlooking the bay, across which rise the coast mountains to a heighth of three or four thousand feet. There was a fine view across the valley to the camp and on beyond to the bay. [On] the hills, some of which were still covered with snow, the sun shone through gaps in the cloud and cast wonderful lights everywhere. Really the beauty of the sunsets here is indescribable. Coming out of town last week we emerged from the sordid filthy streets and it was glorious to plunge down the last hill on the Svyatlanskaya and look up to the wonderful hills beyond, towering 1000 or 1200 feet above the city—bare of vegetation like southern Alberta and bathed in their soft colours of evening—a pink that gradually deepened to heliotrope. To think that so glorious a country is not appreciated.

Well I am going to give you a long talk some of these times on the country so will reserve what I have to say.

Goodbye, dear, I must get ready for dinner.

Your own

Stuart

Rumours and stories mentioned above found their way into the Alberta press, and the following excerpt from one of her letters suggests that Edna, while not happy about it, would not have been surprised had he stayed on with the Red Cross; she did encourage him to make the trip to China to visit his sister:

Well, the papers say you are all to come home in the spring. Of course that is delightfully indefinite, though I suppose that if you get an opportunity of seeing the country you'll make the most of it. Louise says the fare to [visit] them would only be about $50 so that wouldn't be bad. I hope you are able to go. [4]

While the letter below again reflects the prevailing racial attitudes of the time, the keen powers of observation, insight, and objectivity of the scholar are apparent in Stuart's assessment of Siberia and its peoples; the last passage bespeaks his tragic view of the revolution.

GORNOSTAI BAY, MARCH 17, L9L9

My Dear Little Girl:—

Here it is a beautiful day in spring and I have done nothing. But to tell the truth I over did it yesterday. . . . I have been working very hard on the books lately and mess work generally so I just decided to beat it in spite of everything, so it was "over the hills and far away" for me to Second River. But more of that later. I must recapitulate the things that have occurred since I last wrote. . . .

Well, I heard from my application for leave to Peking. It was turned down but I was invited to make my application again after the 27th. So it may go through all right. It was very strongly recommended by the O.C. you know. Did I tell you that I heard from Louise; of course, she is very anxious for me to go. Percival would meet me at Tien Tsin [Tianjin] and pilot me up country. However it is all off just now.

There is so much uncertainty in the air just now as to our going anywhere that we have just given up even hoping. It seems generally agreed that we are going home shortly but no doubt there are circumstances that affect our departure of which we know nothing. Some of the men and officers are going up to Omsk tomorrow with trains. I wish I could ring in a trip like that; wouldn't it be fine to go up loaded with films. But never mind I may get some if we go to Pekin. Or there is a rumour that we may stop in Japan for a few days. . . .

Now as to prospects of staying in the country, I don't really know what these are. As I told you there is a crying need for work of such a character [relief work] but I have grave doubts as to whether it will materialize. Of course the Americans are doing most of it now and naturally getting all the credit for it. What the British would do I don't know but I guess there is need for all the countries to do something. I am crazy to get into work of this kind but of course if it does not materialize I wish to get home at once.

I should like to tell you something about the country and the people, as I said in my last letter, but do not know where to begin. There is so much ground to cover. I am not prepared to speak on Soviet Russia or even the inland of Siberia, or of anything which I have not seen with my own eyes. But of course we see enough in Vladivostok and hear enough of what is going on in Dalnyvostok, as this part of the Amur province is called, to realize what a terrible jumble it all is. First of all you have to start with the native population—Manchurians, on whom everything else is superimposed. They form the base, provide the labour for almost all the outdoor work. Then you have the Chinese who have drifted in and who have monopolized not, as with us, the laundry business, but the provision business and several others. They are clerks in the stores, cashiers in the banks, indeed I had a run in with a fresh young chink with a pink face and a green tie the last time I was in town. They are pretty smooth guys and strut around in their silks and furs or else in very up to date English clothes. Just what the Mongolian is I am not quite sure but I understand they are distinguished by a pigtail; if that is the case, they come fairly close to the Manchurians. Then you have the Koreans who dress in white and are decked out with the most outlandish head gear, I have some snaps of them. The Koreans I understand are emigrants, keep much to themselves and are engaged principally in farming, fishing and trapping. They are very well spoken of and of all the Chinese races are the cleanest and most home loving. Then came the Russian and fastened on the east his autocratic military government to which he raised a monument that will endure for long years— the roads and fortifications that guard the approaches to Vladivostok. When you realize that in every valley lie barracks such as you see in the pictures you may begin to realize what the government have spent here. Someone is today going without his interest payments.

Then the revolution. Well it's a case of putting a round peg in a square hole. It doesn't fit and cannot fit and the same applies to Russia everywhere more or less. They are trying to run before they walk and all that happens is that the theorists play into the hands of the unscrupulous and both ride the poor ignorant peasant to a finish.

Well I have wound up the books tonight and am very tired. Goodnight dearest. Your own.

Stuart

13

Journey to China

&❧ APRIL—MAY, 1919 ❧&

The uncertainty of Canada's role in Siberia as well as the chaotic internal conditions there hampered individual members of the C.E.F. in any planning for the foreseeable future. Stuart was torn between his desires to return home as soon as possible and to stay and participate in what he saw as badly needed service to people suffering enormous losses in the early stages of the civil war in Russia.

GORNOSTAI BAY
MARCH 20, 1919

Dearest:—

Well your first letter in reply to mine from Siberia arrived last night but I must tell you I was a very disappointed boy when I found just one letter awaiting me. I was more than disappointed I can tell you; but I determined to heap coals of fire on your head.

. . . But I have a lot of things to write of.

First of all I attended a lecture tonight given by Sir Bernard Pares, on Russia. He was professor of Russian at the University of London before the war and since the war started has spent most of his time in Russia. He was Lord Kitchener's confidential adviser on Russia before Kitchener's death. He was with the armies at the time of the break up and in Petrograd during the troublous times of 1917. Well it was a rare treat to hear him talk on Russia and to hear the naked unvarnished truth. He brands the Bolsheviks without hesitation as an outcast and the enemy of all civilization.

Well Honey a very sad thing has happened in our midst. Sunday when two of our companies went into Vladivostok on guard one of the officers dropped out with the intention apparently of returning to camp as he was sick. He failed however to turn up and when they searched for him yesterday he was found near the road about a mile from camp shot through the head, evidently suicide. It is a terrible thing. [He] was a very fine fellow; I don't know all his troubles but he has been quite unwell since our arrival. He was most popular and I sure liked him, though lately when he took to drinking there was a sort of coolness between us.

Well, darling, about staying in the country. I felt, though I wished to go home, that the only thing for me to do was to offer my services and do anything I could to heal this running sore. I would like to stay but my heart flies back every night to you and to the home we both want off in dear Canada. I get mad sometimes when I think of not going back. Of course it may not go through. There is a bare chance that if I do stay you might come out, but I would not encourage you to build on that. It would certainly be fine. Now I am not going to stay here one minute longer than you want me to or unless I am useful. You don't know how I miss you—oh dear, Honey you don't know what homesickness is. Now don't forget to write. I am going to write every day from now on if I possibly can. As to mother's [financial] assignment, I shall fix it up from this end, i.e. have a remittance put through and then an assignment from March. The papers came all right and were much enjoyed. Goodnight. God bless you.

Stuart

In the spring of 1919, Sir Bernard Pares landed in Vladivostok and embarked on a speaking tour that began with what he described in his memoirs as "the curious addresses that I was to deliver in Siberia." He made preparations there for a long trip west by rail, obtaining stores from the American depot and exceptional travel arrangements from the British Railway Minister. He was given a small private carriage which he was allowed to hitch to any train that he chose. As for the lectures, he said,

I provided myself with enormous posters announcing my lectures, which were designed to give some idea of the nature, spirit, and limits of our co-operation with the Russians. I had planned three and gave them first in Vladivostok. . . . The first was an acknowledgement of the obligation of the Allies to Russia and was a description of what I had seen of the fighting on the Russian front. The second. . . was a historical sketch of the labour movement in England. . . . In these two lectures I wished to make clear first, that the end of the war did not terminate our obligations, and second, the conditions which governed our performance of them and which ruled out any participation of ours in Russian internal affairs. In the third lecture I tackled all the current questions of the moment, and tried to give a view of them which I thought might fairly represent our own [British] public opinion.[1]

Stuart Tompkins attended the third lecture, which was given on 20 March,[2] and he reported it to Edna in the letter above. This chance encounter was the first of several intermittent meetings and dealings between Tompkins and Pares, the last of which occurred in 1945 when Stuart tried unsuccessfully to include Norman, Oklahoma, on Pares' post-war lecture tour of the United States.[3]

Stuart was somewhat in awe of what he was witnessing, and the tone of his letters from Siberia differed a bit from that of previous letters. They were long on descriptive narrative and most were shorter on affirmations of love.

GORNOSTAI BAY, SIBERIA
MARCH 24, 1919

My Dearest:—

Imagine my unadulterated joy when I returned on Saturday morning and found three or was it four letters waiting for me.

I went to town on Friday to get supplies from ordnance. As they could not come out till Saturday and as I had to be there when they were loaded I decided to go out to Second River for the afternoon and sleep in town that night. I got back at ten o'clock, went straight to a comfortable bed at West Barracks and turned in. Early in the morning I was up and away, made arrangements for the supplies and returned to West Barracks for breakfast. There were two other 260th officers there so we decided to drive out together. We got a droshka at the station and drove out. It was a beautiful though rather chilly morning, but we were home at eleven.

Sunday, i.e. yesterday, we decided to walk up the coast to one of the Korean fishing villages. We set off about 9:30 over the hills. The morning was raw and cold. We stopped for lunch in a ravine about 12:00 and reached the Korean village about quarter to one, met the head man and arranged to get tea. Most of the houses were mere mud and wattle houses with hollow logs for chimneys, but this one, whatever the material, was painted white and had a galvanized iron roof. So you must not run away with the idea that these people are all savages. The man himself wore an olive green tunic like the Italians with characteristic breeches. Most of the others were dressed in a fashion that was a compromise. We were ushered into the building through the low entrance and saw across the room a half dozen women squatted on the floor at dinner. They had a couple of low tables or stools in front of them on which their dishes were arranged. They ate with chopsticks and spoons. A very high pitched altercation followed. At least one of the women objected strenuously to our entrance. But that apparently wore off. As our eyes got more used to our surroundings we saw that the room was divided into two parts. One part consisted of a raised platform covered with straw matting. You were supposed to take off your boots when you stepped on to this. But we did not do so. The women were barefoot, dressed in a sort of Western way, waist and skirt. Near the middle of the room we discovered a boiler and from the activities that went on in the basement, we discovered that the fire was built there for supplying the house with heat and hot water. It is of course covered. Across the room was a sort of rack or series of shelves on which they arranged their dishes— mostly bowls, some porcelain some brass. Clothes were hung in quite a civilized manner on the wall. There was an inner room from which people emerged from time to time and to which the women withdrew. There were several Russian men in the building and at least one Russian woman. How they were connected I do not know but the conversation—a good deal of it at any rate—was in Russian. The young Korean who brought us in entertained us with talk about Canada, the States and the present situation. He railed bitterly at the Japs from which you can fairly well gather how popular they are in this country. They hope that the Peace Conference will intervene on their behalf and secure their independence—though heaven only knows what they would do with it.

Well we sipped our tea—left the photograph with which we were charged to present them and came away. We came back along the shore, where some fishermen were working at their boats—one of them came off with a load of very large crabs which he offered to me, two for a rouble. But I did not want a load. I reached home about four; as I was dog tired I went to bed early and have been in bed all day.

I don't know that I have much more to tell you. I hesitated to write very full letters now after your last reference to mine. I suppose I am needlessly sensitive. But everything I have seen I have noted down for you. . . .

Now my own Honey sweetheart, I come to other things and that is myself and yourself. You may not be interested in other things, but you are interested I think in whether I still love you and whether I am changed. Dearest, I think I have run the gamut of emotion's sensations since I came out here and I really think I look on life with a deeper broader view than ever before. You know Browning's "Come and grow old with me." Well it is literally true. You may have thought we plumbed the depths of life when we were first married and we experienced that awe and thrill of our early days together. But we didn't. For Life holds out even greater things. I have often wondered at the course of our love. . . . [A] man from his makeup is subject to peculiar temptations. However I was resolved that at least that one thing our union should be spared. I went through the temptation I told you all about. But I have been surprised at how easy it has become to me. There simply is only one girl for me and I couldn't even remotely dream of any other girl in that way. Now that may not be any satisfaction to you but it is to me. . . . It is a very wicked world around us, but we are the captains of our own souls and I think the masters of our fate.

Now this is very general but I am not preaching at you or want you to be otherwise than what you are. I married you for what you were. Is my ideal of the years to come untrue or vain that we should come to love one another as never before—. . . to know that there is between us perfect devotion because there is between us perfect candour, perfect understanding, a recognition of our mutual needs and a determination to share our great gift with the world. Oh darling, teach me unselfishness and purity that our love may be without blemish.

Now—a practical point. I hear we may be given an opportunity to go up the line. Whether to accept it or not is the question of the hour for me. I feel I could do good—but I am thinking of you. Before you get this I shall have decided.

I am sorry you didn't ask Reith to write. He won't write to me. Where did he go. Do you know.

... My batman is bringing me supper in bed. French toast.

Stuart

GORNOSTAI BAY
MARCH 26, 1919

My own Dearest:—

Here it is Wednesday night and two days since I have written you. But of course things are not exactly exciting. No, I am not going to fall into such a way of talking. But really as far as events go, little enough happens. We have rumours of trouble or attempted trouble but nothing comes of it at all. There is no evidence of the slightest disturbance in town. I was in town yesterday but felt so wretched that it was almost a night mare, but I had to go. I got a lift both in and out so it was at least tolerable and I profited by the occasion to pay a visit to the British Mission and ask them about employment, but I don't think I can stay in the country. I simply get too homesick for words. But I went and interviewed a major who questioned me in Russian to which I answered fluently enough. It looks all right but when I think of months more without seeing you—why I cannot bear the thought. I am sometimes afflicted by a doubt that you may not understand me. I don't set so much store by my own opinion and standards but I have tried to play absolutely fair with you... do you love me? My heart cries out for some answer across the six thousand miles of ocean—and none seems to come. Love is such a terrible burning reality—a flame that will not be quenched. . . . But its impelling power is laid on me and I can not say it nay.

Anything I have said I have said out of love... [but] why attempt to put into words what can only be felt.

I was not feeling any too well today so was in bed most of the time—felt much like I did a year ago. However I shall probably be better in the morning.

Good night dearest,

Stuart

❧

The Siberian intervention had never been popular in Canada, and it had soon become apparent that any hopes for Canadian economic advantage in Siberia were ill-founded. By the end of January 1919, Prime

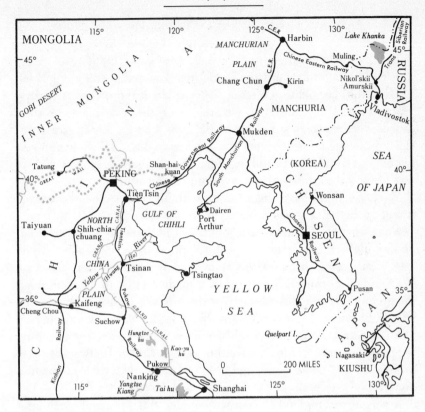

Minister Borden had informed Lloyd George that Canadian forces would be withdrawn from Siberia as soon as possible.[4] By the end of March, coping with the battalion's mess accounts had made life in Vladivostok unpleasant for Stuart, and time was running out on his hopes of visiting his sister Louise in China. But on the first of April he received a two-week leave. He always thought that a deciding factor in his securing the leave was Colonel Jamieson's feeling of obligation to him for having denied him seniority to which he was entitled in the battalion. Jamieson knew Stuart was supernumerary and "excess to the establishment," hence long leave could be granted him. The British Railway Mission in Vladivostok arranged space for him as far as Harbin [Haerphin] on a train that was taking British officers "up country to Omsk to act as trainers of the Russian soldiers that they hoped to use in upsetting the Bolsheviks."[5]

NEARING HARBIN
MANCHURIA, APRIL 5, 1919

My Dearest Little Girl:—

Well I am a bit farther from home than I was, and still going. I left Vladivostok day before yesterday and to put it more correctly, early yesterday morning, and now we are out on the wide plains of Manchuria. The last week at Gornostai Bay was a perfect nightmare. I was closing out the mess accounts and worked night and day, even now I am not over it. There is nothing much to tell about it. However there was always the consolation [leave] might go through.

Well now that I have had a season with my fountain pen I trust that it will go better. It gives promise of so doing.

Now what am I to tell you about? Well I was ready to go on Wednesday night, fairly early [2 April]. I suppose I should really tell you first how I came to be on this train. When I landed up in town on Wednesday morning I first went to Canadian H.Q. to find out about things in general. I was directed by them to the British Railway Mission from whom I got particulars about trains. A train was going up that night and on the advice of the consul, I postponed my arranging for passport until getting to Harbin; so the British Railway Mission promised that I could go on that train so I can save at least so much of my fare.

It was nearly midnight when we boarded the train, and much later when we pulled out of Vladivostok. We awoke in the morning late, and as far as I was concerned, dead dog tired, but I managed to get breakfast and felt very better for it.

Well we have finally reached Harbin and I am leaving tonight for Mukden [Shenyang]. I have given Harbin the once over and was taken in tow by an American who took me to lunch.

Your own,
Stuart

The letter above was never mailed. Stuart later found it, together with the following journal-like entries, in a small notebook that he had carried with him on the trip.

Near Muling, on the Chinese Eastern Railway, April 1919. British officers waited on a siding for track repairs so they could continue on to Harbin.

Places on the Trans Siberian [and the Chinese Eastern] Railway

Nicolsk-CT Nikol'skii Amurskii [Ussuriysk]—Quite a large place, the junction of the Chinese Eastern with the Amur Valley line, formerly a scene of activity against the Bolsheviks. Arrived here during the morning [3 April 1919], took a walk with Captain Archer.

We stopped at another place during the afternoon, where we saw one of [Ataman] Kalmikoff's [armoured] trains, which I snapped from the front—picturesque country.

Muling—a big place where we halted for some hours owing to a smash up in which three trains were involved. A fair amount of interest to be seen. We had a game of football and other amusements while the track [was] being repaired. The country we ran through the afternoon before and this morning [is] extremely like southern Alberta, much open prairie with little sign of cultivation.

Dashmagoya—here a Chinese guard turned out for one of their generals I took a picture of this and of the valley.

Kudan'tsam—took a picture of Archer [illegible]—two kiddies, stockade, [and a] cart; big Manchurian town. The country gradually became rougher, sharp hills rising out of the plains. Towards evening we reached [Khandokhetszi]—a large town in the mountains. Here we were passed by General Jack with his special. Left here at eight o'clock. Next morning we were running through a less picturesque but more wooded and cultivated country around Harbin, more habitations. We reached Harbin about 10:30, and I at once proceeded to make arrangements re going south.

April 4th.

Left Harbin at 8:40 that night, arrived Chang Chun [Changchun] at 8:00 a.m. and left at 12:00—very sick all morning and all day. Since leaving Harbin we have been getting into better and better cultivated country.... I take it we are in China proper—every inch of land cultivated, one vast dust heap, no trees... in the distance, dreary, dusty looking mountains, mud villages, and mud baked cart tracks connecting them. I am anxious to get some pictures but the light is very bad.

Several strange things to be noted.

Enclosures marked with stones and containing piles of earth and sometimes trees.

What look like small shrines scattered everywhere.

While trees are very scarce, you see from time to time groves (very beautiful ones) of fir trees apparently carefully tended. [Stuart later noted that these were obviously cemeteries.]

Everywhere on the fields, little symmetrical piles of earth or fertilizer.

CHANG CHUN
APRIL 7, 1919

Dearest:—

For the first time in four days I am travelling in comfort and am taking advantage in the circumstances to write a short letter. Really the last few days have been so crowded that I have not had leisure or energy to write. But I have the whole afternoon before me until we reach Mukden to write. We reached Harbin about 10:30 yesterday morning. The weather was overcast but became warm and sultry as the day wore on. As soon as possible I got out and visited the Royal Transport Officer to get particulars from him about trains and soon learned that I should not be able to get away that day. Warren (Sgt) who accompanied us from Vladivostok came with me to hunt up a restaurant. I accosted a young American in civies who was talking to an officer. At first he offered to give us directions but afterwards insisted on us coming to his own apartments. He first took me over to the American hospital and there I met some American girls. From there we returned about 1:30 and reached his rooms at 2 o'clock. There lunch was served by his Chinese servants and a very nice lunch it was. I went down to the station again and reported to the R.T.O. but was advised to go up and see the British consul. That I did but he was not at home. On my way back I stopped at a tea room where I met a young Italian officer. Having a sort of introduction to a Captain LeHain, I hunted up his car which stood on the siding. He insisted on taking me up to the consul to settle the question of the credentials I should have. That decided I went around with LeHain calling on a young Canadian couple who are living in Harbin, Major Carvell formerly of the Princess Pats. It was just like getting home and we had a most enjoyable time after which I returned to the station and arranged the details of my departure. I left Harbin last night for Chang Chun in a first class coupe which means a compartment. I had it all to myself but guided by the conductor a young Russian couple intruded themselves. I should not have tolerated it only the woman could get nowhere to sleep and I really needed only half of it. But they were most rude and ungracious. We reached Chang Chun about eight. I was sick as a dog and to make things worse I could get no room at the hotel. However a young South African whom I met allowed me to wash and shave in his room. I had no breakfast but got a cold lunch before leaving. So am all right. I am now in a real honest to goodness train—a typical Canadian 1st class carriage and I have two seats with a table to write on. Everything is beautifully clean and the only thing to remind me I am in the East is the gibberish of Chinese going on. They don't all travel third class I can tell you.

Now how can I describe to you all about this wonderful, wonderful trip. From the moment we left Vladivostok, it has been crowded with interest. The first two days took us over the rolling plains of Manchuria, an extraordinarily fertile country so much like Alberta—miles and miles of rolling grass lands with the sun sinking in a golden haze behind the horizon. Gradually we left the Russians behind and there was nothing but Chinese. As you near Harbin the country gradually becomes more broken. Ragged broken hills rise from the plain in all directions half covered with trees but that does not prevent the most intense cultivation. Harbin is in the centre of a vast uninteresting plain—sprawling out like another Winnipeg to the four points of the compass. It impresses you so much like a Western boom city which of course it really is. There are four cities—Old Harbin, New Harbin, Prislan and Leng Chin or something of the kind—the Chinese part. I saw only the new town where are the railway offices, consular offices etc etc all housed in up to date buildings some of them very fine. But there is no water system nor sewage system. The roads are wide but ill paved and unwatered and the dust rolls up in cyclones. Though Russian influence is strong, the Chinese predominate—coolies every where and Chinese sentries at every street corner. Really I thought Vladivostok wonderful but it is a back woods town compared with Harbin—so much wealth, poverty, misery, vice jostling one another every where. It was indescribable. I did not get any pictures but hope to have some time when I go back. Now I am out of the Russian sphere of influence which ends at Chang Chun—have changed to the standard gauge Japanese line and am on my way for Mukden which we will reach tonight. Really I do not like the Japs. I was told that a passport would not be necessary and came away from Harbin strong in confidence. However a little undersized Jap came past me in the car, slid into one of my seats and began to interrogate me. I was fairly civil to him but became exasperated and turned on him and asked him who he was. He admitted he was a gendarme so I asked him why he didn't come through with that information before. A train official came down the car and said something to my friend in Japanese. He answered and then apologized to me for the man interrupting. He had been asking whether the train should start. In spite of the gendarme's explanation that the man was a new comer, I believe that the train has to be held till he gives the say so. Just while I have been writing this we stopped and a Japanese soldier came aboard and patrolled up and down the car. I don't like them at all, but they do run a real train. Ain't I going to have a good sleep this afternoon. I had a good lunch and should be able to sleep.

Well Honey I wish you were here—such a hurrying scurrying— mad ancient modern—topsy turvy country I never saw. While I was at the station last night, a train load of coolies came in—thousands of them in herds like cattle. They scuttled off the train when it stopped and swarmed across the yards. Many got lost in the gathering dusk and they called to one another like cattle. What a strange land.

Well I am very tired, must close now to have a sleep.

Stuart

[Journal entry in small notebook]

The train I am on today April 8th is an English train in contradistinction to the very fine American one that brought me down from Chang Chun to Mukden—with every comfort in the world. Last night I got dinner at the Yamata Hotel and left myself too little time, was almost bundled into the train by my coolie. I expected at least a sleeper, but no such luck—was bundled into a compartment with a Chinese officer and his servant. Thank God his nibs left at daybreak, since which time I have been comfortable.

TIEN TSIN
APRIL 9TH, 1919

Dearest, dearest Honey:—

Two years ago tonight we were lying out in the wet and snow too miserable and cold even to sleep and here I am tonight in a most comfortable hotel in the most peaceful part of the East. That statement may sound exaggerated when you think of what you have read in the papers, but I find that the idea here is that Vladivostok is the centre of disturbance while in the north we thought Tien Tsin [Tianjin] was the seat of trouble and so goes the world. Now I could sit down and write you a most interesting letter if I thought you wanted to hear them. My last letter was written in a blue funk and wrung from my pen by sheer will power.

So I am going back to [start at] Mukden. I shook the dust of that ancient city off my shoes within an hour of reaching it. The Japanese train rolled in about 8:30 and at 9:30 we were on our way south. It was nearly a tragedy for me as a conversation I had with an American officer kept me late. I know I boarded my train in great confusion and it was only [by] the coolie's instinct and not my own prevision that I found my baggage there. And when I boarded the train my nerves were even more badly upset. I found there was no sleeper. It was an English corridor train and every compartment was full of Chinamen who had all the doors locked. I stamped from end to end of the first class carriage and finally dumped my luggage down in the aisle of the big, though over crowded, rear smoking compartment while I went forward and stood in the darkened corridor. Then along comes a chink mind you—a brakie or a guard and abused me roundly for leaving it there. Maybe I didn't feel sore at the world in general—to be talked to like that and in addition to be cursed I suppose for a stupid idiot for not understanding him. The tables were indeed turned on the white race. Finally I did enlist the services of a civilized Chinaman who spoke English and tackled the aforesaid porter. The latter assured me a place so soon as some of the Chinese officers left the train at one of the first stations. So I possessed my soul in patience for the first ten or fifteen miles. You really mustn't mind the writing, my pen is acting abominably tonight. Well in a few minutes the train stopped and there was a bowing and scraping in one of the near compartments and next minute I was bundled unceremoniously into a compartment. Here sat what looked like an ancient Chinese general. He was dressed in civilized clothes as far as that went but he might otherwise have stepped out of the Ming dynasty. He seemed to resent my intrusion but I didn't mind and the first opportunity I had I pacified him with cigarettes, for which he was grateful. It was quite neatly done and I don't think any of the great powers have it on me for diplomacy. Well I didn't mind the old fellow except his smell. I did want to get that window open. However, I was on my good behaviour that night, insisted on the young aide lying at full length while I propped myself against the end of the seat and slept. At four a.m. a porter shoved in his head and the Ming dynasty aroused himself and got out. Again a bowing and scraping. This time I saluted. The younger Ming and I then shared the compartment and both stretched at full length. I slept till about six. When I looked out the land was already awake. We were sliding through a vast gray country—ridge and furrow, ridge and furrow—the country roads made spider tracks across its expanse and the little villages were like dusty islands in a sea of dust. Smoke curled from the mud roofs of the houses and John Chinaman went afield with his donkey to till the land. Never did one behold such vast and tireless energy. The whole prairie for unbroken hundreds of miles worked and reworked until the humus was gone and there is nothing but a dust heap over which the wind plays as over the desert. Honey it was awe inspiring. It took you back through the long centuries and called up the countless generations whose lives have been bounded by one village who have sown and tilled and reaped and died, like the human ants they are.

Well this is China—indescribable but overwhelming in its antiquity. The impression it made I shall not soon forget. At every station now the platforms were crowded with a yelling gesticulating mob trying to sell you something—fruit cakes, eggs, fried chicken—anything to tempt the hungry traveller. But I was so interested I could not be hungry. I shoved up the window while the young officer slept and fairly drank in the scenes. About nine o'clock he awoke, brushed his boots, put on his belt and then started a pantomime for my benefit apparently intimating that I should do likewise. I resented it at first but thought better of it. In a few minutes the train stopped—the door opened, a coolie rushed in, grabbed my baggage and disappeared with it. I rushed after him but he was half way up the stairs to the railway bridge across which all the travellers were hurrying so I decided to go with the crowd and sure enough we found another train waiting for us across the platform to take us to Tien Tsin. I had not known of this transfer though I suspected something would happen when we reached—I can't supply the name [Shanhaikwan]. I was on the lookout for the Great Wall and as we rolled into the town I snapped the wall on the off chance—and later discovered it to be the real wall.

Well I take back all I said about the Chinese Government railways. I again found myself on a real honest to goodness train with a real dining car on. Say didn't I have a real breakfast. Then I sat in the smoker and languished. It kept getting hotter and hotter—the wind rose and the atmosphere became heavy with great clouds of dust that rolled to heaven. All afternoon we travelled through a hot flat dusty plain and at 4:45 rolled into Tien Tsin—where I found—no Percival. But that begins my story of Tien Tsin which I must reserve.

I had a long, philosophic, homely thought out for you tonight but you will be spared. Oh dear, I wish I were with you tonight. I could take you in my arms and tell you all about it. I am afraid otherwise you wouldn't understand me. But of this be assured darling I love you more than ever, not less, and some day I shall prove it and meanwhile I am doing without mail from you.

Well goodnight sweetheart, it is now 10:30 and I must to bed.

Your own
Stuart

Stuart wrote no more letters until he reached his sister's home, the Presbyterian mission at Siu Wu [Siuwu] in the north of Honan Province, where he then recounted the rest of his journey. Before leaving Vladivostok he had agreed to buy fabric and souvenirs for his fellow officers, and as the letter below indicates, he took the first opportunity to shop for them.

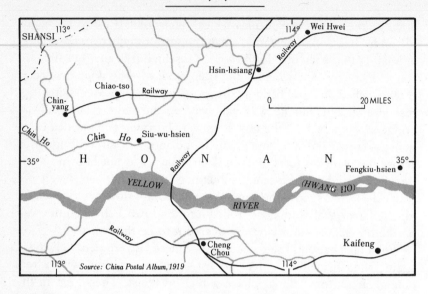

SIU WU HSIEN   HONAN CHINA
APRIL 14, 1919

My Dearest Honey:—

Well here I am in Honan of which you have heard so much and of which no doubt you are bored to death. I don't want to tell you a lot of things you have heard before, strange as they may seem to me. But I am not exaggerating when I say that I have enjoyed every minute of my trip sick and all as I was. I forget where I left myself in my last letter sent from Tien Tsin. But I think it must have been at Chang Chun or was it Mukden. At any rate I left Chang Chun at 12 noon on the Japanese train—a real train once more with American coaches and engines and we ticked off the rails just as you would between Edmonton and Calgary. Side seats—double just as you would at home. I just lay back and enjoyed it all and ate my dainty Japanese lunch. We reached Mukden at 8 o'clock and I got dinner at the station where I changed to the Mukden-Peking line. At dinner I met an American officer Colonel Baldwin just over from Tokyo. I caught the night train for Peking [Beijing]—was amazed that there was no sleeper but arranged to get along, reaching Tien Tsin the next afternoon about 4:45. No Percival to meet me, so I made enquiries at the station and was recommended to go to the Imperial Hotel. Here I had my first ricksha ride, a delightful experience I assure you. We reached the hotel in five minutes, I had tea, a bath and dinner. I talked with some people around the hotel, got their advice as to buying and then went to bed—not however before wiring to Percival. Next morning I was hardly up before I had a reply from him saying he would be up next day; so I got fixed up and proceeded to do some shopping. Oh I wish you had been here for that. I revelled in silks and satins all day besides buying a few things for myself—gloves, etc. Everything imported was of course dear but not more so than in Edmonton I think. But of course I had to fall for some of the stuff trumped up for tourists around the hotel. Whether I was stung or not I do not know and do not care. I satisfied myself. I really had a great day. Must tell you more about it later. I got a few pictures in the morning but in the afternoon another terrible dust storm such as was raging on my arrival came up and obliterated everything. So had another bath and went to bed early. Thursday morning I was up early hired a ricksha and was away with my camera, into the Italian concession to take some pictures of the beautiful houses there. I had a fine time for about an hour then had breakfast and went out to do a bit more shopping. I finished my rounds early and got back in good time for tiffin. By the way, tiffin is the word used here for lunch. I don't know why and I don't like it but people stare at you if you say lunch. I was just getting ready to go down to eat when Percival was announced and came up. I don't need to tell you all we had to say to one another; we had to cut that part of it short as he had a good deal of business to do. We went out got rickshas and made our rounds, getting back about two. We decided to go on to Peking that day and at 4:45 got away, travelling third class. I had a great shock at first getting in among the Chinese but I guess it did me good. I saw their habits and manners at closer range and saved money. Our run was through a flat sandy uninteresting country apparently at all times liable to flood from the waters of the Pei Ho. It was nearly dark when we ran through the outer wall of Peking and we soon found ourselves at a very modern station in the heart of that ancient city. You won't be interested in knowing the details of the difficulties we had in getting accommodation. We did however get accommodation for the night and after a large and substantial dinner sank away into a dreamless sleep, not disturbed by the the moon or the weird night cries of this extraordinary city.

Well I was up betimes in the morning and the first thing I saw was a camel train going down the street out towards the East gate of the city with the tinkling of bells. Well Honey do you remember those days of sightseeing in London; well I lived them over again in Peking. Percival is a driver and we just set our teeth and saw everything we set our hearts on. First the cloisonne works on the Hataman Street a little

Peking street scene, April 1919.

place back in a maze of court yards where we saw the cloisonne in the process of manufacture under the direction of a fat pleasant faced Chinaman who spoke English. The equipment looked very crude but they do beautiful work. I bought one or two articles. Then to the Imperial and the Forbidden cities. It is pretty hard to describe without a diagram and I shall try to get one, also a bit of history. The arches and palaces which were in great profusion are most beautiful but the effect is rather gained by the arrangement of courtyards and stair ways and approaches than by the grandeur of the building itself. The forbidden city has of course been accessible ever since it was entered in 1900. I won't attempt to describe these things. We then rode around the north side of the Imperial City to the drum and bell towers then to the Confucian and Buddhist temples. The former was very remarkable for its grove of ancient and stately cypresses of which I took a picture. I also took a picture of a prayer wheel in the Buddhist temple which should be of interest. We got home for tiffin at two and did not leave again till four when we visited the temple of Heaven away south in the Chinese city. This completed our day and we left on the night train for the south. Well, goodnight dear.

Your own—
Stuart

SIU WU HSIEN

APRIL 17, 1919

Dearest:—

How the days do slip away in spite of everything and I have not yet got caught up with my narrative. I think I got you up to Peking and our day's peregrinations. I often thought of our first days in London. I was done out by five o'clock when we dragged ourselves away from the Temple of Heaven. Our rickshas took us next into the shopping district but it was too late to do much. I bought only a couple of trifles. We had dinner and made ready to get away on the night train for the south. I urged [Percival] to go third class. I wanted to save money and I know he did so we packed ourselves in amid a crowd of Chinese and slept sitting up. It was close and uncomfortable but most interesting. I was the centre of attraction for the whole car for the Chinese don't hesitate to show their curiosity. One old gentleman with a long beard leaned over and asked in a voice loud enough for the whole train to hear, why we didn't travel second class so Percival answered quite frankly that it cost too much—it was of course unanswerable logic.

Morning found us still rolling over a monotonous plain cut only by roads and dry river beds. We gradually got elbow room as the crowds thinned. Percival shaved and I washed. We had breakfast and settled down. The day was fairly cool which was most providential. We filled in the time mostly by eating—Chinese buns and cakes and once a basin of rice and eggs. We had one change, at Shin Shang Shien [Xinshang] and at five thirty or so reached Siu—we had now I may say left all white behind—nothing but yellow grinning faces.

Louise came over in a Sedan chair with the kiddies and we all walked back through the wheat fields. Say I had a sleep that night after a bath—slept in till noon next day—oh boy. In the afternoon we went in state to call on the local mandarin—some side eh. Well I am a local lion you know. We rode in state in a donkey cart such as you might see in the west of Ireland—a terrible thing. It looks like a dog kennel on wheels—you crawl inside and curl up while the thing rocks you from side to side. Well that was one conversation I did not monopolize. But I horned in now and again. By the way, though, when I sent my card over the gate keeper who took it proclaimed me a brigadier so I got not only a present [arms] from the sentry but all the good man's hangers on turned out to see me. I am sure I am the only British officer that they had seen.

Louise and Percival certainly have a nice home here. They live in a real European house in an immense compound with a great retinue of servants—formidable and impressive in number only. The grounds of course suffered in last year's flood. They are nearly half a mile from town and a mile and a half from the station. Siu is a walled town population probably 1500 exclusive of animals. We would call it a wretched huddle of buildings. I shall get some photos of it. Otherwise it will be impossible to describe it. The buildings with the exception of the very best are of mud. The country here is a great wheat growing plain—a range of mountains to the north. If I were to be here longer I should explore them. Monday was a quiet day—but yesterday, Tuesday, we went up to Chiao Tso [Tsiatso], a mining town with something of a European population. Here is where Percival expects to settle in the fall. He took me around and showed me everything including the mines and pumps. We had dinner at Dr. McCullough's, the mine doctor, where I was right royally entertained. Percival having to be absent at a class I stayed with the doctor until called for at ten. We went back on a late freight train and walked home in the moonlight at 1:30 a.m. to find Louise up. She had hot milk for us and we rolled in to find a sweet oblivion.

Today the mandarin called on me, but more of that later. He was announced about two p.m.—in fact we were still loitering over dinner—fortunately I was in war paint. Louise and the kiddies disappeared. Percival and I went down to meet him in approved Chinese style and kow-towed—not literally of course. Well sir we had one fine thing. He smoked cigarettes till he oozed smoke at every pore and sitting in the Morris chair talked on every subject under heaven—in fact he railed at the Japs; their oppression of Korea and their harsh dealings with China; the opium trade—the missionaries—the corruption in public life in China—the trouble between North and South. In fact Percival was amazed at his frankness. As I couldn't talk to him I plied him with cigarettes which his secretary lit for him in his long cigarette holder. When he got up to go I got a photograph of him. Honey, you will scream when you see it. But I must go to bed. Percival and Louise have already gone.

Your own
Stuart

SIU WU HSIEN CHINA
APRIL 18, 1919

Dearest:—

The proper time for me to have started this letter was last night when we were sitting around but I felt tired and relaxed. Well I took you along in my last letter to the visit of the mandarin and the subjects he discussed; really Percival was surprised at his frankness—he admitted the corruption at Peking. When he displayed his hatred of the Jap, I asked him whether if the Jap were run out the people of China could really keep him out; he admitted it depended on north and south getting together. Then he discussed Christianity and ancestor worship; he thought mission work would be more successful if some concessions were made to Chinese prejudice on the latter line. Well he talked and smoked and drank. You know the custom is not to drink your tea till you are ready to go, but he drank his, then forgot about going. Finally at four o'clock he rose to go and I nudged Percival to ask him if he would like his picture taken. So he posed and his secretary came up and put his little derby on straight. I hope it is a good picture. Then we escorted him to the gate and I snapped his equipage.

Well the next day, that was Thursday, we went up to Chiao Tso for dinner. There was nothing of particular interest unless you would call a big dinner so.

Yesterday was another red-letter day. We went to a country fair near here. We followed the railroad track all the way and found the "fair" overflowing from a village out on to the prairie. We ate our lunch at a good safe distance and did not venture into the fair until afterwards. When we did it seemed as though the whole fair came out to meet us and as we entered the village a sea of blue which is the colour the Chinese wear just flowed round us and closed us in. Of course, the crowd was mostly kiddies curious to see our wheels. By jostling, pushing, threatening and at intervals grabbing someone by the throat, we managed to make progress and to hold them at a safe distance when buying. There was not much to buy as it was just a peasant's fair, but I bought some interesting jim cracks and took some photos. But it was at an awful price for that sweating mob just shut us in and choked us with dust. Well our progress continued for over an hour. Finally just as we were going, Percival had the poor judgment to throw some pennies among the crowd and they broke loose. We were too far from the outskirts and could not jump on our wheels so before we cleared out there was a most unruly mob after us, chasing over the ground on either side of the mob. I had trouble mounting and some of those cheeky kids grabbed my wheel and held it back. I could have bumped their heads together with great glee. However we got away though they did follow us for nearly half a mile or more. Such a crowd I never saw in my life. Their live stock—donkeys, mules, cows, horses, sheep, goats,

Rev. Percival Luttrell escorted his guest, the local mandarin, to the gate of the Presbyterian Mission at Siu Wu, Honan, China, April 1919.

pigs—the greatest rabble, and not one of them worth anything. A couple of hundred dollars would buy them all up.

Well, I will not write more now but I have a lot more to tell you of our trip to the Yellow River yesterday. I am very tired today as a result, but am having a good rest.

Well good bye Honey,

Stuart

[Later]

Well my dear little girl, I am going to continue this letter and tell you what happened yesterday. We went to the Yellow River—striking it at its closest point about 17 miles south of here. It was a long hard

Stuart Tompkins, his sister Louise Luttrell, and her sons Colborne and Kenneth, Siu Wu, Honan, China, April 1919.

hike across country through villages and towns. We had lunch at Moolandyen about eleven miles away—then crossed the Chin River and followed it down to its confluence with the Yellow. It is a very extraordinary country. The rivers are silted up till they are many feet above the surrounding country, so that standing on the dikes which are just above high water level you are looking down on the roofs of the villages. This has disastrous results as you may imagine when the dikes are broken. The Yellow River is very low so that we had to travel for a mile or more across the flood plain before we reached the banks of the river. A few Chinese barges were sailing leisurely down the stream gliding between the sand bars. Across in the distance we could just see through the haze the distant hills. There was nothing entrancing in the scenery. It was a warm lazy afternoon and I think John Chinaman felt the mollifying influence for there was little life. We came back in quite a hurry. It was getting late and we had to make the return journey before dark. We saw a number of interesting things—such as their irrigation pumps and a mill grinding corn. The going was good in the morning but coming back I was tired and we didn't get off to rest just kept going. Wasn't I glad when we hove within sight of the compound and saw Louise and the kiddies waiting for us. I was not sorry to get into some clean things either. We didn't wash before dinner—I mean "oliver" but I was so tired I could not stay up but disappeared.

I was pretty tired this morning but am now feeling better. Percival has gone up to Chiao Tso for his regular Sunday service. Tomorrow Louise, the kiddies and I go on to Wei Hwei [Chihsien] where I give an address. . . .

Well good bye dear,
Stuart

When Stuart found that a two-week leave was not long enough for the trip he had undertaken, he wired back to Vladivostok for an extension and it was granted quite readily.[6] He did not write again until he reached Harbin on the return trip. That letter, more a combination of entries made along the way, was the last from Siberia; written in the small notebook that he carried, it was never mailed. When he returned to Vladivostok, he distributed the silks and other goods that he had bought for friends in the battalion.

HARBIN, APRIL 27, 1919

My Dearest Little Girl:—

Here I am on the home stretch and I have not written you for nearly a week it seems. I have had a terrible time here; it really is the worst part of the trip but I guess I made it worse than it need have been. Well why go into the harrowing details. Everything has been so hurried in the last week. To begin with we went a week ago yesterday to the Yellow River. I really did not feel like going at all but you know Percival was insistent and it seemed a real pity not to take advantage of the opportunity to go when I was there so against my better judgment I went. It was a lovely day and it was keen delight to mount and to speed away through the fields of standing wheat. A pleasant breeze was stirring and it cooled us quite perceptibly. I stood the racket fairly well but a long stretch of sand tired me.

We did not get away till eleven so it was after one when we reached Moolandyen where we had lunch in the chapel. At Moolandyen we visited a couple of Chinese baths. This operation alone occupied an hour or more. The chapel gate keeper led us through a maze of back streets, lanes, alleys, byeways, mews, courtyards, everything. We found one place closed. It had apparently been turned into a gaming joint so we could not observe its operation. We were more fortunate at the other. It was open and in full blast. We went through an outer room to an inner and then into the baths, i.e. the first class ones where you had a cubicle and tub to yourself. The second class ones were a tank in the ground just off the outer room, here the water was in two compartments, one hot, the other warm. How it was heated I do not know but it was boiling hot.

Well, honey, this letter has been neglected. It is now Monday night and getting dark We are just leaving Manchuria, crossing the line into Siberia proper. Well, to resume my story. We left Moolandyen, climbed rather a steep hill to get to the gate, and found ourselves looking out on the level of the Chin River. These rivers all run above the level of the surrounding country. We had another wade through sand to the bridge, a frail timber structure covered with sods and mud. Another stretch of sand and we reached the dikes which we followed to the junction of the Chin with the Yellow River which we reached about three. The Huang Ho leaves very much to the imagination. A wide valley faced with hills on the southern bank but now nearly dry, its several channels winding over its muddy surface. Down the stream were floating the lazy barges with their curious Chinese sails. It was very interesting but we did not stay long. We left for home about four. It was a long hard grind and the edge was worn off our enthusiasm. Once started we stayed with it and reached home at seven. I was very tired but stayed up to dinner, and went to bed at nine.

Next day I felt all right but stayed in all day. In the afternoon I began to feel ill and went to bed good and sick. Next morning we were due to leave for Wei Hwei. I did not like to disappoint them so I pulled myself together and went. Percival had gone to Chiao Tso, however Louise and I looked after things. I rode over in a chair. I note a mistake above. Percival went to Chiao Tso at five o'clock Sunday afternoon but returned late that night. However as he was very tired he elected to remain over in Siu and look after the children.

We reached Wei Hwei Fu at 11 [o'clock] or so, I should explain as you may not know, that this is one of the very large compounds and as Louise and Percival were so long connected with the work there and knew all the people, they were very anxious to show me around. I had a nice time I must admit, was given a dinner that night. . . . I had a good sleep and felt fairly rested when morning came. It brought however rather startling news—a bad railway accident which might prevent Percival joining me on my way to Peking. However we had a later wire from him that he would come down to the junction on a light engine or a wrecking train in time to catch the train for Peking. This he did and we met him at four o'clock when he turned the kiddies over to Louise and came on with me. Goodbyes were all said and my visit was at an end.

We reached Peking early next morning, as we rode into the city through the west wall, we saw numerous trains of camels heavily laden with goods from the interior. On reaching the station we went straight to a hotel, engaged a room, washed, shaved, etc. My stay in Peking was not quite so interesting as the first but I did considerable shopping. In the afternoon [we] walked on the Tartar Wall where so much trouble occurred in 1900. We left at 8:35 from Peking, arrived at Tien Tsin at midnight, when Percival left me. I travelled third class as far as Mukden where I changed to the Japanese line—got away that night for Chang Chun and made Harbin late Friday night.

This letter is being resumed in Vladivostok on Thursday morning.

To return to Harbin. We did not get in till 10:30. I was quite agitated about the possibility of getting quarters so I accepted the offer of a young Jew to take me down to Pristan, the new town and do what he could for me. It was quite the wrong decision as it turned out. A friend of his had a car so we loaded in my baggage and drove off to the Hotel Moderne. They had no rooms but I was directed round the corner to a kind of cheap rooming house and this had to do me. My room was about 8 × 8, had a table, bed, couch, and commode. There was a bed you will note but no bedding and except for a spread and pillow it was quite innocent of such extravagances. However I would have slept on top anyway so that did not matter. In spite of conditions I slept late; I did not mind as I had no money for breakfast, and really wanted to postpone my meal till I could change my Chinese currency.

I had some difficulty in finding a bank but found an American officer who took me in tow. We found a bank—a branch of our old friend the Hong Kong Shanghai—but they would not give me enough so I went out on the street, in fact to the Chinese money changers. We found a street where there was a good deal of this going on so we went from one to another till we got what seemed a reasonable offer. It was only after we had gone down four or five blocks that we began to realize what an enormous amount of business was being done. The street on one side was lined with hundreds of little stands where money was being bought and sold. Who else besides the Chinese were in business was quite obvious from the Hebraic cast of features among Mammon's worshippers. Well I took a picture of it and otherwise occupied considerable time before I realized that it was noon, the time for the departure of my train. But I was hungry and had to eat so I listened to the voice of the tempter in the person of the Yank who assured me the train was travelling late and that I would have time. So I went in the Moderne and ordered my dejeuner—fried chicken, potatoes, compote of fruit, etc. I was a little nervous so as soon as my bill was paid I grabbed a droshka, packed my luggage and paid my bill at the boarding house and started for the station. Of course, the broken-down old ponies travelled like snails, but everything comes to an end and I did reach the station, turned my luggage over to a porter, and rushed out to the platform. A train was standing on one of the tracks and I headed for it. I enquired of a guard if this was the train for Vladivostok and was dumbfounded to hear the word [illegible]. It has gone. However my feelings would not bring it back so I pocketed my mortification and went down to the R.T.O. office. They laughed at my chagrin but assured me I was fortunate to have missed it as I could not have got a seat. They agreed to put me up for the night and get me a good seat next day. So there was nothing for it but to spend the rest of the day and the night in Harbin.

After tea I went out and did a little more money changing and bought some things then went to the Moderne for supper—steak, onions, chips, and tea. I went back to the station for an hour or two watching the crowds passing in and out, saw a Chinese general come down with his retinue to leave for Chang Chun, then located my car and rolled in in a real honest to goodness bed. Next morning after cleaning up I went up town with the R.T.O.'s assistant who is a young Canadian for breakfast. I discovered again what I should have known, that the Russians do not breakfast early or at all. I had some difficulty finding a place where we could have breakfast—however we did get some French toast and coffee. I then went up to get some pictures of the Sungari River after which I returned to the station. The train was not coming in till five, so we went and had lunch then went back and waited. I had a very interesting talk with a Captain Howley who was in the Ural Mountains mining until a few months ago. Well the train came in and if I live to be a hundred I never expect see such a sight— hundreds of struggling angry people—Chinese, Russians, soldiers trying to get on the train, and the sentries and guards using their batons to keep order. It took me nearly ten minutes to find the right car. My coupe had been secured by Lieutenant Wiggins so I moved in and made myself comfortable till the train went at six. I later had to share my coupe but had a bunk to myself so I should worry. We had no diner on the trains so I had to rustle grub at the stations. The second day we stopped at Pogranichnaya [Progranichnyy] where our luggage was examined and a few minutes later crossed the frontier between Manchuria and Siberia. We reached Vladivostok without incident Tuesday morning to find it cold and raining. I reached the camp with a truck about noon and had a great welcome, found 15 letters, three parcels—eight packages of papers. However the fellows persecuted me all afternoon so I decided to divide the stuff and get it off my hands. Hardisty helped me and after making an inventory and assigning stuff to various officers, I made out accounts, etc. After everything was done I finished reading my letters and opened my parcels. It was 12:30 when I rolled into bed thoroughly done out. Next day and today I have been no good and spent most of the time in bed but hope to be better in the morning.

The last entry ended abruptly, and the collection contains no letters written on the return trip to Vancouver. When Stuart undertook to edit those "Letters from Afar," he wrote a postscript to cover the final days of his Siberian adventure.

... Preparations were well under way for our departure. We went back (Hardisty and I) to Second River to bid farewell to our friends there. This farewell was in no sense an *Au revoir* for it was a final and tragic leave taking, as unquestionably they felt that we were leaving them to the tender mercies of the Bolshevik mobs in Vladivostok, hitherto held in check only by the Allied armed forces. On May [9th][7] . . . *the Empress of Japan* entered the Golden Horn. Embarkation proceeded smoothly. We enjoyed the return voyage across a placid Pacific. Not the least part of that enjoyment was association with the civilian passengers, most of whom had come from the British colony of Hong Kong. . . .

On May 20th we entered the Strait of Juan de Fuca, arriving at William Head at midnight where we took on a pilot together with immigration and customs officers. Here we anchored for some hours in order not to reach Victoria during the hours of darkness. Victoria was reached at seven thirty. We berthed at the outer docks where it seemed the whole of Victoria was waiting for us. The *Daily Colonist* reported that the welcome was somewhat more subdued than that received by the 259th Battalion, when the S.S. *Monteagle* docked some days before, though it seemed to my unpracticed ears, noisy enough.

Only those officers and men who had signed on in Victoria were allowed off the ship. Enough time was allowed for reunions and an hour later, the *Empress of Japan* left for Vancouver. Here at the headquarters for Military District 11, the formalities of discharge were gone through with. In addition each man received a travel warrant to his home. So the 260th Battalion was disbanded, and with this the Canadian Expeditionary Force, Siberia, after a somewhat inglorious existence passed into history.[8]

Stuart Ramsay Tompkins, Research Professor of History, Emeritus, University of Oklahoma, 1956. Professor Tompkins spent the academic year 1956–57 as Visiting Professor at the University of Toronto, and then he and Edna retired to Victoria, B.C.

Epilogue

The Siberian experience remained with Stuart all his life, as both a personal and a professional matter. Early in his career at Oklahoma, he undertook an article on that phase of the Allied intervention, and in the course of his search for sources he called on Sir Robert Borden in Ottawa in June of 1935. The former prime minister was well advanced in age by then, and when Stuart asked him why Canada had sent the Siberian Expedition his initial vague response was, "Well, now why *did* we do that?" He went on to give Stuart some background and material relating to Canada's participation, but Stuart's article did not materialize, and the subject waited until after World War II for further exploration by other historians.[1]

In the autumn of 1954 there was an additional epilogue of sorts to Stuart's stay in Siberia. He wrote to the manager of the Russian Center in San Francisco, telling him:

Towards the end of the First World War I was in Siberia and while there became acquainted with a number of Russian families, who lived out at Second River, eight miles from Vladivostok. During this time I took Russian lessons from a young lady who belonged to one of these families. [That] part of my life had been consigned to oblivion when it was suddenly recalled by an incident that occurred last summer. Friends of mine while in San Francisco, having occasion to ask for directions from a woman, struck up an acquaintance with her. She noticed the [Canadian] insignia worn by the man . . . and recalled that she had known a a former Canadian officer in Vladivostok at the end of World War I and mentioned my name. I was astonished that any of my former Siberian acquaintances should be in this country, but I have no way of tracing the woman in question except through some organization such as yours. However, I can give you the name of the girl from whom I took Russian lessons, and it is probable that it is she or one of her family. Her maiden name was Ol'ga Alexandrovna Krasnopol'ska. . . . I should be very glad to renew acquaintance with some of these people after all these years.

I should be very glad to hear from you if you have any suggestions. I might add that if I cannot trace her through you, I will advertise in the Russian Language newspaper in San Francisco.[2]

The advertisement which he later placed in the Russian Language paper brought an answer from Ol'ga, his tutor of thirty-five years past. It obviously was a positive response, and Stuart relied on it when he sought to be excused from Oklahoma's commencement exercises in June of 1955:

I have recently heard from a Russian woman I knew as a girl long ago in Siberia when she gave me my first lessons in Russian. She is now living in San Francisco and her wish to see me is a natural one and one that is not easy to deny in view of the tragic experiences through which she later passed. These may be sentimental reasons but they are none the less insistent.[3]

He received the early leave from campus and he and Edna drove to California, on their way to Edmonton where he would teach the summer term. Apparently Ol'ga had occasion to read his latest book before they arrived, and Edna later recalled clearly the day that they drove to her home:

We drove over from Oakland to San Francisco and found her address. Stuart got out of the car and went in, and she wouldn't talk to him—she wouldn't have anything to do with him. He came back out looking very crestfallen and said, "She won't talk to me.". . . She said it was because he had spoken harshly of her people in his book. Stuart said that wasn't the fault, he said, "We ran out on them and left them to the mercies of the Soviets." And he felt strongly that was the reason she was so resentful.

Stuart personally felt that the Allies' intervening in Russia was a mistake, a mistake that, once made, was compounded by their not staying long enough or doing what was necessary to prevent the "triumph of Bolshevism."[4]

Notes

PREFACE

1. Stuart Tompkins, "The Riddle of Communism: The Quest for an Answer," 1955, typescript, copy in possession of the author, pp. 1–3, emphasis in the original.
2. Stuart Ramsay Tompkins, *Russia through the Ages: From the Scythians to the Soviets* (New York: Prentice Hall, 1940), p. vii.
3. S. E. D. Shortt, *The Search for an Ideal: Six Canadian Intellectuals and Their Convictions in an Age of Transition, 1890–1930* (Toronto: University of Toronto Press, 1976), p. 85.
4. Carl Berger, *The Sense of Power: Studies in the Ideas of Canadian Imperialism* (Toronto: University of Toronto Press, 1970), p. 260 (quotation), and 147.

INTRODUCTION

1. Stuart Tompkins, interview with Jane Fredeman, Vancouver, December 1976.
2. Ibid.
3. Martha Jane Tompkins to Stuart Tompkins, 9 February 1934, letter in possession of the author.
4. Stuart Tompkins, interview with Jane Fredeman, December 1976.
5. Ibid.
6. Stuart Tompkins to Elizabeth A. H. John, 13 November 1974, copy in possession of the author.
7. Martha Jane Tompkins to Stuart Tompkins, 9 February 1934.
8. Edna Tompkins, interview, Edmonton, 2 June 1983.
9. Stuart Tompkins, interview with Jane Fredeman, December 1976.

10. Ibid.

11. Ibid.; Stuart Tompkins to Elizabeth A. H. John, 6 September 1976 (quotation), copy in possession of the author.

12. Stuart Tompkins, interview with Jane Fredeman, December 1976.

13. Ibid.; Edna Tompkins, interview, 2 June 1983.

14. Stuart Tompkins, interview with Jane Fredeman, December 1976.

15. Ibid.

16. Ibid.

17. Edna Tompkins, interviews, 1 and 2 June 1983.

18. Stuart Tompkins, interview with Jane Fredeman, December, 1976.

19. Stuart Tompkins to Elizabeth A. H. John, 13 November 1974.

20. Ibid.

21. Edward Brado, *Cattle Kingdom: Early Ranching in Alberta* (Vancouver: Douglas and McIntyre, 1984), p. 258.

22. Stuart Tompkins to Edna Tompkins, 16 December 1913.

23. Howard Palmer, *Patterns of Prejudice: A History of Nativism in Alberta* (Toronto: McClelland and Stewart, 1982), p. 21; Gerald Friesen, *The Canadian Prairies: A History* (Toronto: University of Toronto Press, 1984), pp. 285 and 339.

24. Friesen, pp. 286 (first quotation), 342 (second quotation), and 343 (third quotation).

25. Ibid., p. 350.

26. Edna Tompkins, interview, Victoria, 3 May 1984.

27. Edna Tompkins, interview, 1 June 1983; Eleanor Houston and Amy Moorhead, interview, Norman, Oklahoma, 17 August 1983; Elizabeth A. John, interview, Santa Rosa, N.M., 17 October 1984.

28. Edna Tompkins, interview, 1 June 1983.

29. Dorothy Mawdsley, interview, Victoria, 3 May 1984.

30. Ibid. (quotation); Edna Tompkins, interview 3 May 1984.

31. Edna Tompkins, interview, 1 June 1983 (first quotation); Dorothy Mawdsley, interview, 3 May 1984 (second quotation). Unless otherwise noted, the information concerning the years in the Yukon is from the author's interview with Edna Tompkins in Edmonton, 1 June 1983.

32. Edna Tompkins, interview, 3 May 1984.

33. Edna Tompkins, interview, 1 June 1983.

34. Jean Potter, review of *Alaska: Promyshlennik and Sourdough*, *New York Times Book Review*, 3 February 1946 (first quotation); Jay Monaghan, review of *Alaska: Promyshlennik and Sourdough*, *Mississippi Valley Historical Review* 32 (March 1946): 609 (second quote); Richard L. Neuberger, review of *Alaska: Promyshlennik and Sourdough*, *Saturday Review*, 29 December 1945 (third quote).

35. Edna Tompkins, interview, 1 June 1983.

36. Ibid.

37. Ibid. (first quotation); Dorothy Mawdsley, interview, 3 May 1984 (second quotation).

38. Edna Tompkins, interview, 1 June 1983.

39. Ibid.

40. Dorothy Mawdsley, interview, 3 May 1984 (quotation); Edna Tompkins, interview, 3 May 1984.

41. Edna Tompkins, interview, 1 June 1983; Stuart Tompkins to Carl Wittke, 24 October 1943, Box: General File A–Z, Stuart R. Tompkins Papers, University of Oklahoma Library.

42. E. E. Dale to Stuart Tompkins, 9 May 1932 (first quotation), E. E. Dale to Stuart Tompkins, 4 April 4 1932 (second quotation), Stuart Tompkins to E. E. Dale, 7 July 1933 (third quotation), all in Box 67, E. E. Dale Papers, University of Oklahoma Library; Edna Tompkins, interview, 3 May 1984; George L. Cross to Stuart Tompkins, 17 May 1954, Box 7, Tompkins Papers.

43. E. E. Dale to Stuart Tompkins, 4 May 1932, Box 67, Dale Papers.

44. E. E. Dale to Stuart Tompkins, 28 June 1932, Box 67, Dale Papers.

45. Stuart Tompkins to E. E. Dale, 16 May 1932, Box 67, Dale Papers.

46. Stuart Tompkins to Carl Wittke, 24 October 1943, Box: General File A–Z, Tompkins Papers.

47. Edna Tompkins, interview, 2 June 1983; Eleanor Houston and Amy Moorhead, interview, 17 August 1983.

48. Stuart Tompkins to W. H. Alexander, 6 July 1945 (quotation), and Stuart Tompkins to George L. Cross, 14 July 1945, Box: General File A–Z, Tompkins Papers.

49. Edna Tompkins, interview, 2 June 1983.

50. Ibid.

51. Ibid.

52. Stuart Tompkins to Alan Crawley, 13, October 1954, Box 7, Tompkins Papers.

53. Elizabeth A. H. John, interview, 17 October 1983.

54. Stuart Tompkins to A. B. Sears, 19 January 1954, Box: General File A–Z, Tompkins Papers.

55. William E. Livezey, interview, Norman, Oklahoma, 19 August 1983.

56. Ibid.

57. Carl Rister to Stuart Tompkins, 7 December 1945 and 29 July 1951 (quotations), Box: General File A–Z, Tompkins Papers; Eleanor Houston and Amy Moorhead, interview, 17 August 1983.

58. Gilbert Fite, interview, Salt Lake City, Utah, 14 October 1983.

59. Elizabeth A. H. John, interview, 17 October 1983; W. E. Fredeman, Foreword to *The Secret War*, by Stuart R. Tompkins (Victoria: Morriss Publishing, 1981), p. 5 (quotation).

60. Edna Tompkins, interview, 2 June 1983.

61. Stuart Tompkins to G. Bernard Noble, 5 December 1950, Box 2, Tompkins Papers.

62. Michael T. Florinsky, review of *Russia through the Ages, New York Times Book Review*, 26 May 1940.

63. Ivan A. Lopatin, review of *Russia through the Ages, World Affairs Quarterly* 11 (4, 1941): 441; James G. Allen, review of *Russia through the Ages, Journal of Central European Affairs* 1 (April 1941): 105; Jesse D. Clarkson, review of *Russia through the Ages, American Historical Review* 46 (April 1941): 603.

64. W. E. Fredeman, interview, Vancouver, 5 July 1984 (quotation); Hans Kohn, "European History," *Saturday Review*, 4 April 1953, 18 and 47.

65. Elizabeth A. H. John interview, 17 October 1983; W. E. Fredeman, interview, 5 July 1984.

66. Stuart Tompkins to Warren S. Walsh, 7 November 1955, Box 7, Tompkins Papers.

67. Stuart Tompkins to Walter Fitzmaurice, 19 November 1955, Box 7, Tompkins Papers.

68. Stuart Tompkins, "Moscow and the West," 1953, typescript, p. 16, Box 7, Tompkins Papers.

69. Ibid., p. 5.

70. W. E. Livezey, interview, 19 August 1983; Gilbert Fite, interview 14 October 1983; Stuart and Edna Tompkins's citizenship application papers, 1951, in possession of the author. For a full discussion of the loyalty-oath bill (House Bill 8), see George L. Cross, *Professors, Presidents, and Politicians: Civil Rights and the University of Oklahoma, 1890–1968* (Norman: University of Oklahoma Press, 1981), pp. 183–222.

71. Stuart Tompkins to Savoie Lottinville, 8 February 8, 1946, Box 112, University of Oklahoma Press Records, University of Oklahoma Library.

72. Ernest J. Simmons, review of *The Russian Mind: From Peter the Great through the Enlightenment, Saturday Review*, 4 April 1953, 29 (first and second quotations); Murray Polner, review of *The Russian Intelligentsia: Makers of the Revolutionary State, Annals of the American Academy* 318 (July 1958): 167 (third quotation); and Marvin L. Kalb, review of *The Russian Intelligentsia, Saturday Review*, 8 March 1958, 15 (fourth quotation).

73. See, for example, Walter Laqueur, review of *The Triumph of Bolshevism: Revolution or Reaction? New York Review of Books*, 15 June 1967, 25.

74. Ralph Carter Elwood, review of *The Triumph of Bolshevism, Slavic Review* 27 (December 1968): 653; Theodore H. Von Laue, review of *The Triumph of Bolshevism, American Historical Review* 73 (December 1967): 543.

75. W. E. Fredeman, Foreword to *The Secret War*, p. 9.

76. W. E. Livezey, interview, 19 August 1983.

1 COURTSHIP AND MARRIAGE OF A CIVIL SERVANT

1. Elizabeth A. H. John, interview, Santa Rosa, N.M., 17 October 1983.
2. John Herd Thompson, *The Harvests of War* (Toronto: McClelland and Stewart, 1978), pp. 87–94; James G. MacGregor, *A History of Alberta* (Edmonton: Hurtig Publishers, 1981), p. 188.
3. Paul Fussell, *The Great War and Modern Memory* (New York: Oxford University Press, 1975), p. 23; Grace Morris Craig, *But This Is Our War* (Toronto: University of Toronto Press, 1981), p. ix.
4. MacGregor, pp. 229–30.
5. Ibid., pp. 178–80 and 233.
6. Vincent J. Esposito, ed., *A Concise History of World War I* (New York: Praeger, 1964), pp. 340–41.
7. Edna J. Tompkins, interview, Victoria, 3 May 1984.
8. Edna J. Tompkins, interview, Edmonton, 1 June 1983; Dorothy Mawdsley, interview, Victoria, 3 May 1984; Eleanor Houston and Amy Moorhead, interview, Norman, 17 August, 1983.

2 ONE MAN'S MOBILIZATION

1. George F. G. Stanley, *Canada's Soldiers: The Military History of an Unmilitary People* (3rd ed.; Toronto: Macmillan, 1974), pp. 307–11; Desmond Morton, *Canada and War: A Military and Political History* (Toronto: Butterworth's, 1981), pp. 52 and 55; G. W. L. Nicholson, *Canadian Expeditionary Force, 1914–1919: Official History of the Canadian Army in the First World War* (Ottawa: Queen's Printer, 1962), pp. 18–32.
2. Nicholson, p. 20; Morton, p. 60 (quotation).
3. Edna Tompkins, interview, Victoria, 26 September 1984.
4. Esposito, p. 347
5. Esposito, pp. 86 and 341; Nicholson, pp. 105 and 120–22.
6. MacGregor, pp. 229–31; Nicholson, p. 23.

3 TROOP TRAIN AND STEAMSHIP

1. Edna Tompkins, interview, Edmonton, 1 June 1983.
2. Correlli Barnett, *The Sword-bearers: Studies in Supreme Command in the First World War* (London: Eyre and Spottiswoode, 1963), pp. 181–83.
3. Nicholson, p. 36.

4 SHORNCLIFFE

1. Esposito, p. 347.
2. Edna Tompkins, interview, Victoria, 3 May 1984.
3. Esposito, pp. 341–42.
4. Edna Tompkins, interview, Edmonton, 1 June 1983.
5. Nicholson, p. 167; MacGregor, p. 231.

6. Esposito, pp. 348–49.

7. Edna Tompkins, "Journal" (fragment), in possession of the author.

5 IMPRESSIONS OF FRANCE: AT THE FRONT WITH ALBERTA'S 31ST

1. Nicholson, p. 176

2. Stuart R. Tompkins, interview with Jane Fredeman, Vancouver, December, 1976.

3. Alan Lloyd, *The War in the Trenches* (London: Hart-Davis, MacGibbon, 1976), p. 42.

4. John Ellis, *Eye-Deep in Hell: Trench Warfare in World War I* (New York: Pantheon, 1976), p. 16.

5. Ibid., pp. 17–19.

6. Esposito, p. 355.

7. Edna Tompkins, interview, Victoria 3 May 1984.

8. John Brophy and Eric Partridge, *The Long Trail: What the British Soldier Sang and Said in the Great War of 1914–18* (London: Andre Deutsch, 1965), p. 147.

9. Nicholson, p. 200.

10. Nicholson, pp. 210–11; Morton, pp. 67–78.

6 FURTHER IMPRESSIONS: TRANSFER TO THE TRENCH MORTARS

1. Esposito, p. 342.

2. Lloyd, p. 33.

7 NEW YEAR, OLD WAR

1. Stuart Tompkins, "Diary," Box 4, Tompkins Papers.

2. Ibid.

3. Ibid.

4. Craig, pp. 102 and 103.

5. Nicholson, p. 233.

6. Stuart Tompkins, "Diary."

7. Brophy and Partridge, p. 194 and p. 117 (quotation).

8. Barbara W. Tuchman, *The Zimmerman Telegram* (New York: Ballantine Books, 1979), p. 121.

9. Brophy and Partridge, p. 89.

10. Stuart Tompkins, "Diary."

11. Nicholson, pp. 220 and 344; McGregor, pp. 237 and 249 (Murphy).

8 PREPARING THE SPRING ASSAULT: REHEARSAL FOR VIMY RIDGE

1. Tuchman, pp. 147–49; Stuart Tompkins, "Diary."

2. Stuart Tompkins, "Diary."

3. Nicholson, pp. 241–42.

4. MacGregor, p. 235.

5. Nicholson, p. 234.

6. Stuart Tompkins, "Diary."

7. Nicholson, pp. 223–24.

8. Esposito, p. 351; Nicholson, p. 118 (casualty figures).

9. Stuart Tompkins, "Diary."

9   OVER THE TOP AND RETURN TO "BLIGHTY"

1. Stuart Tompkins to Editor, Calgary *Herald*, 1 January 1955, Box 7, Tompkins Papers, University of Oklahoma Library.

2. Nicholson, p. 244.

3. Ibid., p. 265.

4. Stuart Tompkins, "Diary."

5. Ibid.

6. Ibid.

7. Edna Tompkins, interview, Edmonton, 1 June 1983.

8. Stuart Tompkins, interview with Jane Fredeman, Vancouver, December 1976.

9. Ibid.

10. Stuart Tompkins's Service Orders, Box 4, Tompkins Papers.

11. Edna Tompkins, interview, Edmonton, 1 June 1983 (quotation); Stuart Tompkins's Certificate of Service, copy in possession of the author.

10   C.E.F. SIBERIA

1. Stuart Tompkins, "Letters from Afar," 1975, photocopied, p. 1, copy in the possession of the author.

2. Roy MacLaren, *Canadians in Russia* (Toronto: Macmillan, 1976), p. 178.

3. Edna Tompkins, interview, Edmonton, 1 June 1983 (quotations); Stuart Tompkins, "Letters from Afar," p. 2.

4. Stuart Tompkins's Certificate of Service; Edmonton *Journal*, 29 August 1918, p. 1 (quotation).

5. Betty Miller Unterberger, *America's Siberian Expedition, 1918–1920* (Durham: Duke University Press, 1956), pp. 54–56; Donald W. Treadgold, *Twentieth Century Russia*, 5th ed. (Boston: Houghton Mifflin, 1981), pp. 148–50; Gaddis Smith, "Canada and the Siberian Intervention, 1918–1919," *American Historical Review* 64 (July 1959), p. 868.

6. Unterberger, pp. 35, 60, and 69; Smith, p. 871.

7. C. F. Just, quoted in Smith, p. 871.

8. Smith, pp. 872–73.

9. MacLaren, p. 147; Edmonton *Journal*, 29 August 1918, p. 1.

10. Edmonton *Journal*, 28 October 1918, p. 2.

11. Ibid., 21 October 1918, p. 1, 23 October, p. 2, 4 November, p. 1 and 5 November, p. 6.

12. MacLaren, pp. 228–31.

13. Edna Tompkins, interview, Victoria, 26 September 1985; Victoria *Daily Colonist*, 10 December 1918, p. 4.

11   ACROSS THE NORTH PACIFIC: 260TH RIFLES REACH VLADIVOSTOK

1. MacLaren, p. 177.

2. Ibid., p. 177.

3. Tompkins, "Letters from Afar," p. 13.

4. Raymond Massey, *When I Was Young* (Toronto: McClelland and Stewart, 1976; Halifax: Formac Publishing, Goodread Biographies, 1983), chapter 24, n.p.

5. MacLaren, p. 178.

6. Tompkins, "Letters from Afar," p. 8.

7. Stuart Tompkins, interview with Jane Fredeman, Vancouver, December, 1976.

12   BREAKING THE LANGUAGE BARRIER: LIVING AMONG RUSSIANS

1. Tompkins, "Letters from Afar," p. 45.

2. Ibid., p. 45.

3. Edna Tompkins to Stuart Tompkins, 8 and 13 February 1919, letters in possession of the author.

4. Edna Tompkins to Stuart Tompkins, 16 February 1919, letter in possession of the author.

13   JOURNEY TO CHINA

1. Bernard Pares, *My Russian Memoirs* (London: Jonathon Cape, 1931; Academy Books, 1935), pp. 501, 506, and 507.

2. Ibid., p. 506.

3. M. L. Wardell to Stuart Tompkins, 6 November 1945, Tompkins Papers, Box 14.

4. Smith, "Canada and the Siberian Intervention," p. 875.

5. Stuart Tompkins, interview with Jane Fredeman, Vancouver, December 1976.

6. Ibid.

7. MacLaren, p. 207.

8. Tompkins, "Letters from Afar," p. 75.

EPILOGUE

1. Edna Tompkins, interview, 1 June 1983; Stuart Tompkins Papers, Box: Correspondence and General Subjects, A–Z, folder: history; Stuart R. Tompkins to Borden, 24 June 1935.

2. Tompkins Papers, Box 14, file: Russian Center, Anatole Mazour to Stuart R. Tompkins, 5 October 1954, and Stuart R. Tompkins to Manager of Russian Center, 11 October 1954.

3. Tompkins Papers, Box 7, file: Misc III, Stuart R. Tompkins to W. E. Livezey, 25 April 1955.
4. Edna Tompkins, interview, 1 June 1983.

Bibliography

Ackerman, Carl W. *Trailing the Bolsheviki: Twelve Thousand Miles with the Allies in Siberia.* New York: Charles Scribner's Sons, 1919.

Allen, James G. Review of *Russia through the Ages: From the Scythians to the Soviets,* by Stuart R. Tompkins. *Journal of Central European Affairs* I (April 1941): 603.

Barnett, Correlli. *The Swordbearers: Studies in Supreme Command in the First World War.* London: Eyre and Spottiswoode, 1963.

Berger, Carl. *The Sense of Power: Studies in the Ideas of Canadian Imperialism.* Toronto: University of Toronto Press, 1970.

————. *The Writing of Canadian History: Aspects of English-Canadian Historical Writing: 1900–1970.* Toronto: Oxford University Press, 1976.

Brado, Edward. *Cattle Kingdom: Early Ranching in Alberta.* Vancouver: Douglas and McIntyre, 1984.

Brophy, John, and Eric Partridge. *The Long Trail: What the British Soldier Sang and Said in the Great War of 1914–18.* London: Andre Deutsch, 1965.

Chalmers, John W. *Schools of the Foothills Province: The Story of Public Education in Alberta.* Toronto: University of Toronto Press, 1967.

————. *Teachers of the Foothills Province: The Story of the Alberta Teachers' Association.* Toronto: University of Toronto Press, 1968.

Clarkson, Jesse D. Review of *Russia through the Ages,* by Stuart R. Tompkins. *American Historical Review* 46 (April 1941): 603.

Craig, Grace Morris. *But This Is Our War.* Toronto: University of Toronto Press, 1981.

Cross, George Lynn. *Professors, Presidents, and Politicians: Civil Rights and the University of Oklahoma, 1890–1968.* Norman: University of Oklahoma Press, 1980.

Dale, E. E. Papers. University of Oklahoma Library, Norman.

Ellis, John. *Eye-Deep in Hell: Trench Warfare in World War I.* New York: Pantheon, 1976.

Elwood, Ralph Carter. Review of *The Triumph of Bolshevisim: Revolution or Reaction?,* by Stuart R. Tompkins. *Slavic Review* 27 (December 1968): 653.

Esposito, Vincent J., ed. *A Concise History of World War I.* New York: Frederick A. Praeger, 1964.

Florinsky, Michael T. Review of *Russia through the Ages: From the Scythians to the Soviets,* by Stuart R. Tompkins. *New York Times Book Review,* 26 May 1940.

Fredeman, W. E. Foreword to *The Secret War,* by Stuart R. Tompkins. Victoria: Morriss Publishing, 1981.

Friesen, Gerald. *The Canadian Prairies: A History.* Toronto: University of Toronto Press, 1984.

Fussell, Paul. *The Great War and Modern Memory.* New York: Oxford University Press, 1975; Oxford Press paperback, 1977.

Graves, William S. *America's Siberian Adventure, 1918–1920.* New York: Peter Smith, 1941.

Harper, Paul V., ed. *The Russia I Believe In: The Memoirs of Samuel N. Harper, 1902–1941.* Chicago: University of Chicago Press.

Kalb, Marvin. Review of *The Russian Intelligentsia: Makers of the Revolutionary State,* by Stuart R. Tompkins. *Saturday Review,* 8 March 1958, 15.

Kohn, Hans. "European History," *Saturday Review,* 4 April 1953.

Langer, William L. *Gas and Flame in World War I.* New York: Alfred A. Knopf, 1965.

Laqueur, Walter. Review of *The Triumph of Bolshevism: Revolution or Reaction?,* by Stuart R. Tompkins. *New York Review of Books,* 15 June 1967, 25.

Liddell Hart, Basil. *The War in Outline, 1914–1918.* New York: Random House, 1936.

Lloyd, Alan. *The War in the Trenches.* London: Hart-Davis, MacGibbon, 1976.

Lopatin, Ivan A. Review of *Russia through the Ages: From the Scythians to the Soviets,* by Stuart R. Tompkins. *World Affairs Quarterly* 11, no. 4, (1941): 441.

MacGregor, James G. *A History of Alberta*. Edmonton: Hurtig Publishers, 1986.

MacLaren, Roy. *Canadians in Russia, 1918–1919*. Toronto: Macmillan of Canada, 1976.

Manning, Charles A. *The Siberian Fiasco*. New York: Library Publishers, 1952.

Marwick, Arthur. *The Deluge: British Society and the First World War*. London: The Macmillan Press Ltd., 1965; Macmillan Student Edition, 1973.

Massey, Raymond. *When I Was Young*. Toronto: McClelland and Stewart, 1976; Halifax: Formac Publishing Company, Ltd., Goodread Biographies, 1983.

McKee, Alexander. *The Battle of Vimy Ridge*. New York: Stein and Day, 1967.

Monaghan, Jay. Review of *Alaska: Promyshlennik and Sourdough*, by Stuart R. Tompkins. *Mississippi Valley Historical Review* 32 (March 1946): 609

Morton, Desmond. *Canada and War: A Military and Political History*. Toronto: Butterworth's, 1981.

Neuberger, Richard L. Review of *Alaska: Promyshlennik and Sourdough*, by Stuart R. Tompkins. *Saturday Review*, 29 December 1945.

Nicholson, G. W. L. *Canadian Expeditionary Force, 1914–1919: Official History of the Canadian Army in the First World War*. Ottawa: Queen's Printer, 1962.

Palmer, Howard. *Patterns of Prejudice: A History of Nativism in Alberta*. Toronto: McClelland and Stewart, 1982.

Pares, Bernard. *My Russian Memoirs*. London: Jonathan Cape, 1931; Academy Books, 1935.

———. *A Wandering Student: The Story of a Purpose*. Syracuse: Syracuse University Press, 1948.

Polner, Murray. Review of *The Russian Intelligentsia: Makers of the Revolutionary State*, by Stuart R. Tompkins. *Annals of the American Academy* 318 (July 1958): 167.

Potter, Jean. Review of *Alaska: Promyshlennik and Sourdough*, by Stuart R. Tompkins. *New York Times Book Review*, 3 February 1946.

Shortt, S. E. D. *The Search for an Ideal: Six Canadian Intellectuals and Their Convictions in an Age of Transition, 1890–1930*. Toronto: University of Toronto Press, 1976.

Simmons, Ernest J. Review of *The Russian Mind: From Peter the Great through the Enlightenment*, by Stuart R. Tompkins. *Saturday Review*, 4 April 1953, 29.

Snow, Russell E. *The Bolsheviks in Siberia, 1917–1918*. Cranbury, N.J.: Associated University Presses, 1977.

Stanley, George F. G. *Canada's Soldiers: The Military History of an Unmilitary People*. 3rd ed. Toronto: Macmillan of Canada, 1974.

Stewart, George. *The White Armies of Russia: A Chronicle of Counterrevolution and Allied Intervention*. New York: Macmillan, 1933.

Swettenham, John. *Allied Intervention in Russia, 1918–1919: And the Part Played by Canada*. London: Allen and Unwin, 1967.

Thompson, John Herd. *The Harvests of War: The Prairie West, 1914–1918*. Toronto: McClelland and Stewart, 1978.

Tompkins, Stuart Ramsay. *Russia through the Ages: from the Scythians to the Soviets*. New York: Prentice Hall, 1940.

———. "Moscow and the West." Typescript, 1953.

———. *The Russian Mind, from Peter the Great through the Enlightenment*. Norman: University of Oklahoma Press, 1953.

———. "The Riddle of Communism: The Quest for an Answer." Typescript, 1955.

———. *The Russian Intelligentsia: Makers of the Revolutionary State*. Norman: University of Oklahoma Press, 1958.

———. *The Triumph of Bolshevism: Revolution or Reaction?* Norman: University of Oklahoma Press, 1967.

———. "Letters from Afar." Photocopy, 1975.

———. *The Secret War*. Victoria: Morriss Publishing, 1981.

———. Papers. University of Oklahoma Library, Norman.

Treadgold, Donald W. *Twentieth Century Russia*. 5th ed. Boston: Houghton Mifflin, 1981.

Tuchman, Barbara W. *The Zimmerman Telegram*. New York: Macmillan, 1966; Random House, Bantam Books, 1979.

University of Oklahoma Press Records. University of Oklahoma Library, Norman.

Unterberger, Betty Miller. *America's Siberian Expedition, 1918–1920*. Durham: Duke University Press, 1956.

Von Laue, Theodore H. Review of *The Triumph of Bolshevism: Revolution or Reaction?*, by Stuart R. Tompkins. *American Historical Review* 73 (December 1967): 543.

Warth, Robert D. *The Allies and the Russian Revolution: From the Fall of the Monarchy to the Peace of Brest-Litovsk*. Durham: Duke University Press, 1954.

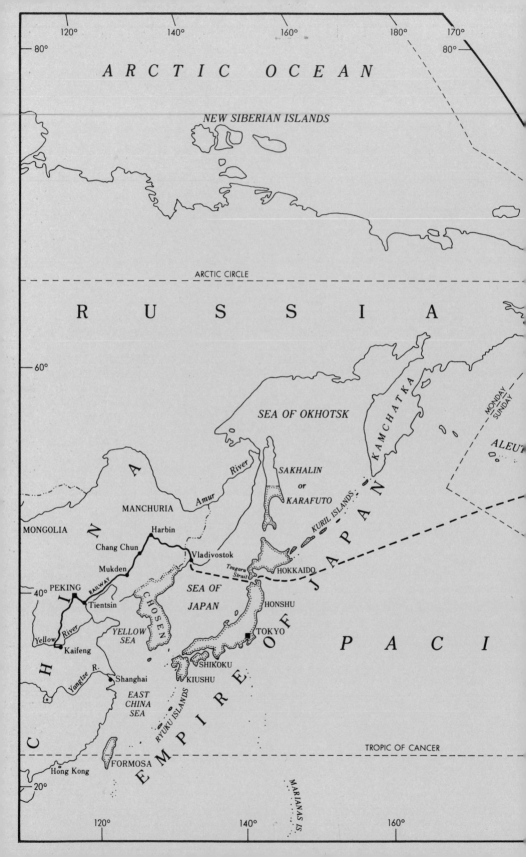